THE AMERICAN INSTITUTE OF ARCHITECTS

AIA 2010~2012
DESIGNS FOR THE NEW DECADE

DESIGN MEDIA PUBLISHING LIMITED

©2012 by Design Media Publishing Limited
This edition published in July 2012

Design Media Publishing Limited
20/F Manulife Tower
169 Electric Rd, North Point
Hong Kong
Tel: 00852-28672587
Fax: 00852-25050411
E-mail: Kevinchoy@designmediahk.com
www.designmediahk.com

©2012 The American Institute of Architects
1735 New York Avenue, NW
Washington, DC 20006
www.aia.org

All rights reserved. No part of this publication may be reproduced or transmitted in any form or by any means, electronic or mechanical, including photocopy, recording or any information storage and retrieval system, without prior permission in writing from the publisher.

The information in this book has been obtained from many sources. The American Institute of Architects has made every reasonable effort to make this reference work accurate and authoritative, but does not warrant or assume any liability for the accuracy or completeness of the text, or its fitness for any particular purpose.

Design/Layout: Chunling Yang
Cover Photo: ©Timothy Hursley
Printing: Toppan Leefung, Shenzhen

ISBN 978-988-15661-3-3

Printed in China

007 Foreword

008 A History of the AIA Honor Awards Program

010 Introduction

012 2010 Institute Honor Awards Jury

156 2011 Institute Honor Awards Jury

304 2012 Institute Honor Awards Jury

438 Index

2010

ARCHITECTURE

016 Alice Tully Hall

020 Austin E. Knowlton School of Architecture

028 Beauvoir

030 Brochstein Pavilion and Central Quad: Rice University

034 Camino Nuevo High School

038 Campus Restaurant and Event Space

044 Macallen Building

048 Outpost

054 Serta International Center

060 Skirkanich Hall

068 Step Up on 5th

072 TKTS Booth and the Redevelopment of Father Duffy Square

076 Urban Outfitters Corporate Campus

082 Yale University Art Gallery, Kahn Building Renovation

INTERIOR ARCHITECTURE

086 CHANEL Robertson Boulevard

092 Craftsteak

096 Data

100 Exeter Schools Multipurpose Space

104 Historic Central Park West Residence

108 The Cathedral of Christ the Light

114 Vera Wang Boutique

REGIONAL & URBAN DESIGN

118 A Civic Vision for the Central Delaware River

124 Connections: MacArthur Park District Master Plan

128 Greenwich South Strategic Framework

132 Monumental Core Framework Plan

138 Ryerson University Master Plan

142 Savannah East Riverfront Extension

148 The U.S. House Office Buildings Facilities Plan and Preliminary South Capitol Area Plan

TWENTY-FIVE YEAR AWARD

152 King Abdul Aziz International Airport – Hajj Terminal

2011

ARCHITECTURE

160 AT&T Performing Arts Center Dee and Charles Wyly Theater

166 Ford Assembly Building

172 Horizontal Skyscraper Vanke Center

180 New Acropolis Museum

184 North Carolina Museum of Art

188 One Jackson Square

194 San Francisco Museum of Modern Art Rooftop Garden

198 The Barnard College Diana Center

204 University of Michigan Museum of Art

210 U.S. Land Port of Entry

INTERIOR ARCHITECTURE

216 Alchemist

220 Armstrong Oil and Gas

226 Conga Room

234 FIDM San Diego Campus

240 Moving Picture Company

246 Registrar Recorder County Clerk Elections Operations Center

250 The Academy of Music

254 The Power House, Restoration/Renovation

258 Vancouver Convention Center West

264 Washington Square Park Dental

270 John E. Jaqua Center for Student Athletes

REGIONAL & URBAN DESIGN

276 Beijing CBD East Expansion

278 Chicago Central Area DeCarbonization Plan

284 "Community | City: Between Building and Landscape Affordable Sustainable Infill for Smoketown, Kentucky"

290 Gowanus Canal Sponge Park

292 "Low Impact Development: A Design Manual for Urban Areas"

298 Townscaping an Automobile-Oriented Fabric

TWENTY-FIVE YEAR AWARD

302 John Hancock Tower

2012

ARCHITECTURE

308 8 House

320 41 Cooper Square

324 The Gates and Hillman Centers for Computer Science

330 Ghost Architectural Laboratory

334 LumenHAUS

338 Pittman Dowell Residence

342 Poetry Foundation

348 Ruth Lilly Visitors Pavilion

352 The Standard, New York

INTERIOR ARCHITECTURE

360 ARTifacts

364 Children's Institute, Inc. Otis Booth Campus

370 David Rubenstein Atrium at Lincoln Center

374 HyundaiCard Air Lounge

380 The Integral House

384 Joukowsky Institute for Archaeology & the Ancient World

388 Memory Temple

392 Prairie Management Group

396 Record House Revisited

400 The Wright at the Guggenheim Museum

REGIONAL & URBAN DESIGN

404 Fayetteville 2030: Transit City Scenario

408 Grangegorman Urban Quarter Master Plan

412 Jordan Dead Sea Development Zone Master Plan

418 Master Plan for the Central Delaware

420 Miami Beach City Center Redevelopment Project

424 Portland Mall Revitalization

428 Reinventing the Crescent: Riverfront Development Plan

430 SandRidge Energy Commons

TWENTY-FIVE YEAR AWARD

434 Gehry Residence

FOREWORD

Since 1949, the American Institute of Architects has encouraged design excellence through its Institute Honors Awards program. Hundreds of projects, firms, and architects have been honored for their ingenuity in a range of categories. Yet, all of them have achieved the same high standard of rigor, clarity, and spirit.

The projects that were premiated in 2010, 2011, and 2012 are no different and speak to the quality of global architectural production in the first decade of the new century. They also speak to a few interrelated themes: regional adaptation to climate, soil, infrastructure, and culture; a sense of context and place that drives the project, conceptually; a strong desire on the part of the design architect to balance the building typology with local tradition and community.

Of course, there are some global themes that connect the work here, however diverse it may be: the urgency of finding sustainable solutions, the economy of systems-thinking in design, and the urbanity of public spaces to bring us all together.

As you learn more about these projects, consider the whole to be a survey of talent and a good overview of the quality that an AIA member brings to the project at hand. Naturally, the scale of work in countries like China is much larger than in the United States. But, the finer grain work that happens in the United States represents a living laboratory – constantly examining, re-examining, building, and evolving. I think you'll understand more fully what that laboratory looks like as you mine the pages of this book.

Robert A. Ivy, FAIA
Executive Vice President/Chief Executive Officer
The American Institute of Architects

A HISTORY OF THE AIA HONOR AWARDS PROGRAM[i]

The Institute Honor Awards program of The American Institute of Architects encourages distinguished design by recognizing it and celebrating its architects. Yet this is only part of the meaning of this awards program, as a study of the recipients from 2010 through 2012 will reveal. It is a striking representation of where architecture stands today and where it promises to lead.

The importance of this portfolio is not limited to the architect, whose natural preoccupation is design, nor is it limited to the critic. It is not limited to engineering or construction, which are both guided by and informed by the design process.

Architecture is about making and re-making of the physical environment in which we live, work, play, and learn. It's about designing at all scales and inspiring others to think from the spoon to the city, to paraphrase the architect Ernesto Rogers. It's about the synthesis of past lessons and today's aspirations for the benefit of future generations.

Since its inception in 1857, the AIA has helped advance all of these ideas for an architecture profession in service to society. As it neared its centennial anniversary, the Institute's leadership realized that encouraging good design among its members was not enough; it must also encourage public notice and acclaim for good design if the profession was to continue making a difference in the built environment.

In 1948, at the convention held in Grand Rapids, Michigan, the AIA Board of Directors formed a committee to bring before the Institute a concrete proposal for an honor awards program centered on current work.

A year later, in 1949, the AIA launched its Honor Awards for Current Work program.

There are two main ways of narrowing the field of entrants in an awards program – by membership type and by awards category. The AIA diligently experimented with both. At first, organizers solicited only corporate members of the Institute to submit. By 1950, they lifted that restriction and accepted entries from anyone legally entitled to call themselves an architect. Over the next few years, the program was governed by categories rather than membership type. Those categories (based on building type) rotated annually based on the AIA Board or Executive Committee's recommendations based on what was most desirable for the upcoming annual convention: schools, churches, hospitals, residences, commercial buildings, and so on.

But, as Edmund Purves, FAIA, the consulting director for the AIA's awards program in 1962 acknowledged, even this arrangement had its limitations. "The categories were poorly balanced one with another," noted Purves, "and there were one or two rather sad occasions when the category failed to achieve a single mention. Unexpectedly the use of categories became a rather invidious restriction."[ii] The Honor Awards were opened to any type of architecture.

---

i. Adapted from Philip Will, Jr.'s forward and Edmund R. Purves, FAIA's, introduction to Mid-Century Architecture in America: Honor Awards of the American Institute of Architects, 1949-1961. Baltimore: Johns Hopkins University Press (1962): 5-7, 29-30.

ii. Purves, Edmund R., FAIA, "The AIA 'Honor Awards for Current Work' and its Juries," in Wolf Von Eckardt (ed.), Mid-Century Architecture in America: Honor Awards of the American Institute of Architects, 1949-1961. Baltimore: Johns Hopkins University Press (1962): 30.

One of the first Honor Award recipients was Skidmore Owings and Merrill for Lever House in New York. Completed in 1952, the building is now regarded as the quintessence of International Style office buildings, certainly owing to its appearance, but also to its commitment to a civic ideal. While an office building's "public plaza" is commonplace today, Bunshaft and de Blois set a generous standard here that remains, in many ways, peerless. Design architects Gordon Bunshaft, FAIA, and Natalie de Blois, FAIA, incorporated New York's first curtain wall system, making Lever House an engineering touchstone as well as an icon of Modernism.

Over the years, additional sub-categories have come and gone, such as the Bartlett Award to recognize Barrier-Free Architecture in the early 1970s, before handicapped access was a legal requirement. One of the notable recipients of the Barlett Award was Louis Kahn, FAIA, for his Kimball Museum of Art in Fort Worth, Texas in 1975. The Kimball's 16 cycloid vaults, spread out over one level make it a model of accessibility. It's also a model of innovation and collaboration. From the skylight baffles (which diffuse the sun evenly to produce a silvery glow) to the surrounding landscape, Kahn worked closely with the engineer August Komendant, the landscape architect George Patton, and the lighting designer Richard Kelly to create what is regarded as a critical turning point in museum design.

In some cases, buildings have repeatedly surfaced as touchstones of good design for generations of architects. The Santa Monica home of Frank Gehry, FAIA, which he renovated (for the first time) in 1978, received an honor award in 1980. In 2012, it emerged in the award rolls again to receive the AIA 25 Year Award. The irony, of course, is not lost – for such a modest, highly personal project, constructed with unglamorous materials on a shoestring budget, to have lasting impact and widespread significance is a testament to Gehry's particular talent.

Architecture's ability to adapt, as evinced by Gehry's home, was not lost on awards organizers, either. A separate division for "Extended Use" was added in the early-1980s to recognize the reuse of historic structures and restoration. In 1994, categories to recognize Interior Architecture and Regional and Urban Design were also added. Inclusiveness aside, the focus of the Institute Honor Awards has remained singular – to recognize the best examples of contemporary architecture.

In the pages of this book, the AIA presents recipients in the Architecture, Interior Architecture, and Regional and Urban Design categories within the Institute Honors Program. The breadth of architectural production is on full display here in a series of fine projects completed in the first decade of the 21st century. These projects are standard bearers for good design, in keeping with the mission of the AIA's awards programs. But, each one also represents the fruits of a collaborative and rigorous design process. In doing so, they transcend our expectations for what architecture can achieve

INTRODUCTION

Peer recognition drives professional excellence. That's true in every profession and in all creative endeavors – and architecture uniquely draws from both of those worlds. It is bound by the ethical codes, rigorous training, and licensure process like law or medicine; it is also the art of building in service to the global population. Although the demographics of its membership have shifted over time, the American Institute of Architects has always represented the professionals who practice this art. The AIA's Institute Honor Awards program annually chronicles excellence in thinking, collaboration, and ultimately, design.

In the pages that follow, the AIA recognizes three years worth of award recipients across four categories: architecture, interior architecture, regional and urban design, and its esteemed Twenty-five Year Award. On one hand, these projects from 2010, 2011, and 2012 constitute a snapshot of architectural production – a moment in time and a record of "excellence" in that moment. On the other hand, it is a snapshot that speaks more broadly about evolving design trends – what has come before, in the first decade of the 21st century, and what we might expect more of in the following decade. As one juror noted, these projects were selected from a portfolio of exceptional work that survived rigorous critique, discussion, site visits, and extensive deliberations. Although all of the entries were conceived with passion and commitment, those that garnered an award uniquely demonstrated a single, compelling idea and purpose. In essence, they constitute design excellence both in this moment and despite the vicissitudes of an age-old art form.

Across the four categories contained in this book, there are some constants worth noting: projects are considered individually within their categories, rather than relatively to other projects in the same category. Projects must also be more than simply unique or interesting; they must be attentive to their contexts and the environmental issues that deeply affect us all. However, each entry in the Institute Honor Awards program is judged against the degree to which it has met the category's individual requirements.

Additionally, for each of the following categories, all submissions must include the project's percentage of energy reduction and energy consumption (per square foot) as defined by the U.S. Environmental Protection Agency's (EPA) Energy Star Target Finder Tool and/or documentation of specific material choices to address the needs for indoor environmental quality and diversion of materials from the waste stream. This is in recognition of the AIA Sustainable Architectural Practice Position Statement, which sets a goal of at least 50-percent reduction of fossil-fuel energy use by 2010 and carbon neutrality by 2030.

For the Institute Honor Award for Architecture, projects must exhibit design achievement that demonstrates exemplary skill and creativity in resolution and integration of formal, functional, and technical requirements, including ecological stewardship and social responsibility that acknowledges and advances social agendas. Projects should reflect a strong sense of place, of ecology, of history, or of purpose as an integral part of the demonstrated design excellence.

In addition to design achievement, projects may be exemplary in the following subcategories: technical advancement, which includes engineering achievements (structural, mechanical, transportation, computer, etc.) as well as innovative use of materials; and/or preservation/restoration, including demonstration of exemplary skill, sensitivity, and thoroughness in preservation, restoration, or alternative use of existing buildings regardless of their original architectural significance.

The Institute Honor Awards for Interior Architecture acknowledges the excellence of building interiors created by architects licensed in the United States. Program organizers intend to draw attention to the full range of completed interior architecture: entries may be large or small in scope; they may involve renovation or adaptive use; they may also represent new construction. Submissions in such areas of residential, institutional, commercial, corporate, retail, hospitality, or other focus are welcome. And all entries are judged on merit regardless of scale or budget.

The purpose of the Institute Honor Awards for Regional and Urban Design is to recognize distinguished achievements that involve the expanding role of the architect in urban design, city planning, and community development. The awards seek to identify projects and programs that involve public participation and contribute to the quality of the urban environment.

Owners, individual practitioners, private design firms, public agencies, civic organizations, and public interest groups may submit nominations for projects and programs in which they were involved. Applicants do not need to be architects or members of the AIA, but an architect licensed in the United States must be the author of the project.

Submissions may include urban design projects, planning programs, civic improvements, environmental programs, and redevelopment projects. Since many urban design projects are never "completed" in the traditional sense, "incomplete" projects or ongoing programs may be recognized if a significant portion has been completed, implemented, or adopted by a local jurisdiction.

Design achievement can be evidenced by the exploration of new approaches to ecological planning, urban form, or sensitive reinforcement of successful historical development patterns. Entries should address ecological issues by describing (preferably with graphics) how the design captures, collects, stores, and distributes resident renewable resources and energies. Entries may also exhibit improvements in the quality of life, the environment, and/or the technical advancement of urban systems.

For the Twenty-five Year Award, projects that receive this recognition have stood the test of time, having been completed between 25 and 30 years ago. They may be built in the United States or in some other country, but they must have been designed by an architect licensed in the United States. The award is open to architectural projects of all classifications and may be one building or a related group of buildings forming a single project.

The project must be standing in a substantially completed form and in good condition and it must still carry out the original design. Change of use is permitted when it has not basically altered original intent. The project must have excellence in function – in the distinguished execution of its original program and in the creative aspects of its statement by today's standards. Building and site together should be examined.

As you review these projects, remember that they represent countless hours of work by thousands of individuals working across time zones and, in all cases, over many years. They represent what a jury of architect peers has deemed worthy of recognition. It is recognition of accomplishment, to be sure, but also of the promise that tomorrow's architecture will have taken a cue from the best of today's excellent work.

William Richards,
The American Institute of Architects

2010 INSTITUTE HONOR AWARDS FOR ARCHITECTURE JURY

Richard L. Maimon, FAIA, Chair
KieranTimberlake Associates, LLP

Jeanne Gang, FAIA
Studio/Gang Architects

Sam Grawe
Dwell/At Home in the Modern World

Jeffrey Lee, FAIA
Pearce Brinkley Cease & Lee P.A.

Justine N. Lewis
Georgia Institute of Technology/
American Institute of Architecture Students
Representative

Miguel A. Rivera Agosto, AIA
Miró Rivera Architects

Mark Simon, FAIA
Centerbrook Architects & Planners

H. Ruth Todd, AIA
Page & Turnbull Architects

William R. Turner, Jr., Associate AIA
Shears Adkins Architects

2010 INSTITUTE HONOR AWARDS FOR INTERIOR ARCHITECTURE JURY

Daniel H. Wheeler, FAIA, Chair
Wheeler Kearns Architects, Inc.

David H. Hart, FAIA
Utah Capitol Preservation Board

Audrey A. Matlock, AIA
Audrey Matlock, Architect

Audrey Stokes O'Hagan, AIA
Audrey O'Hagan Architect

Clive R. Wilkinson, AIA, RIBA
Clive Wilkinson Architects

2010 INSTITUTE HONOR AWARDS FOR REGIONAL AND URBAN DESIGN JURY

John F. Torti, FAIA Chair
Torti Gallas & Partners, Inc.

Lance Jay Brown, FAIA
Lance Jay Brown Architecture & Urban Design

Brenda Scheer, AIA
University of Utah
College of Architecture + Planning

Edward K. Uhlir, FAIA
Uhlir Consulting, LLC

Debby Wieneke
Habitat for Humanity of Benton County, Inc.

Richard L. Maimon, FAIA, LEED AP
2010 Chair,
Institute Honor Awards for Architecture

© Ed Wheeler

Richard Maimon is a Principal at KieranTimberlake, an internationally recognized architecture firm noted for its integration of research and practice guided by a deep environmental ethic. He has been with KieranTimberlake for over twenty years, participating in the growth of the firm and deeply involved in the breadth of its work. He currently oversees a range of projects including the Embassy of the United States in London, UK, the Center City Building for the University of North Carolina at Charlotte, the Kimmel Center Master Plan, a housing prototype for the Make It Right Foundation in New Orleans, and the redesign of Dilworth Plaza in Philadelphia. He has been responsible for highly acclaimed projects including Melvin J. and Claire Levine Hall at the University of Pennsylvania, Atwater Commons at Middlebury College, F. Otto Haas Stage at the Arden Theater Company, and the Philadelphia Theater Company's Suzanne Roberts Theatre. Projects he has been responsible for have been published internationally and have received national design awards.

Mr. Maimon served as jury chair for the 2010 AIA Institute Honor Awards and the 2010 Twenty-Five Year Award. He is a frequent guest lecturer, with appearances at colleges and universities, AIA Chapters and national conferences including the AIA Convention in Boston, the North American Theatre Engineering and Architecture Conference in New York City, and the United States Green Building Council Convention. He serves on the board of the Arden Theater Company, a leading regional theater in Philadelphia, is on the Charter High School for Architecture and Design Business Advisory Council, and is active with other nonprofit organizations in Philadelphia.

Mr. Maimon earned a Bachelor of Architecture, magna cum laude, from Columbia University in 1985 and a Master of Architecture from Princeton University in 1989. He was awarded the Phi Beta Kappa Award from Columbia University in 1985.

KieranTimberlake creates beautifully crafted, thoughtfully made designs which are holistically integrated to site, program and people. The firm is recognized for its research-based practice that focuses on new materials, processes, assemblies and products, receiving over one hundred design citations, including the 2008 Architecture Firm Award from the American Institute of Architects and the 2010 Cooper-Hewitt National Design Award.

Daniel H. Wheeler, FAIA
2010 Chair,
Institute Honor Awards for Interior Architecture

© Julie Wheeler

Daniel H. Wheeler, FAIA, is principal of Wheeler Kearns Architects, and Professor of Architecture at the University of Illinois at Chicago. He has served as Interim Director for the UIC School of Architecture and the Graham Foundation for the Advanced Studies in the Fine Arts, and has been a collaborator with Auburn University's Rural Studio for the past ten years. A graduate of RISD, he worked in the early studio of Machado Silvetti in Boston. Prior to founding WKA in 1987, he was a Studio Head/Associate at Skidmore, Owings, and Merrill in Chicago.

John Francis Torti, FAIA, LEED AP
2010 Chair,
Institute Honor Awards for Regional & Urban Design

© Torti Gallas and Partners, Inc.

As President of Torti Gallas and Partners, Mr. Torti has provided the strong conceptual leadership to bring his firm to national recognition. His firm has been the recipient of 95 national design awards in the last 15 years. With offices on both coasts and a liaison office in Istanbul, Turkey, he and his partners have built a firm that understands the inextricable tie between urban design and architecture, and between conceptual thinking and creating value for clients and for communities.

Mr. Torti joined the firm in 1973. His conceptual design leadership is key to the success of the firm's projects. As the leader of a market-focused firm, he and his partners have specialized expertise in the development and design of new towns and villages, neighborhoods, homes, main streets, workplaces and civic and institutional buildings.

Prior to joining Torti Gallas and Partners, Mr. Torti was affiliated with NASA and the National Capital Planning Commission, where he worked on numerous designs to rebuild Washington after the 1968 riots. He also was a Principal in an architectural firm in the Midwest and was the director of a non-profit housing and community development corporation.

In recognition of his many design contributions in architecture and urban design, Mr. Torti was elected to the American Institute of Architects College of Fellows in 2001. Mr. Torti is a graduate of the University of Notre Dame with a Bachelor of Architecture degree. He is also a member of the Advisory Council for the School of Architecture at the University of Notre Dame. In 2004, Mr. Torti became a LEED Accredited Professional.

Mr. Torti's teaching credentials include:
-Assistant Professor of Architecture, Catholic University of America, 1970-1973
-Lecturer and Visiting Critic, University of Maryland, University of Virginia, Ohio University, Harvard University

A selected listing of Mr. Torti's recent speaking venues includes:
-American Institute of Architects • The Mayor's Institute on City Design: Northeast
-Urban Land Institute • National Conference of the American Planning
-Congress for the New Urbanism Association
-Multi Housing World Info Expo • Multi-Family Housing Conference
-National Apartment Association • University of Notre Dame
-National Association of Home Builders • University of Maryland International Builders' Show • Andrews University
-The 21st Century Neighborhoods Conference University of Miami

Alice Tully Hall

Jury Comments:
This project takes an introverted anti-urban building and engages it with the city, bringing a sense of performance and theater right out to the sidewalk.

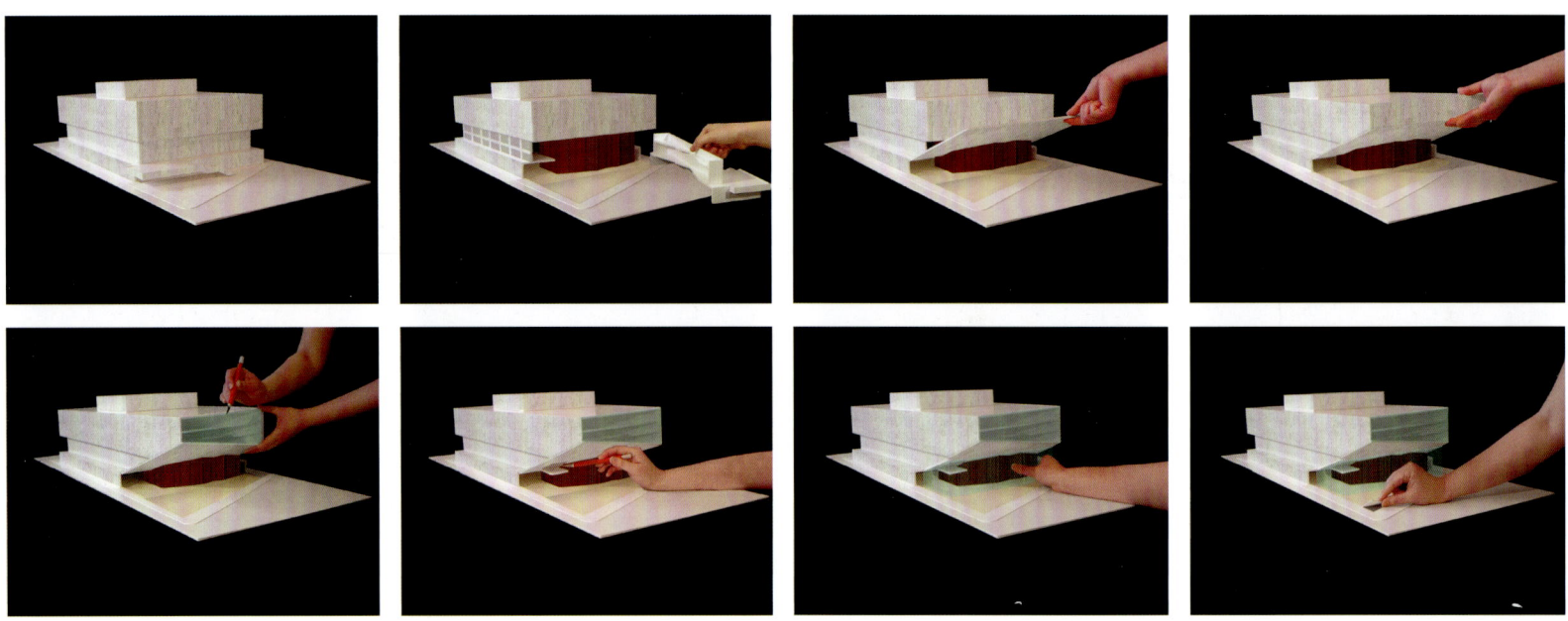

Notes of Interest
The redesign of Alice Tully Hall transforms the venue from a good multi-purpose hall into a premiere chamber music venue with street identity and upgraded functionality for all performance needs. The sloped underside of Juilliard's expansion serves as a canopy framing the hall, its expanded lobby, and box office; the opaque base of Pietro Belluschi's building is stripped away to reveal the hall's outer shell and a shear one-way cable net glass façade puts the hall on display.
Illumination emerges from the wood skin of the hall much the way a bioluminescent marine organism exudes an internal glow. A percentage of wood liner is constructed of translucent custom-molded resin panels surfaced in veneer to match and blend seamlessly with the wood, binding the house and stage with light. Like raising a chandelier signaling the start of the performance, the blush will be part of the choreography.

Consultant: L'Observatoire International, Fisher Dachs Associates
Engineer: ARUP
General Contractor: Turner Construction Co.
Owner: Lincoln Center Development Project

Architect
Diller Scofidio + Renfro and FXFOWLE Architects

Location
New York City, New York

Photo Credit
© Iwan Baan

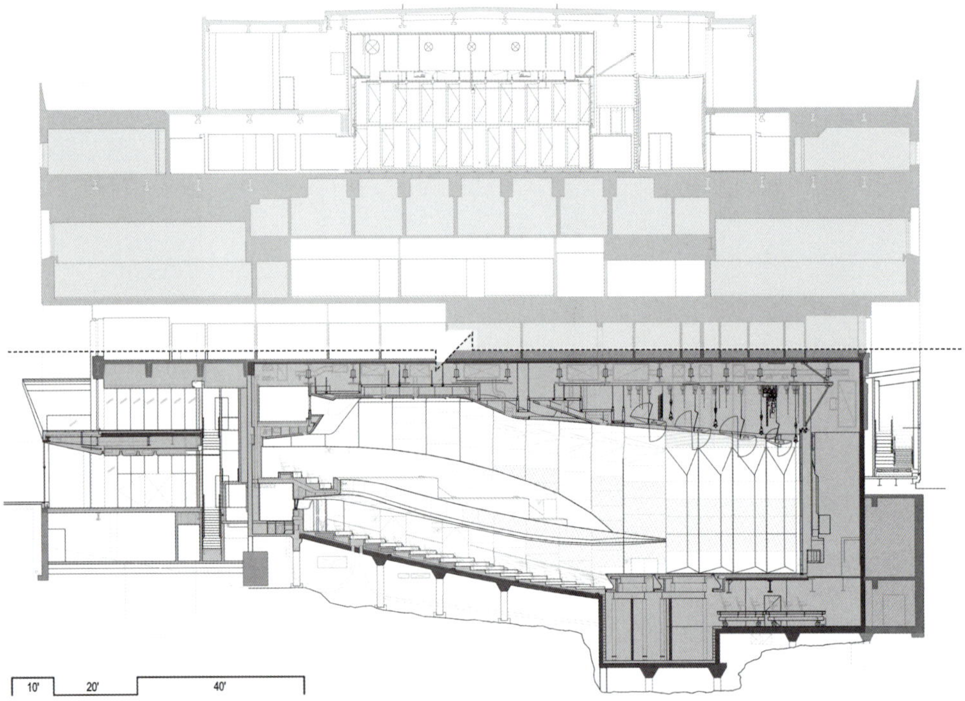

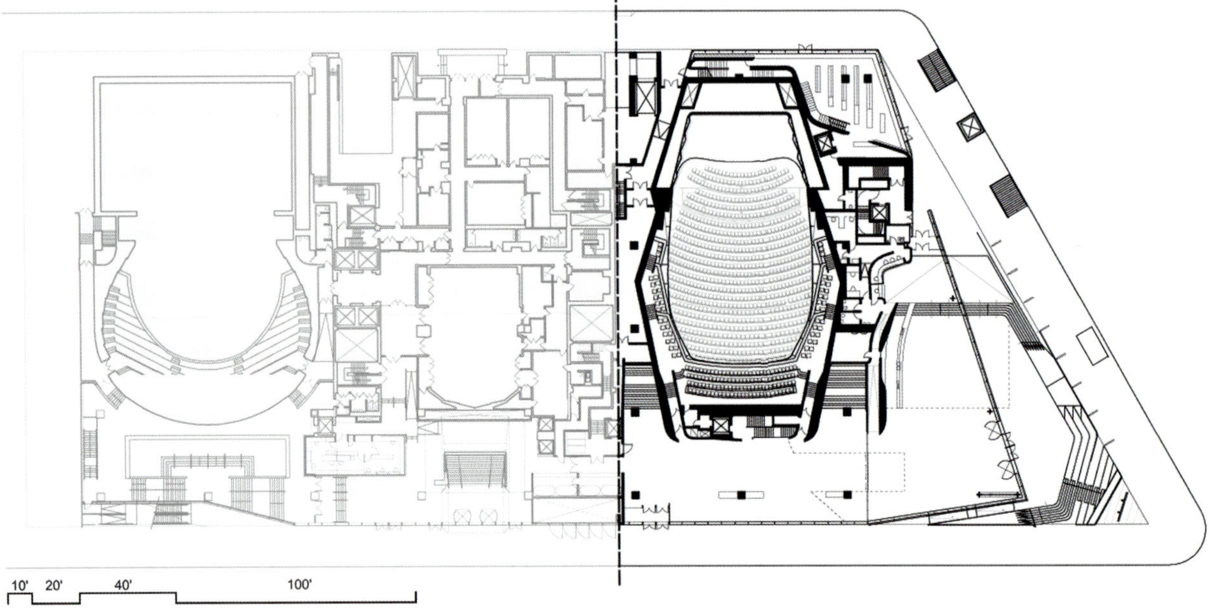

Austin E. Knowlton School of Architecture

Jury Comments:
This project embodies everything I would want in an architecture building. It is full of unique spaces, an open flexible hall that beckons people to participate, and seems to have surprises around every corner.

Level One, Ground:
1. Jury Space and Lecture Rooms
2. Café
3. Center Space
4. Gallery
5. Classroom
6. Administration
7. Front Entry
8. Forecourt
9. Bus Stop/North Gardens
10. South Court
11. North Porch

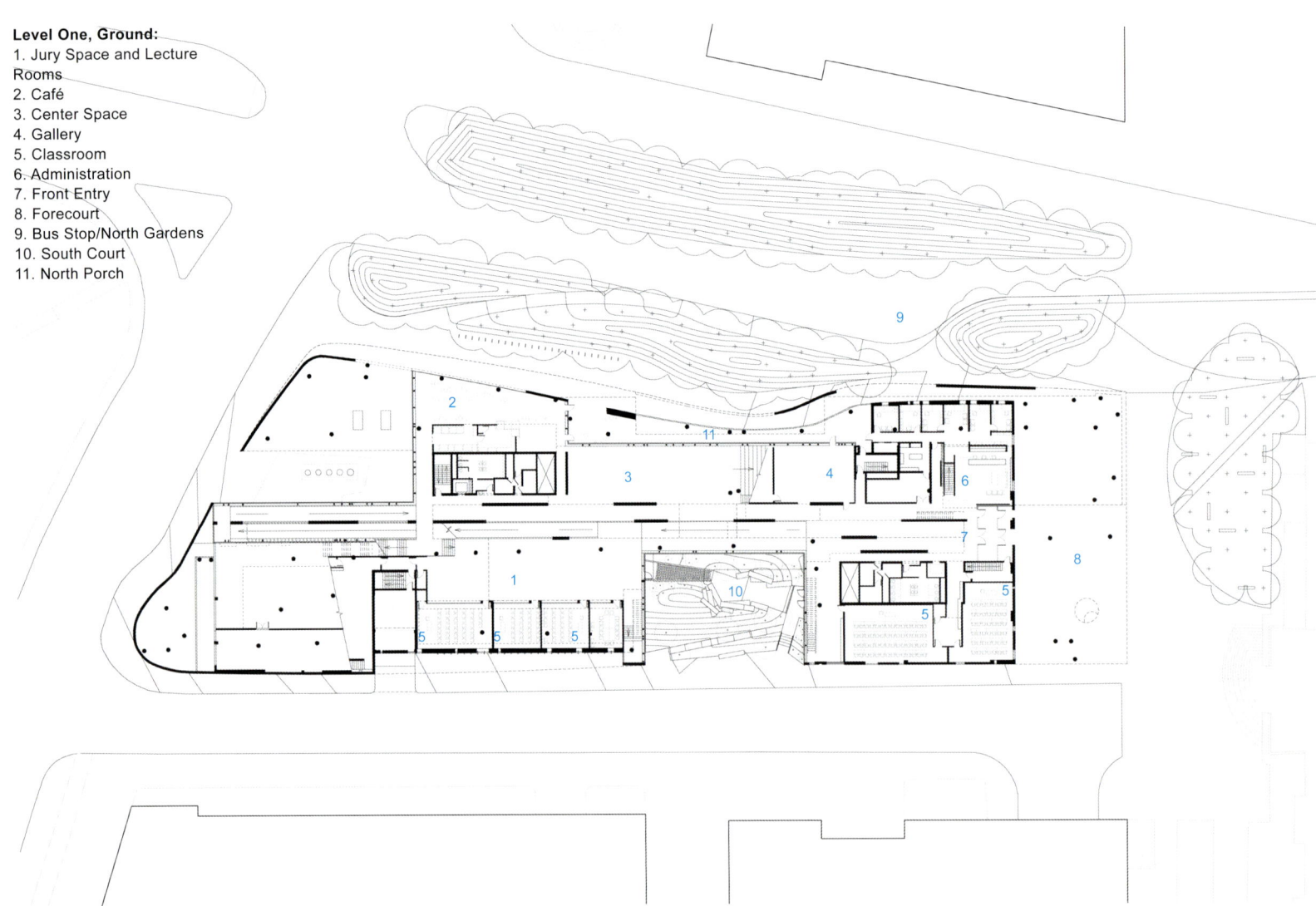

Notes of Interest

The site of the new school of architecture is at the western edge of the old campus, close to the river and the football stadium, at the happily congested corner of West Woodruff Avenue and Tuttle Park Place. Bounded by existing buildings and crossed by major campus pedestrian thoroughfares, the site is a dynamic zone, capable of sustaining a connective architecture and landscape and an inclusive urban form.

Asserting the belief that a school of architecture has a commitment to teach by example to both students within and the community at large, the architectural form and urban positioning of the new school is strategically active and interactive. The building form is generated by enclosing, defining and confronting the spaces and existing buildings of the larger site. Studios overlook the newly captured spaces. Students are in the midst of the urban activity which they will study and will eventually help form and influence.

Consultant: Bird + Bull, Ramon Luminance Design
Engineer: Shelley Metz Baumann Hawk, HAWA Consulting Engineers
General Contractor: P.J. Dick, Inc.
Landscape Architect: HAWA Consulting Engineers
Owner: The Ohio State University

Architect
Mack Scogin Merrill Elam Architects and WSA Studio

Location
Columbus, Ohio

Photo Credit
© Timothy Hursley Photography

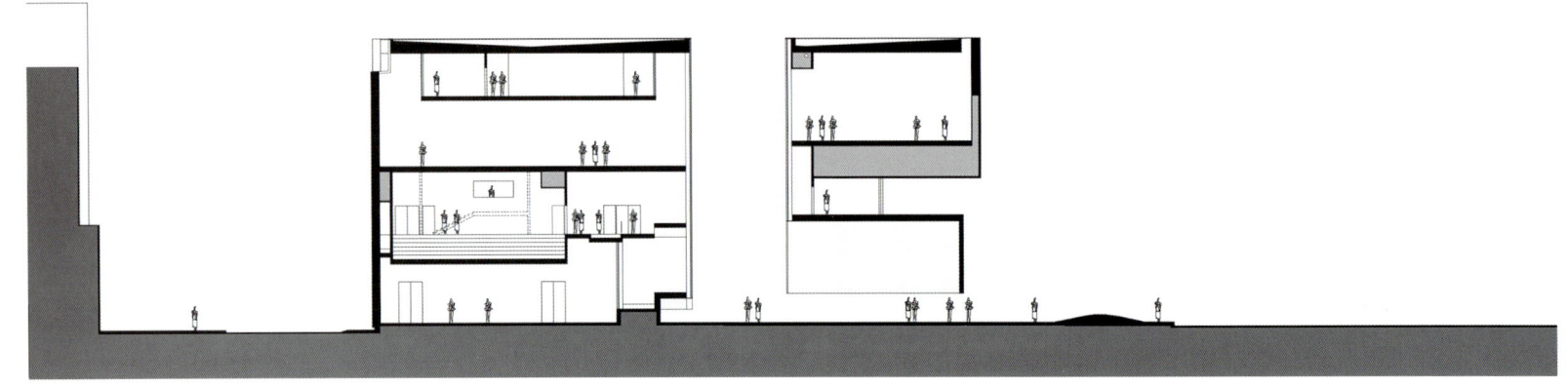

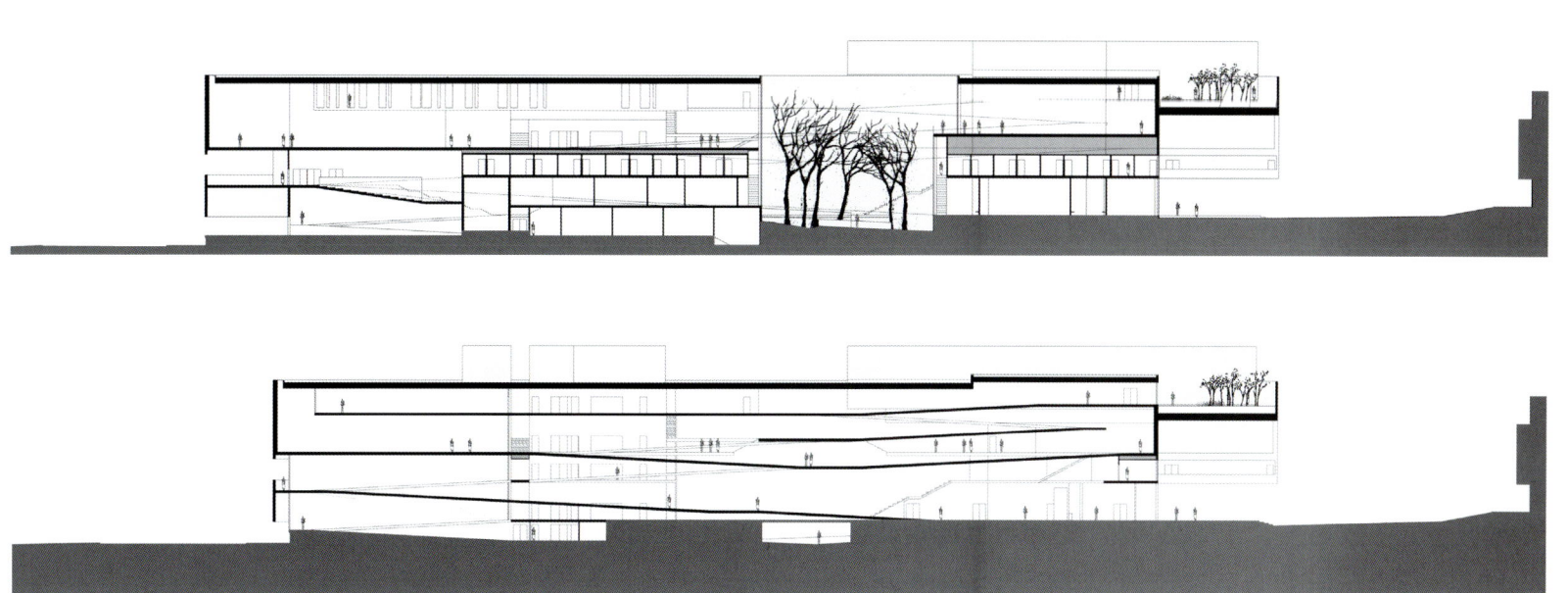

Lower Level:
1. Workcourt
2. Woodshop
3. North Courtyard
4. Mechanical
5. Unexcavated
6. Knowlton Columns
7. Archives

Beauvoir

Jury Comments:
This is a great example of a successful effort that included finding the funds, doing the research and implementing the work with great skill, discipline and love. As a victim of Hurricane Katrina this project is significant culturally, historically and architecturally. The clarity of the commitment led to a remarkable restoration.

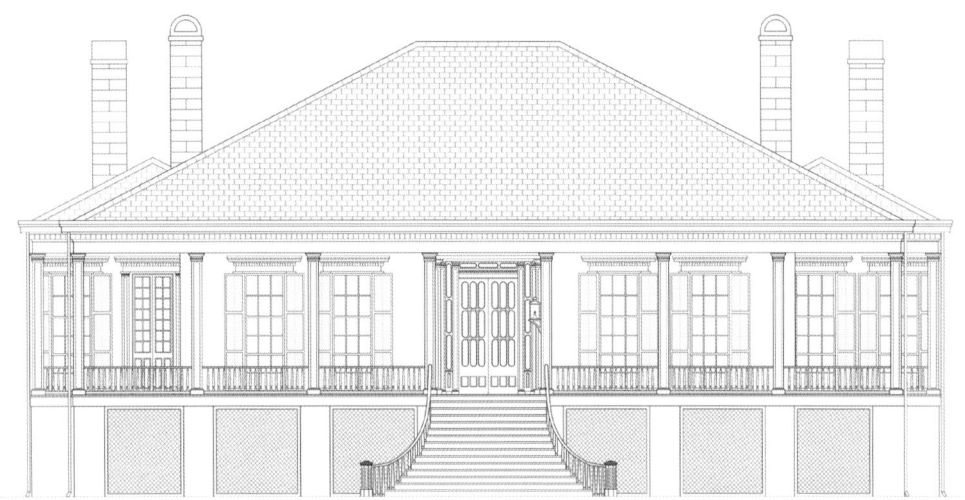

Notes of Interest
The home that would become known as Beauvoir (meaning "beautiful view") was constructed in 1852 by James Brown, a planter from Madison County, Mississippi. It was owned by the Mississippi Division of the Sons of the Confederate Veterans (SCV) and operated by the State of Mississippi. In 1973, Beauvoir was designated a National Historic Landmark by the National Park Service.
On August 29, 2005, Hurricane Katrina made landfall approximately 60 miles west of Biloxi. The storm surge ripped the piers out from under the porches causing structural failure of the entire front porch and the roof over the front porch, as well as compromising the integrity of the chimneys. Failure of the roof over the front porch also caused extensive damage to adjacent interior ceilings. Ultimately, the mansion had barely survived the worst weather event in its 153 year history with a severely compromised foundation and an overly vulnerable envelope.

Consultant: George Fore
Engineer: Sparks Engineering, Inc
General Contractor: The Lathan Company Inc.
Owner: Mississippi Division Sons of Confederate Veterans

Architect
Albert & Associates Architects

Location
Biloxi, Mississippi

Photo Credit
© Sarah A. M. Newton

Brochstein Pavilion and Central Quad: Rice University

Jury Comments:
The only non-brick building at Rice University, the Brochstein Pavilion is a deceivingly simple glass, aluminum and steel jewel that solves complex issues on campus and activates the open space of this important circulation area. Its transparency, lightness and immaculate detailing make this structure a refreshing destination on campus.

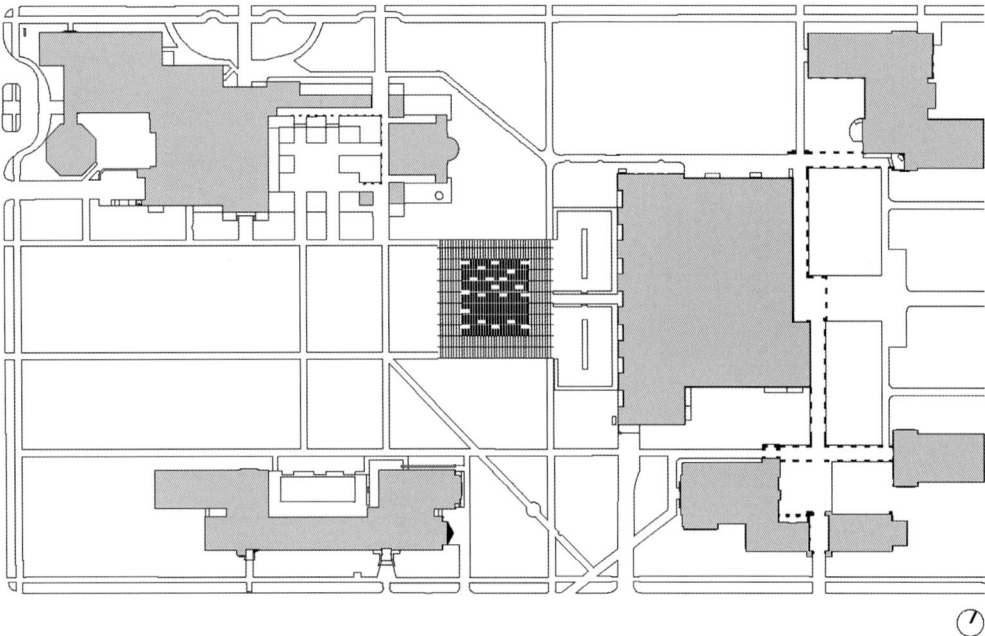

Notes of Interest
Centrally located on Rice University's campus, the Raymond and Susan Brochstein Pavilion was conceived as a destination for students and faculty to interact and share ideas in a relaxed environment. Carefully sited at an important intersection of campus pathways to create a new hub of activity, the Pavilion encourages interaction without interrupting pedestrian movement through campus. The sensitive addition of trees, fountains, and garden seating areas seamlessly blends the new pavilion into the existing quadrangle.

The Brochstein Pavilion is capped by a steel trellis structure which protects the building and extends in all directions to cover and shade the surrounding seating terrace. Shading the entire structure pavilion consisting of an array of small aluminum tubes, the trellis cuts the direct sun by an average of 70 percent. This extensive shade protection reduces the required mechanical cooling load by 30 percent and allows the structure to be open and naturally ventilated throughout much of the year.

Consultant: Fisher Marantz Stone (Lighting), Walter P. Moore (Structural)
Engineer: AltieriSeborWieber LLC, Haynes Whaley Associates
General Contractor: Linebeck Group, LLC
Landscape Architect: The Office of James Burnett
Owner: Rice University

Architect	Location	Photo Credit
Thomas Phifer and Partners	Houston, Texas	© Scott Frances

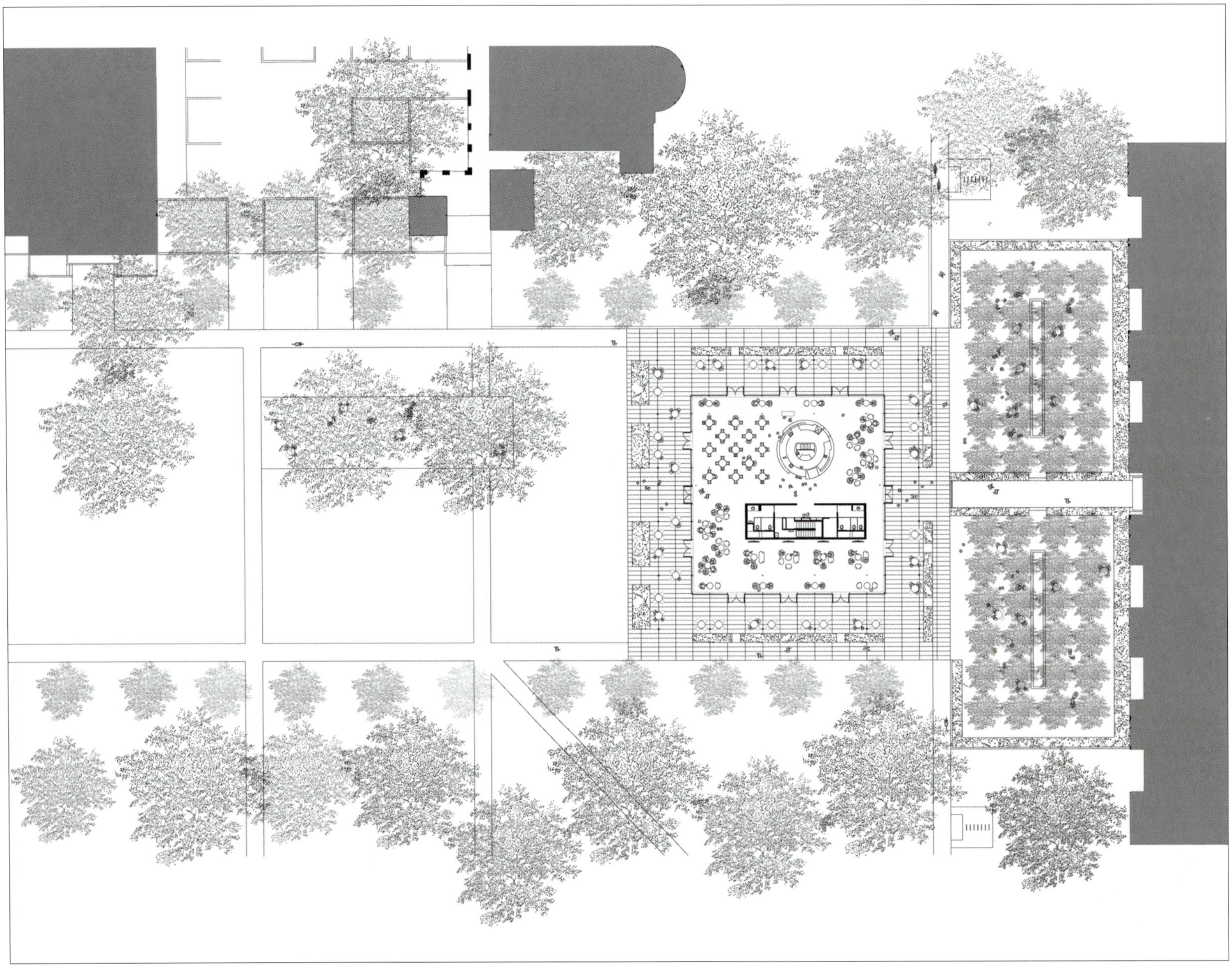

Camino Nuevo High School

Jury Comments:
Architecturally responsive to program and difficult (thin) site on very tight budget, while solving social and sustainability desires with single loaded exterior circulation and maximum daylighting opportunities... creates an educational haven within a busy urban environment.

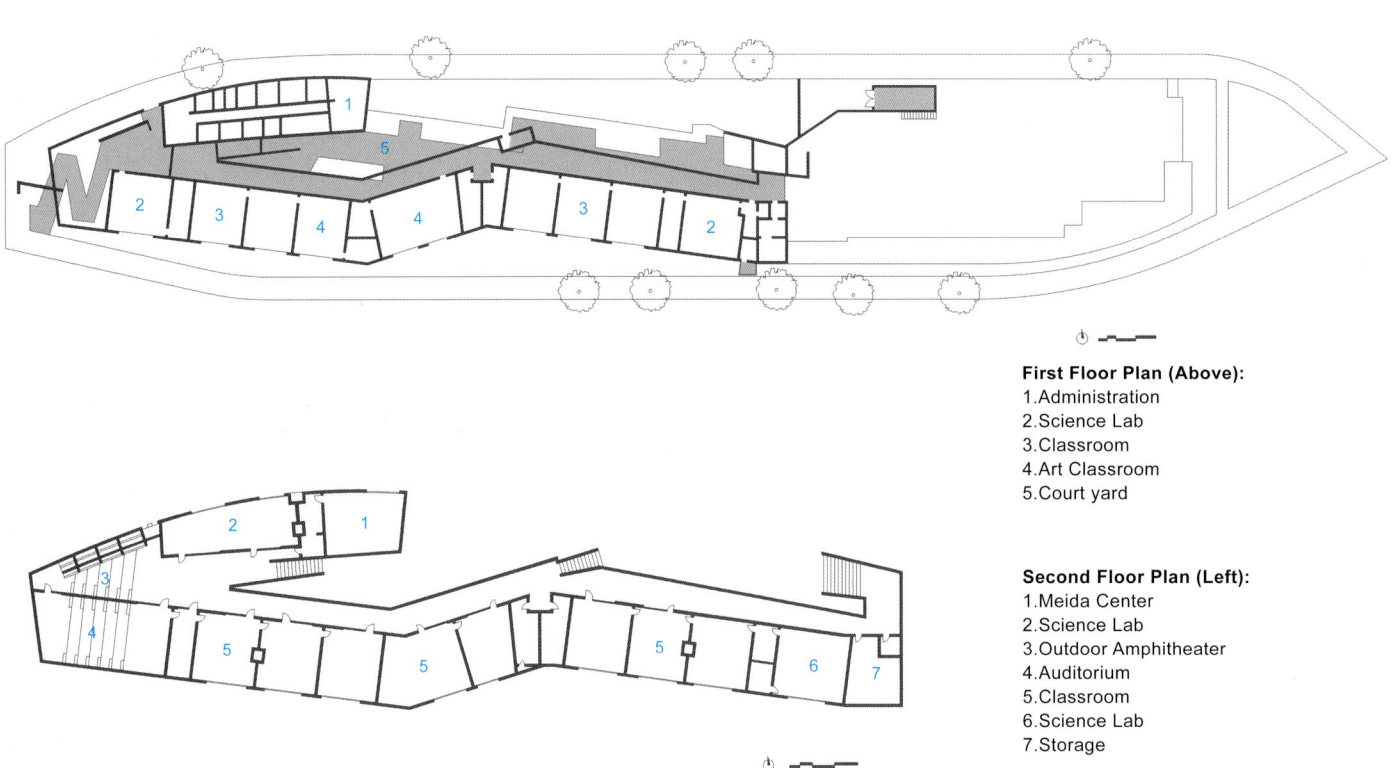

First Floor Plan (Above):
1. Administration
2. Science Lab
3. Classroom
4. Art Classroom
5. Court yard

Second Floor Plan (Left):
1. Meida Center
2. Science Lab
3. Outdoor Amphitheater
4. Auditorium
5. Classroom
6. Science Lab
7. Storage

Notes of Interest

This charter high school houses 500 students in Silver Lake, a multi-cultural community adjacent to downtown Los Angeles. It is the third project, in a series of four that the firm has designed for the charter school client. The schools were launched by a nonprofit community development corporation to provide small, focused schools for children in a dense and underserved urban Los Angeles neighborhood. In 2000 and 2003 the office completed an elementary and a middle school on a single block campus in MacArthur Park.

A winding form for the 30,000 square foot, 18-classroom building maximizes the space available on the oddly shaped site. Additionally, by single-loading the one, main classroom building, two important social and sustainable functions were accomplished with simple solutions: direct visual connections are established between the classrooms and the inner courtyard and natural light flows into each classroom from both the windows on the street side and courtyard side. This courtyard has become the hub of the school.

Consultant: Konsortum 1, Pfeiler and Associates
Engineer: John Labib + Associates, Tsuchiyama Kaino Sun & Carter
General Contractor: Turner Special Projects
Landscape Architect: Ah be
Owner: Pueblo Nuevo Development

Architect
Daly Genik

Location
Los Angeles, California

Photo Credit
© Tim Griffith

Campus Restaurant and Event Space

Jury Comments:
Crisp, elegant and ordered with a fantastic floating canopy that engages the campus landscape, this project brings together company staff of all types into a light-filled, open gathering place.

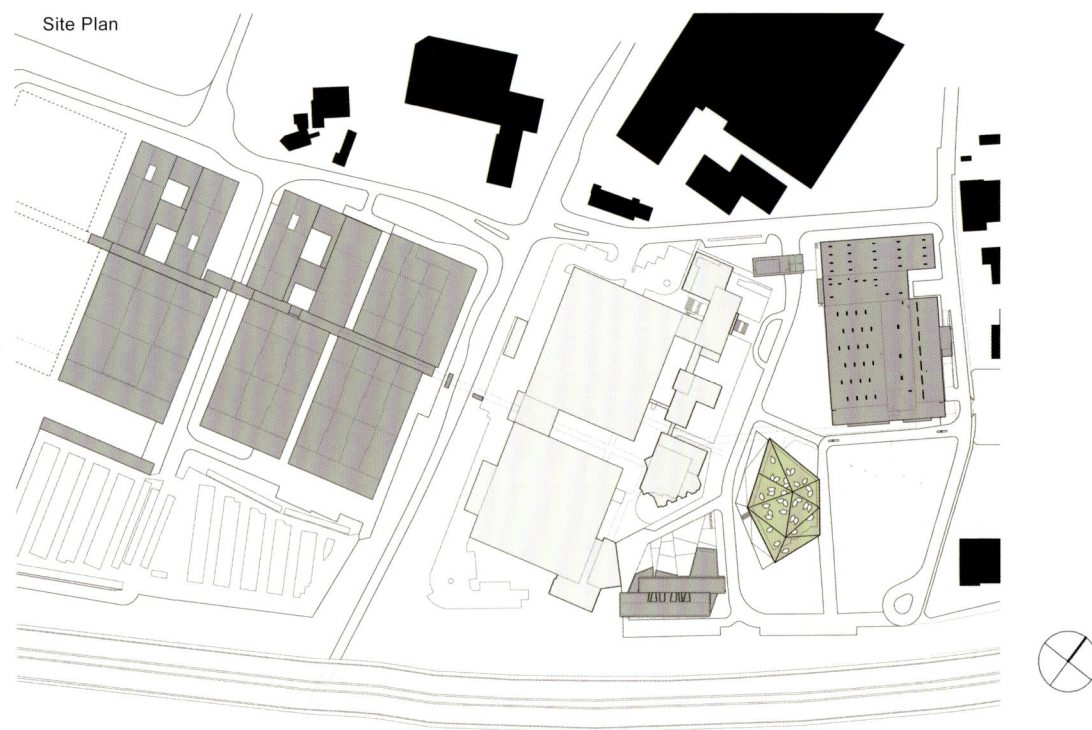
Site Plan

Notes of Interest
This pavilion provides a new central cafeteria and event space for a Stuttgart-based industrial campus. It is the new social center for the company for both blue- and white-collar workers. The pavilion, with seating for 700, enables the company's 2,000 employees to lunch around three time slots in the large central space with reserve seating in a mezzanine. When programmed for events the space functions as an auditorium with seating for 800.

A floating roof hovers over the central dining space and mezzanine that are placed in an excavated hollow. The intention was to create a polygonal leaf-like canopy that wide-spans over column-groups. Aesthetically, the roof as a fifth facade, is carefully organized with skylights, and air-vents, as it is highly visible from the mid-rise office buildings adjacent to it.

Neither a factory nor an office building, this freestanding pavilion introduces a new typology to the campus. Urbanistically the new restaurant helps to complete spatially the entrance courtyard. Formally its crystalline pentagon plan is a continuation of the crystalline ground plans of the new office building to which it is adjacent.

Consultant: Transsolar Energietechnik GmbH (Climate), Gassmann + Grossmann (Management)
Engineer: Werner Sobek Stuttgart (Structural; Facade) Schuckertstrasse 27
Landscape Architect: Buero Kiefer
Owner: TRUMPF GmbH + Co.KG

Architect
Barkow Leibinger Architects

Location
Stuttgart, Germany

Photo Credit
© Amy Barkow

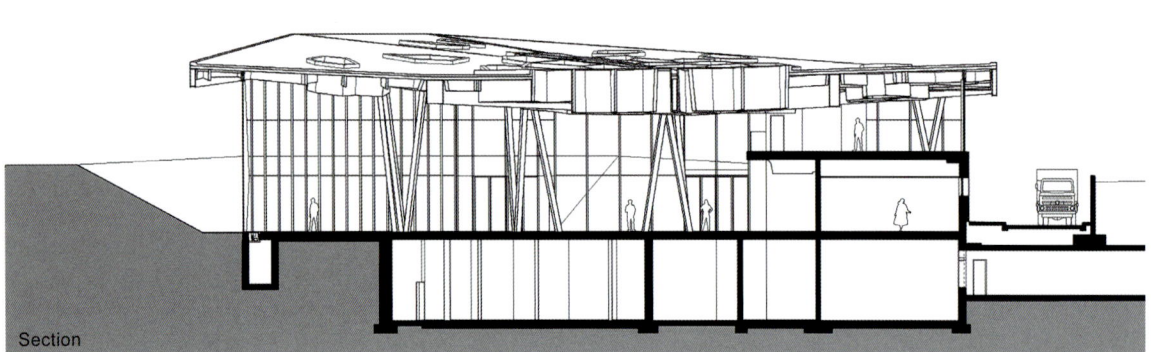
Section

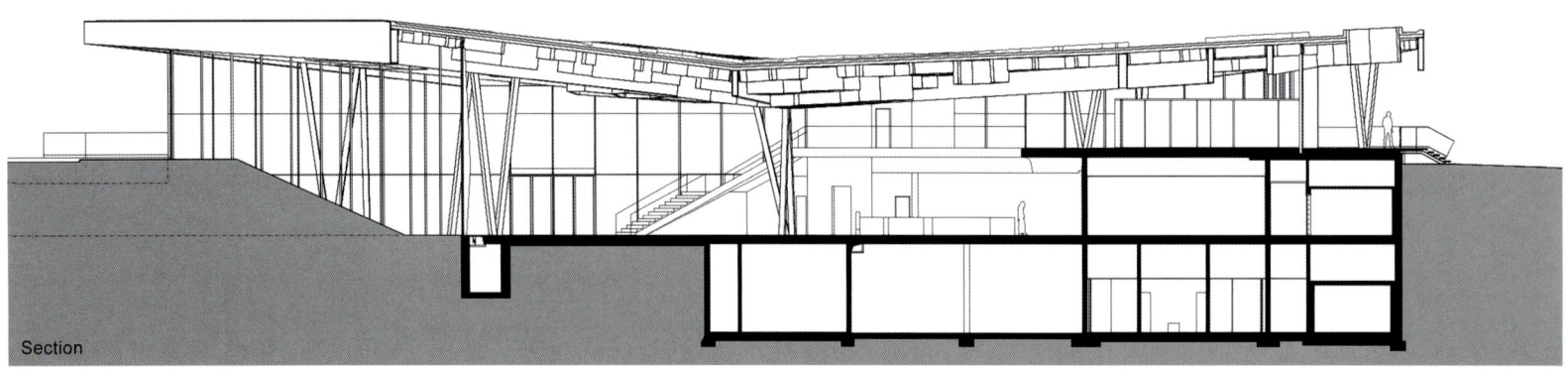
Section

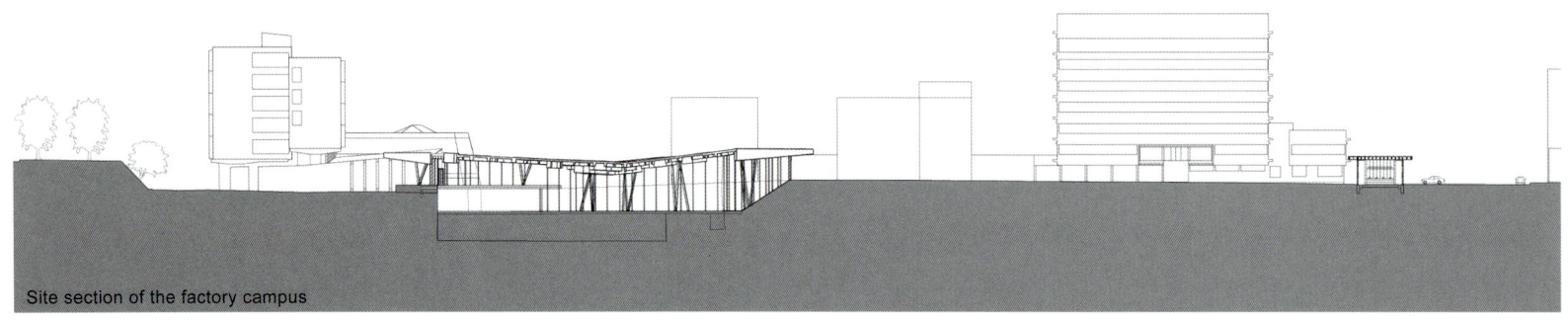
Site section of the factory campus

CAMPUS RESTAURANT AND EVENT SPACE

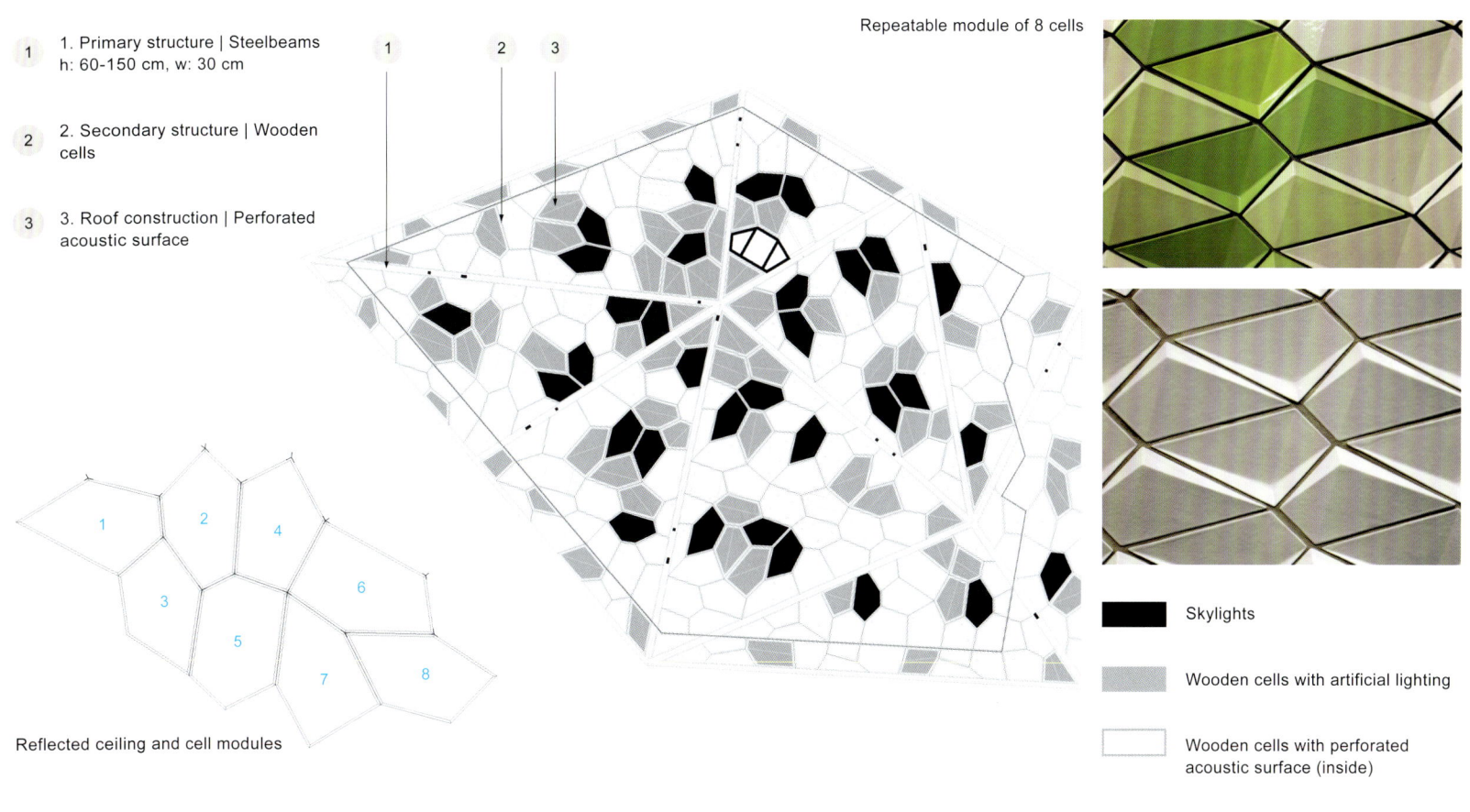

1. Primary structure | Steelbeams
   h: 60-150 cm, w: 30 cm
2. Secondary structure | Wooden cells
3. Roof construction | Perforated acoustic surface

Repeatable module of 8 cells

Reflected ceiling and cell modules

■ Skylights
▨ Wooden cells with artificial lighting
☐ Wooden cells with perforated acoustic surface (inside)

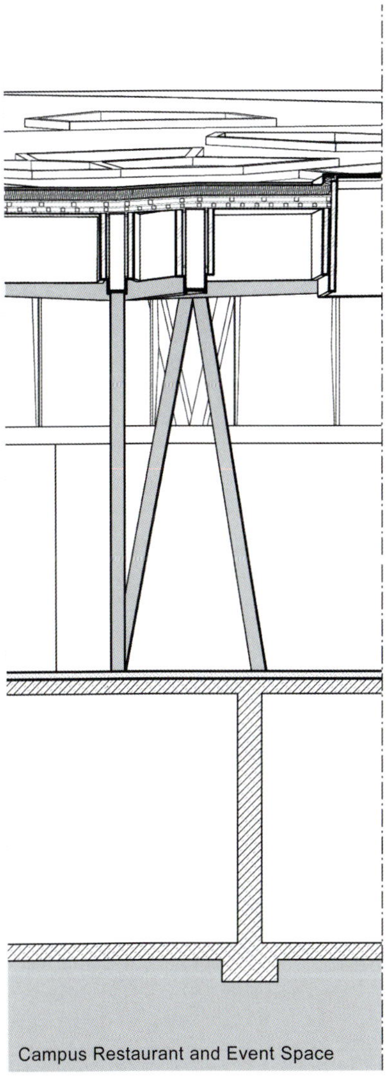

Campus Restaurant and Event Space 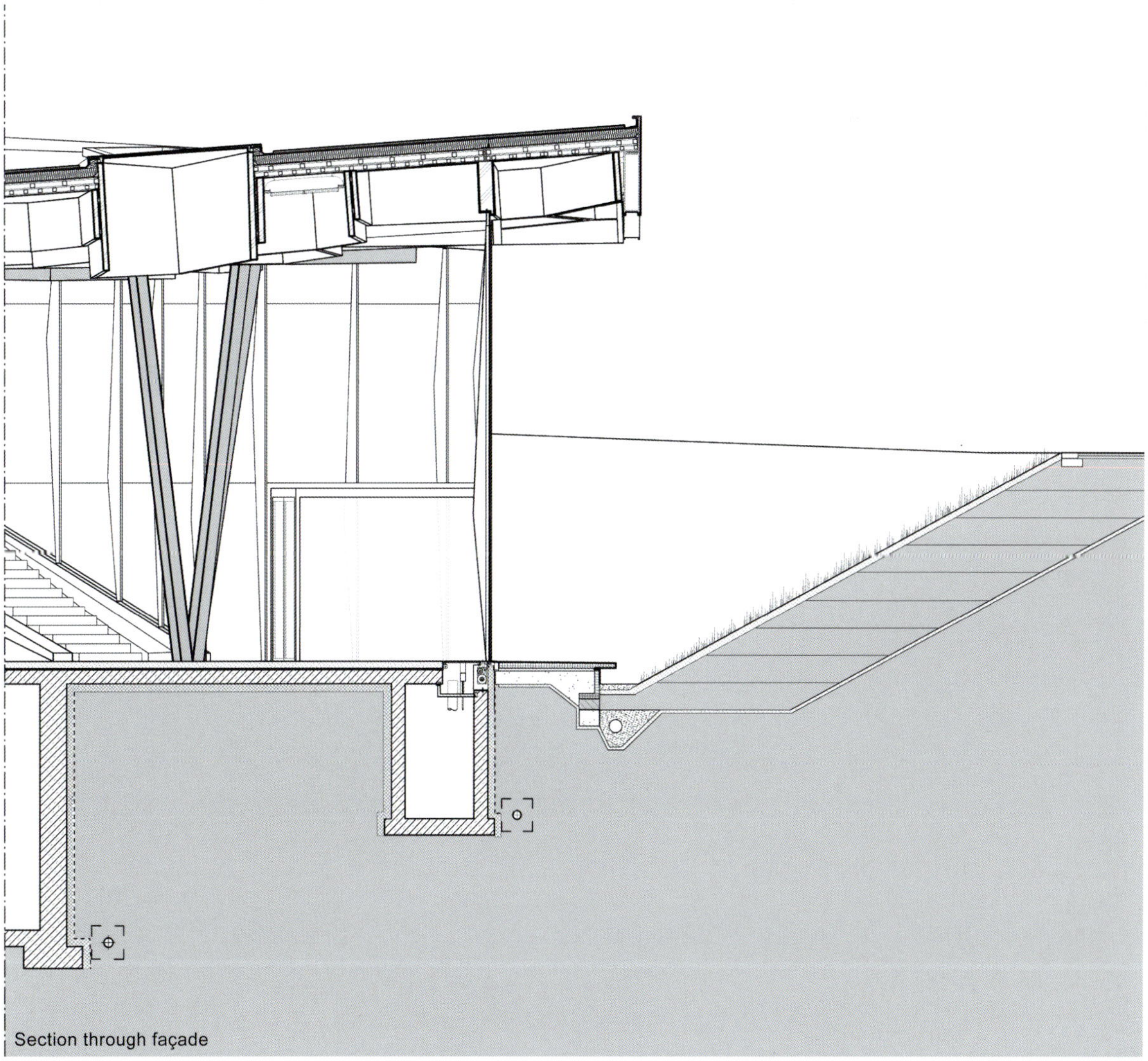 | Section through façade

041

Floor Plan: Mezzanine (+ 1m):
1. Restaurant
2. Terrace
3. Caféteria
4. Air supply
5. Leaving air, return cooling tower

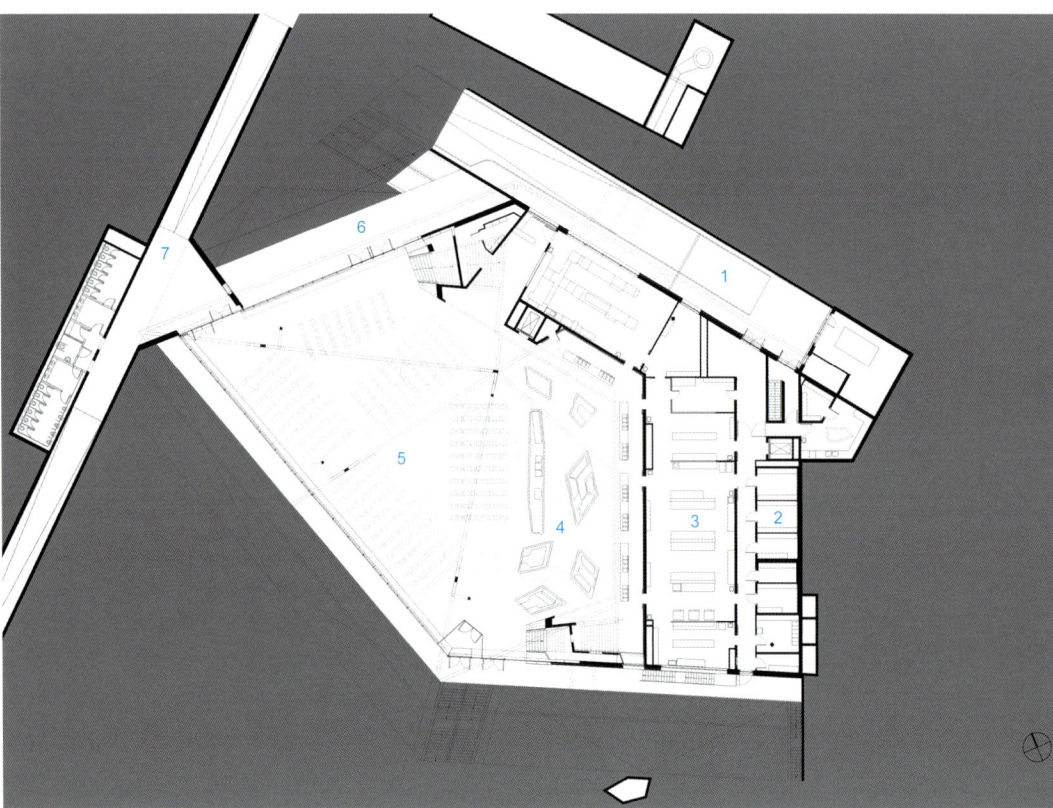

Floor Plan: Level 1 (- 4m):
1. Delivery
2. Storage
3. Kitchen
4. Foodcounters
5. Restaurant and Auditorium
6. Lounge
7. Tunnel connection of factory campus

Macallen Building

Jury Comments:
This is a bold architectural statement in which the architects and the client did not shy away from taking risks. The building is inventive and at times, ingenious.

Notes of Interest
As a pivotal building in the urban revitalization of South Boston, the Macallen's design required a reassessment of conventional residential typologies to produce an innovative and sustainable building that worked within a developer's competitive budget. Occupying a transitional site that mediates between highway off-ramps, an old residential fabric, and an industrial zone, the building negotiates different scales and urban configurations through varied spatial conditions, various ways of reacting to the public sphere, and different material and façade articulations.

On the western end, the building responds to the highway and Boston skyline with a glass curtain wall yielding panoramic views for the residents inside. On the eastern end, brickwork mirrors that of the neighborhood's building fabric, extending the logic of the storefront and pedestrian scale elements. On the north and south façades, bronzed aluminum panels reflect the industrial zone and express the structural system within.

The Macallen is fully integrated – in structure, and sustainability – and is replete with sustainable features to make it the first LEED gold certified building of its type in Boston.

General Contractor: Bovis Lend Lease
Landscape Architect: Landworks Studio
Owner: Pappas Enterprises, Inc.

Architect
Office dA, Inc. and Burt Hill

Location
Boston, Massachusetts

Photo Credit
© John Horner Photography

Outpost

Jury Comments:
A severely simple building evokes ages-old images of oases and paradisiacal gardens transported to the American west. Industrial materials, while rough, are thoughtfully detailed and crafted, and are handled with great skill to make a sublime place.

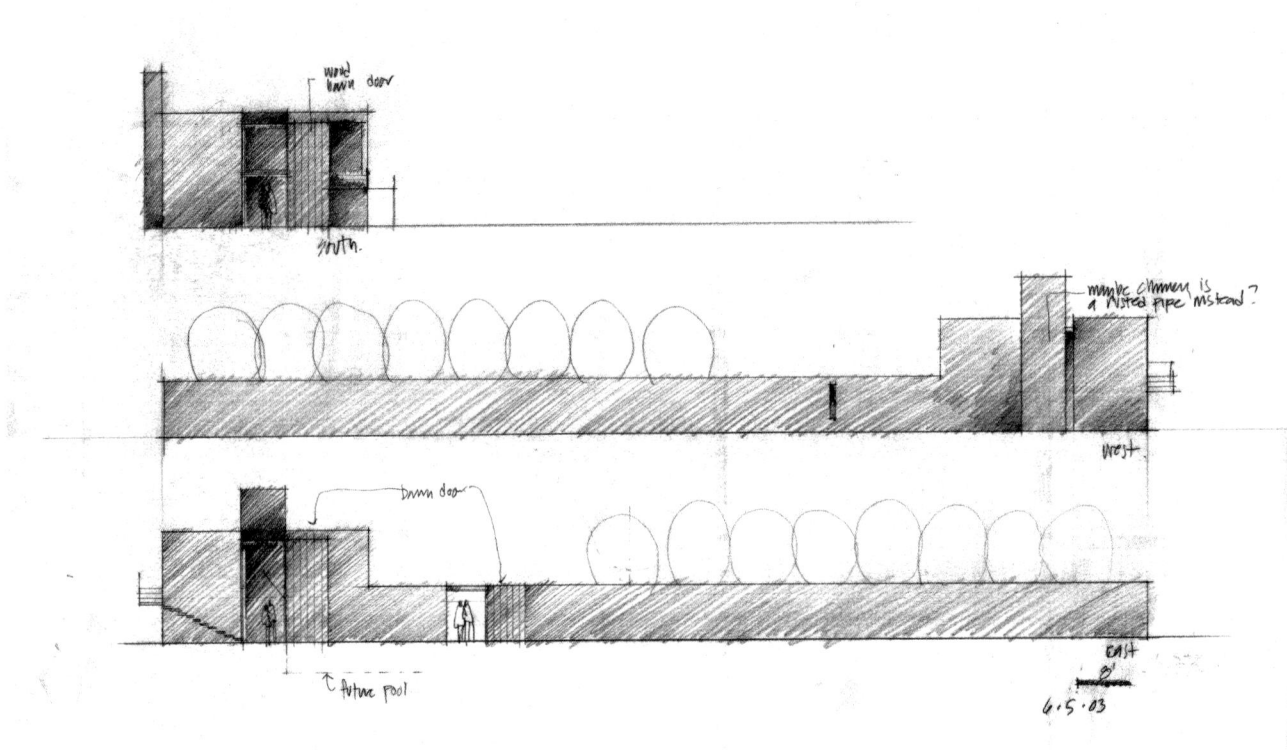

Notes of Interest

Set in the remote and harsh high desert landscape of Idaho, Outpost is an artist live/work studio and sculpture garden for making and displaying art. An important aspect of the complex is the protected "paradise garden", which is separated from the wild landscape by thick masonry walls. The materials used in the structure, including concrete block, car-decking, and plywood, require little or no maintenance, and are capable of withstanding the extreme weather that characterize the desert's four seasons.

Outpost's compactness limits site impact and reinforces the desire to be outside. The architects chose a readily available construction material – concrete block – for the primary structure; commercial builders were able to quickly and cheaply assemble the building. Interiors are exposed and unfinished. In a windy environment, the enclosed garden provides protection to develop a cultured space. Nothing outside the walls is modified. The footprint of the building is the limit of intrusion into the landscape – a simple, clearly defined space within the landscape.

Engineer: Monte Clark
General Contractor: Upham Construction
Owner: Jan Cox

Architect
Olson Kundig Architects

Location
Central Idaho

Photo Credit
© Tim Bies

future loft
exterior courtyard
interior room
big glass door
exterior courtyard
Main floor
6-5-03
N

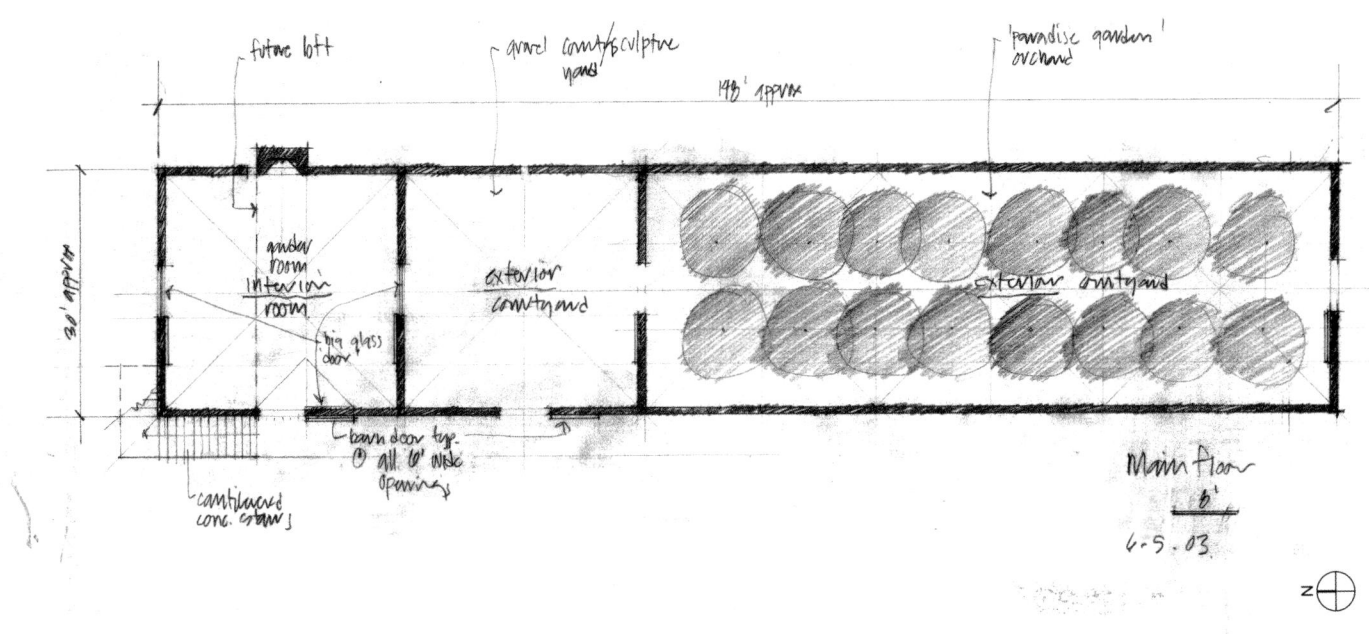

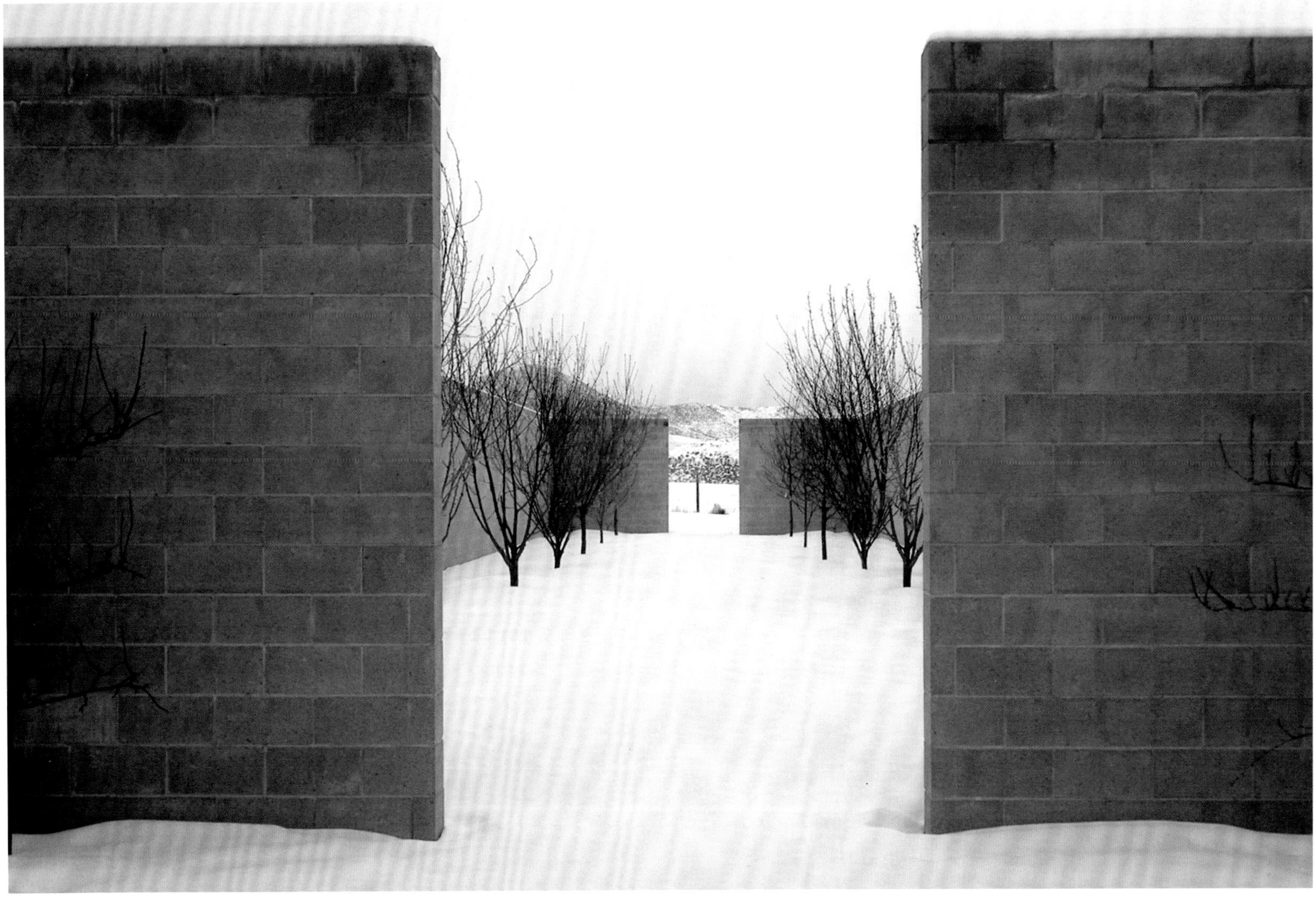

50'
30'
tool area
office
pool equip
7'
mech equip
laundry
clo.
powder.
lower.
1/16" = 1'-0"
11·15·04
N

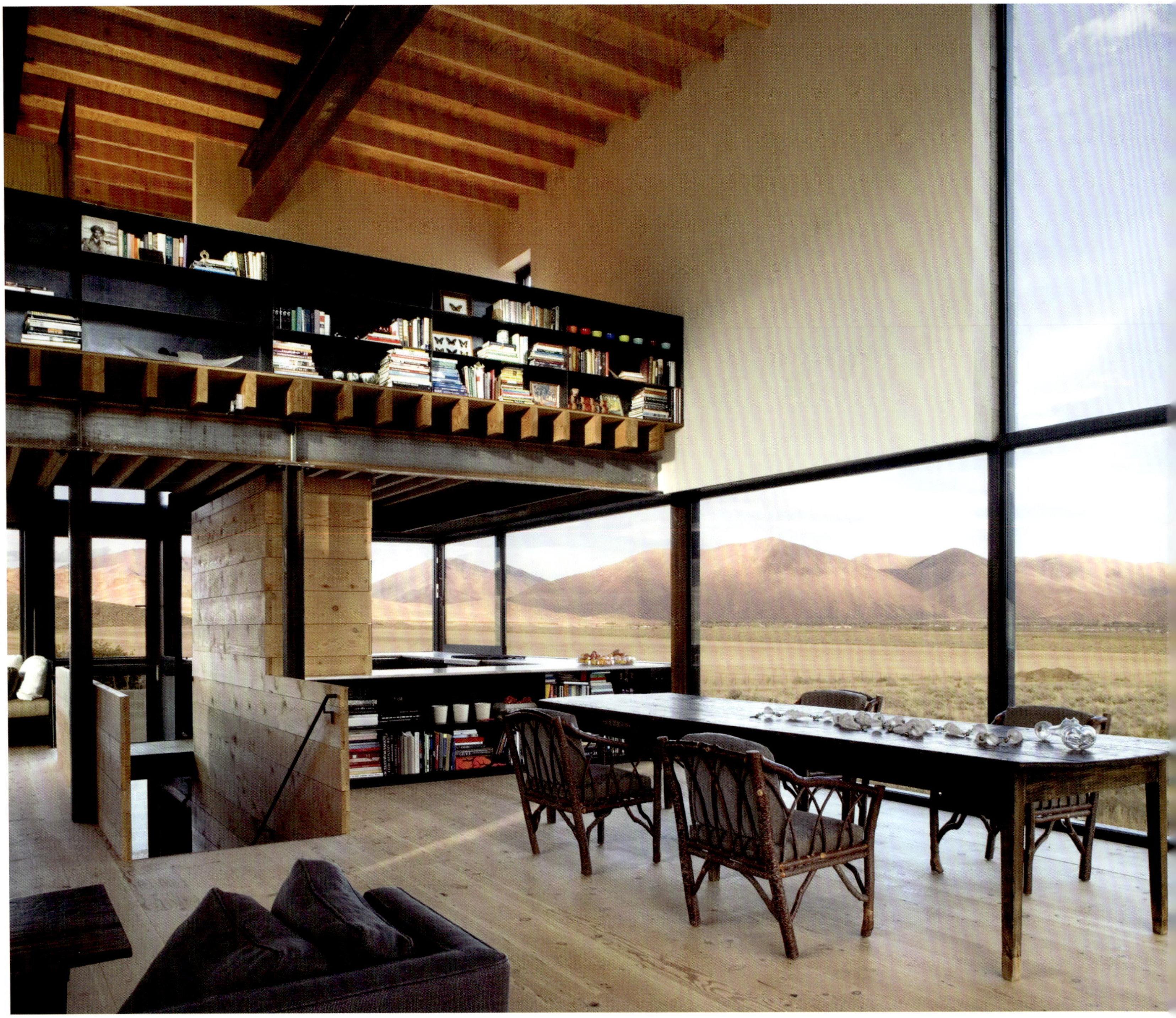

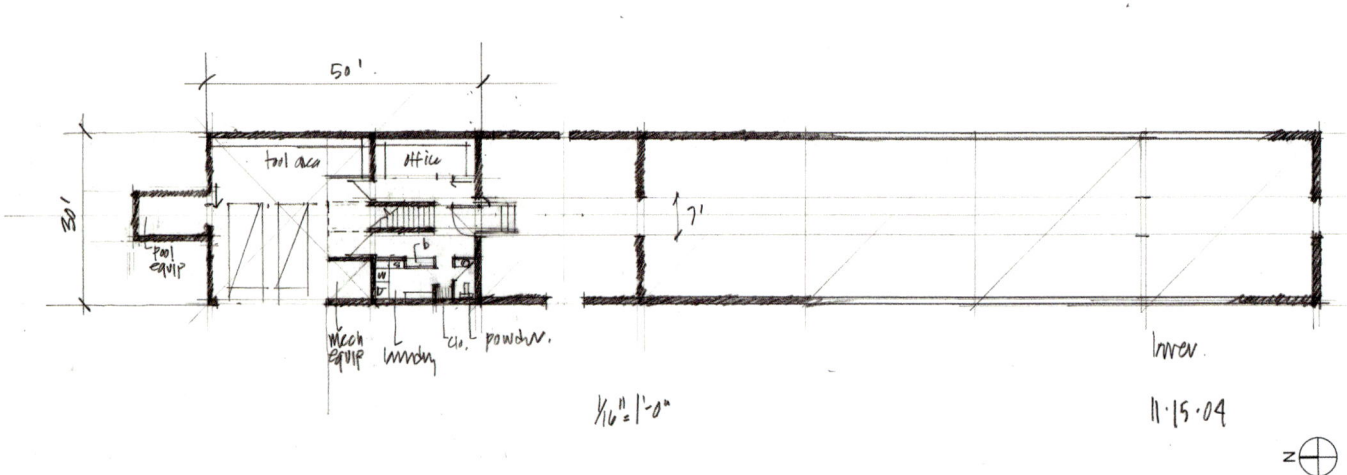

Serta International Center

Jury Comments:
A corporate headquarters that goes beyond trying to project a "powerful" corporate image... Not only is the building beautiful and functional, but it is a testament to Serta's commitment to their employees and providing them with an inspiring workspace and to the preservation of the environment around them.

Notes of Interest
The project is a 90,000 square foot world corporate headquarters for Serta International Mattress Company located on a 20-acre Illinois prairie site. The program combines a 65,000-square-foot office wing and a 25,000-square-foot-high bay R&D facility.

The building (700 feet long x 67 feet wide) has been designed to facilitate equal access to natural light, ventilation, and views of the wetlands for all employees. To accomplish this, the floor plan has been layered from a glass edged public circulation path on the east, to an open office area on the west toward the wetlands. The design also takes advantage of the variations in the topography of the site, to weave together the building and the landscape into a strong holistic composition. The design intent of the building is to float lightly on the landscape, reinforcing the notion of environmental sustainability and echoing the lines of the prairie.

Engineer: Epstein
General Contractor: G.A. Johnson and Sons
Landscape Architect: Jacob/Ryan Associates
Owner: Serta International

Architect
Epstein | Metter Studios

Location
Hoffman Estates, Illinois

Photo Credit
© Metter Photography, © Epstein, © Andrew Metter

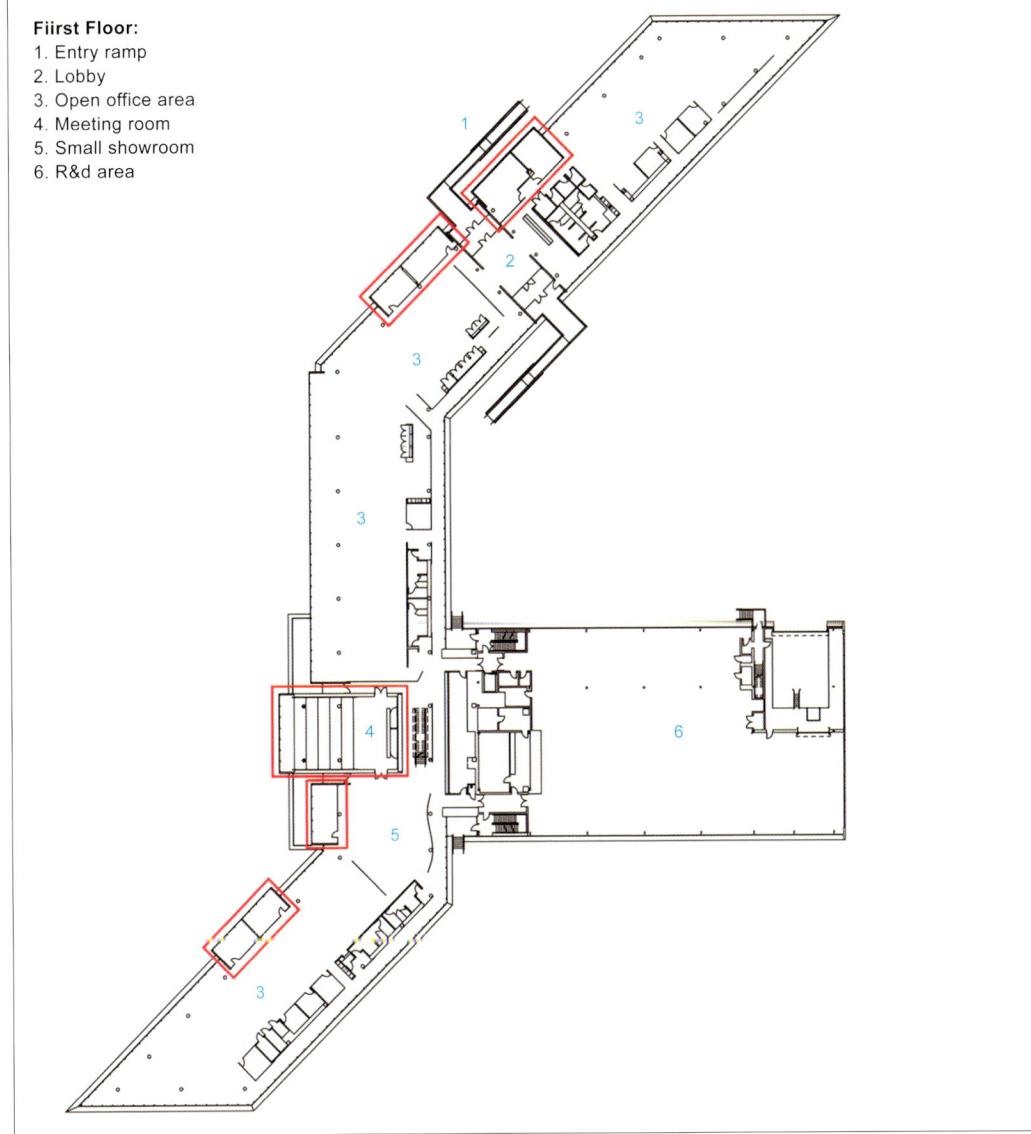

Fiirst Floor:
1. Entry ramp
2. Lobby
3. Open office area
4. Meeting room
5. Small showroom
6. R&d area

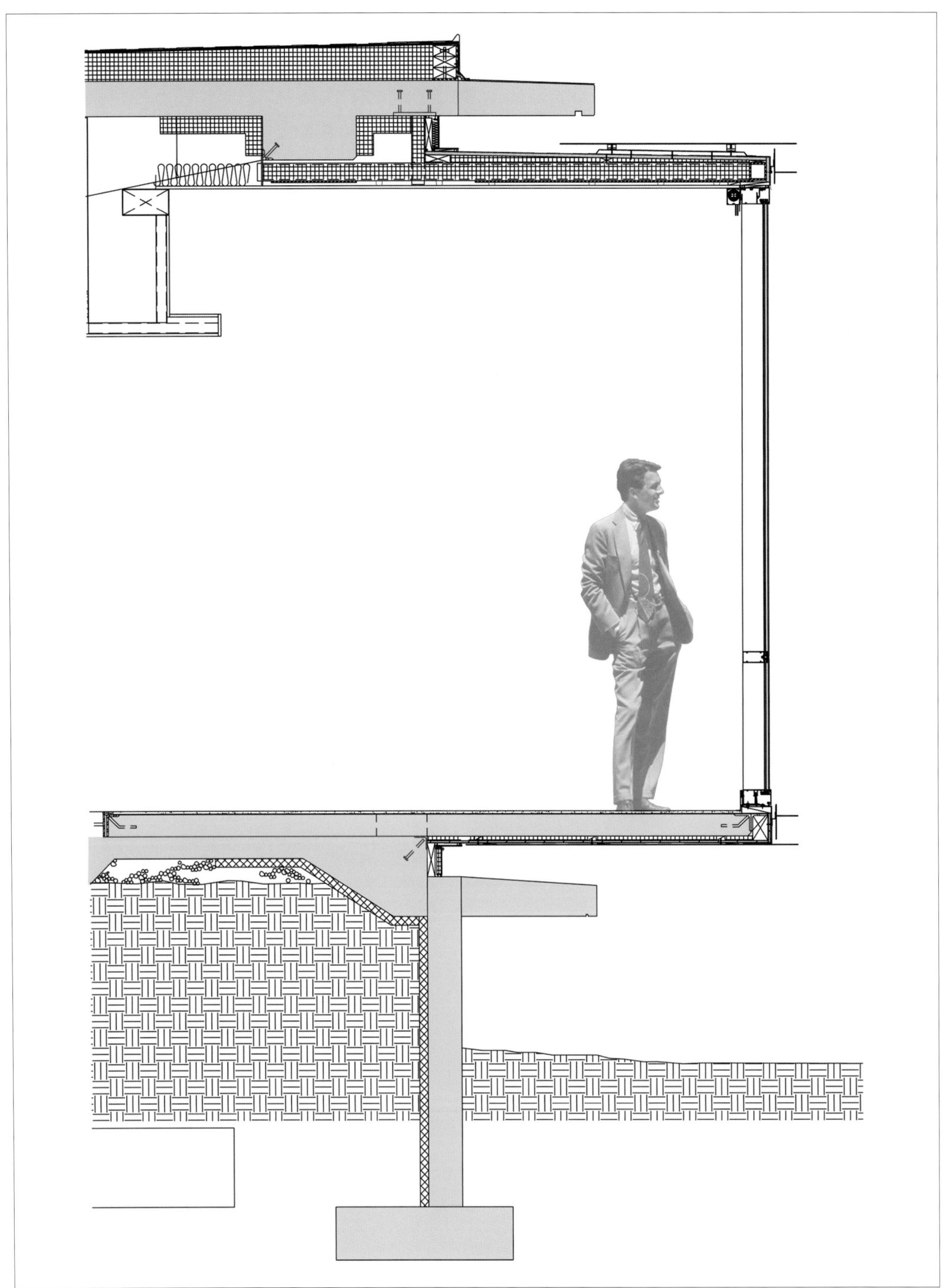

Skirkanich Hall

Jury Comments:
There is a thoughtful use of materials, genius in vertical circulation, solid programmatic resolution... both delicate and dramatic, all in all a beautiful project.

Notes of Interest

Located in the heart of the University of Pennsylvania, Skirkanich Hall is home to the Bioengineering Department. It is an infill building that functions as a connector by creating a new public quadrangle and entry for the School of Engineering and Applied Sciences. Movement and interaction is emphasized with generous circulation spaces that offer places to sit and gather.

The building is cantilevered over the street and descends twenty feet below grade to minimize vertical impact. An open atrium continues up from the ground through five floors above. The laboratories are placed on either side. A vibrant yellow tile with a changing pattern enhances the core space.

To subtly stand out from the red brick buildings next door, a new kind of brick was developed through an extensive process to balance texture, color, durability, and stability. The mossy green colored brick changes with the light of the day. Giant glass shingles contrast the density of the surrounding masonry and bring filtered light into the laboratories.

Associate Firm: The Rose + Guggenheimer Studio
Consultant: GPR Planners Collaborative, Fisher Marantz Stone
Engineer: Ambrosino DePinto & Schmeider, Severud Associates
General Contractor: Skanska USA Building, Inc.
Landscape Architect: Edmund Hollander
Owner: The University of Pennsylvania

Architect
Tod Williams Billie Tsien Architects

Location
Philadelphia, Pennsylvania

Photo Credit
© Michael Moran

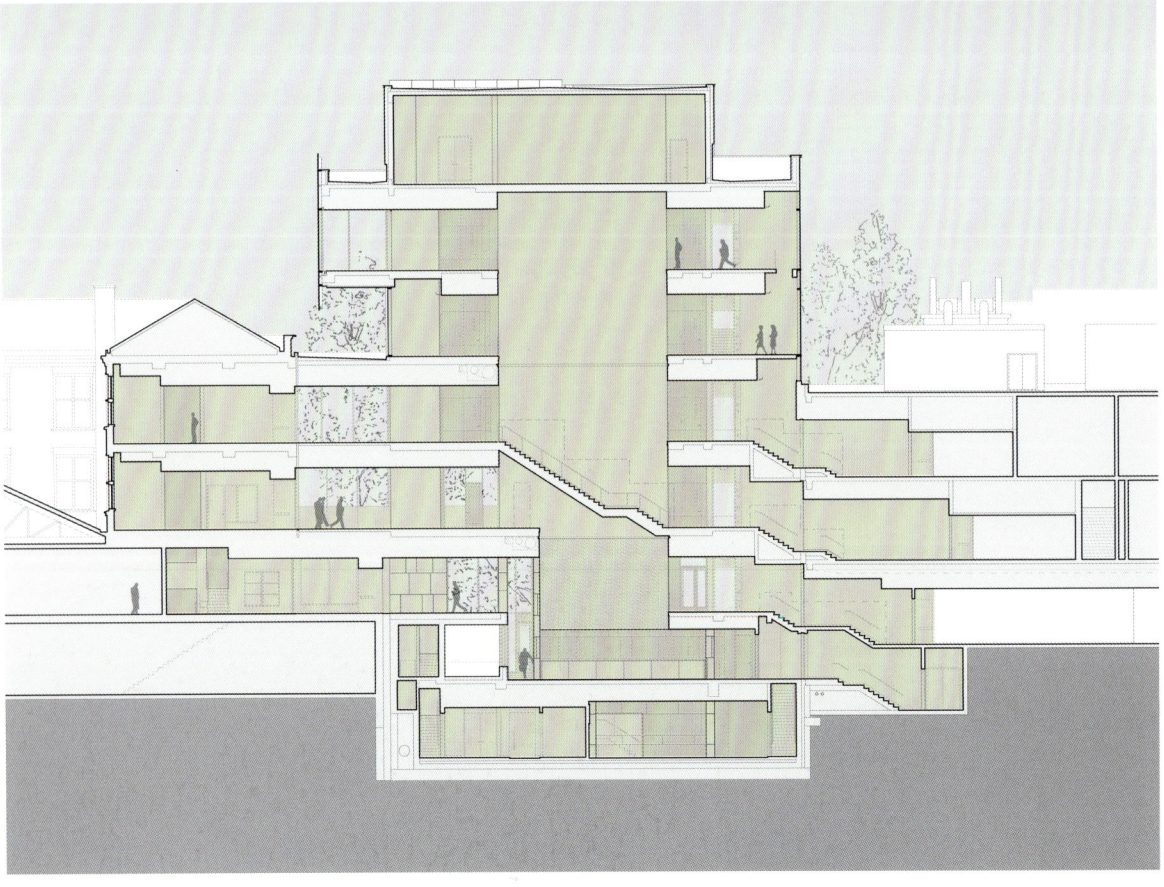

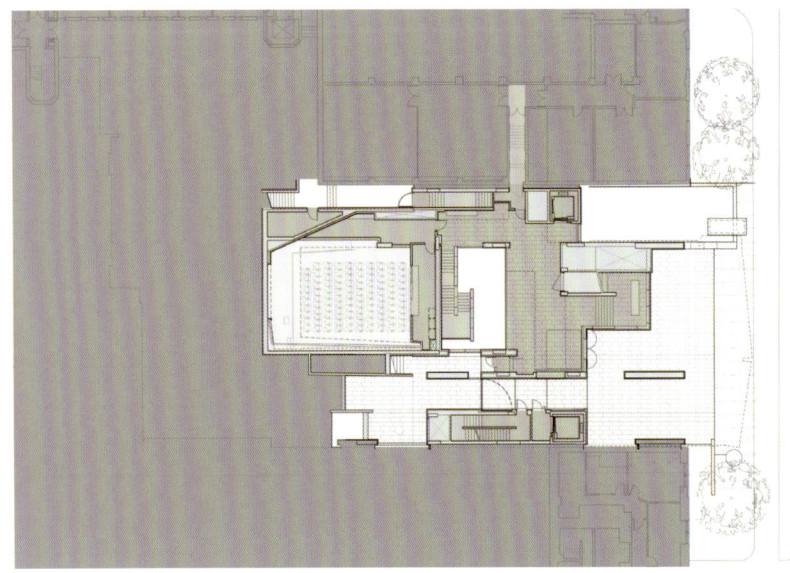
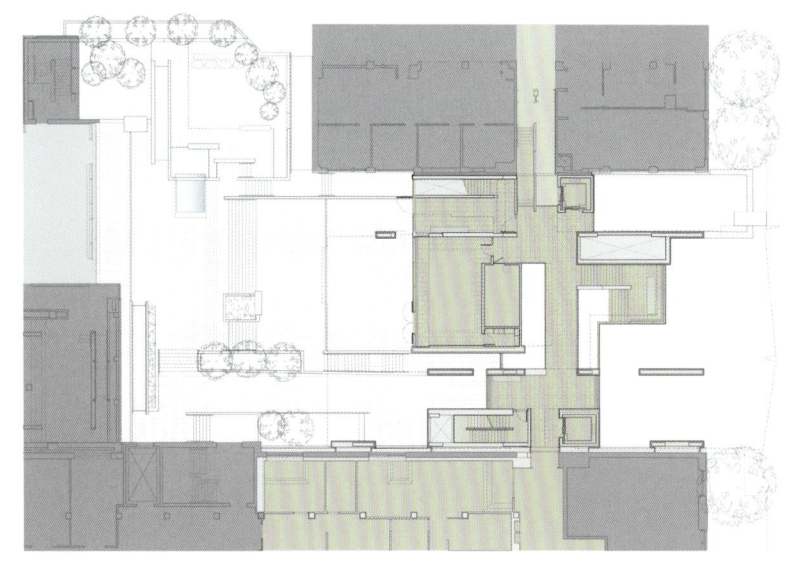
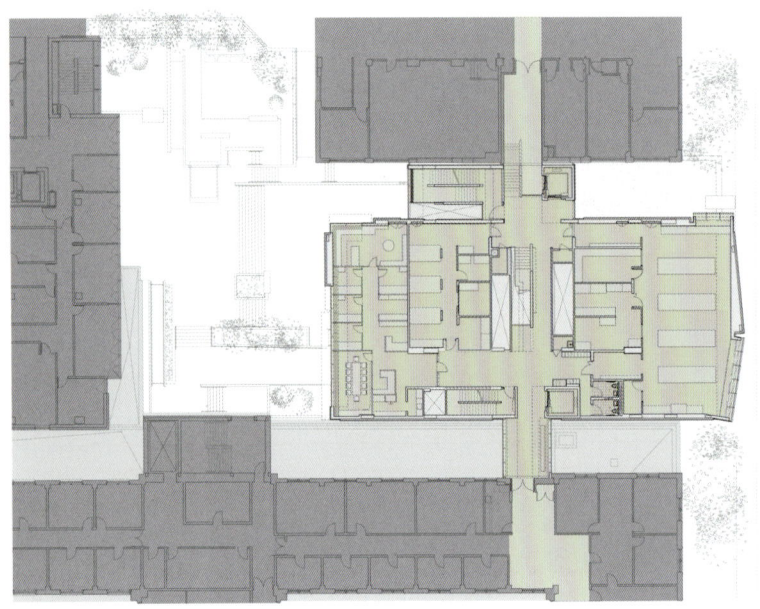
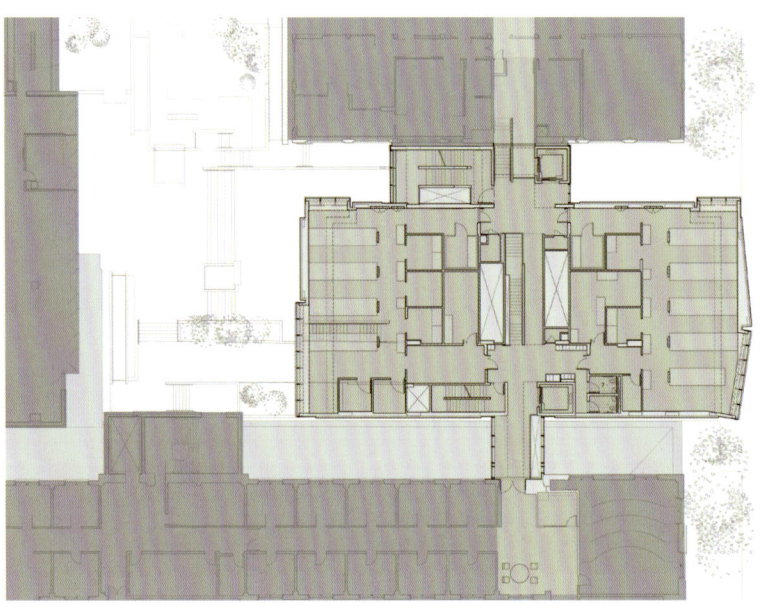
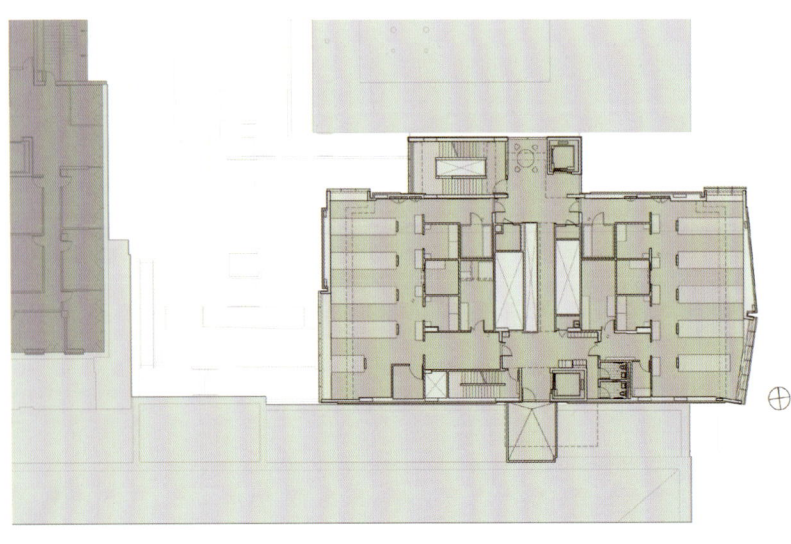
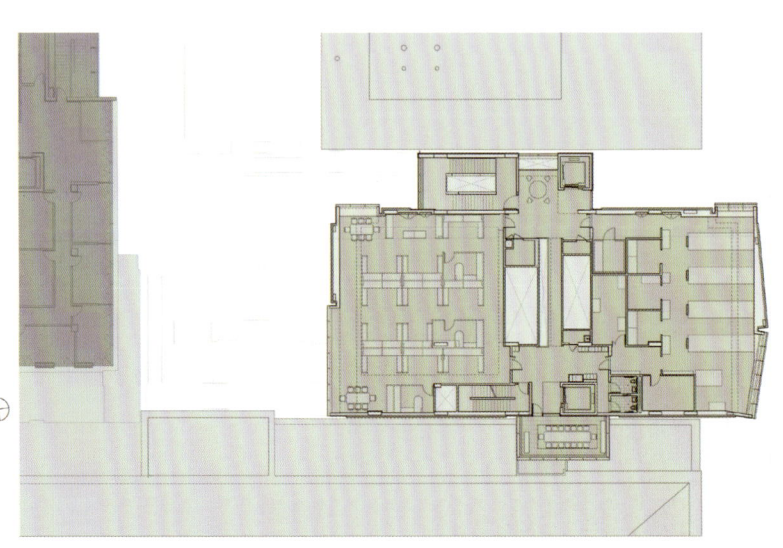

Step Up on 5th

Jury Comments:
Step Up on 5th is a very conscious piece of architecture in general. Not only a refuge for the homeless and mentally disabled, it is also an incredibly dense and sustainable piece of architecture. It's an example of a project with a lot of thought and care put into the design of it for the betterment of the community and the inhabitants.

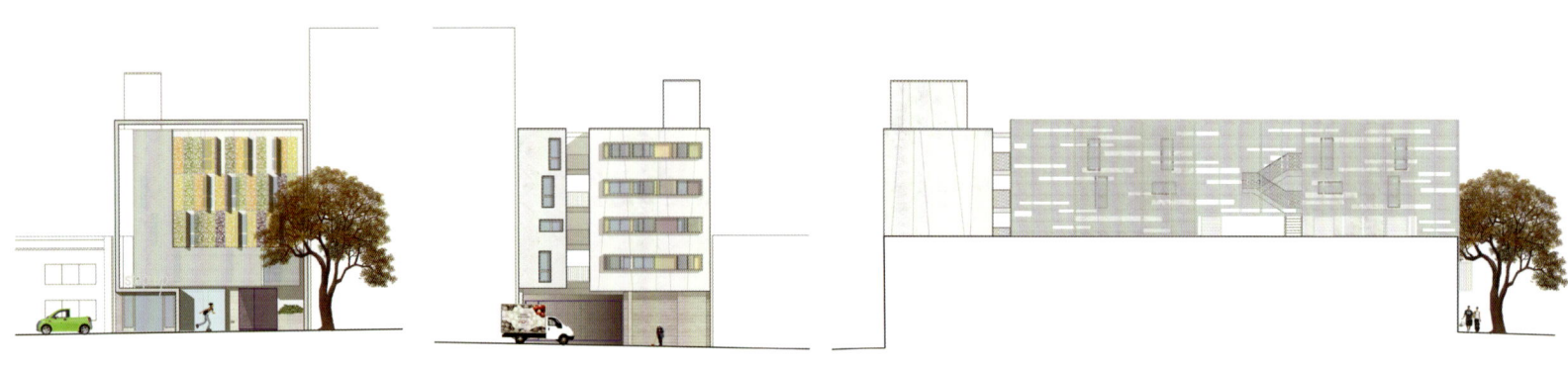

East Elevation	West Elevation	South Elevation

Notes of Interest
The new 46-unit mixed-use building provides a home and support services for the mentally disabled homeless population.
The main façade made from custom water jet anodized aluminum panels creates a screen that sparkles in the sun and glows at night, while also acting as sun protection and privacy screens. The material reappears as a strategic arrangement of screens lending a subtle rhythm to the exterior circulation. South-facing walls filter direct sunlight creating a sense of security for the emotionally sensitive occupants.
The project incorporates energy efficient measures that exceed standard practice, optimize building performance, and ensure reduced energy. The design emerged from close consideration and employment of passive solar design strategies that make this building 50 percent more efficient than a conventionally designed structure. While California has the most stringent energy-efficient requirements in the United States, the building exceeds LEED standards and state mandated Title 24 energy measures by more than 30 percent.

Consultant: Laschober + Sovich, Helios International, Inc.
Engineer: John Martin and Associates, IBE
General Contractor: Ruiz Brothers
Landscape Architect: LAND Studio
Owner: Step Up on Second

Architect
Pugh + Scarpa

Location
Santa Monica, California

Photo Credit
© John Linden

Sections

Ground Level Floor Plan (Below):
1. Residential entry lobby
2. Mail boxes
3. Public restroom
4. Elevator
5. Cookline
6. Pot wash
7. Cold prep
8. Refridgerator
9. Dry storage
10. Trash room
11. Parking

Fourth Level Floor Plan (Left Buttom):
1. Unit living space
2. Unit kitchen
3. Unit bathroom
4. Community room
5. Laundry room
6. Trash room
7. Elevator
8. Perforated screen
9. Manager's unit

Second Level Floor Plan (Below):
1. Unit living space
2. Unit kitchen
3. Unit bathroom
4. Community room
5. Laundry room
6. Trash room
7. Elevator
8. Perforated screen
9. Manager's unit

TKTS Booth and the Redevelopment of Father Duffy Square

Jury Comments:
With its elegant conception and realization, its refined design stands up to the cacophony of Times Square; this is as much a 21st Century art piece as a building.
The very idea of the building is playful: a structure for selling tickets to shows while also being a vehicle for watching the very "theater" of activity in Times Square. It will be a catalyst for ongoing pedestrian enhancements of the Square.
A simple building, whimsical in nature… it is efficient and functional… sculptural and energetic.

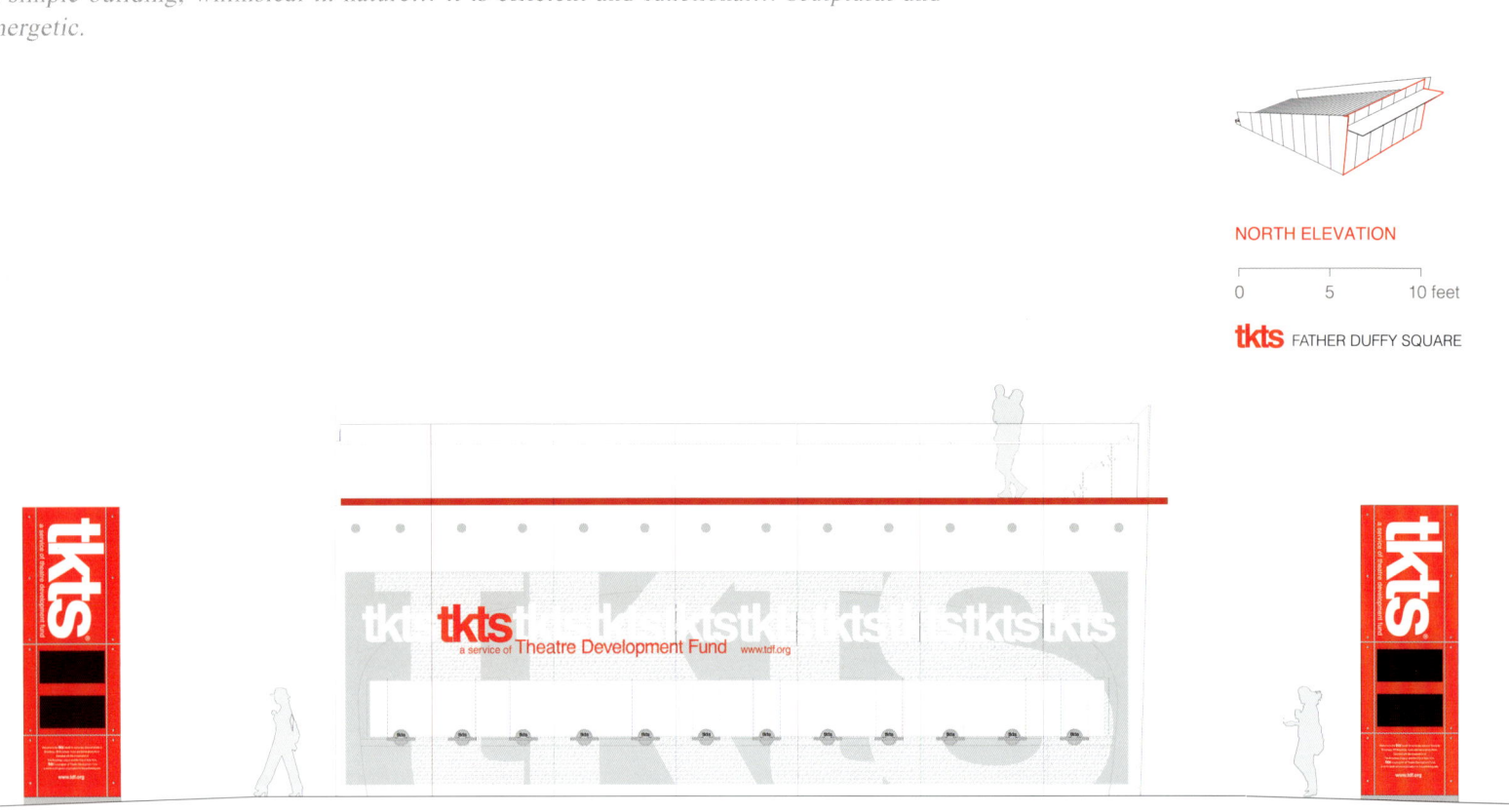

NORTH ELEVATION

0   5   10 feet

tkts FATHER DUFFY SQUARE

Notes of Interest

The new TKTS Booth, including the redevelopment of Father Duffy Square, creates a new center for Times Square, one of the world's most popular and iconic destinations. The project began in 1999 with a design competition to re-design the popular TKTS booth. While the competition brief simply requested designs for a small scale architectural structure to replace the existing ticket booth, the concept-winning design reframed the problem as one requiring a broader urban design response to invigorate and provide a center for Times Square, and won the competition.

In 2001, the client commissioned a firm to conduct a feasibility study to evaluate the conceptual design scheme. The final design was informed and inspired by the original concept but also used a distinctly 21st Century set of approaches: glass would now be employed as the TKTS Booth's sole structural component for the steps and the TKTS Booth itself would be free-standing within the glass enclosure. The transformation of the public space of Father Duffy Square by the Plaza architect allows for increased pedestrian traffic and more prominence for Father Duffy's commanding statue.

Consultant: Dewhurst MacFarlane and Partners, Fisher Marantz Stone, Bresnan Architects, PC
Engineer: Dewhurst MacFarlane and Partners, Schaefer Lewis Engineers, PC, DMJM Harris, Haran Glass, with IG Innovation Glass LLP
Landscape Architect: Judith Heintz Landscape Architects
Owner: Times Square Alliance, Theatre Development Fund, Coalition for Father Duffy and City of New York

Architect
Perkins Eastman, Choi Ropiha, and PKSB Architects

Location
New York City, New York

Photo Credit
© Paúl Rivera

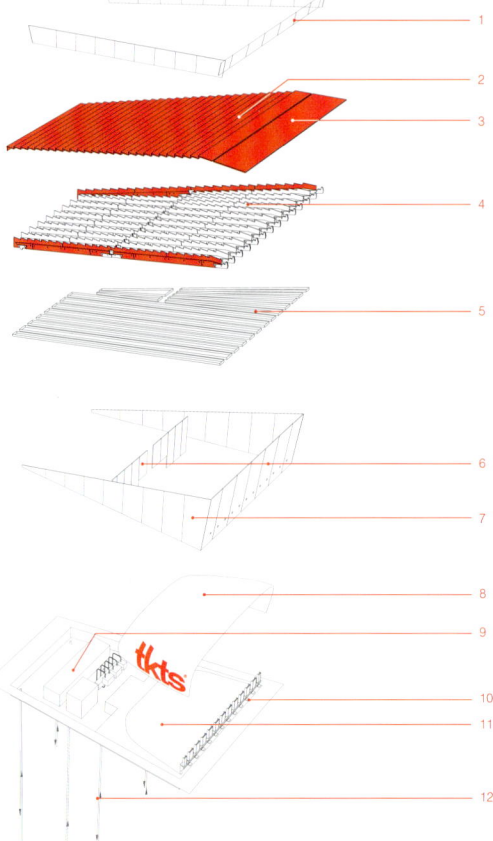

1. Glass Balustrades
2. Laminated Glass Treads
(Ticket Slot Assembly Grouted into Position)
3. Glass Cantilevered Canopy
4. Glass Stringer Beams
5. Radiart Panels + Reflector Parts + LEDs
6. Load Bearing Glass Walls
7. Glass Sidewalls
8. Prefabricated Fiberglass Booth
9. Skid Mounted Mechanical Equipment
10 TKTS Counters
11. Raised Form Assembly
12. Geothermal Wells

AXON

tkts FATHER DUFFY SQUARE

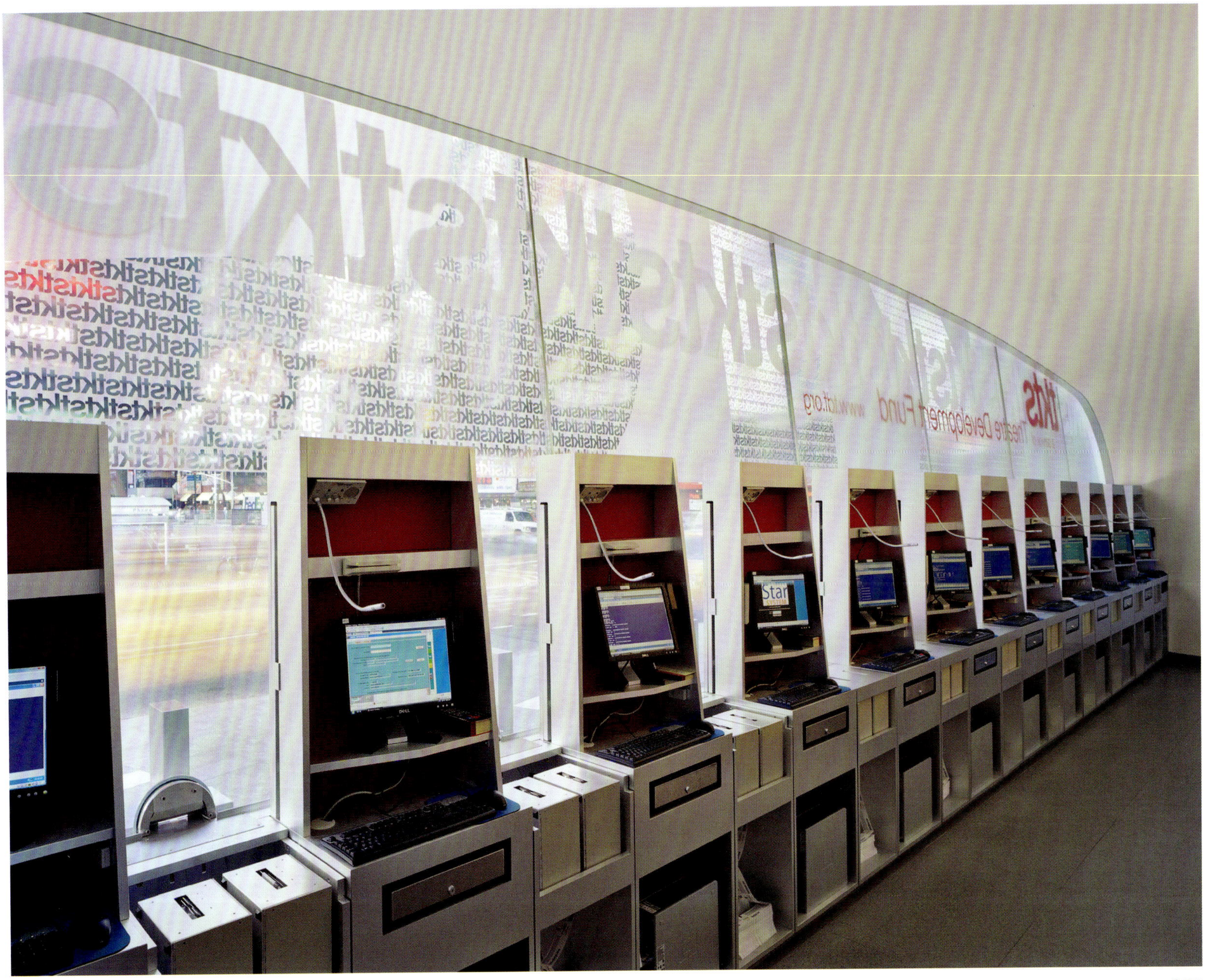

Urban Outfitters Corporate Campus

Jury Comments:
This is a great example of a reuse project. The industrial buildings were beautifully renovated, resulting in an open, collaborative environment that reflects the image of the company that they portray in their clothing stores.

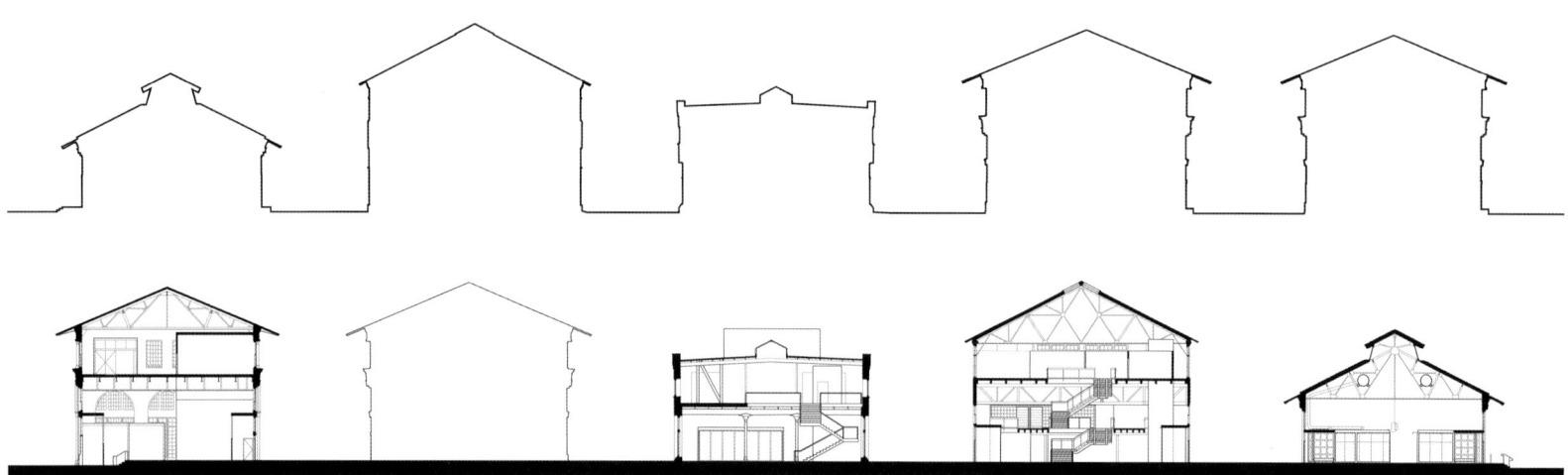

Notes of Interest

The Urban Outfitters Corporate Campus, housed in five rehabilitated buildings in the historic Philadelphia Navy Yard, provides design studio and office space for the company's distinctive retail brands while celebrating the idiosyncratic remnants of more than 125 years of ship-building.

When Urban Outfitters first considered the site, the existing structures were dilapidated. Despite the decay, the soul of the Yard spoke to the company's founder. Each building now houses a different division of the company. Design, documentation, and renovation were completed within 23 months.

The design centers on utilizing the factory characteristics of the buildings – industrial materiality, open volumes and access to daylight – to repurpose the buildings' major function from production to creativity. The synthesis of four measures – art, culture, economy, and environment – results in the transformation from a public, production-based yard to a private, creativity-based one.

Associate Architect: H2L2 Architects Planners, LLC
Consultant: Advanced GeoServices, Jim Larson
Engineer: Paul H. Yeomans, Inc., Meyer, Borgman, and Johnson, Inc.
General Contractor: Blue Rock Construction
Landscape Architect: D.I.R.T. Studio
Owner: Urban Outfitters, Inc.

Architect
Meyer, Scherer & Rockcastle, Ltd.

Location
Philadelphia, Pennsylvania

Photo Credit
© Lara Swimmer Photography

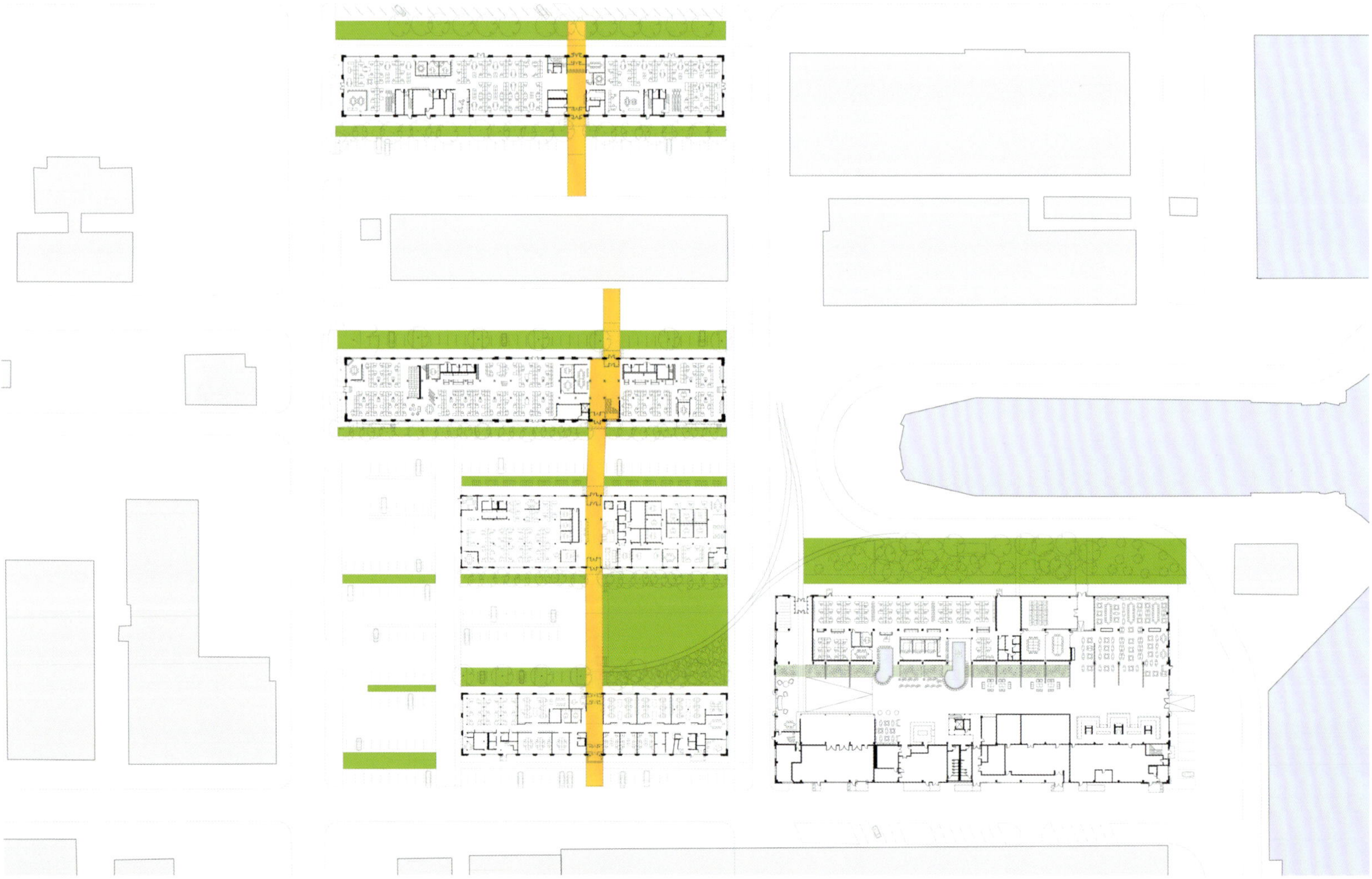

078

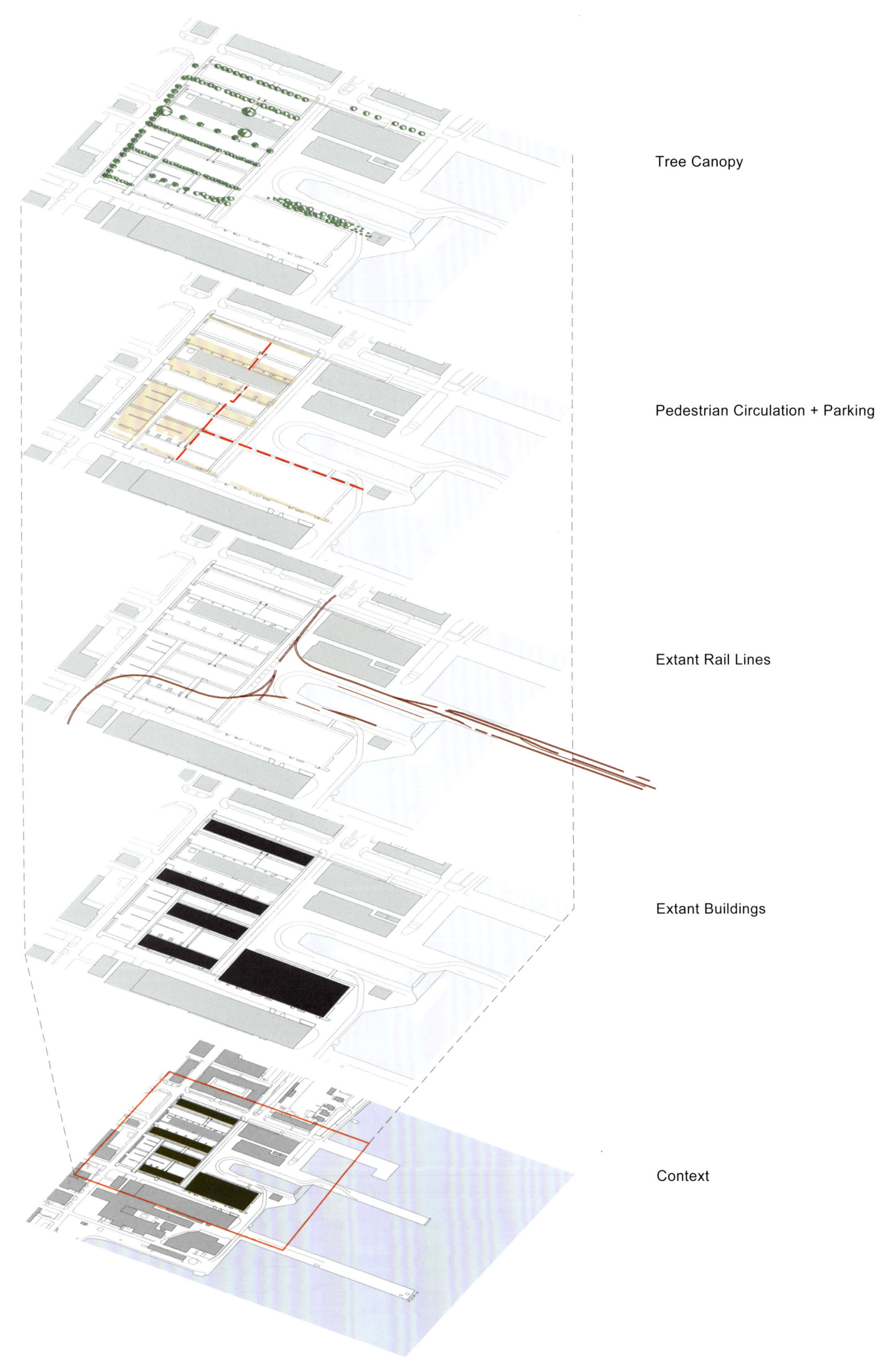

Yale University Art Gallery, Kahn Building Renovation

Jury Comments:
The architectural clarity of the building had been greatly compromised over the years... The original intent is now, once again, perfectly clear... A masterful response to the work of a master.

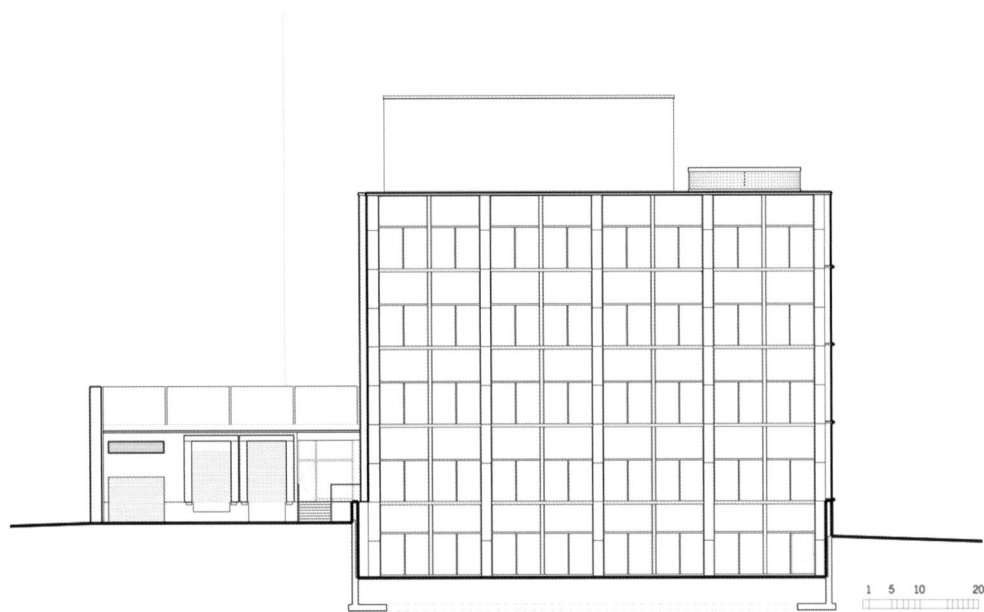

Notes of Interest

Completed in 1953, the Kahn Building is widely considered to be the visionary American architect's first masterpiece and a significant turning point in the history of American museum architecture. Constructed of masonry, glass, and steel, the building has been acclaimed for the bold geometry of its design, its daring use of space and light, and its technical innovations.

The renovation of the landmark building reestablishes its original purity and integrity, restoring many original design features that had become altered or obscured over the years. Roofed over in the 1970's to create additional gallery space, an exterior courtyard has been restored as an open exterior sculpture space. On the second and third floors, extraneous partitions have been removed, and the individual galleries are now revealed in spacious, unobstructed vistas according to Kahn's original vision.

Consultant: Wolf & Company, Robert Schwartz & Associates Shen Milsom & Wilke, Hughes Associates
Engineer: Robert Silman Associates PC, Altieri Sebor Wieber Consulting Engineers, David DeLong
General Contractor: Barr & Barr Builders
Landscape Architect: Towers | Golde
Owner: Yale University

Architect
Polshek Partnership Architects

Location
New Haven

Photo Credit
© Elizabeth Felicella

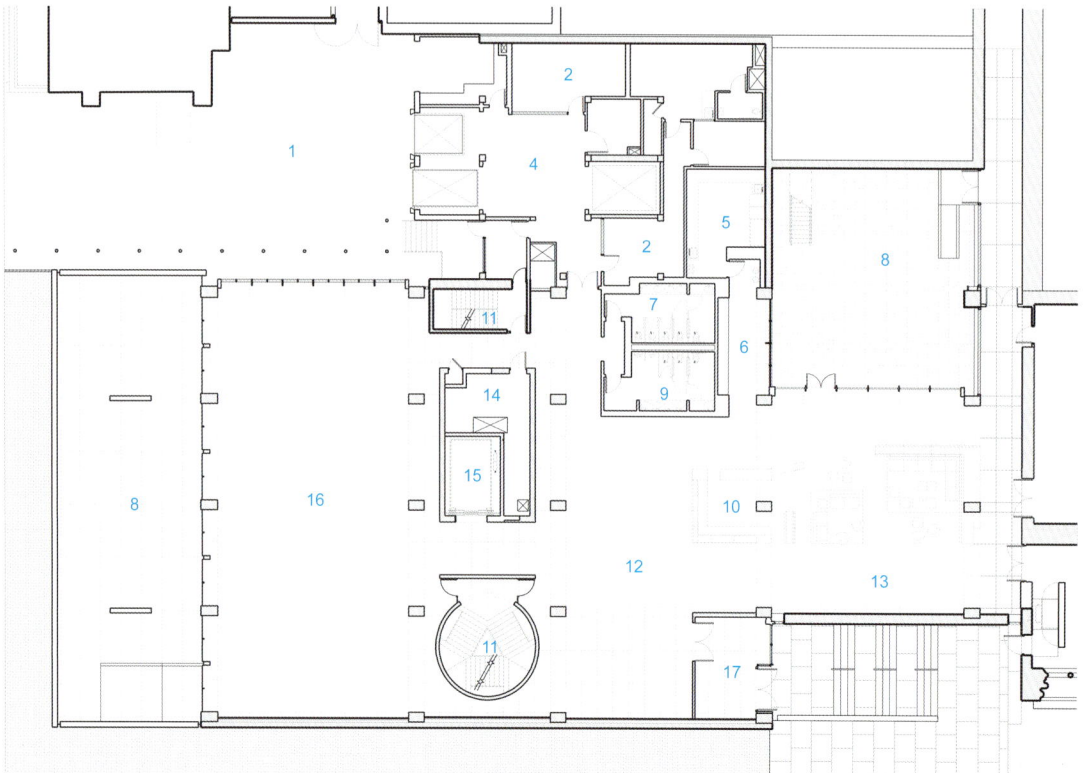

For Reference Only
Site & Ground Floor Plan:
1. Driveway
2. Admin.
3. York st.
4. Loading dock
5. Catering
6. Lockers
7. Women
8. Court
9. Men
10. Reception
11. Stair
12. Lobby
13. Media lounge
14. Mech.
15. Elev.
16. Temporary exhibition gallery
17. Vest.
18. Chapel st.

CHANEL Robertson Boulevard

Jury Comments:
What great restraint-elegantly understated; the content is beautifully executed.

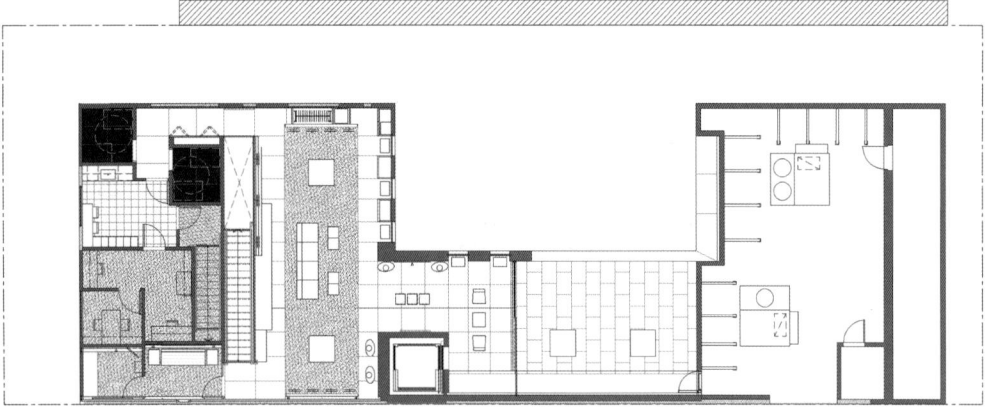

Notes of Interest
The monolithic white plaster façade above the entry references Chelsea galleries as do the clean, spare finishes within. Zoning restrictions dictated preservation of an existing building, which was stripped down to the bare wood frame.
Through the open street façade a gently rising promenade passes through three distinct "zones" to a semi obscured stair hinting at continued exploration above. The entrance, with its high glossy black and white barrisol ceilings, corresponding black and white polished stone floors and stage lighting, is exuberantly theatrical. Next, a series of lighted coves running up one wall, across the ceiling, and down the opposite wall orients the customer to the courtyard and the Southern Balifornia light.
The U-shaped first floor is organized around an exterior courtyard with a plaster façade punctured by 17 uniformly sized openings. The unifying courtyard is present in each "room", but always freshly orientated in both plan and section.

Engineer: Murphy Burr Curry, Rosini Engineering
General Contractor: Dickinson Cameron Construction
Owner: CHANEL

Architect
Peter Marino Architect

Location
Los Angeles, California

Photo Credit
© Paul Warchol Photography

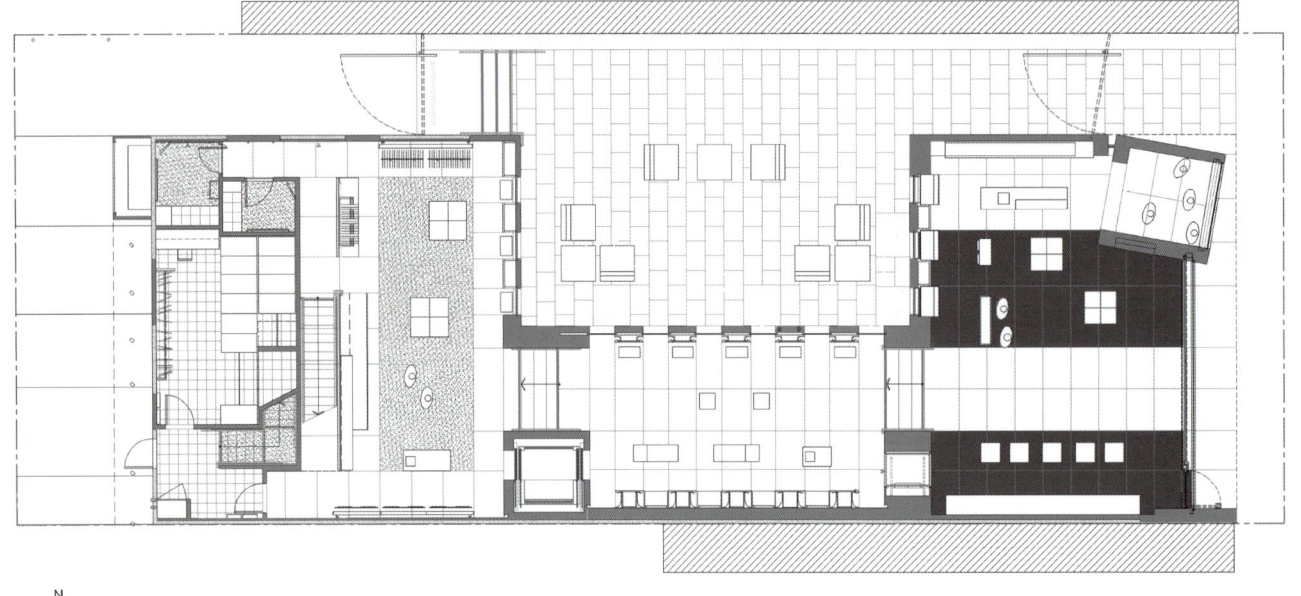

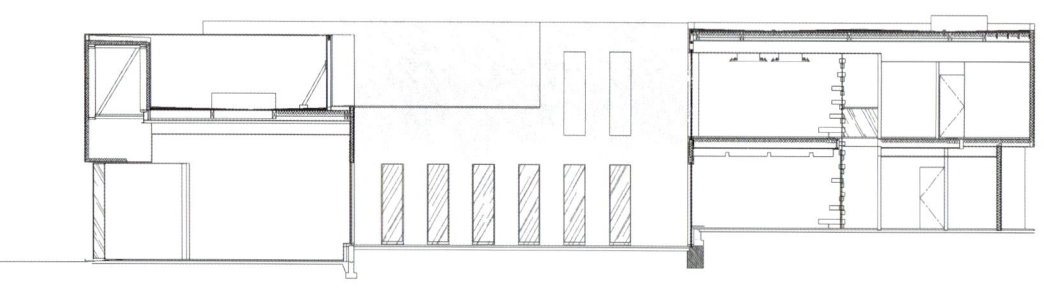

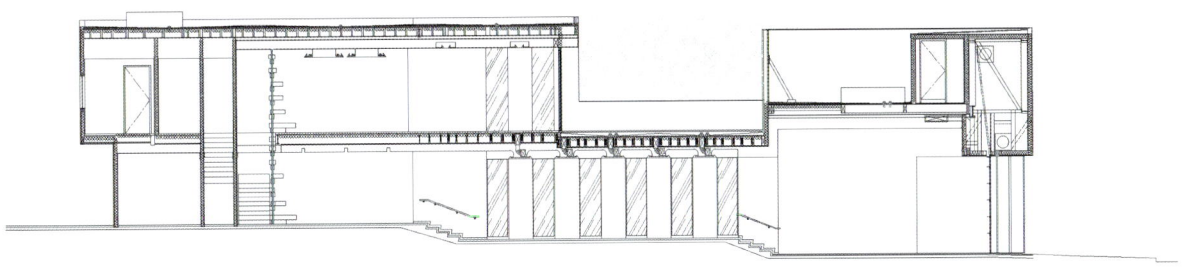

091

Craftsteak

Jury Comments:
It very successfully takes a large volume of space and makes it comfortable. It is lovingly crafted with attention to detail which brings the scale down by humans for humans.

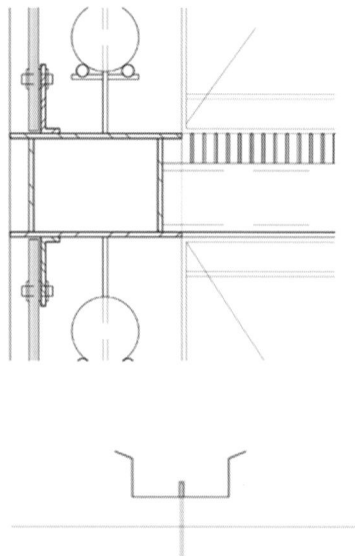
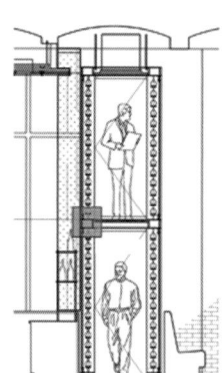
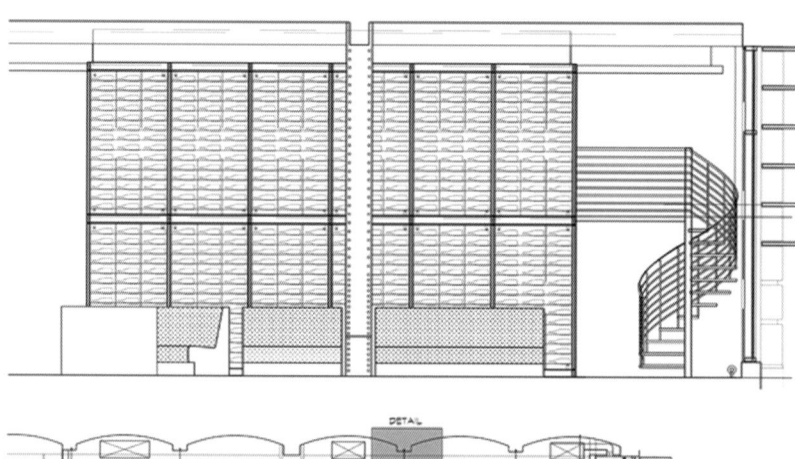
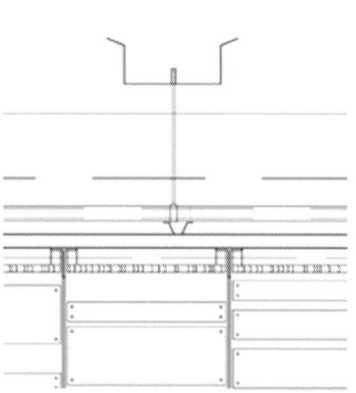
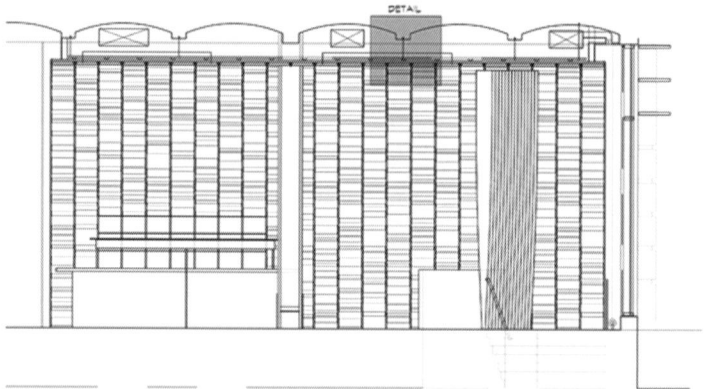

Notes of Interest

The architect's ultimate goal for the restaurant project was to shape, within the one hundred year old shell of this previous National Biscuit Company bakery building, a simple yet texturally and spatially rich interior that integrates the context with the food service both functionally and metaphorically.

Inspired by chef and owner Tom Colicchio's culinary approach of uncomplicated respect for the ingredient, all furnishings and fittings, such as the walnut and steel dining tables, were designed to celebrate their materials and the simple craftsmanship used to assemble them. In addition to this self-assigned goal, the architect also accommodated Colicchio's desire for 225 total seats, 2,000-bottle wine storage, and 3,000-square-foot kitchen, contained within a 3,500-square-foot first floor and a 4,500-square-foot cellar.

Consultant: Alliance Food Equipment Corp., Archetype Consultants Inc.
Engineer: Koutsoubis, Alonso Associates, P.E., P.C., AMA Consulting Engineers, P.C.
General Contractor: MG & Company
Owner: FoodCraft LLC

Architect
Bentel & Bentel Architects

Location
New York City, New York

Photo Credit
© Eduard Hueber

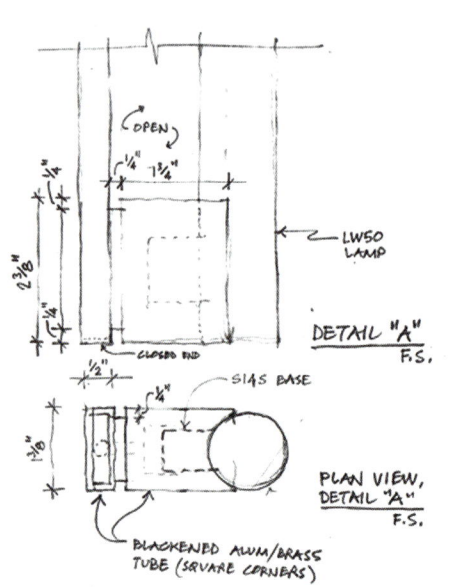
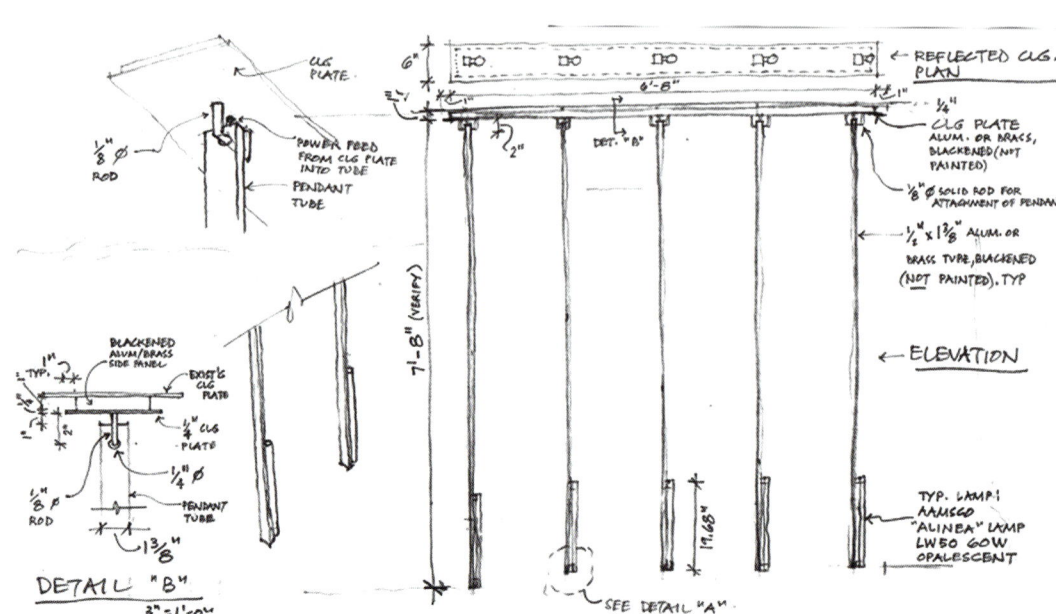

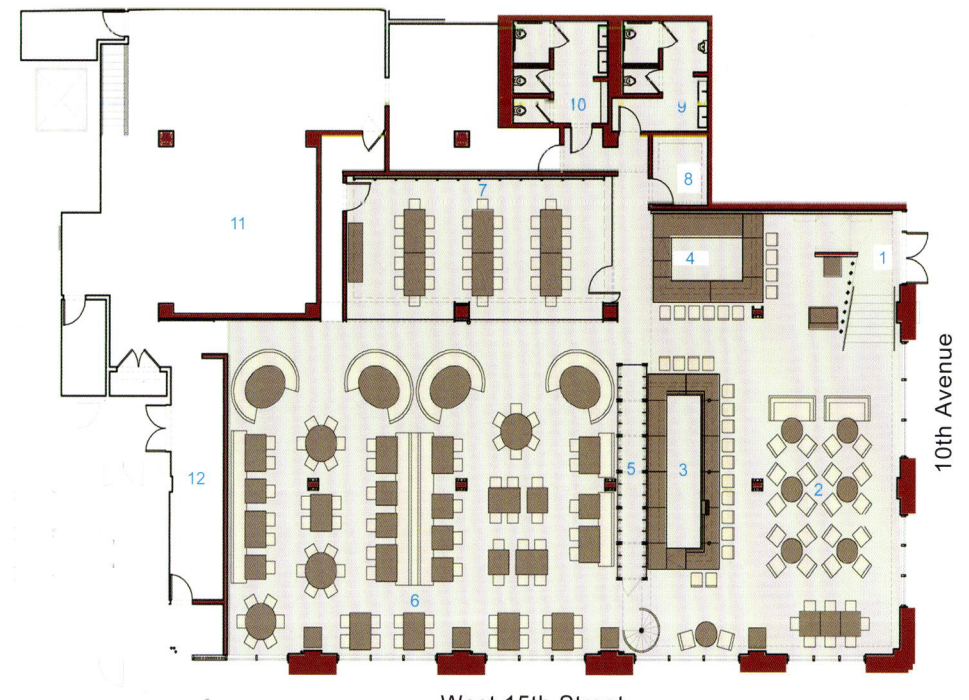

Plan:
1. Entry
2. Lounge
3. Bar
4. Raw bar
5. Wine vault
6. Main dining area
7. Private dining room
8. Coats
9. Men
10. Women
11. Kitchen
12. Service station

Data

Jury Comments:
The project is well executed with a certain level of craft; the details are nice, clean, and edgy, yet a fun work environment.

Notes of Interest

The client is one of America's leading providers of mailing lists, marketing data, sales leads, and research data. The client's challenge to the architect was to create a fresh new design for their office that expresses who they are.

The organizational strategy was to create a centrally located circulation core that sets the mood for the office and connects all of the spaces together. The design energy and most of the $28 per square foot budget was focused on three elements: an etched glass conference room wall expressing the company's data, a cut and bent wall/ceiling form which connects the office together, and galvanized metal shed wall panels to express both ideas of technology and the Midwest rural vernacular of the company's founding location.

Engineer: Alvine and Associates, Canelli Engineering, Inc.
General Contractor: KSI Construction
Owner: US Data

Architect
Randy Brown Architects

Location
Omaha

Photo Credit
© Assassi 2009

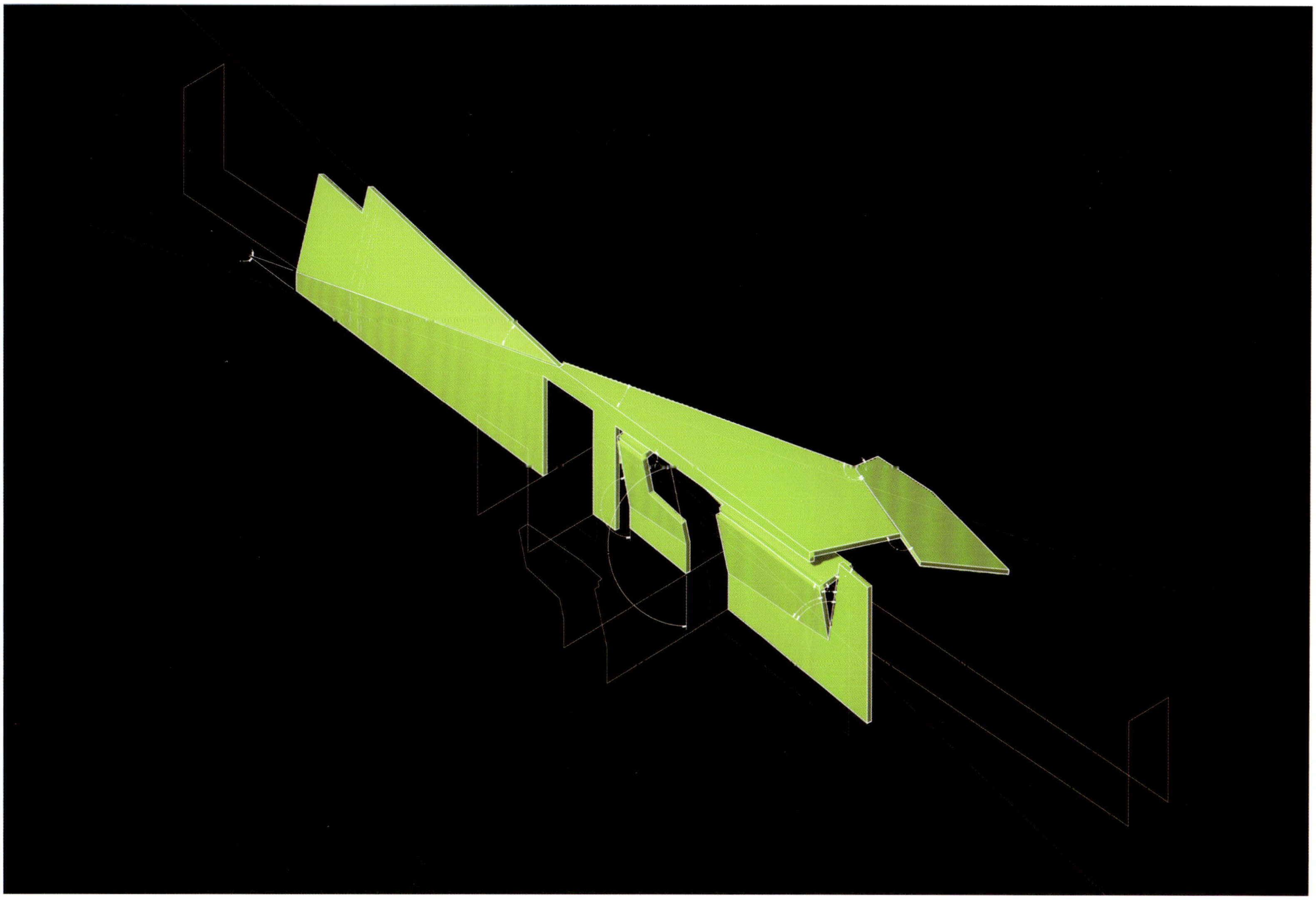

099

Exeter Schools Multipurpose Space

Jury Comments:
Such a joyful, bountiful amount of architecture, achieved under constraints of site and budget... turning a small budget into a functional and beautiful place is outstanding to see.

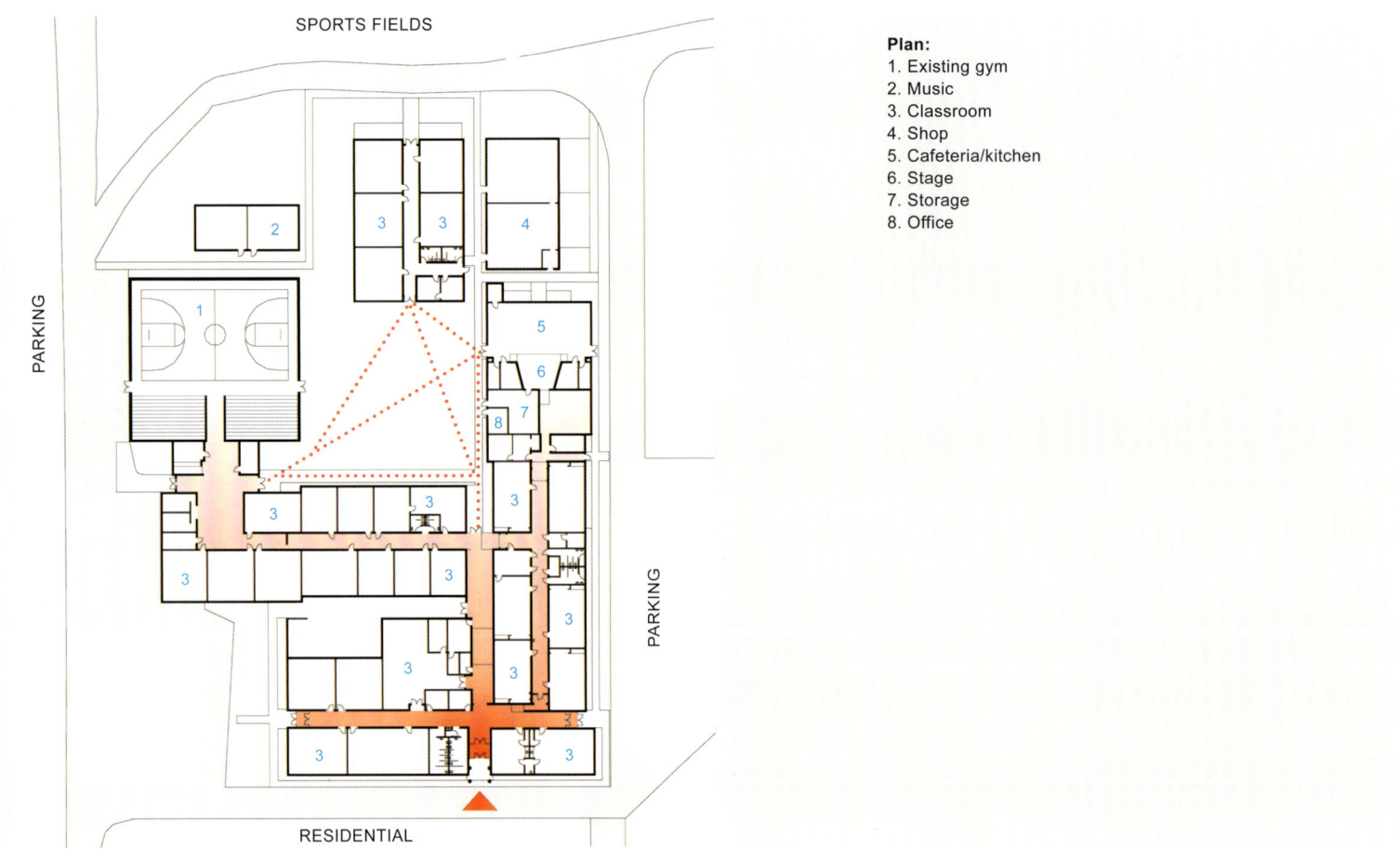

Plan:
1. Existing gym
2. Music
3. Classroom
4. Shop
5. Cafeteria/kitchen
6. Stage
7. Storage
8. Office

Notes of Interest

The challenge was to design a single space that functions well as a cafeteria, practice gym and performance hall for a rural K-12 school district on a limited budget.

Solving the acoustic challenges of these varied uses led to a solution derived from a sushi roll – absorptive on its outermost layer with a thin, reflective inner layer. The solution is executed as a simple steel frame structure inserted into an existing courtyard with an outer layer of Tectum and an inner layer of perforated wood panels. Attention is paid to detailing the wood panels to distribute sound appropriately for performances while protecting light fixtures and mechanical systems for use as a gymnasium.

Consultant: Environmental Market Solutions, Inc., Bruce Moore, AIA
Engineer: Jones & Associates Structural Engineers, Genesis Mechanical
General Contractor: Springfield Builders, Inc.
Owner: Exeter R-VI School District

Architect
Dake Wells Architecture

Location
Exeter, Missouri

Photo Credit
© Gayle Babcock; Architectural Imageworks, LLC

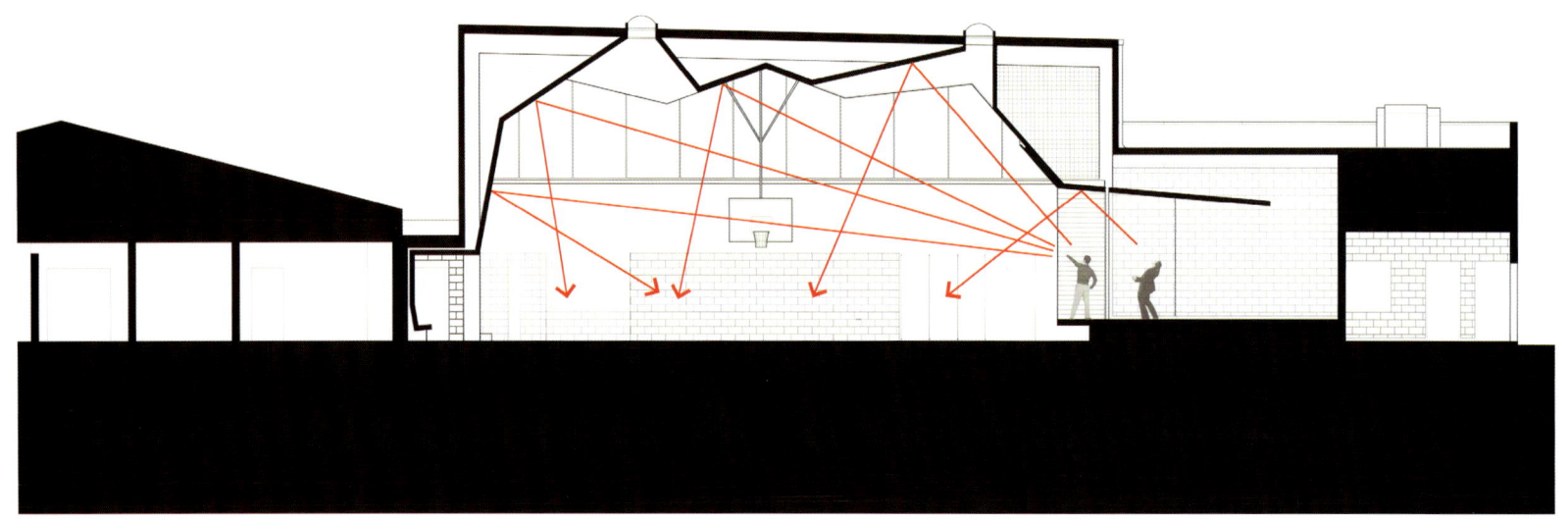

Historic Central Park West Residence

Jury Comments:
Historic elements are re-detailed with the white panels, allowing them to simultaneously exist and recede, and the dialogue with the modern elements of dark wood reinvigorates the architecture.

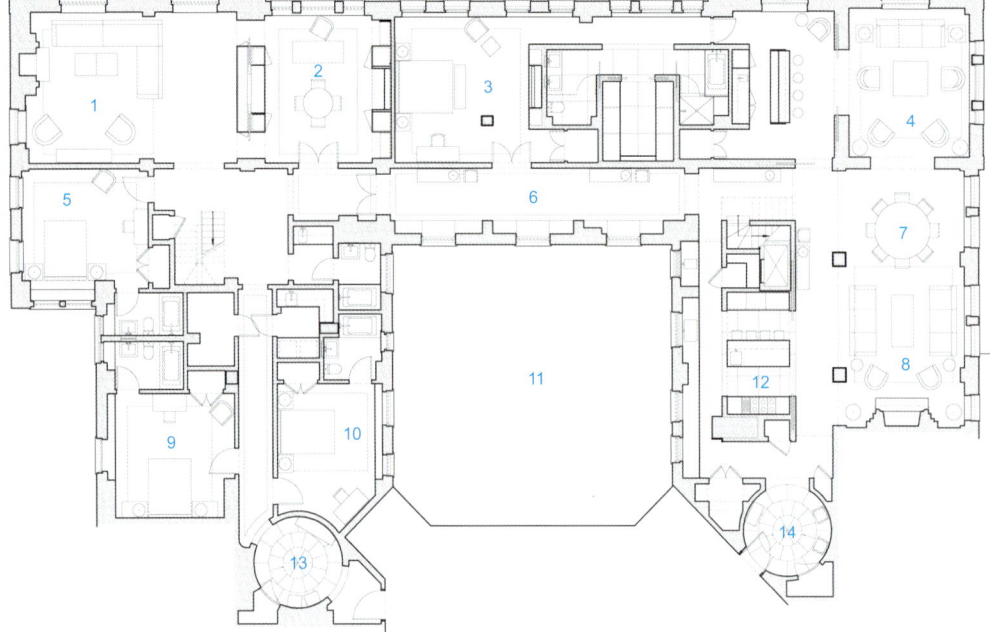

12th Floor Plan:
1. Guest living room
2. Study
3. Master bedroom
4. Sitting room
5. Guest bedroom 1
6. Gallery
7. Dinning room
8. Living room 1
9. Guest bedroom 2
10. Guest bedroom 3
11. Courtyard
12. Kitchen
13. Entry 2
14. Entry 1

Notes of Interest
This project called for combining two untouched, disparate penthouses (circa 1920) in one of Manhattan's noted landmark beaux-arts revival buildings to create one cohesive, seamless residence. It had to retain the best of the historic past, while still being appropriate to our time.
Additional goals involved taking full advantage of the four exposures of light, mezzanine, conservatory, rooftop access and views of Manhattan's Central Park. In addition, the architect provided the philanthropist owner with a residence easily maneuvered and divided into "public" and "private" spaces for work and family.

Consultant: Schwinghammer Lighting
Engineer: I.P. Group, Ross Dalland, P.E.
General Contractor: 3-D Laboratory, Inc
Landscape Architect: R/F Landscape Architecture P.C.
Owner: Jon Stryker

Architect
Shelton, Mindel & Associates

Location
New York City, New York

Photo Credit
© Michael Moran Photography

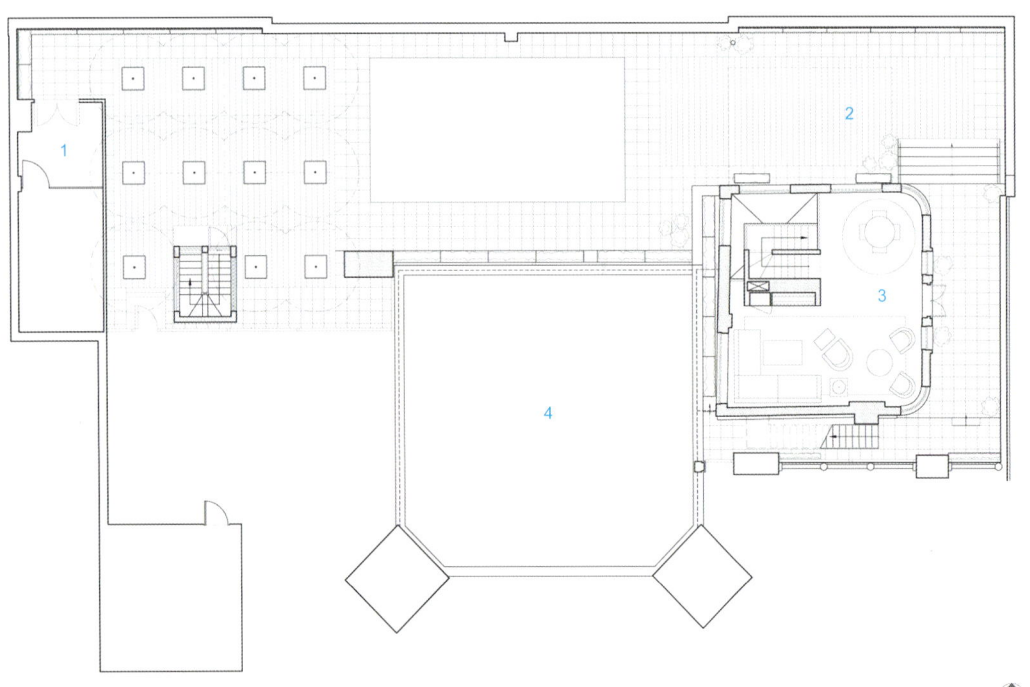

Penthouse Floor Plan:
1. Utlts Utilities
2. Terrace
3. Media Room
4. Courtyard

The Cathedral of Christ the Light

Jury Comments:
The project exhibits some of the most original rethinking of architectural enclosure and form since the Gothic period.

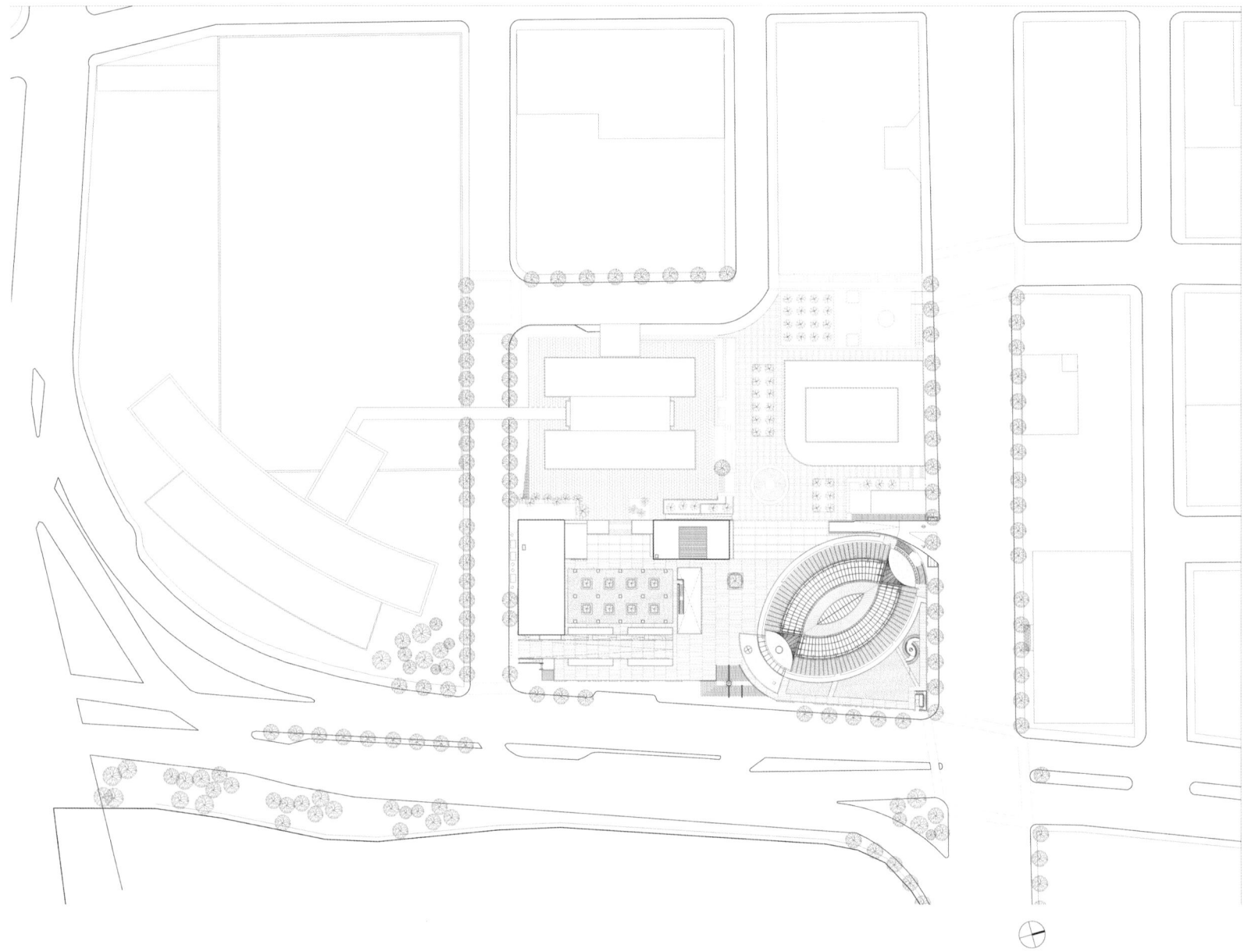

Notes of Interest

The Diocese challenged the design team to create a building for the ages. As a result, the 1,350-seat sanctuary, with its side chapels, baptistery, health and legal clinics and dependencies, will honor its religious and civic obligations to the Catholic Diocese and the city for centuries to come.

Through its poetic introduction, indirect daylight ennobles modest materials-primarily wood, glass and concrete. Triangular aluminum panels form the petal-shaped Alpha Window, which diffuses light 100 feet above the Cathedral's entrance. The Omega Window resonates with the surrounding structure metaphorically and physically through its experimental use of light, re-imagining a 12th-century depiction of Christ from the façade of Chartres Cathedral in France through over 94,000 pixels cut into the Window's triangular aluminum panels.

Associate Architect: Kendall/Heaton Associates, Inc.
Consultant: Conversion Management Associates, Inc., The Engineering Enterprise, Claude R. Engle Lighting Consultants, Shen Milsom & Wilke, Inc.
Engineer: Skidmore, Owings & Merrill LLP, Taylor Engineering
General Contractor: Webcor Builders, Oliver + Co.
Landscape Architect: Peter Walker and Partners
Owner: Roman Catholic Diocese of Oakland

Architect
Skidmore, Owings & Merrill LLP

Location
Oakland, California

Photo Credit
© Cesar Rubio, © Timothy Hursley
All drawing are © SOM

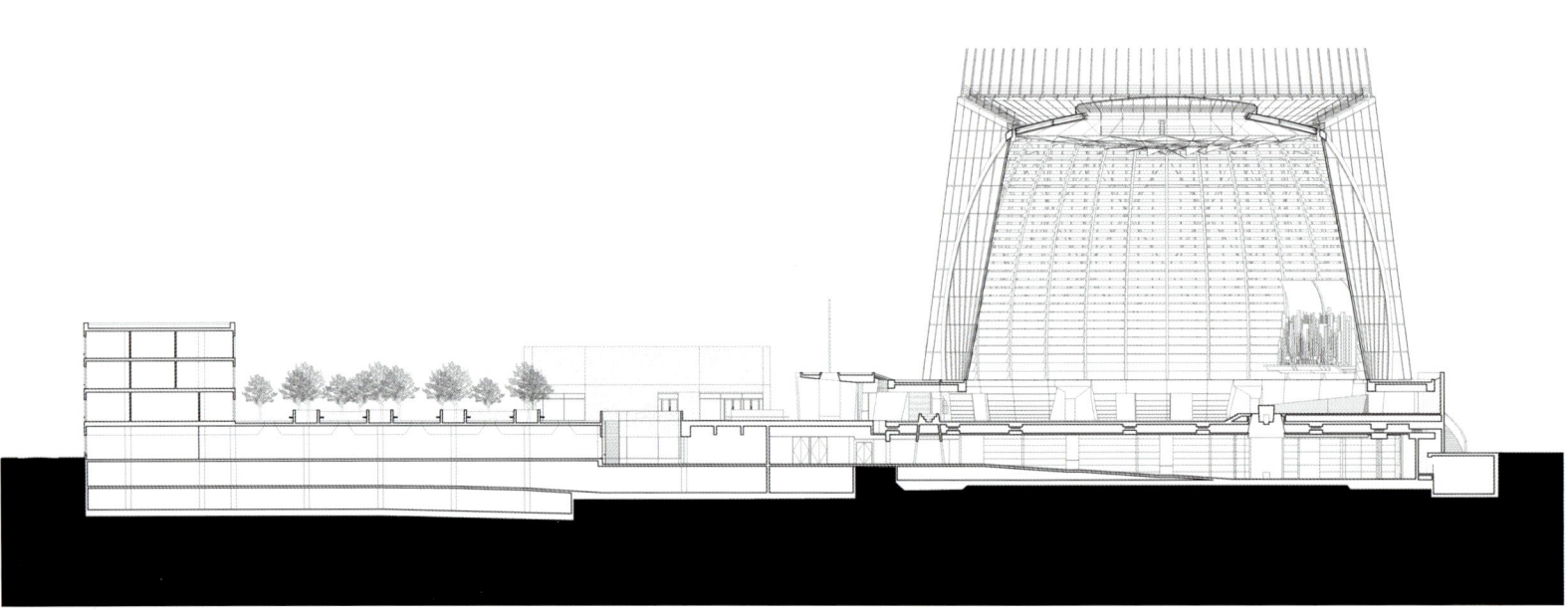

© Cesar Rubio

© Timothy Hursley
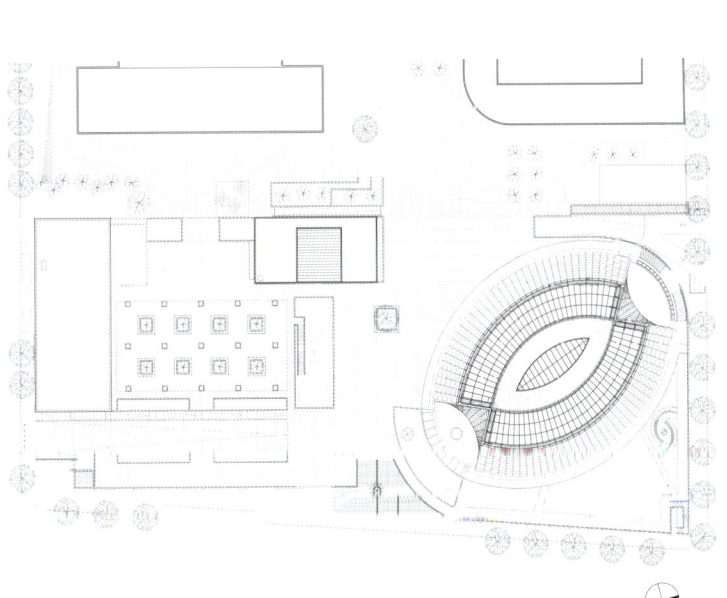

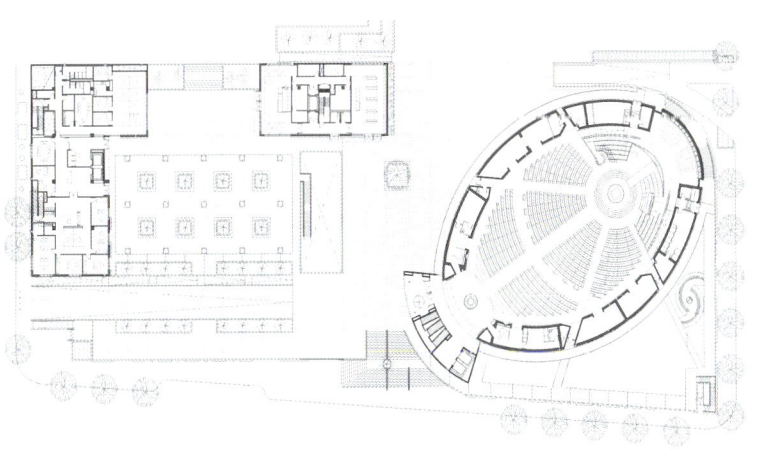

111

Vera Wang Boutique

Jury Comments:
It is all about the subtlety – of the details that are very, very refined. You don't see them at first and they reveal themselves as you move within the space.

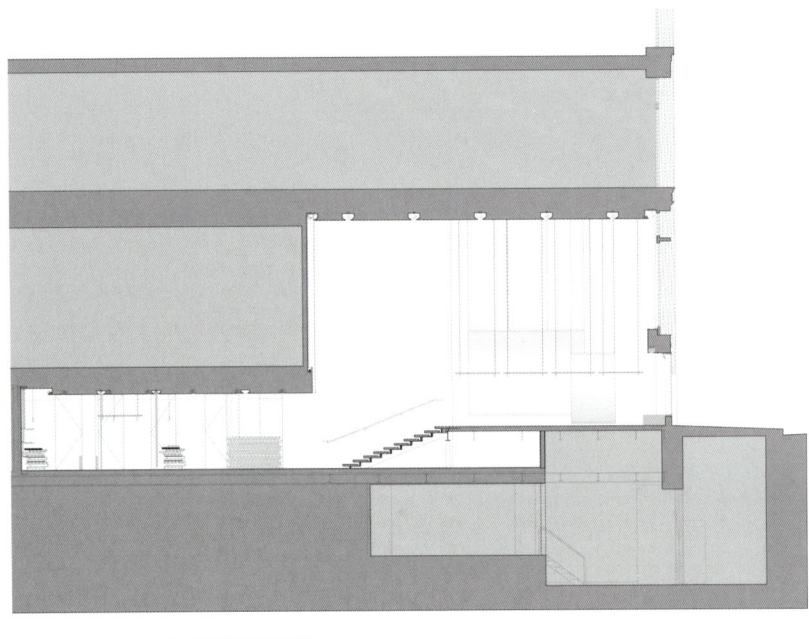

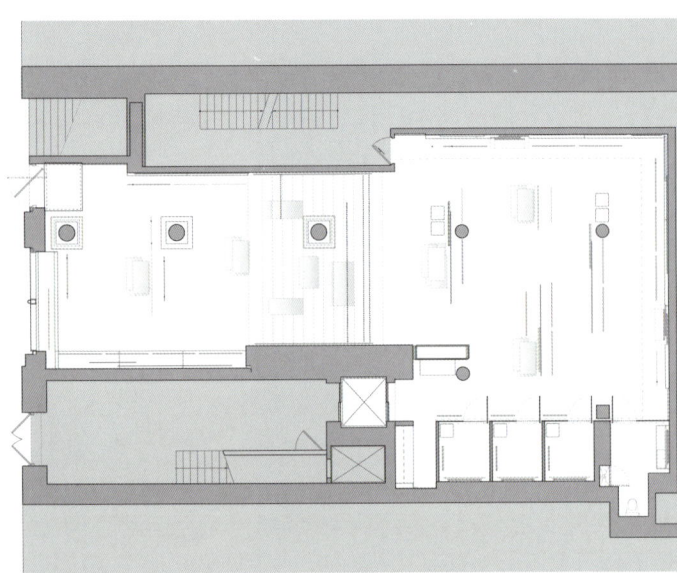

Notes of Interest

Customers enter as performers on a stage, stepping into the elevated, double-height proscenium at the front of the store. The spatial sequence unfolds down a full-width, white Corian grand stair, which transitions into the more intimate display and changing area at the rear of the space.

With LED backlighting, the steps appear to float; they double as seating for special events or a display riser with translucent acrylic platforms.

Reflecting the juxtapositions that characterize Vera Wang's fashion design, the material palette is based on a series of complementary contrasts. High-gloss, white epoxy flooring contrasts with diaphanous scrims; synthetic acrylic partitions feature hand-sculpted, curved edges, while natural architectural plaster is polished to the point of abstraction. Lighting is as much a physical material as the plaster and steel, and is used to simulate a range of atmospheric states.

Consultant: Tillotson Design Associates
Engineer: Robert Silman Associates, Edwards & Zuck Consulting Engineers
General Contractor: Michilli, Inc.
Landscape Architect: R/F Landscape Architecture P.C.
Owner: Vera Wang Group

Architect	Location	Photo Credit
Gabellini Sheppard Associates	New York City, New York	© Paul Warchol

A Civic Vision for the Central Delaware River

Jury Comments:
Focusing on seven miles of Philadelphia's former industrial waterfront, this concept for reclaiming severely dilapidated real estate is long overdue. This is a very appropriate set of solutions to a set of longstanding problems and a sustainable approach to the re-invigoration of existing facilities.

Notes of Interest
As the lead design consultant for this mayoral initiative, the firm created a new vision for seven miles of the Delaware River in Philadelphia. Currently cut off from the city by the intrusion of I-95, this riverfront is comprised of underutilized post-industrial land and big-box development, and is subject to unregulated residential speculation. The plan emphasizes the ecological and economic value of the waterfront and sets forth a framework that the city can follow to generate new, cohesive, and sustainable development. This new growth will be organized around parks and open space, providing access to the river and a new movement system, including the decking-over of I-95 and a grand civic boulevard complete with public transit. For the ability of the plan to accommodate the future needs of the city and its people, this project has received numerous endorsements.

Consultant: Penn Project on Civic Engagement, Philadelphia City Planning Commission
Owner: PennPraxis, University of Pennsylvania

Architect
Wallace Roberts & Todd, LLC

Location
Philadelphia, Pennsylvania

Photo Credit
© Wallace Roberts & Todd

PARKS AND OPEN SPACE

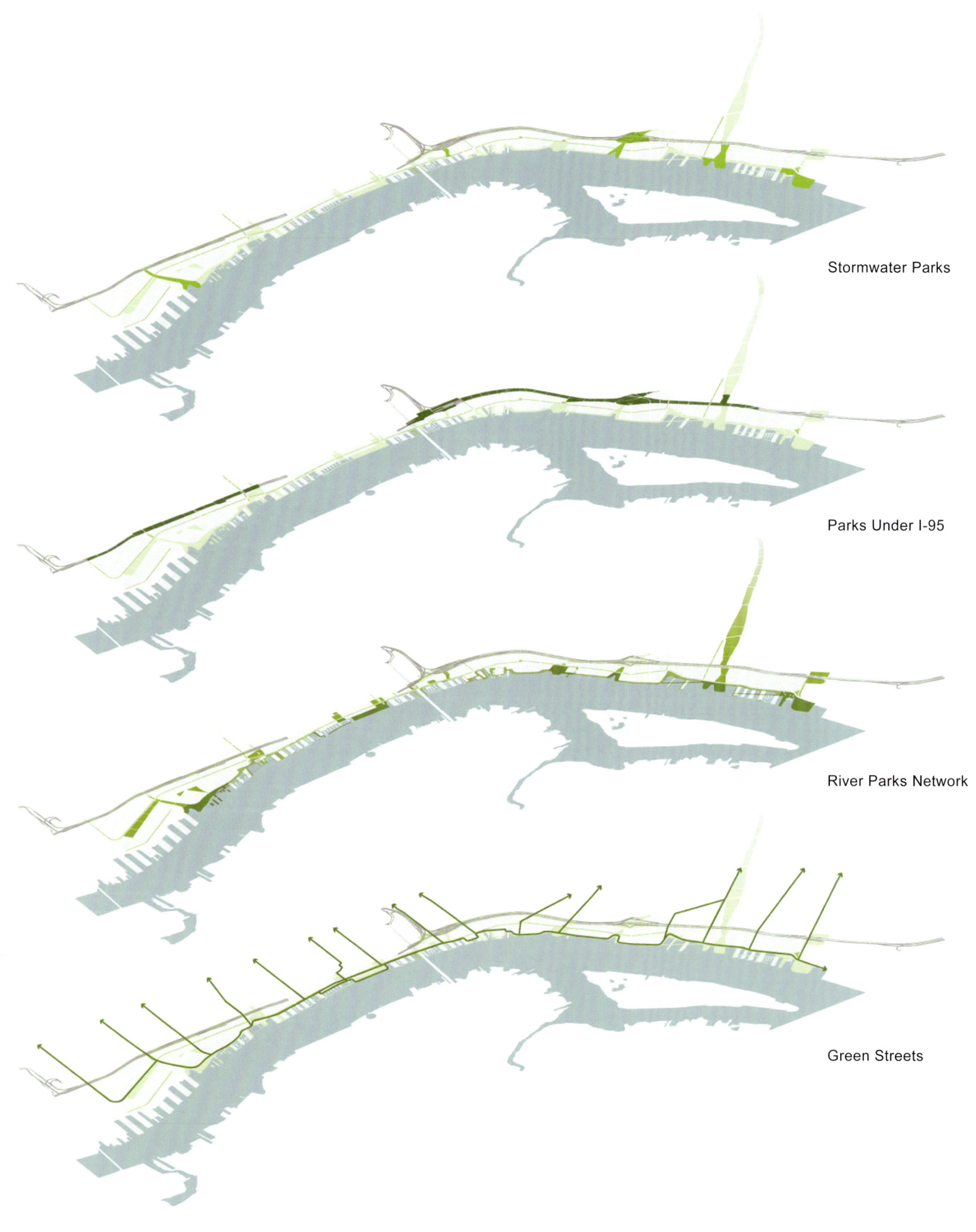

Movement Systems

Parks and Open Space

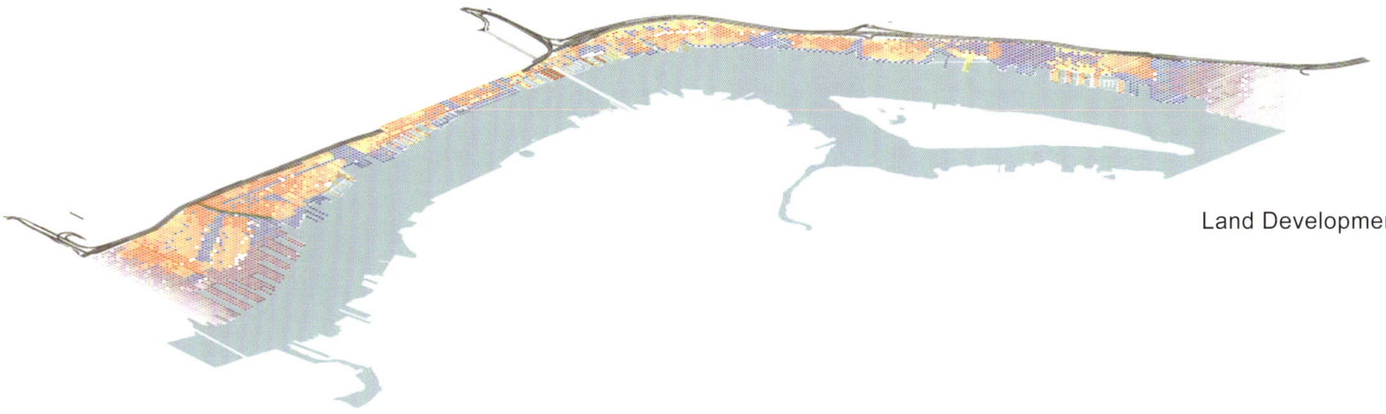

Land Development

Connections:
MacArthur Park District Master Plan

Jury Comments:
Connecting a historically residential area of Little Rock in a way that also extends the park beyond its highway-induced isolation, this is an excellent endeavor to mitigate the effects of other-scaled urban infrastructures and use connective landscape amenities to enhance the quality of the urban experience and "eyes on-the-street" security.

Notes of Interest

Like waterfronts and transit stops, parks leverage value in urban areas. While much recent attention has been given to the signature mega-park, the value of the small-scale neighborhood park in reinventing the city has been overlooked. Once connecting neighborhoods of differing character, and sponsoring more than 80 residential structures along its edges, the historic MacArthur Park at the edge of downtown Little Rock is radically underutilized as an urban neighborhood asset. Severed from its neighborhoods along two edges by interstate construction in the 1960s, this moribund 40-acre municipal park is left with only 16 residential structures along its frontage. The planning concept optimizes the park's latent economic, environmental, and social potential through improvements to the district's neighborhood infrastructure, enhancing the delivery of ecological and urban services. This counters the greatest ongoing threat to MacArthur Park District's irreplaceable legacy – incompatible low-density, suburban-type development that fails to define street edges, and is inherently cynical of the city. The planning goal is to align the park's capacity to sponsor denser and higher quality mixed-use housing fabric throughout the district with improvements to the park grounds. Rather than treat MacArthur Park as a discrete project, planning for the district's four neighborhoods extends the park's landscape into a larger urban landscape network with MacArthur Park as the anchor.

Associate Architect: University of Arkansas Community Design Center
Consultant: University of Arkansas Little Rock Urban Studies, Donjek Public Finance
Engineer: McClelland Consulting Engineers
Landscape Architect: Oslund and Associates
Owner: City of Little Rock, Parks and Recreation

Architect
Conway+Schulte Architects, PA

Location
Little Rock

Photo Credit
© Conway+Schulte Architects

125

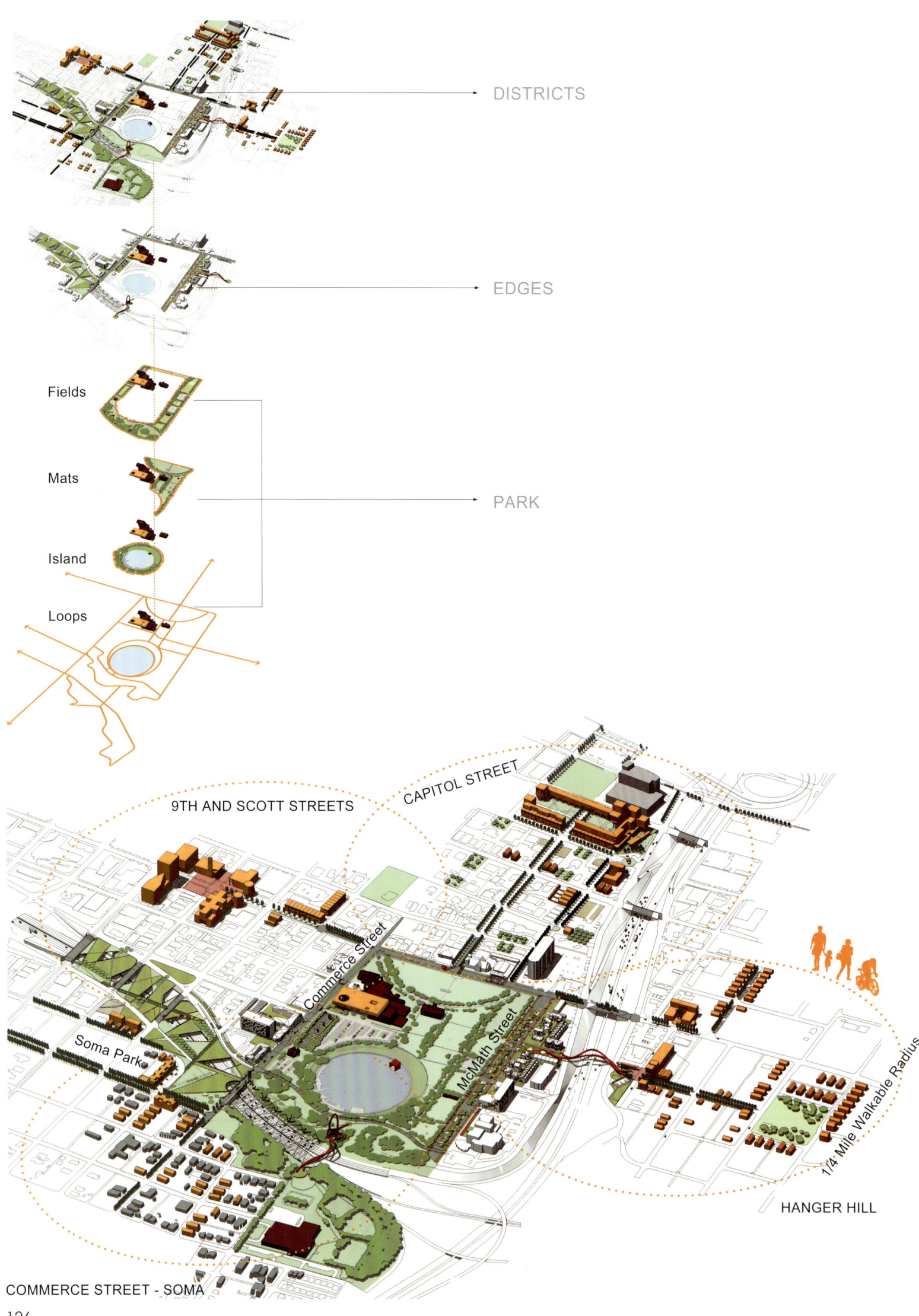

Site Plan:
1. North Loop
2. North Lawn
3. Fountain
4. Play Space
5. Parking
6. Hanger Hill Pedestrian Bridge
7. McMath Plaza
8. Row Housing
9. McMath Boulevard
10. Active Recreation
11. Parade Grounds
12. Arkansas Arts Center Addition
13. Patio Housing
14. Walk-up Housing
15. Sculpture Garden
16. Entry Plaza
17. Pier Pavilion
18. Landscape Amphitheater
19. Restroom
20. Firehouse Hostel and Museum
21. Pond
22. Pier
23. MacArthur Lane
24. Freeway Park
25. Pedestrian Plaza Bridge
26. Freeway Bosque
27. Freeway Arbor
28. Observation Bridge
29. Housing
30. Southern Bosque
31. Southern Loop
32. Observation Tower
33. Memorial Walk

Greenwich South Strategic Framework

Jury Comments:
A critical element to the sustainability of the design is that it invites the public to imagine and participate! The potential of this extraordinary large parcel, essentially forgotten for decades, could result in a reconnection that opens up millions of square feet of developable air rights.

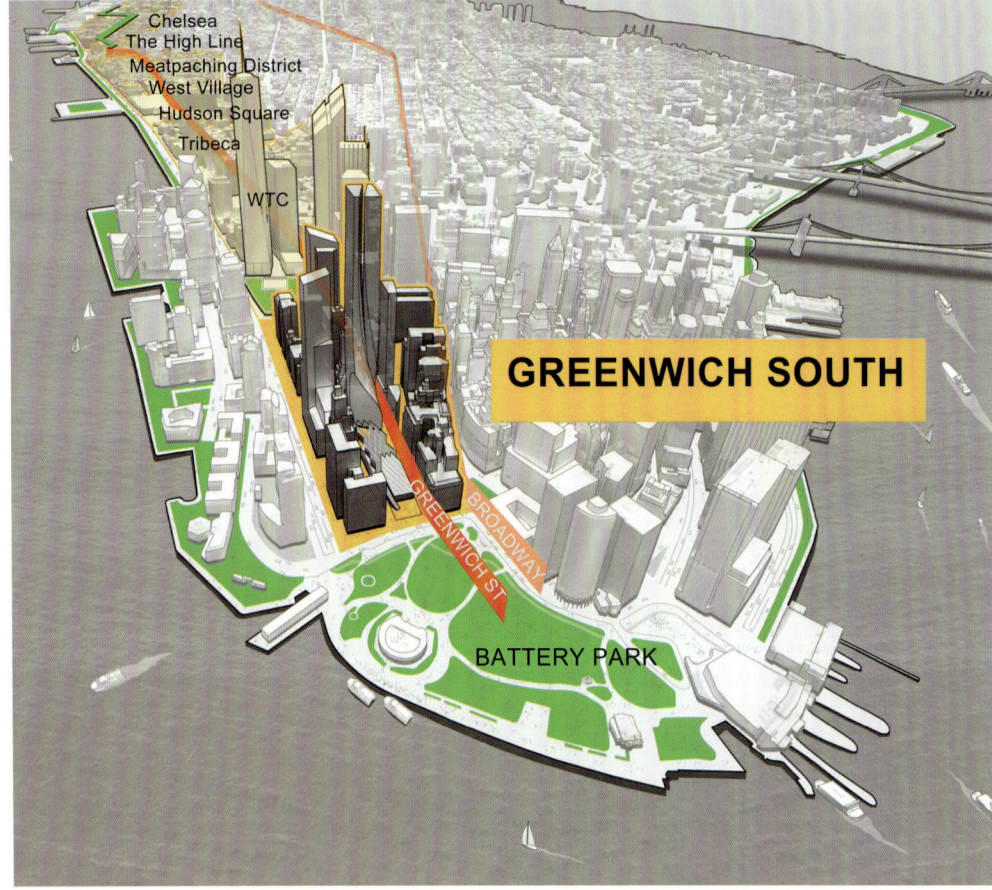

Notes of Interest
The primary goal of a study by the Alliance for Downtown New York was to produce a strategic framework for Greenwich South by establishing a set of key principles and objectives to guide both immediate and long-term growth. The architecture firm developed Five Principles to define a vision for the future of Greenwich South as a dense, reconnected, mixed-use neighborhood and lynchpin for Lower Manhattan. Each principle is comprised of a set of clear objectives to be achieved within these goals. In addition to establishing principles and setting goals, the firm also identified a series of clear opportunities for action – from the subtle, genius and immediate to the huge, radical and visionary – to achieve these goals. The project was highly collaborative, employing a Brain Trust as well as a Design Challenge charrette.

Associate Architect: Beyer Blinder Belle
Consultant: OPEN, Marc Kristal
Owner: Alliance for Downtown New York

Architect
Architecture Research Office

Location
New York City, New York

Photo Credit
© Architecture Research Office

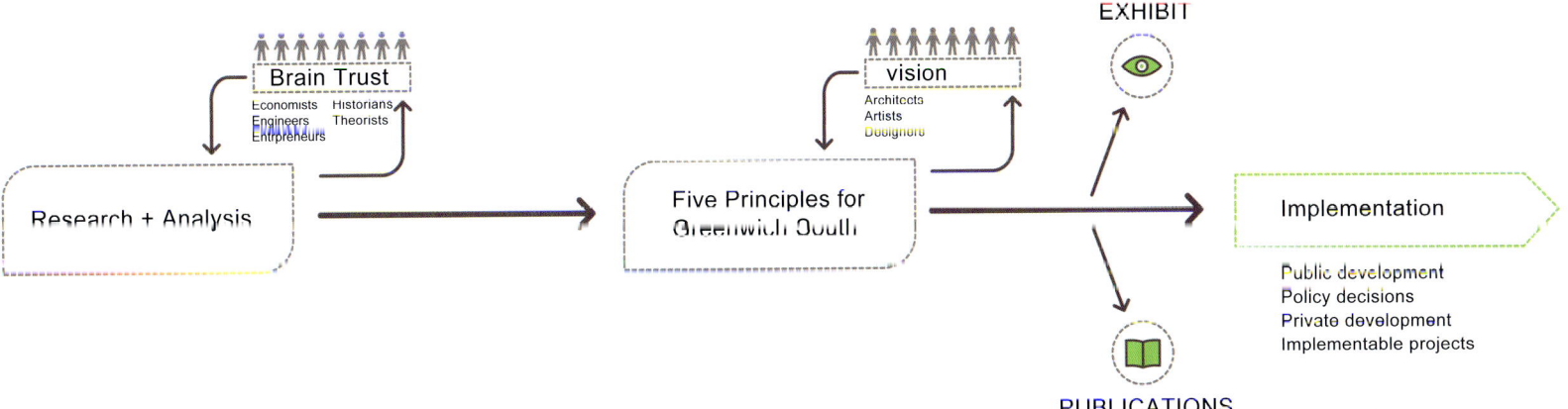

Monumental Core Framework Plan

Jury Comments:
Marking the bicentennial of the original L'Enfant/Ellicott plan and centennial of the McMillan Plan, which created the Mall as we know it today, this phased framework promises to stop degradation of heavily used areas and open less-used venues to greater appreciation and public enjoyment – all within the context of Washington's expanding downtown.

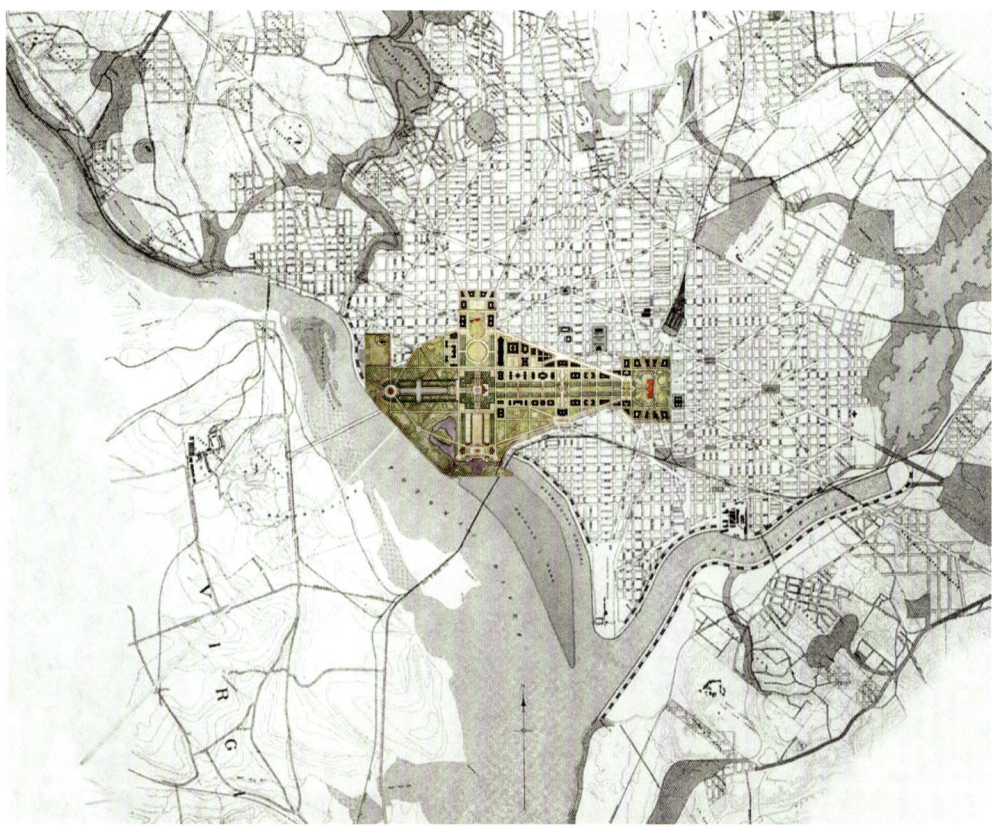

Notes of Interest

The Monumental Core Framework Plan is a proposal sponsored by two federal agencies, the U.S. Commission of Fine Arts and the National Capital Planning Commission, to transform federal precincts surrounding the National Mall into vibrant destinations and to improve connections between the city, the National Mall, and the waterfront. Proceeding from the context of visionary planning for the national capital, the Framework Plan is a practical tool to guide decisions and investment over the next thirty years and complements concurrent planning efforts in Washington.

The Plan proposes a series of sector-by-sector strategies that are designed to protect the National Mall, create distinctive settings for cultural facilities and commemorative works, overcome barriers between the National Mall and the surrounding city, and enhance the monumental core of Washington as a symbolic and sustainable place to work, visit, and live. Initiated to address immediate needs of accommodating national commemorative sites in the monumental core, the Framework Plan also maintains the federal workplace in the central city while providing opportunities for new parks, infrastructure and transportation improvements, and mixed-use public and private development. The Plan is guided by a foundation of best practices to achieve a high quality of urban design, smart growth, and sustainability in strategies for buildings and infrastructure as well as the urban ecological environment.

Associate Architect: EDAW-AECOM
Owner: U.S. Commission of Fine Arts, National Capital Planning Commission

Architect
U. S. Government

Location
Washington, D.C.

Photo Credit
© National Capital Planning Commission

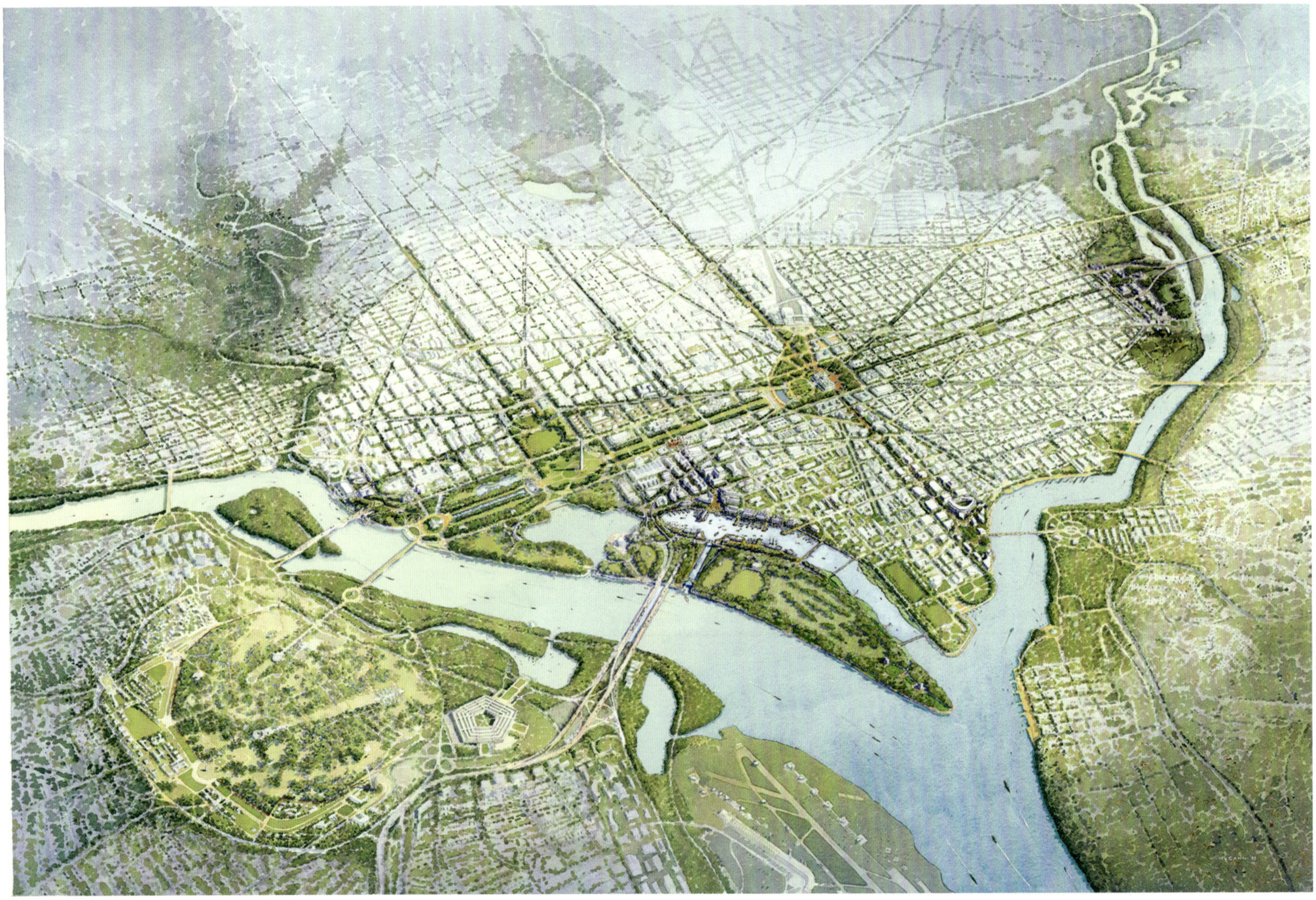

134

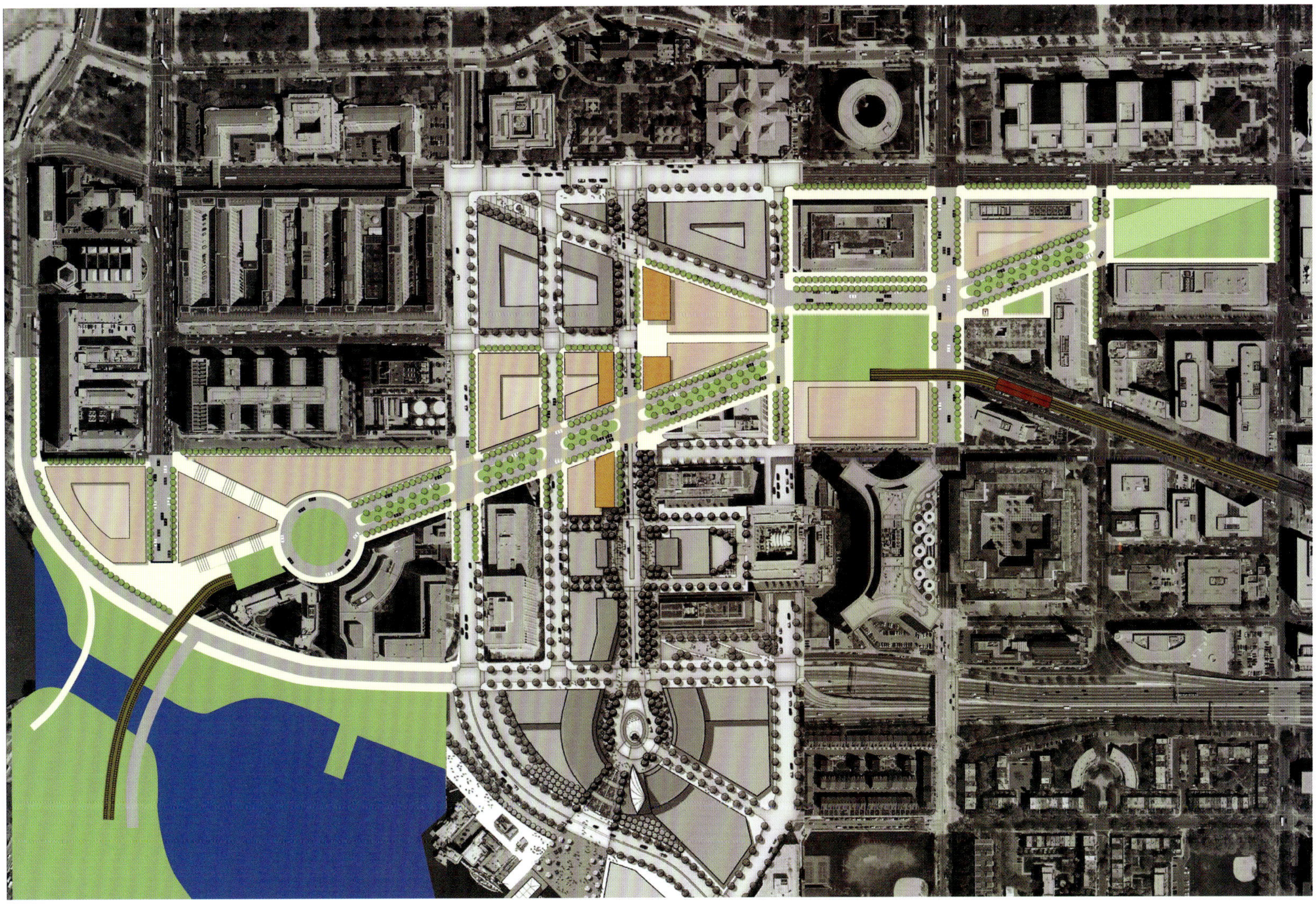

135

Ryerson University Master Plan

Jury Comments:
With its thoughtful connection to the area transportation system and extensive integration with the city, this plan is a decidedly 21st Century response to co-development, including funding and potential integrations of uses within a tight timeframe.

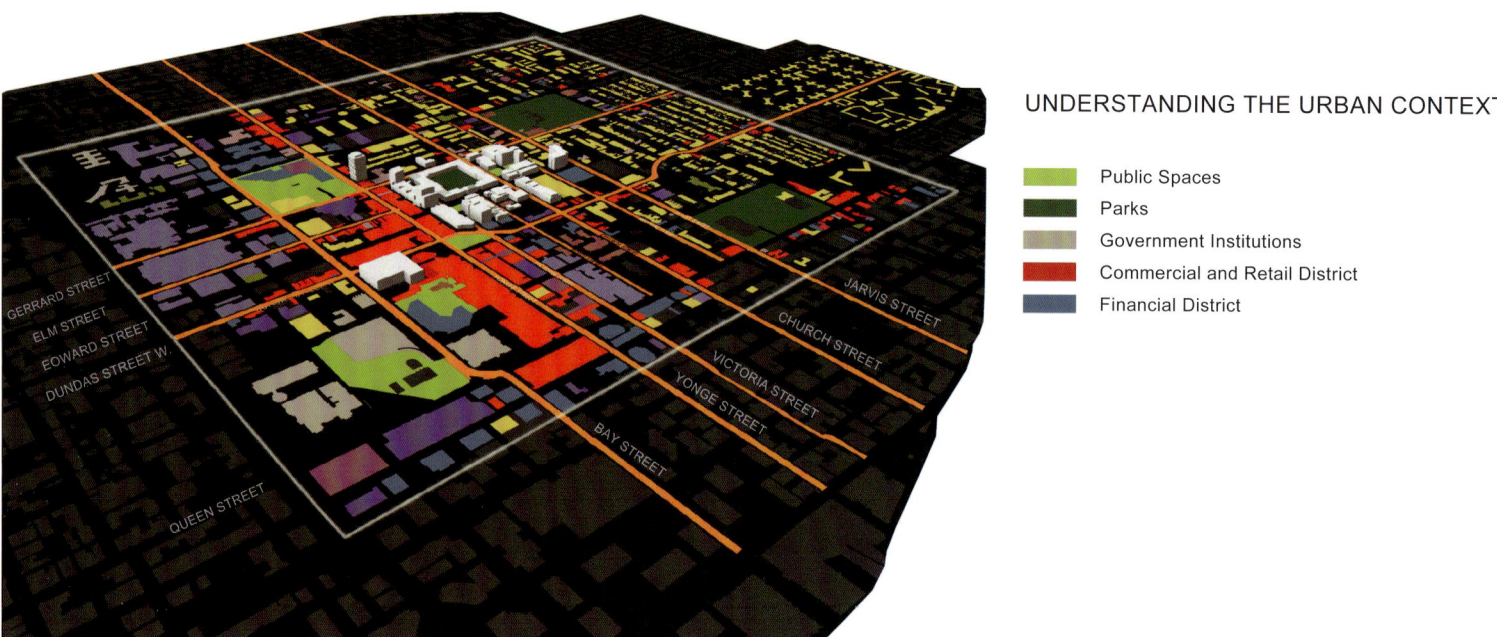

UNDERSTANDING THE URBAN CONTEXT

- Public Spaces
- Parks
- Government Institutions
- Commercial and Retail District
- Financial District

Notes of Interest

While the Master Plan was developed to deal effectively with the Ryerson University (RU) campus' deficiencies, it ultimately foregrounds Ryerson as a city building, and a model for the 21st Century urban university. Each goal of the Master Plan is defined by a series of principles, and together, they form the flexible framework which will guide the growth of Ryerson University. These goals are: urban intensification, people first (pedestrianization of the urban environment), and a commitment to design excellence.

The Master Plan represents the collective input of the entire University community over an 18-month development period. The consortium architects/urban planners/financial advisors worked closely with Ryerson University senior administration, faculty, students, and the RU Board to articulate the university in clear, concise and implementable terms. Unlike conventional master plans that approach a site and provide specific guidelines in terms of use and density, massing, etc., the RU Master Plan uses demonstration sites, a building site, street, or open space, to demonstrate the application of goals and guidelines. Given the demands of an evolving academic program, the economic imperative to look at "co-development" with commercial or residential development partners, the demonstration sites are presented in the Master Plan document as tools to suggest design directions consistent with the principles.

Consultant: Curran McCabe Ravindran Ross Inc., Gottschalk+Ash International
Engineer: Stantec Consulting, Halcrow Yolles, Crossey Engineering
Owner: Ryerson University

Architect
Kuwabara Payne McKenna Blumberg Architects and Daoust Lestage, Inc. in association with Greenberg Consultants, Inc. and IBI Group

Location
Toronto, Ontario

Photo Credit
© Kuwabara Payne McKenna Blumberg Architects,
© Daoust Lestage Inc. ,
© Greenberg Consultants Inc., © IBI Group

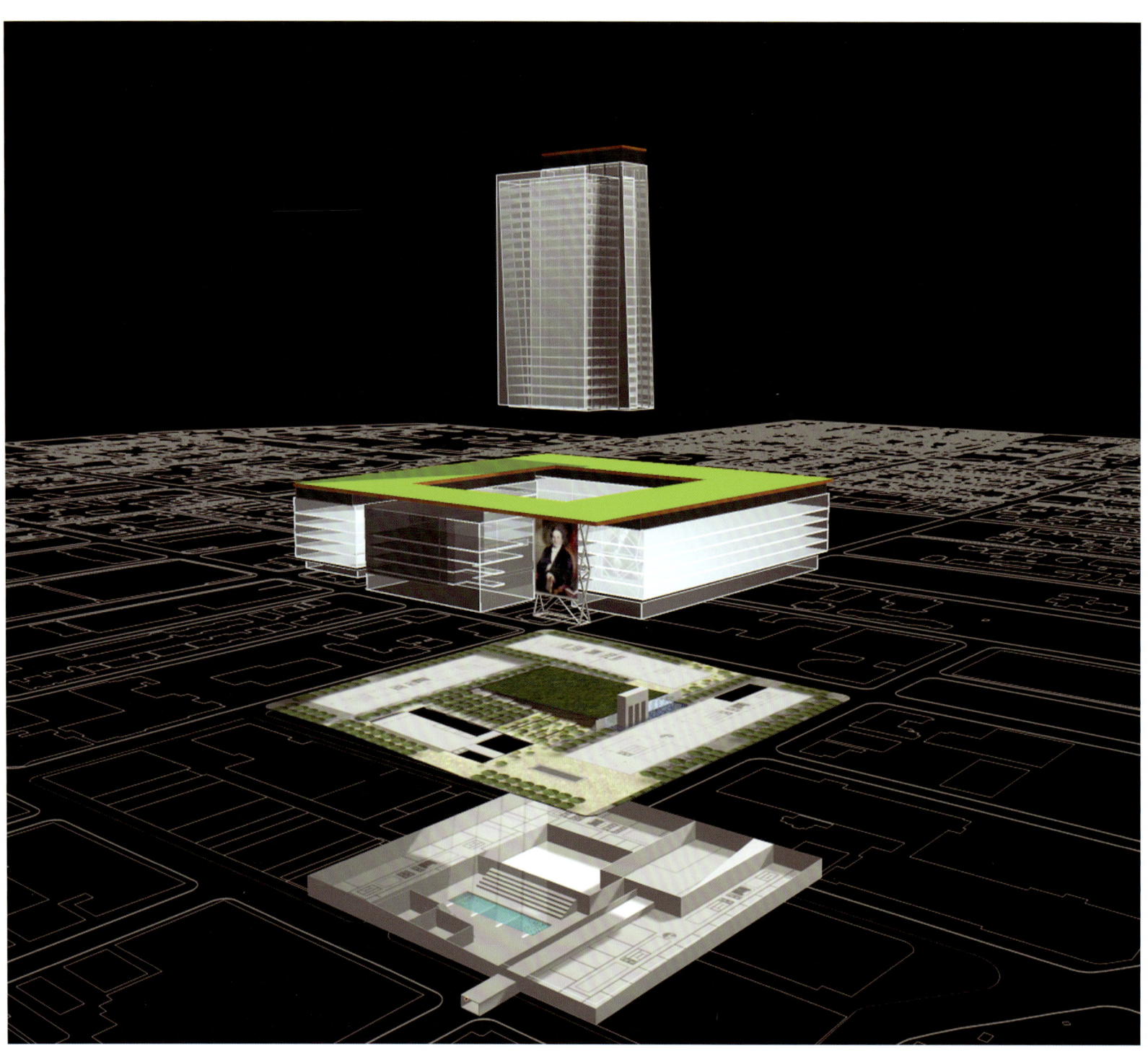

Savannah East Riverfront Extension

Jury Comments:
This very sensitive addition to one of America's historic treasures is simply the right thing to do and is carried out with a real understanding, pride, and careful analysis.

CIVIC MASTER PLAN

Historic view of the East Riverfront

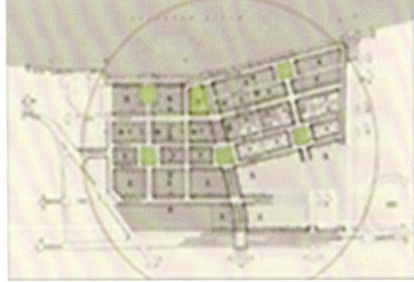

COMPATIBLE BUILDINGS

Architectural standards should follow to the extent possible the Manual for Development in Savannah's Historic District.

BUILD-TO LINES AND ENTRANCES: Continuity of building frontage produces a sense of defined space in the public realm. Build-To Lines are established within each block designating a range for required number of minimum entrances in each block. Blocks intended for retail uses have the most permeable building fronts with minimum access occurring every 50 feet, those intended for residential or large commercial uses provide minimum access every 50 to 100 feet.

HEIGHT AND MASS: Consistency of building heights and mass create visual continuity in the streetscape and the skyline. Maximum heights measured in stories have been established in each block, ranging from 4 to 10 stories. A parking level is counted as a story. Building façades over 60 feet in width should be broken down vertically to reduce their mass and create a human scale. Horizontal articulation of buildings should include an identifiable base, body and cap.

COLOR AND TEXTURE: Building walls should be of traditional masonry material such as brick or true stucco. Surfaces should be detailed to provide visual texture and human scale. On taller buildings fronting the water, the colors of surfaces above 4 stories shall be darker and visually recessive in order to not dominate the skyline from the river.

MIXED USES & SUBDIVISION OF BLOCKS: Blocks should be subdivided to allow for a diverse range of building types and lot sizes. Primary uses may be mixed within blocks and within buildings. Fee-simple lots may be subdivided within blocks in varied configurations. Subdivided blocks shall allow for each lot to have a minimum of 20 feet of frontage on a primary street or a lane and a minimum lot size of 1,000 square feet.

Notes of Interest

Savannah's Civic Master Plan for the East Riverfront has two goals, one vision: Public Framework and Private Freedom.

The City of Savannah, Georgia identified a series of large vacant parcels along the boundary of its historic City Center for eastward downtown expansion. The first goal was to successfully grow the historic city plan of Savannah after over 150 years. The second goal was a physical and regulatory framework that would allow the expansion district to evolve into a thriving and authentic urban extension.

The Civic Master Plan for the East Riverfront Expansion was implemented by the City in 2006. It defines 54 acres located to the immediate east of Savannah's National Landmark Historic District along the Savannah River. New city blocks, parks, public

Associate Architect: Niles Bolton Associates
Engineer: Thomas & Hutton Engineering Co.
Landscape Architect:
Michael Van Valkenburgh Associates, Inc.
Sasaki, Reed | Hilderbrand
Owner: City of Savannah, ALR Ogelthorpe LLC

Architect	Location	Photo Credit
Sottile & Sottile	Savannah	© Sottile & Sottile

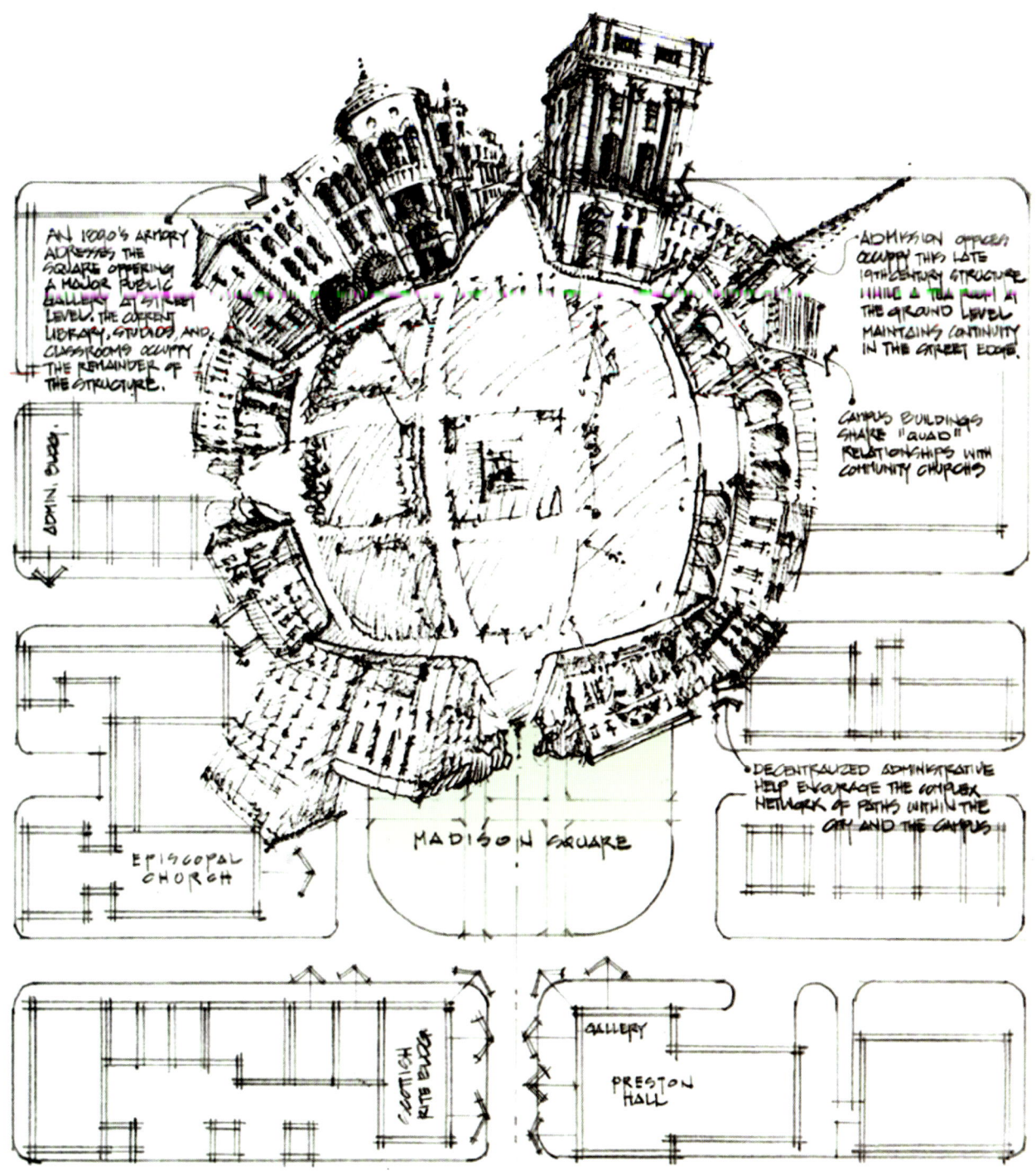

spaces and a 2,000-foot river walk extension are currently under construction. The initial private sector build out is expected in 10 years at an estimated cost of 800 million dollars.

However, the significance of the Civic Master Plan is not the magnitude of the current development effort, but in the longevity of the public realm that is created. The design process evolved over a five-year timeframe including multiple public charrettes between the City, citizens, property owners and development interests. The outcome of the process was a unified agenda of sustainable urban growth and the creation of a Civic Master Plan as the fundamental mechanism for urban expansion.

BLOCK SUBDIVISION

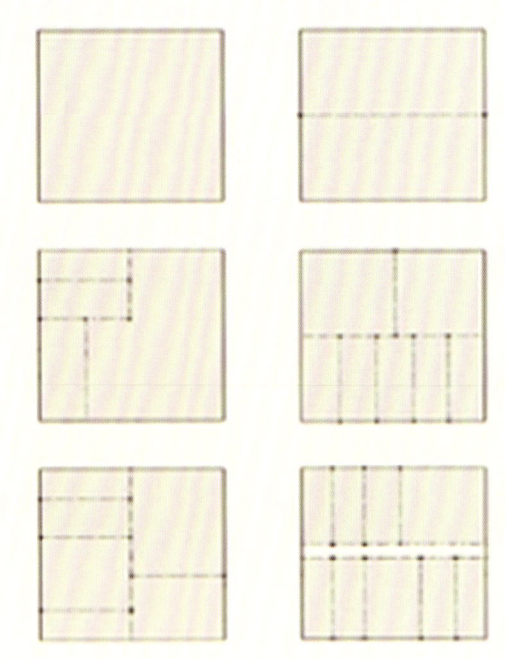

Savannah's East Riverfront Extension adjacent to the Historic City Center

BLOCK PLAN: The single most important defining element of the Civic Master Plan is the street and block plan, connecting this large open property to the historic patterns of the City of Savannah. The street and block plan organizes the site, provides public access to the waterfront, respects view corridors, improves circulation, and creates small blocks to accommodate a range of uses and open spaces. It is the basis for the official mapping of streets, parks, and other public spaces that will shape the future of the public realm.

STREETS AND PARKING: A network of interconnected streets provides circulation throughout the area. Street sections are compact with 10 foot travel lanes on most two-way streets and 12 foot travel lanes on one-way streets. Curb radiuses are minimized to between 6 and 12 feet. Parallel parking is provided on all streets on either one or two sides. Parallel parking is accommodated in 8x20 foot bays. Additional off-street parking may be provided in surface lots with appropriate landscaping or in structured decks. Off-street parking may not front a build-to line.

SIDEWALKS AND STREET TREES: A network of continuous sidewalks on all streets promotes connections and pedestrian-oriented development. Sidewalks are generally 5 to 6 feet in width, ranging up to 20 feet along retail frontage. Street trees are provided in tree lawns are 6 to 13 feet in width and are located between the sidewalk and the street. Regularly spaced and aligned street trees provide human scale, visual continuity, shade for pedestrians, and a barrier between moving traffic. Trees should be Live Oaks at 40 to 50 foot intervals, or other species compatible to those found in the city center.

PUBLIC SPACES: A variety of parks are created with an emphasis on the riverfront. The extension of the river walk is an integral element in connecting these spaces. Parks should be designed to accommodate a variety of passive uses. Multiples focal points should be developed which may include a playground, amphitheater, fountains, or connection to water travel.

Realization of the Plan extension, 2008

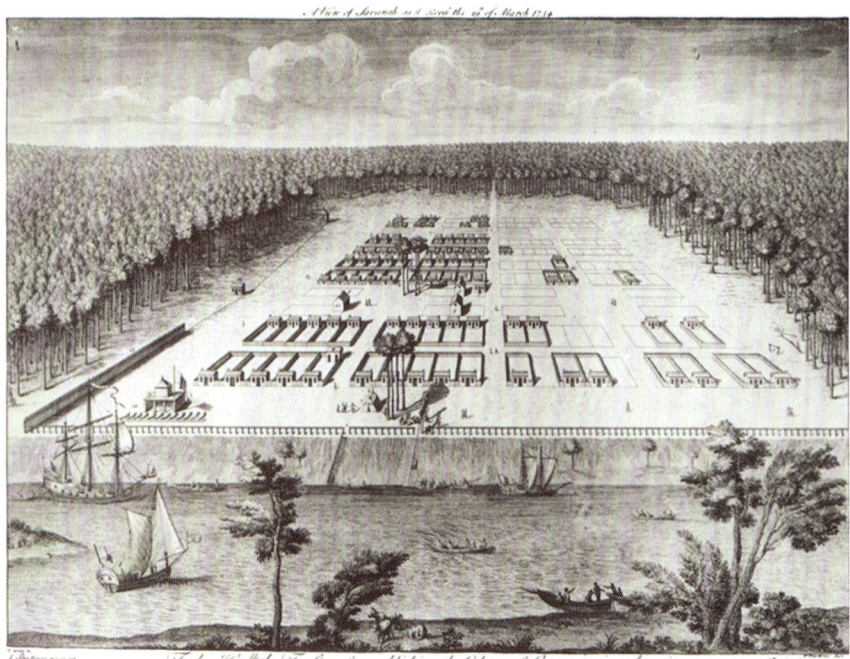

1733

Revisiting the Earliest Ownership Patterns (Above)
Savannah 1798, Highlighting East Riverfront Wards

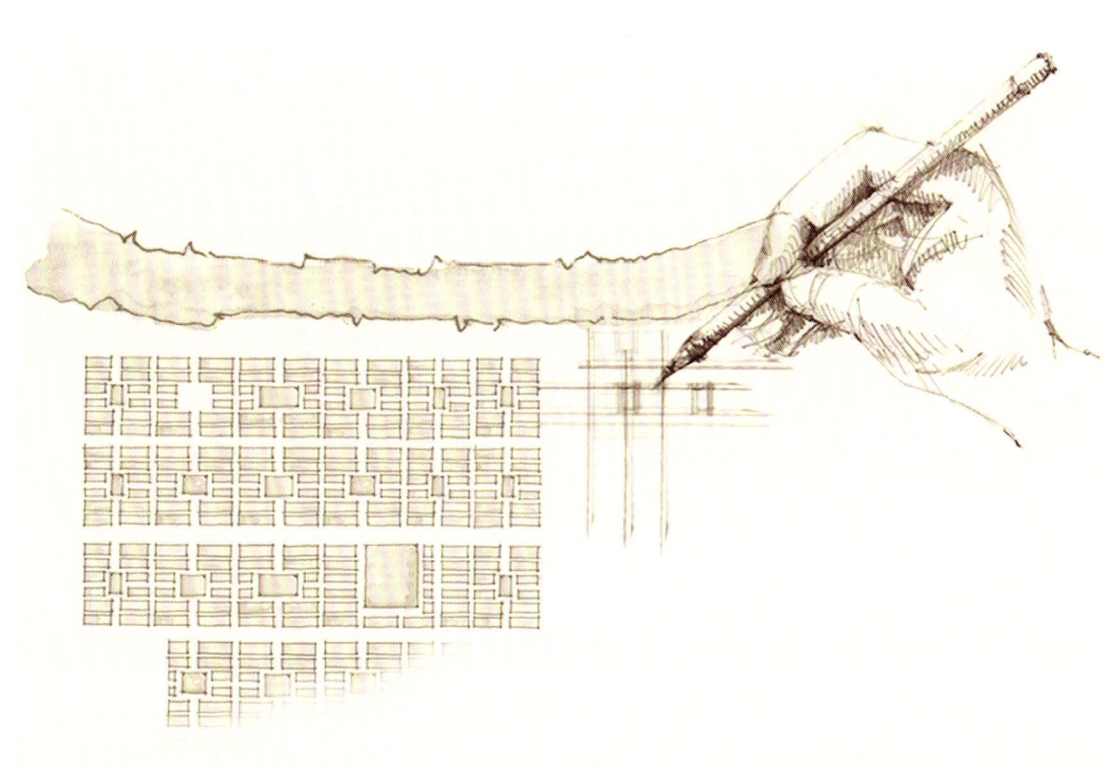

145

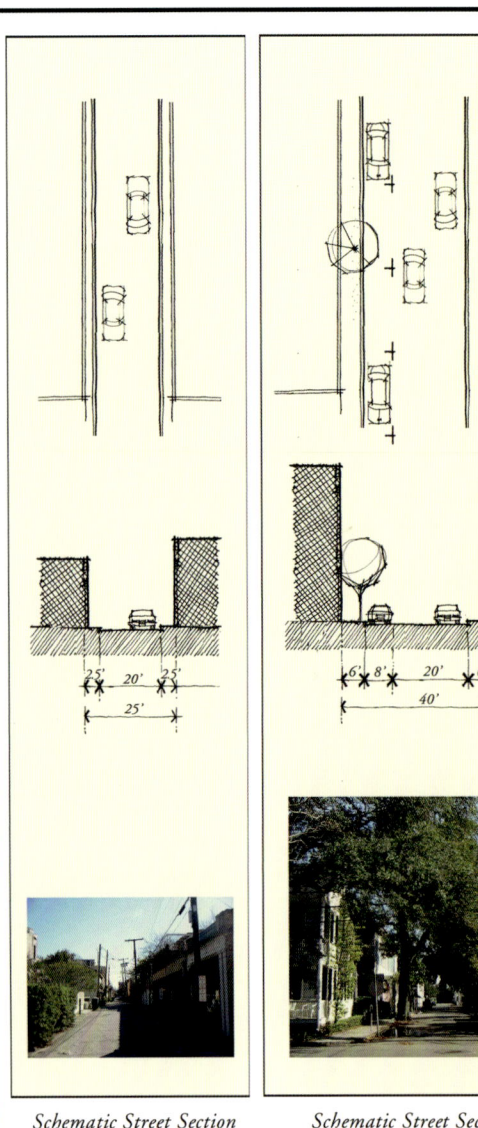

Schematic Street Section

25' LANE

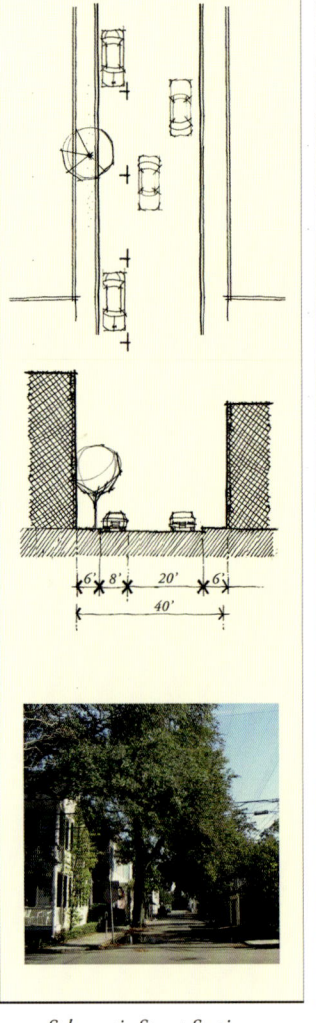

Schematic Street Section

40' STREET

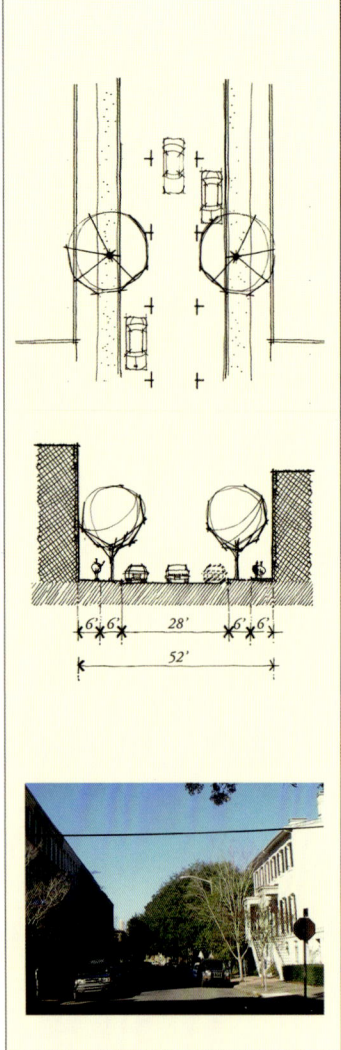

Schematic Street Section

52' STREET

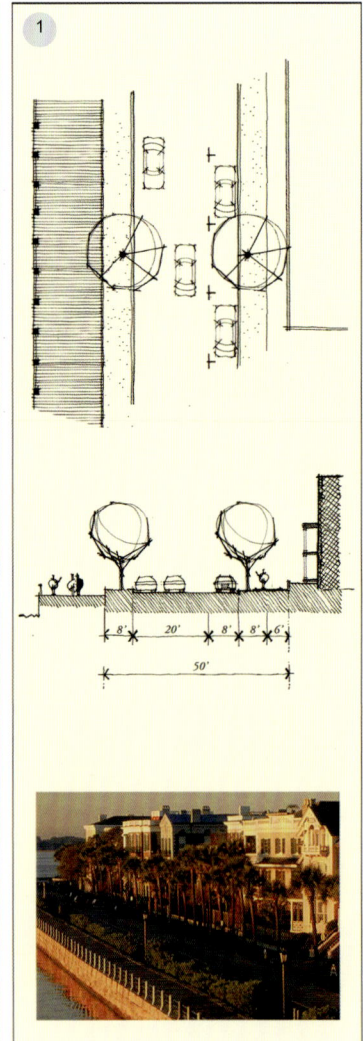

Schematic Street Section

50' RIVERFRONT STREET

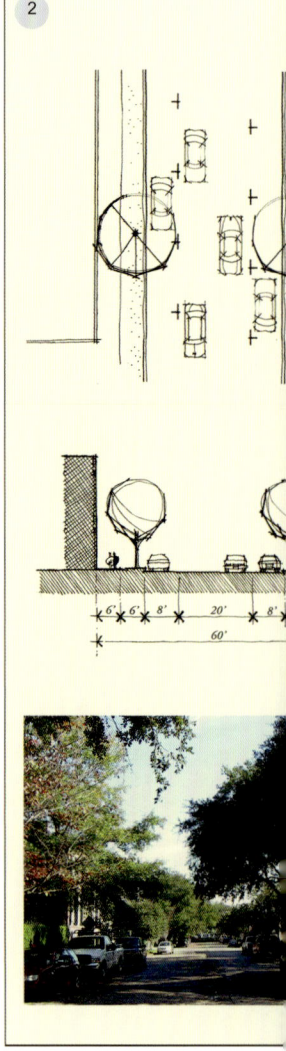

Schematic Street Se...

60' STREET

STREET TYPES
East Riverfront Civic Master Plan

SAVANNAH GEORGIA

EXTENDING CITY STREETS (1 2 3)

Streets, Sidewalks & Street Trees

A network of interconnected streets provides circulation throughout the area. Street sections are COMPACT with 10 foot travel lanes on most two-way streets. Curb radiuses are minimized. Parallel parking is provided on all streets on either one or two sides.

Continuous sidewalks on all streets promote CONNECTIONS and pedestrian-oriented development. Street trees are provided in tree lawns along all primary and secondary street. Regularly spaced and aligned street trees provide HUMAN SCALE, visual continuity, shade for pedestrians and safety from moving vehicles.

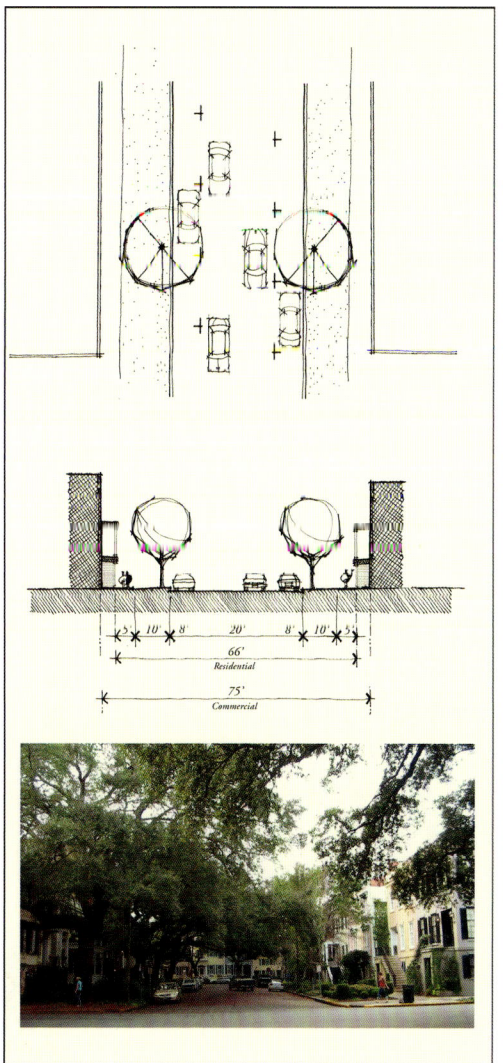

Schematic Street Section

66'/75' STREET

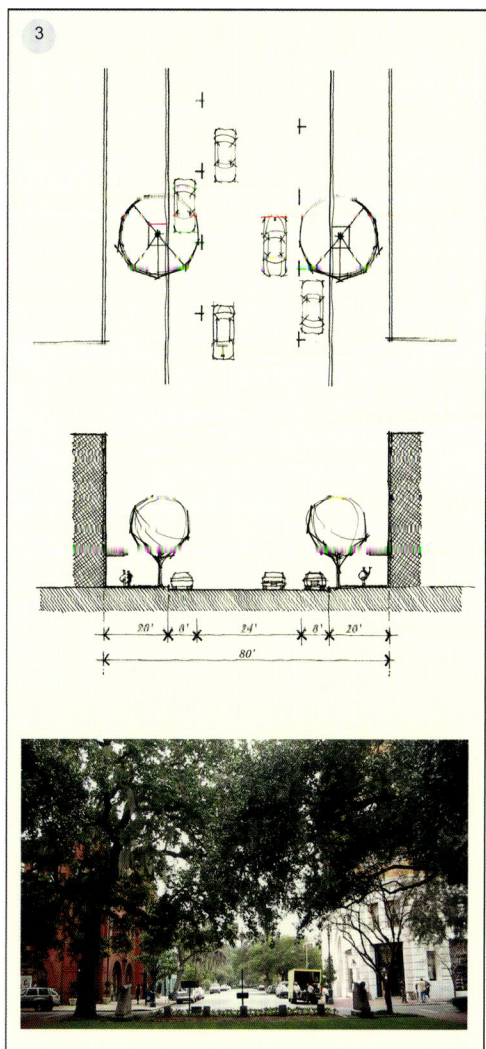

Schematic Street Section

80' STREET

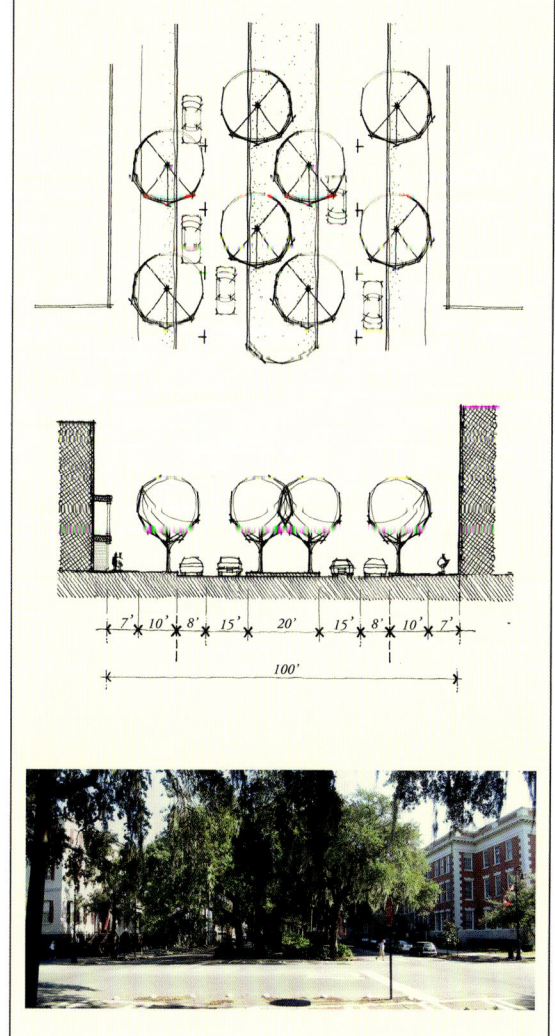

Schematic Street Section

100' BOULEVARD

City of Savannah
Metropolitan Planning Commission
Savannah Development & Renewal Authority

In collaboration with
Savannah River Landing, LLC
The Ambling Companies

Thomas & Hutton Engineering Co.
Sottile & Sottile *Urban Design*

February 24, 2006

Information contained herein has been compiled from various sources. Due to availability of data, it does not claim complete accuracy. It is intended instead to provide an overview and analysis of urban conditions.

© Copyright 2006, Sottile & Sottile

The U.S. House Office Buildings Facilities Plan and Preliminary South Capitol Area Plan

Jury Comments:
From the three adjacent House office buildings south to the Anacostia River, this plan pays a great deal of respect to the original L'Enfant plan, shifts space use to maximize adjacency priorities, and pays considerable attention to facility restoration and the incorporation of sustainable-design elements such as runoff control...

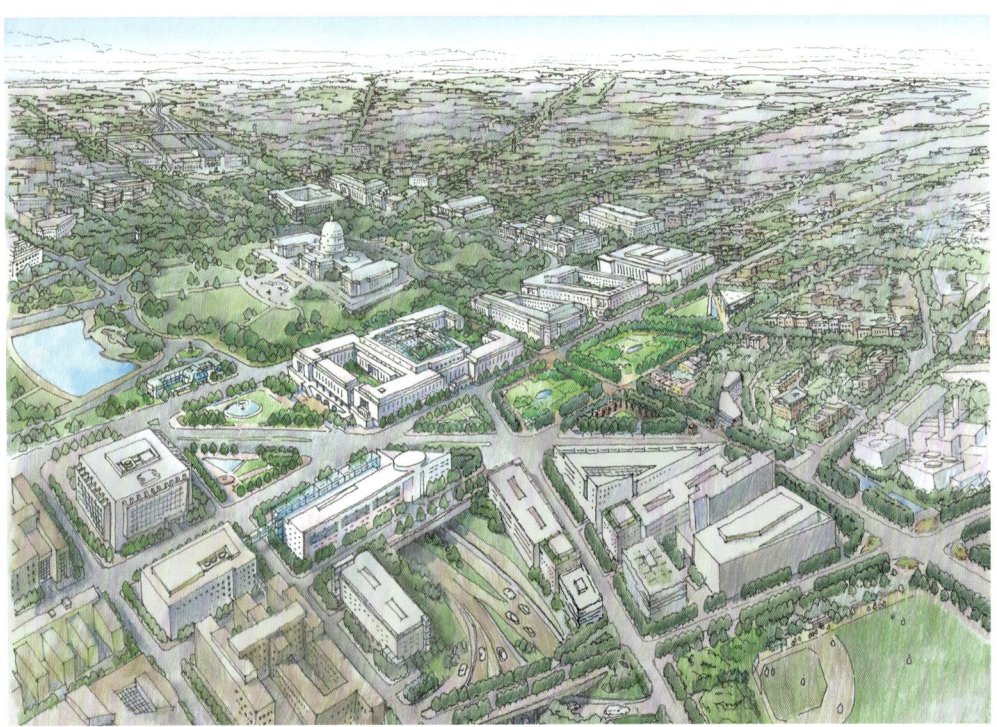

Notes of Interest

The U.S. Capitol Complex in Washington, D.C. is one of the most significant and sensitive places in our country. Within it, the U.S. House of Representatives is its largest component. The House Office Buildings Plan and South Capitol Area Plan defines a vision for fulfilling the current and future space and functional needs of the House, serves as the basis for organizing, budgeting, and funding its long-range capital improvements, and establishes an interface with the future re-development of the South Capitol District from the U.S. Capitol Complex to the Anacostia River.

The project area comprises the 177-acre South Capitol District, and focuses on land within it that is part of the U.S. Capitol Complex, containing some 2.56 million square feet and 5,772 parking spaces assigned to the House, whose needs were projected to grow for 2025 to 3.16 million square feet and 7,283 spaces. The goals, as outlined by Congress, included accommodating growth, improving security, improving transit links, preserving historic assets, upgrading open spaces, complementing new urban development south of the Complex, and developing an overall sustainability framework for the district. The plan also looks beyond 2025 to 2050, to the vision of the National Capitol Planning Commission's Legacy Plan, anticipating the removal of a railroad viaduct and the I-295/395 superstructure. The extension of the Canal Park would complete the integration of the South Capitol District with the U.S. Capitol Complex, to finally heal a scarred urban fabric.

Consultant: Carter Goble Associates, Inc., Booz Allen Hamilton Inc.
Engineer: Louis Berger Group, Inc.
Landscape Architect: Wallace Roberts & Todd
Owner: Architect of the Capitol

Architect
Wallace Roberts & Todd, LLC

Location
Washington, D.C.

Photo Credit
© Architecture Research Office

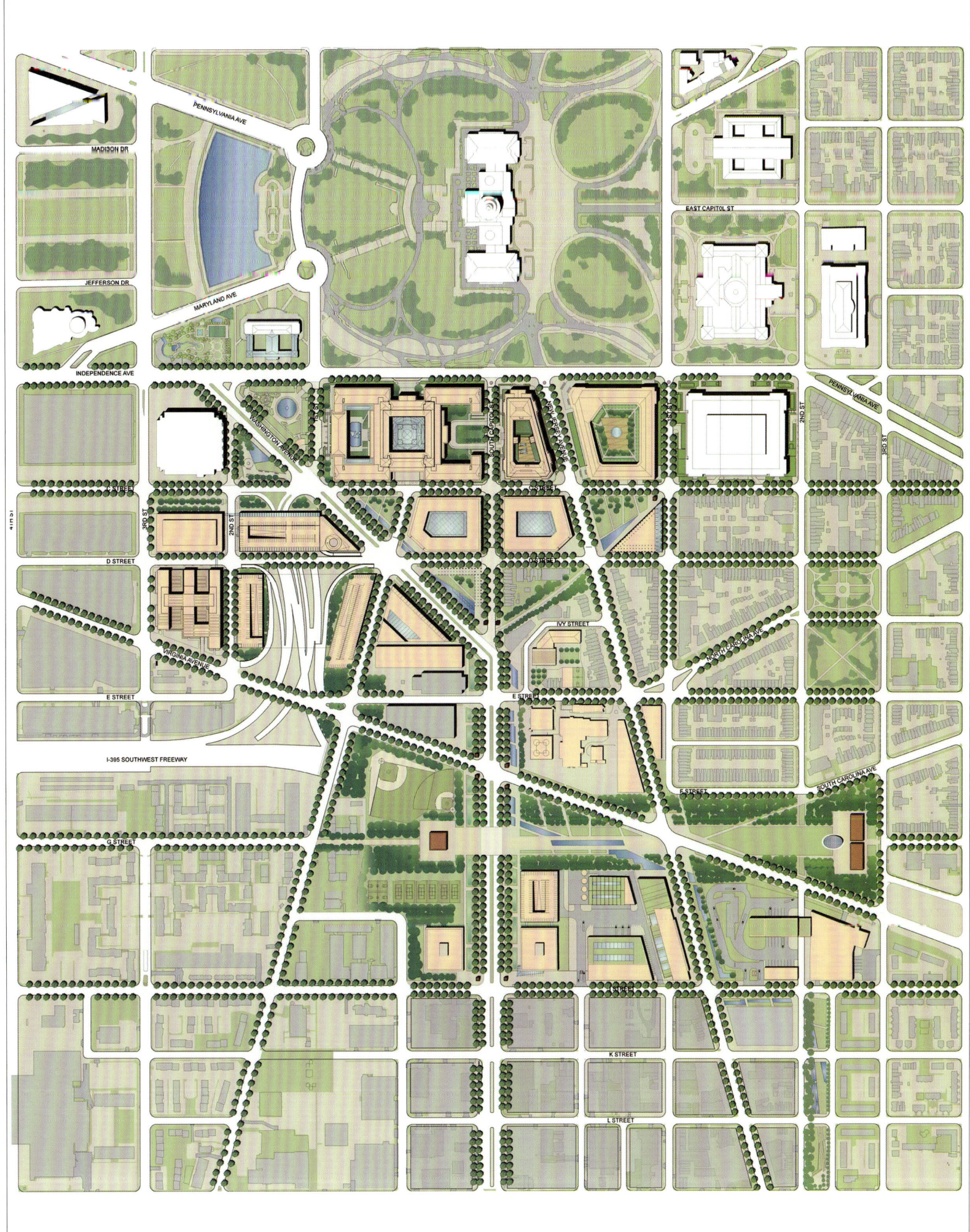

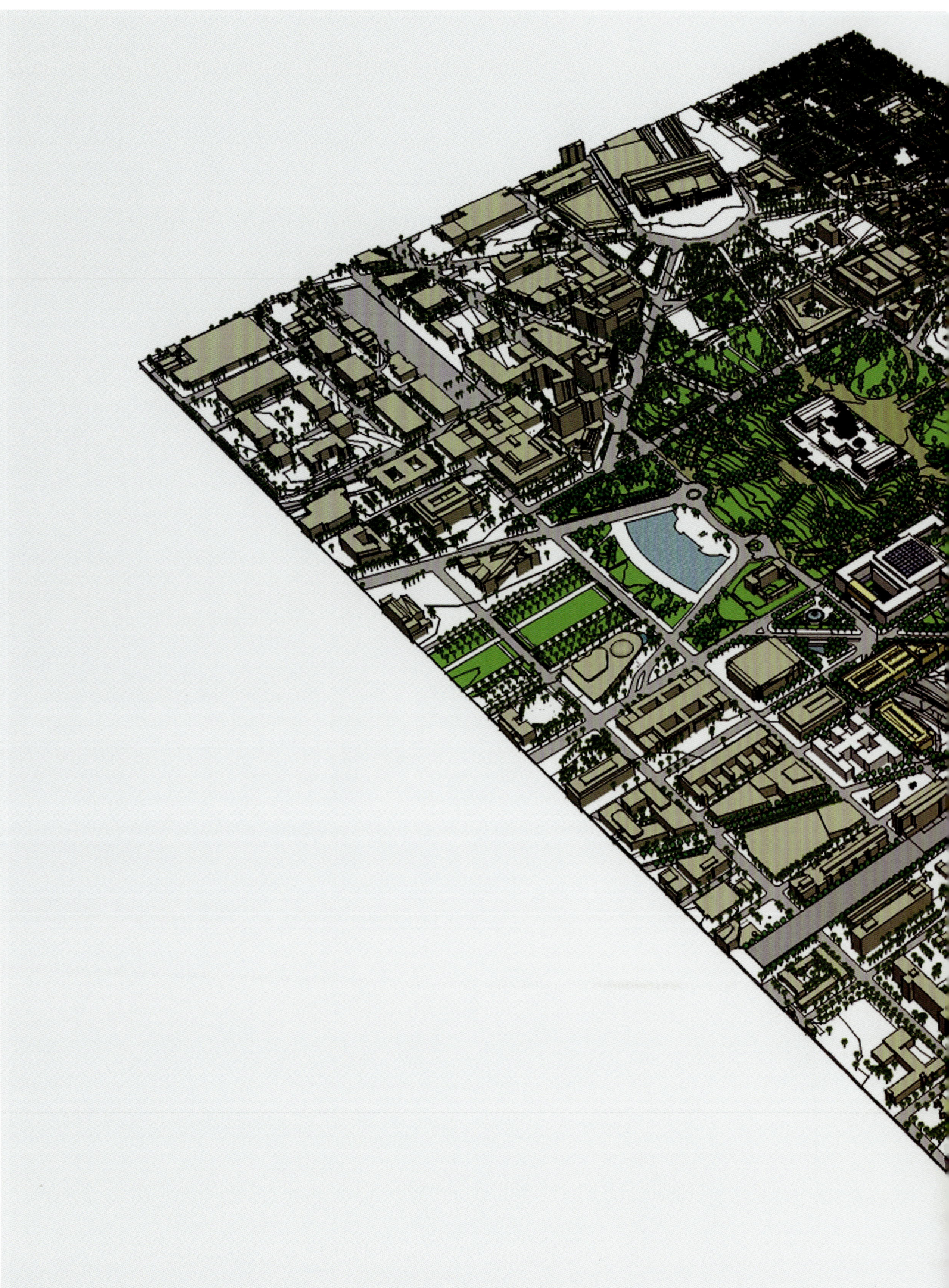

King Abdul Aziz International Airport – Hajj Terminal

Jury Comments:
The architects created a highly sustainable project well ahead of the green movement; they learned from the way people have inhabited the desert since early civilization – screening the sun, allowing natural light and ventilation. They did so much with so little – few materials, a regular rhythm of structural bays, a simple fabric structure that works as shelter, as environmental control and as a tie to tradition.
The great roof still works as originally designed as a plaza for the pilgrimage. The building is highly regarded for what it offers spatially, spiritually, symbolically, culturally – it has acquired landmark status as an airport and in the region.

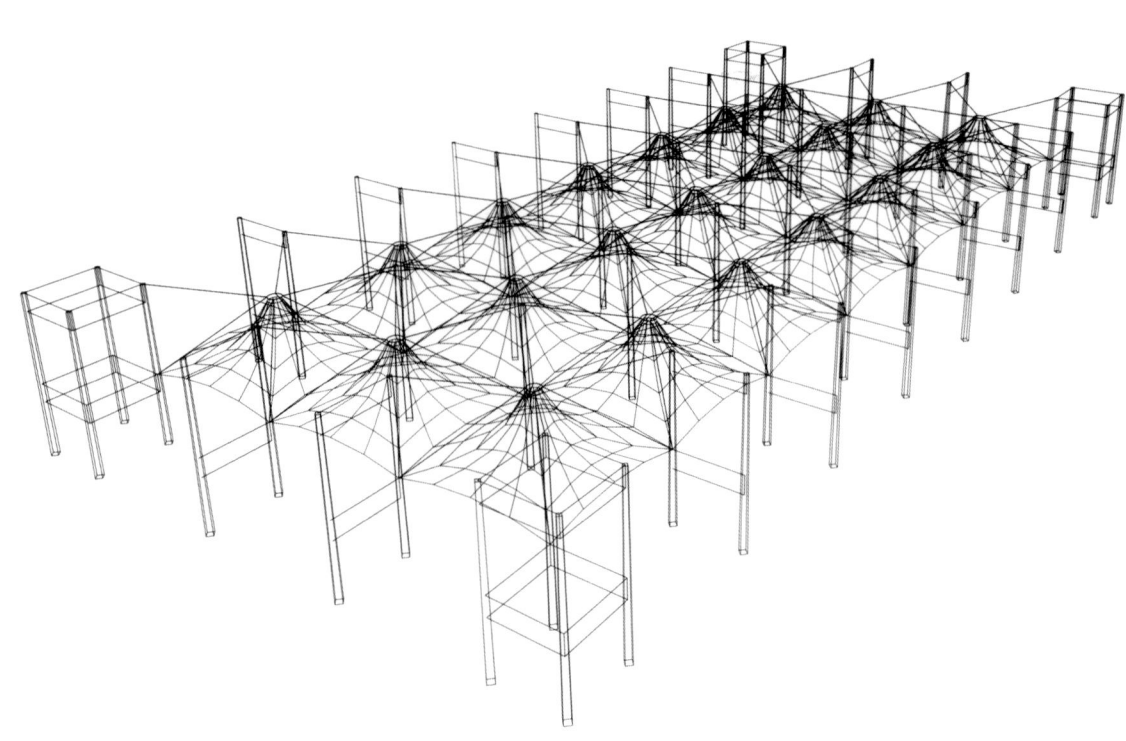

Notes of Interest

The King Abdul Aziz International Airport – Hajj Terminal receives millions of Hajj pilgrims on their way to the Islamic holy site of Mecca through this tented, open-air terminal each year. It was designed and serves as a gathering place of religious fellowship, an improvised campsite for pilgrims waiting to begin their journey, and a point of departure and gateway to Islam's most revered places.

The ritual journey of Muslims to Mecca is one of Islam's five pillars of faith. Pilgrims from around the world travel to Mecca and perform a series of religious rituals. Over a six week span, millions of Muslims undertake this journey. When SOM signed onto the project, the increasing number of Hajj pilgrims had overwhelmed the original Jeddah airport 43 miles west of Mecca, and the firm's Chicago office was commissioned to design a dedicated Hajj terminal there that would only be used during these religious ceremonies. Completed in 1981, the terminal covers 120 acres and 2.8 million square feet.

General Contractor: Hochtief A.G.
Owner: Kingdom of Saudi Arabia Ministry of Defense & Avia

Architect
Skidmore, Owings & Merrill LLP –
New York and Chicago Offices

Location
Jeddah, Saudi Arabia

Photo Credit
© Owens-Corning Fiberglas/S. A. Amin/
Skidmore, Owings & Merrill LLP/Prof. em. Herbert Schmidt

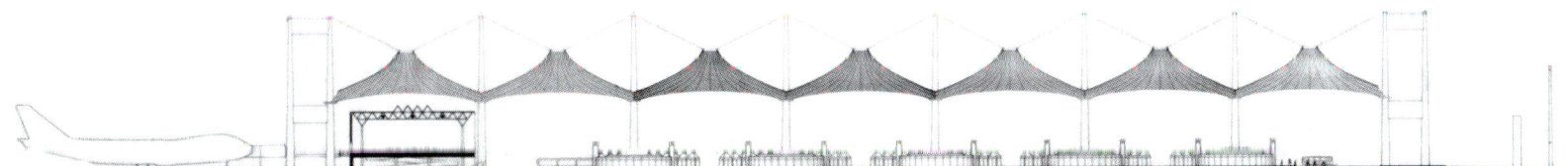

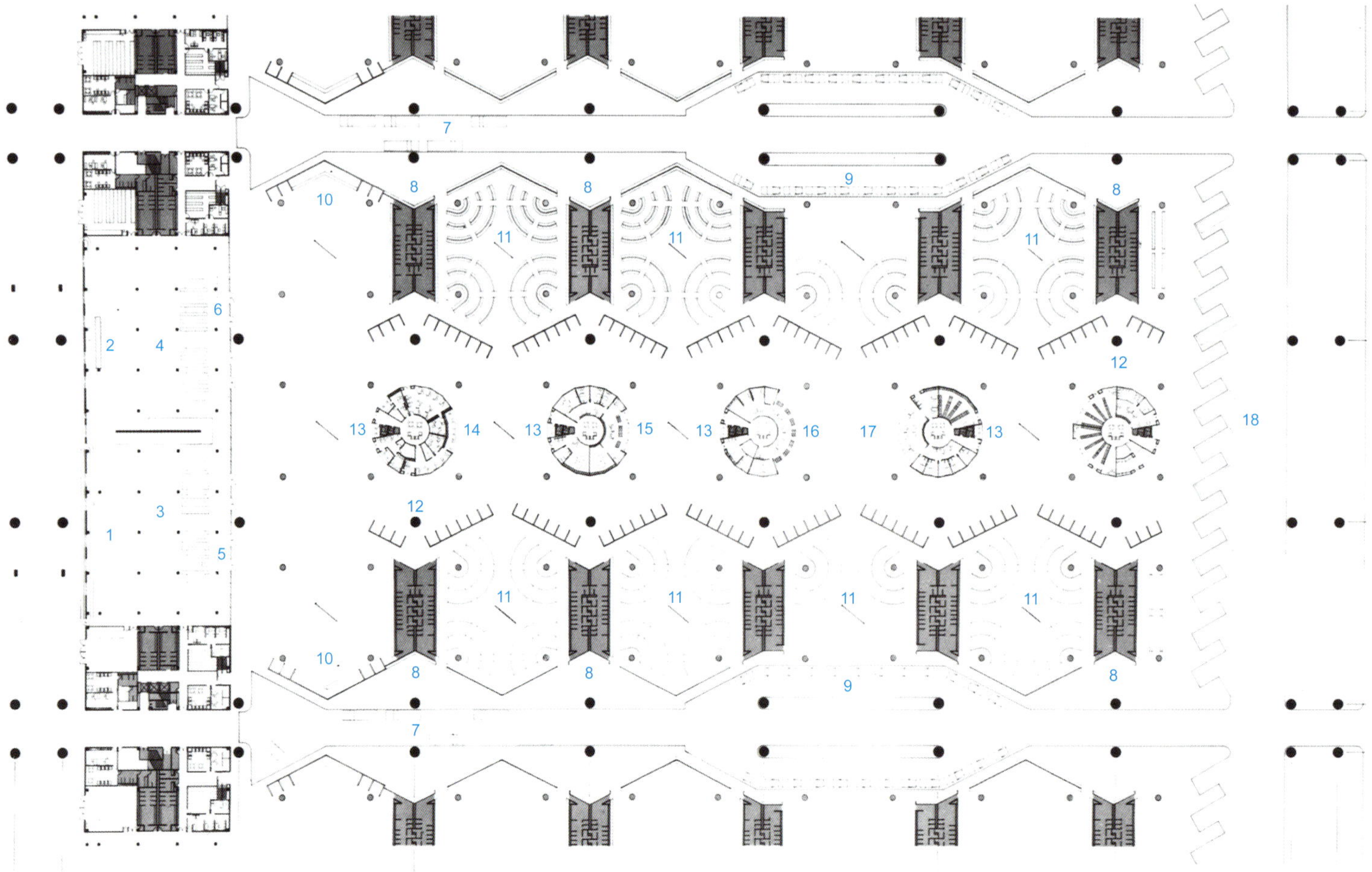

1. Baggage retrieval
2. Ticketing
3. Arrivals
4. Departures
5. Customs
6. Exit check
7. Service road
8. Cooking
9. Taxis
10. Dining
11. Rest area
12. Souk
13. Info
14. Banks
15. Agents
16. Airlines
17. Bus/ taxi
18. Buses

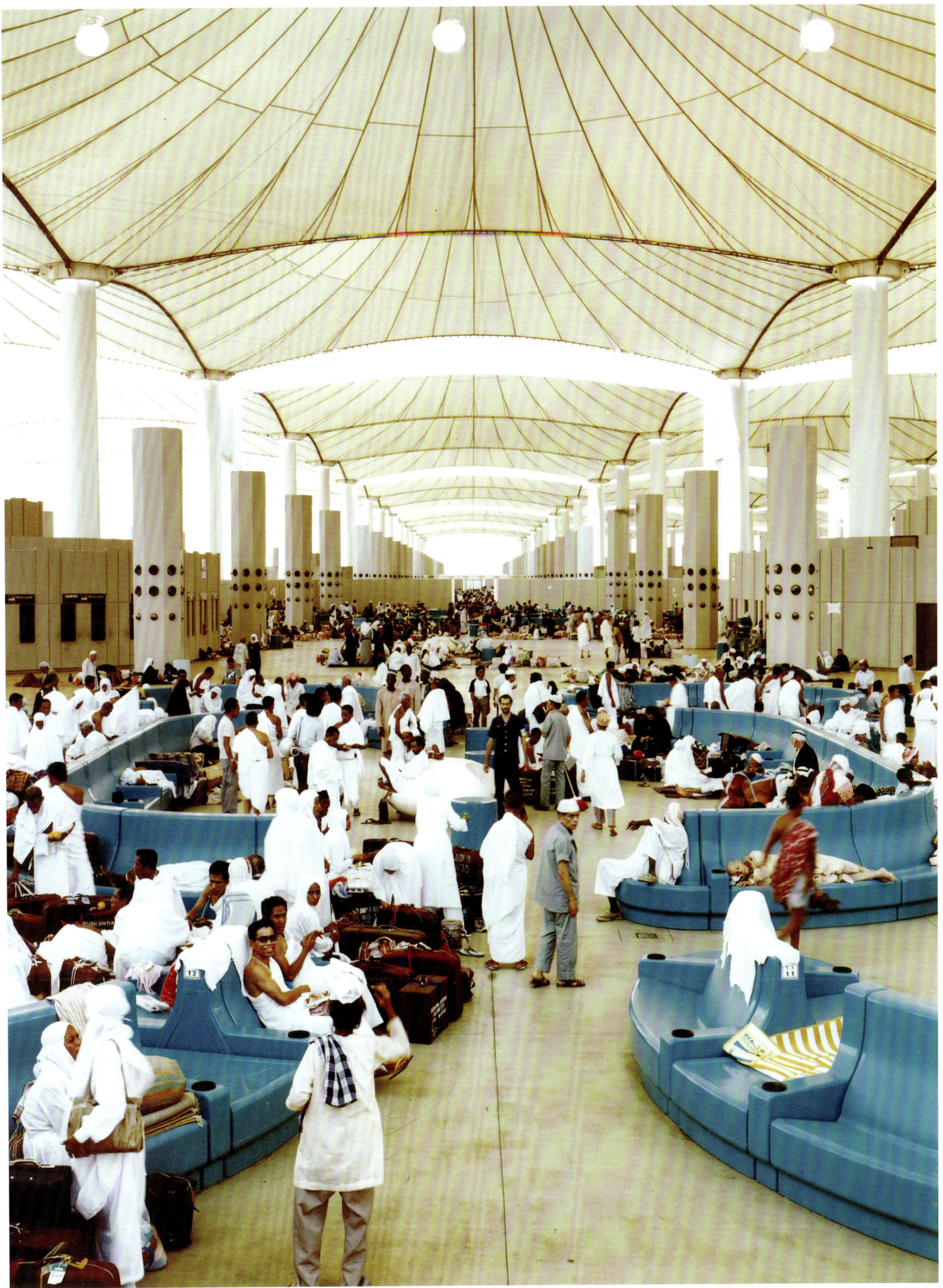

2011 INSTITUTE HONOR AWARDS FOR ARCHITECTURE JURY

David E. Miller, FAIA, Chair
The Miller Hull Partnership, LLP

Ashley Clark, Associate AIA
The Littlejohn Group

Curtis Fentress, FAIA
Fentress Architects

T. Gunny Harboe, FAIA
Harboe Architect, PC

David Neuman, FAIA
University of Virginia

Louis Pounders, FAIA
ANF Architects

Sarah Snodgrass
University of Nevada, Las Vegas/
American Institute of Architecture
Students Representative

Allison Williams, FAIA
Perkins & Will

Jennifer Yoos, AIA
VJAA

2011 Institute Honor Awards

2011 INSTITUTE HONOR AWARDS FOR INTERIOR ARCHITECTURE JURY

John Ronan, AIA, Chair
John Ronan Architects

Jaime Canaves, FAIA
Florida International University,
School of Architecture

Margaret Kittinger, AIA
Beyer Blinder Belle Architects

Bryan Lewis
The Capital Group Companies

Brian Malarkey, AIA
Kirksey

2011 INSTITUTE HONOR AWARDS FOR REGIONAL AND URBAN DESIGN JURY

Daniel E. Williams, FAIA, Chair
Daniel Williams Architect

C.R. George Dove, FAIA
WDG Architecture, PLLC

Vivien Li
Boston Harbor Association

Claire Weisz, AIA
Weisz + Yoes Architecture

Bernard Zyscovich, FAIA
Zyscovich, Inc.

David E. Miller, FAIA
2011 Chair,
Institute Honor Awards for Architecture

David E. Miller, FAIA, is a founding partner of The Miller | Hull Partnership, a sixty-five person firm in Seattle. Miller|Hull is a fundamentally design oriented firm, emphasizing a rational design approach based on the culture, climate and building traditions of a place. In addition to over 200 awards for design excellence, the firm received the 2003 AIA Architecture Firm Award, which is given to one architectural design practice in the U.S. each year. Three monographs have been published on the firm's work; Ten Houses by Rockport Press, 1999; Miller | Hull, Architects of the Pacific Northwest by Princeton Architectural Press, 2001; and Public Works by Princeton Architectural Press, 2009.

David is an excellent and inspirational designer. In 2006, he received two unique awards: the Washington State University Regents' Distinguished Alumnus Award and the BetterBricks Designer Award, recognizing him as a designer who supports, uses and designs sustainable, high performance, commercial buildings. In 2010 he received the AIA Seattle Chapter Medal, the highest individual award bestowed on an architect by the Chapter.

Currently, David is Chair for the Department of Architecture at the University of Washington, where he is also a tenured professor of architecture. In 2005, David authored, toward a New Regionalism (University Press), which promotes environmental architecture and showcases the work of Northwest architects from Portland to British Columbia. For the 2010 year, he is Co-Chair of the National AIA, Committee on the Environment (COTE), Advisory Group.

© David E. Miller

John Ronan, AIA
2011 Chair,
Institute Honor Awards for Interior Architecture

© Michelle Litvin

John Ronan is founding principal of John Ronan Architects in Chicago, founded in 1997. He holds a Master of Architecture degree with distinction from the Harvard University Graduate School of Design and a Bachelor of Science degree with honors from the University of Michigan. In 1999, he was a winner in the Townhouse Revisited Competition staged by the Graham Foundation and his firm was the winner of the prestigious Perth Amboy High School Design Competition in 2004, a two-stage international design competition to design a 472,000 square foot high school in New Jersey. In December 2000, he was named as a member of the Design Vanguard by Architectural Record magazine, and in January 2005 he was selected to The Architectural League of New York's Emerging Voices program. In 2006 he was featured in the Young Chicago exhibition at the Art Institute of Chicago. His work has been exhibited in galleries throughout the U.S., including the Graham Foundation, the Art Institute of Chicago and The Architectural League of New York, and his work has been featured in numerous international publications. A monograph on his work, entitled Explorations, published by Princeton Architectural Press was released in 2010. John is currently an Associate Professor at the Illinois Institute of Technology College of Architecture, where he has taught since 1992.

Daniel E. Williams, FAIA, APA
2011 Chair,
Institute Honor Awards for Regional & Urban Design

© Megan H. Williams

Daniel E. Williams, is a Fellow in the American Institute of Architects and is an internationally recognized expert in sustainable architecture and urban and regional design. Mr. Williams is a member of the experts team for the Clinton Climate + Initiative, advising on projects in Toronto and London. He served as 2006 chair of the AIA's Sustainability Task Group and sat on the national advisory council for United States Environmental Protection Agency – NACEPT.

He participated in the development, the 2010 Council of Mayor's resolution that will reduce carbon emissions by 50%; presented Watershed Planning Initiatives at the Center for Neighborhood Technologies in Chicago; wrote and chaired the AIA/EPA grant Water + Design; co-wrote the Barcelona Declaration on Sustainability; and has worked with dozens of communities around the country, creating master plans with the residents – specifically to assist in the rebuilding of towns and cities after natural disasters and the associated impacts from climate change.

In 2003 he chaired the National Committee on the Environment for the American Institute of Architects and chaired the Task Force on the Environment and Energy for the Congress for the New Urbanism from 1996 – 2000, and won the first passive design award in Architecture from NASA in 1980.

His work on post-disaster smart growth urban and regional design projects won the 1999 and 2000 National Honor Award for Urban and Regional Design from the American Institute of Architects' and the Catherine Brown Award for Urban Design in the American Landscape in 1999. His projects range in scale from "off the grid" residences to regional master plans of thousands of square miles – these designs integrate issues in ecology, economic development, transportation, agricultural preservation, education, water resource protection, smart growth and climate change.

Named Eminent Scholar and Distinguished Alumni in 2000 at the University of Florida, his book Sustainable Design: Ecology, Architecture and Planning was published Earth Day 2007 by John Wiley & Sons. He is presently working on a book titled Design with Climate-Change.

AT&T Performing Arts Center Dee and Charles Wyly Theater

Jury Comments:
This building is an expression of a totally new way to investigate the potential of performative experimentation – completely re-choreographed the way in which one experiences a theater.

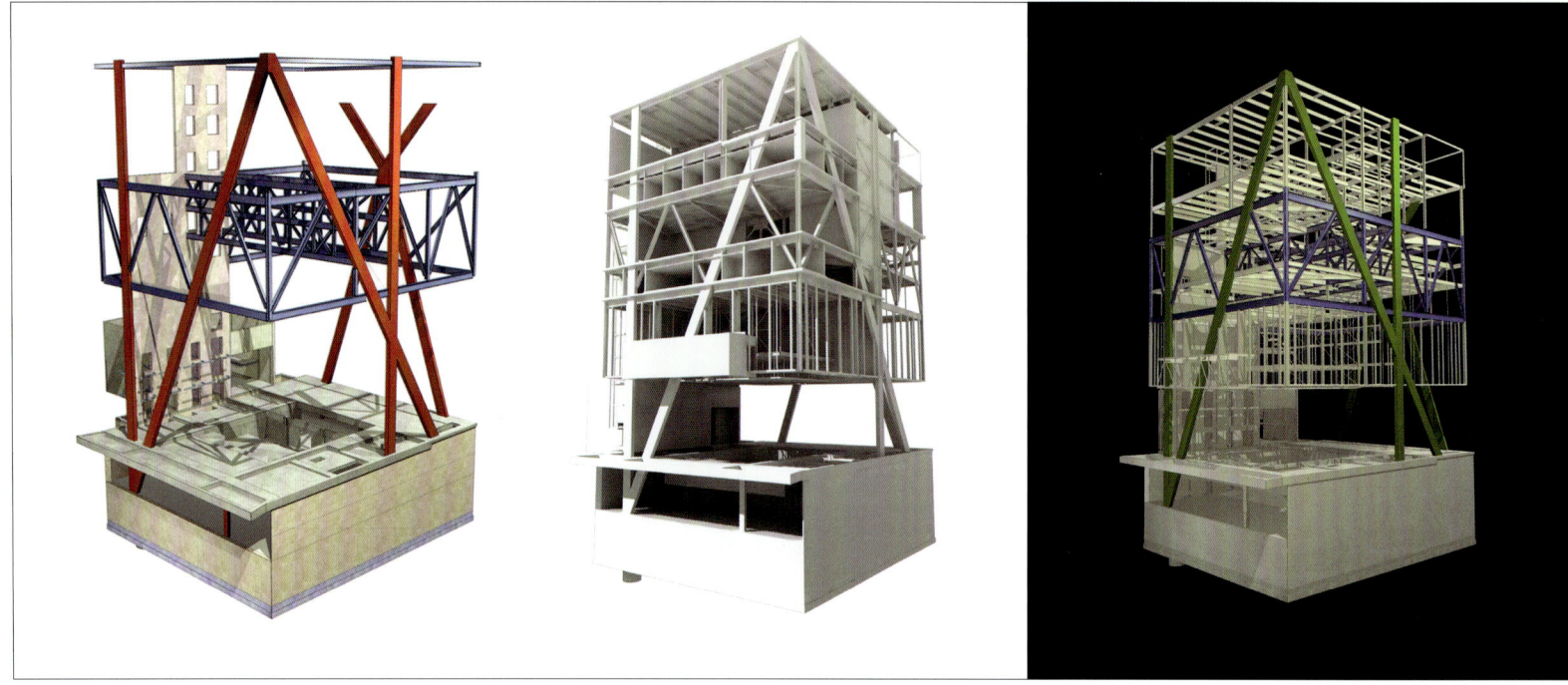

Notes of Interest

The AT&T Performing Arts Center is an 80,300 square-foot, 575-seat "multi-form" theater with the ability to transform between configurations and a performance chamber open to its urban surroundings.

The Dallas Theater Center (DTC)'s previous accommodation – a makeshift metal shed – freed its users from the limitations imposed by a fixed-stage configuration and the need to protect expensive interior finishes.

The Dee and Charles Wyly Theatre overcame these challenges by positioning back-of-house and front-of-house facilities above and beneath the auditorium, instead of encircling it. This unprecedented stacked design transforms the building into a "theater machine" that provides an almost infinite variety of stage-audience configurations and manifests a strong presence in the Dallas Arts District despite its relatively modest size.

Associate Architect: Kendall/Heaton Associates
Engineer: Transsolar Energietechnik, Cosentini Associates, Magnusson Klemencic Associates
Construction Manager: McCarthy Building Companies
Lighting: Tillotson Design Associates
Owner: AT&T Performing Arts Center

Architect
REX | OMA

Location
Dallas, Texas

Photo Credit
© Iwan Baan Photography

164

Ford Assembly Building

Jury Comments:
This renovated facility has improved the region by saving an older building and its embodied energy. It is functioning in a fashion of research and design fabrication not dissimilar to Khan's original intentions.

Section Detail:
1. South facing sun
2. Solar panel
3. Soft north light

Notes of Interest

The restoration and preservation of the Ford Assembly Building on the San Francisco Bay waterfront saved a historic architectural icon from the wrecking ball and converted a long-vacant auto plant into a current-day model of urban revitalization and sustainability. The 525,000 square foot building had been designed by Albert Kahn for Henry Ford, and constructed in 1931. Following the facility's initial car factory function, the Ford Building had many incarnations, including the famous World War II tank factory "manned" by Rosie-the-Riveters.

Design excellence for the restoration of the Ford Assembly Building meant instilling new purpose and function by revitalizing an already rich historic architectural icon while respecting its existing industrial aesthetic. The restoration allows for the considerable mix of uses at Ford, including offices, manufacturing, R&D labs, support space and retail. Along the east side are loading docks, while the west side has the official front doors of several companies. Favorite amenities for both tenants and visitors include The Craneway event space and The BoilerHouse Restaurant for both tenants and visitors to the Ford campus.

Engineer: Charles M. Salter Associates, Mechanical Design Studio, Inc., The Crosby Group, Gregory P. Luth & Associates
General Contractor: Dalzell Corporation
Historic Preservation: Preservation Architecture
Lighting: Lighting Design: Architecture + Light
Owner: Orton Development, Inc.

Architect
Marcy Wong Donn Logan Architects

Location
Richmond, California

Photo Credit
© Billy Hustace

Transverse Section Looking North (Below)

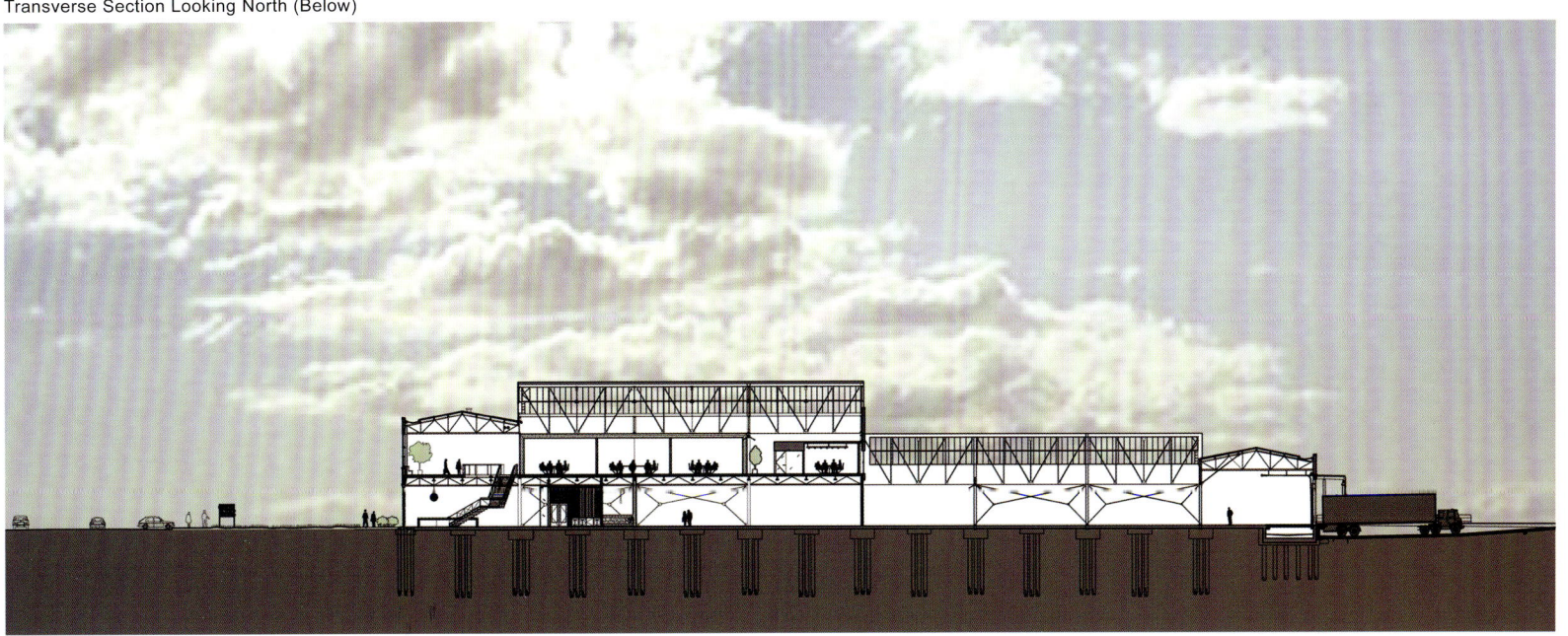

Longitudinal Section Looking West (Below)

Horizontal Skyscraper Vanke Center

Jury Comments:
This project skips along from mound to mound and manipulates the landscape, while letting it breathe — it builds it up and shapes it into a powerful form above the land with inventive manipulation.
The building is shading the landscape and letting it breathe — integrated sustainability.
A reinvented building type with the building floating over the landscape — dancing on the landscape.

Notes of Interest

The Horizontal Skyscraper Vanke Center stands as a new hybrid model that provides ample public space in a unique way. The building also combines the most forward-thinking sustainable technologies with innovative construction techniques.

The building hovers above the landscape, freeing it for public use and for a unique scheme of ecosystem restoration. Of the 60,000-square-meter site, 28,000 square meters are left unbuilt, and people in the surrounding community have already begun inhabiting the space for leisure. By lifting the building off the ground, the project is both a building and a landscape. The landscape scheme works to minimize run-off, erosion, and other types of environmental damage associated with development.

Additionally, the Horizontal Skyscraper Vanke Center employs some of the most forward-thinking sustainable design strategies. It utilizes greywater recycling, rain water harvesting, green roofs, dynamically controlled operable louvers, high-performing glass, and a roof of photovoltaic panels that provide 12.5 percent of the total electric energy demand for Vanke Headquarters.

Associate Architect: CCDI
Engineer: Transsolar, CCDI, CABR, CCDI
Lighting: L'Observatoire International
Owner: Shenzhen Vanke Real Estate Co.

Architect	Location	Photo Credit
Steven Holl Architects	Shenzhen, China	© Iwan Baan

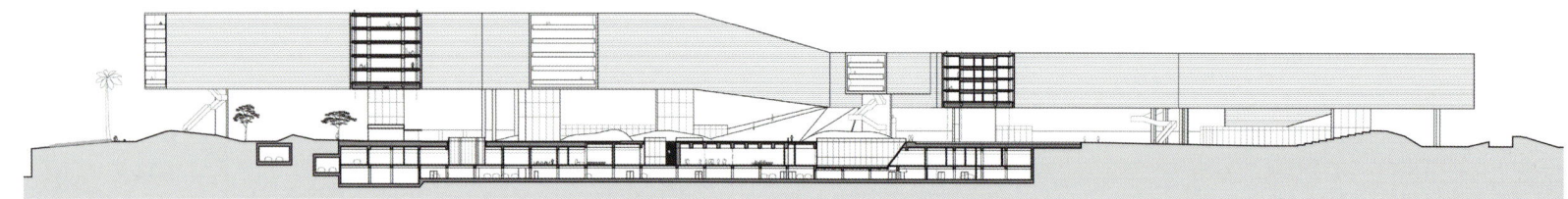

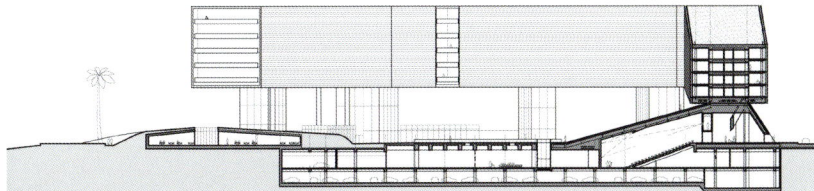
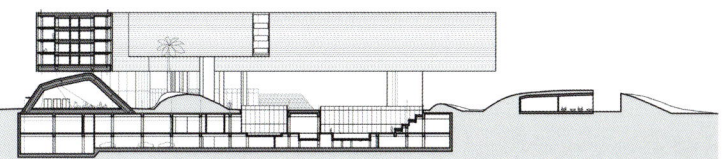

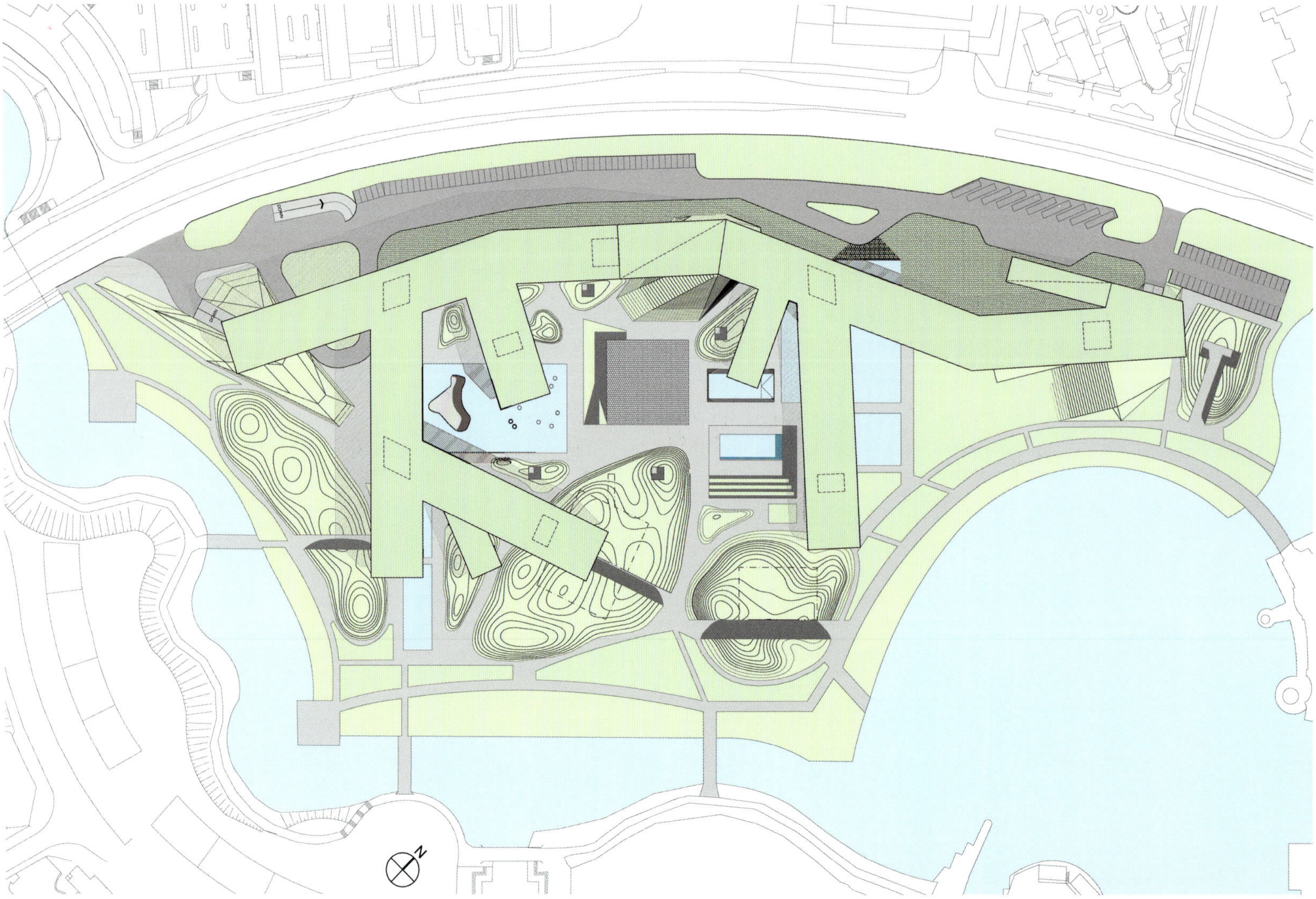

176

SIZE COMPARISON

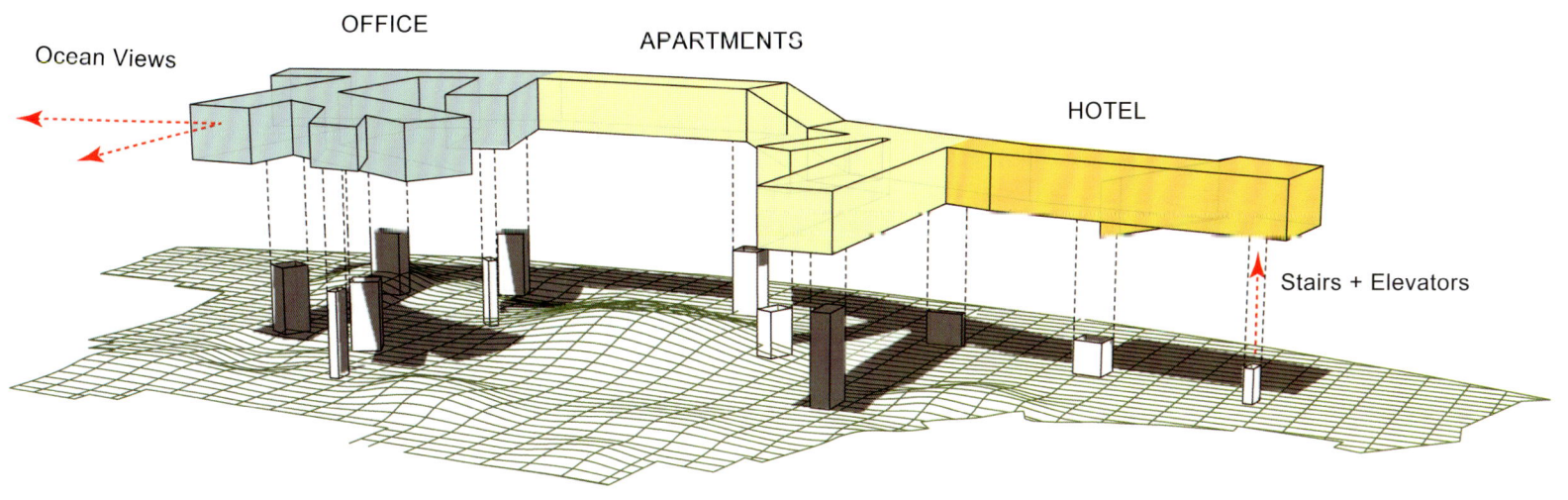

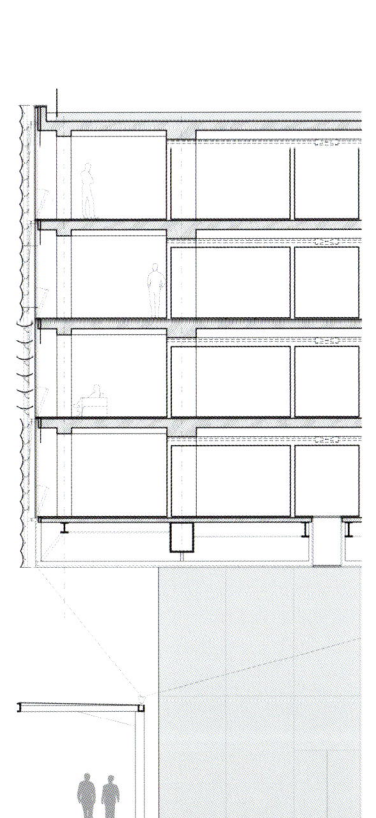
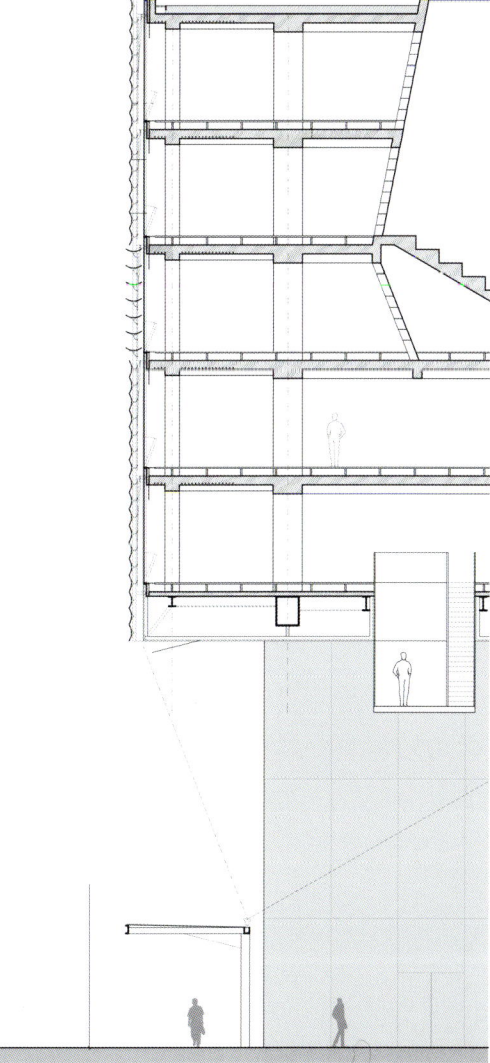

New Acropolis Museum

Jury Comments:
The building rotates in plan to fit the site – it is very contextual and powerfully respectful of the urban fabric of Athens while doing a dance around the ruins.
Not a light building – it is very contextual and powerfully respectful of the urban fabric of Athens while doing a dance around the ruins.
The sculpture from the old museum is much more dramatic than in the old setting with the screen walls and slab edges remaining contextual to the neighborhood and city.

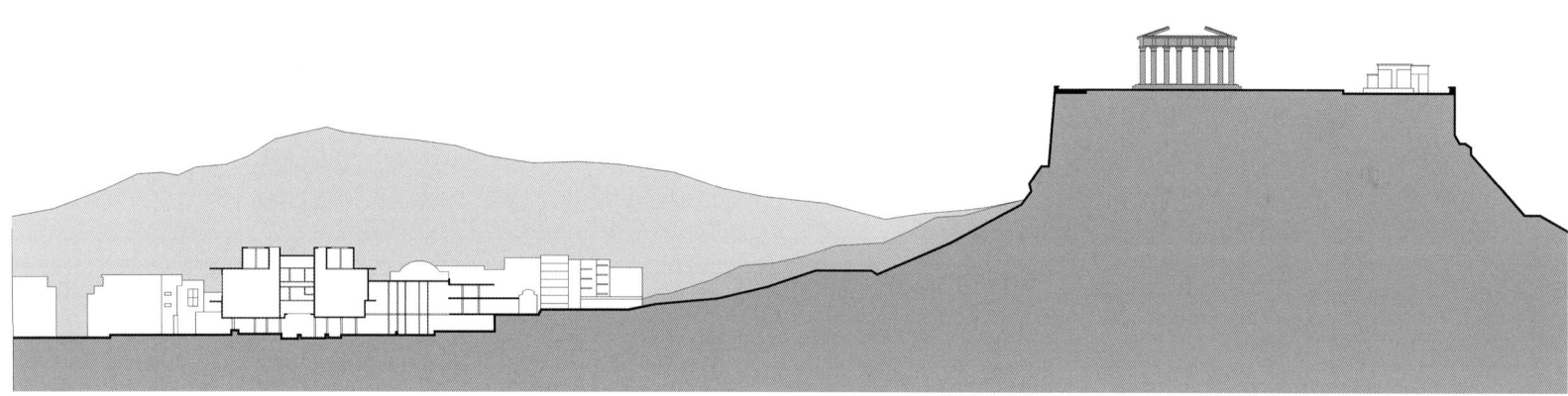

Notes of Interest

Located in Athens's historic Makryianni district, the New Acropolis Museum stands less than 1,000 feet southeast of the Parthenon. The site presented unique challenges, such as the need to accommodate a large existing structures and Athens' largest ongoing archaeological excavation. Additionally and importantly, the site is located in a hot climate in a major seismic zone, requiring state-of-the-art technology to protect visitors, staff, and the irreplaceable artifacts of the Museum collection.

The building was designed in three layers, two of which follow the city grid and existing and ancient pathways. The top-floor Parthenon Gallery, designed to display the Parthenon sculptures, is rotated 23 degrees and dimensioned to approximate the size, orientation, and viewing conditions of the historic Parthenon.

The Parthenon Gallery's glass outer walls allow visitors uninterrupted, 360-degree views of the ancient temple and the surrounding city. Its transparent enclosure provides ideal light for sculpture in direct view to and from the Acropolis, using the most contemporary glass and climate control technology, engineered with a view to sustainability, to protect the gallery against excessive heat and light. One of the goals of the topmost gallery is to eventually reunite the elements of the Parthenon Frieze, currently dispersed among several world museums.

Associate Architect: Michael Photiadis & Associate Architects
Owner: Greek Ministry of Culture

Architect
Bernard Tschumi Architects

Location
Athens, Greece

Photo Credit
© Christian Richters, Exterior; © Peter Mauss/Esto, Interior

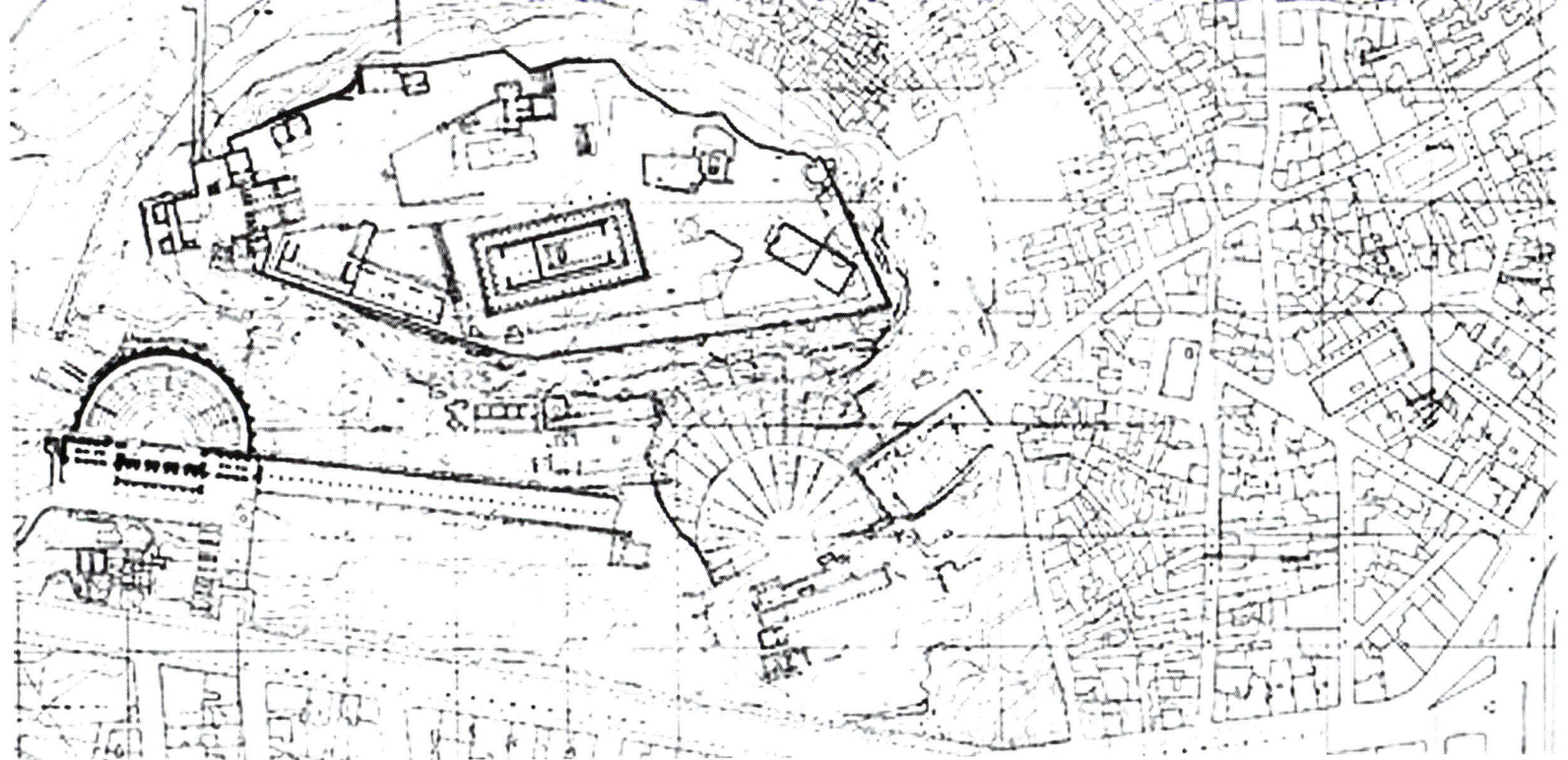

North Carolina Museum of Art

Jury Comments:
Worthy of recognition for the precision and technology that went into the design of the ceiling and light well – the way daylight is brought into this building is ingenious.
From a distance, the building appears as a normal industrial building fitting into its context – upon approach it is an amazingly precise and elegant box.
Very unique for a museum in that it contributes to the overall master plan for this part of the city.

Notes of Interest
Inside the North Carolina Museum of Art, the light of day and the lush surrounding hills have a presence unusual in institutional galleries for art. Overhead, hundreds of elliptical occuli bathe the museum's interior in even, full-spectrum daylight, modulated in intensity by layered materials that filter out damaging rays.
A departure from tradition, the museum in some respects is a single 65,000-square-foot room. Within this spatial continuum, a succession of wall planes delineate separate galleries. The building's skin is a rain screen of pale, matte anodized-aluminum panels that softly pick up surrounding colors and movement, fostering a discourse with the landscape.
The expansion galleries at the North Carolina Museum of Art will provide a distinct visitor experience in a state-of-the-art "energy smart" building. Naturally illuminating the interior environment provides color rendering and light levels ideal for viewing art, while efficient temperature and air quality controls, lighting and envelope systems provide the ideal interior environment for preserving the art.

Engineer: Skidmore, Owings & Merrill LLP
AltieriSeborWieber, Kimley-Horn Associates
General Contractor: Balfour Beatty, Barnhill
Lighting: Fisher Marantz Stone
Owner: Department of Cultural Resources, State of North Carolina

Architect
Thomas Phifer and Partners

Location
Raleigh, North Carolina

Photo Credit
© Scott Frances

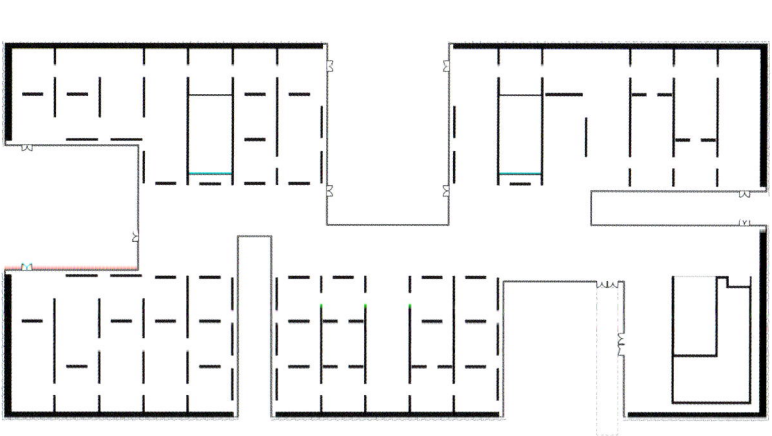

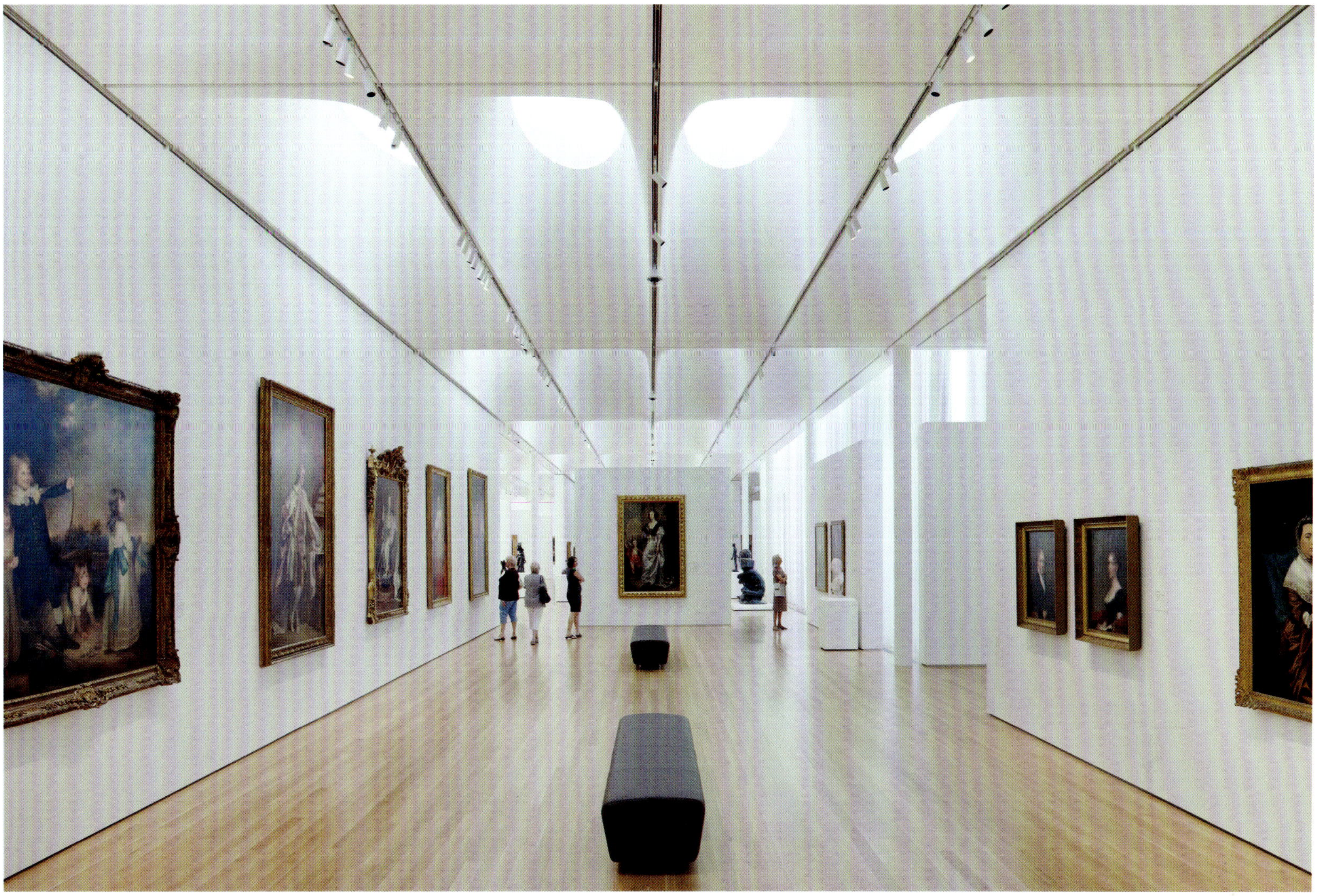

187

One Jackson Square

Jury Comments:
This project is textural and spatial to a high degree.
Great example of using modern digital fabrication techniques.
The execution of the window wall is a strong resolution of the detail nicely resolved.

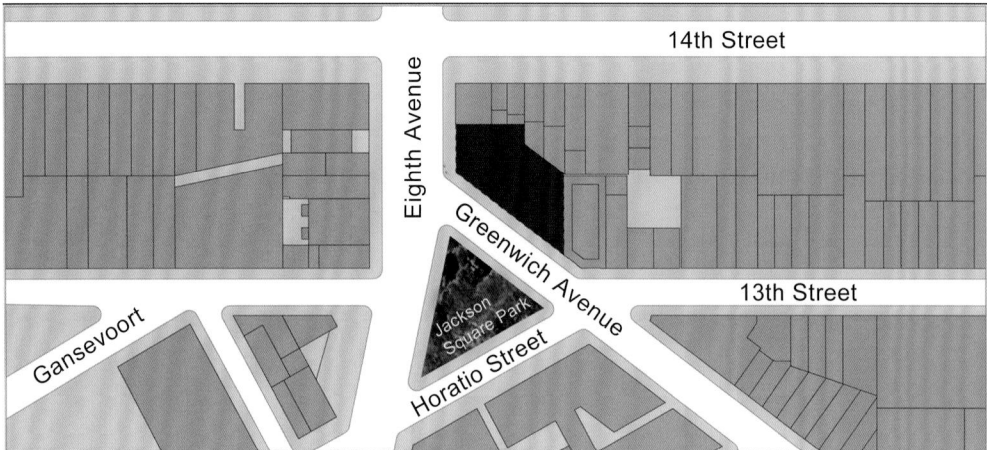

Notes of Interest

One Jackson Square, located in Manhattan's Greenwich Village, is a 35-unit luxury residential development that responds to its celebrated locale. This district is home to the highest concentration of early architecture in New York City, and any new structures introduced to this intricate fabric must respect its existing architecture and history.

Formerly a surface parking lot, the six-sided, split-zone site above two subway tunnels posed significant challenges, which the design negotiates through its massing, material expression, and robust foundation. It also provides a long-missing north edge to Jackson Square Park.

The building volume steps down from 11 stories to seven stories, from north to south, accommodating the zoning laws and mediating the varied scales of the neighborhood. Undulating bands of glass identify individual floors, creating a ribbon-like series of convexities and concavities along the street wall. The predominantly masonry structures of the immediate surroundings, along with the park, are "played back" in the glazed, fluid façade.

Associate Architect: Schuman Lichtenstein Claman Efron
Engineer: RA Consultants, WSP Flack & Kurtz, Gilsanz Murray Steficek
General Contractor: Hunter Roberts Construction Group
Historic Preservation: Higgins & Quasebarth
Owner: Hines

Architect
Kohn Pedersen Fox Associates, PC

Location
New York City, New York

Photo Credit
© Raimund Koch

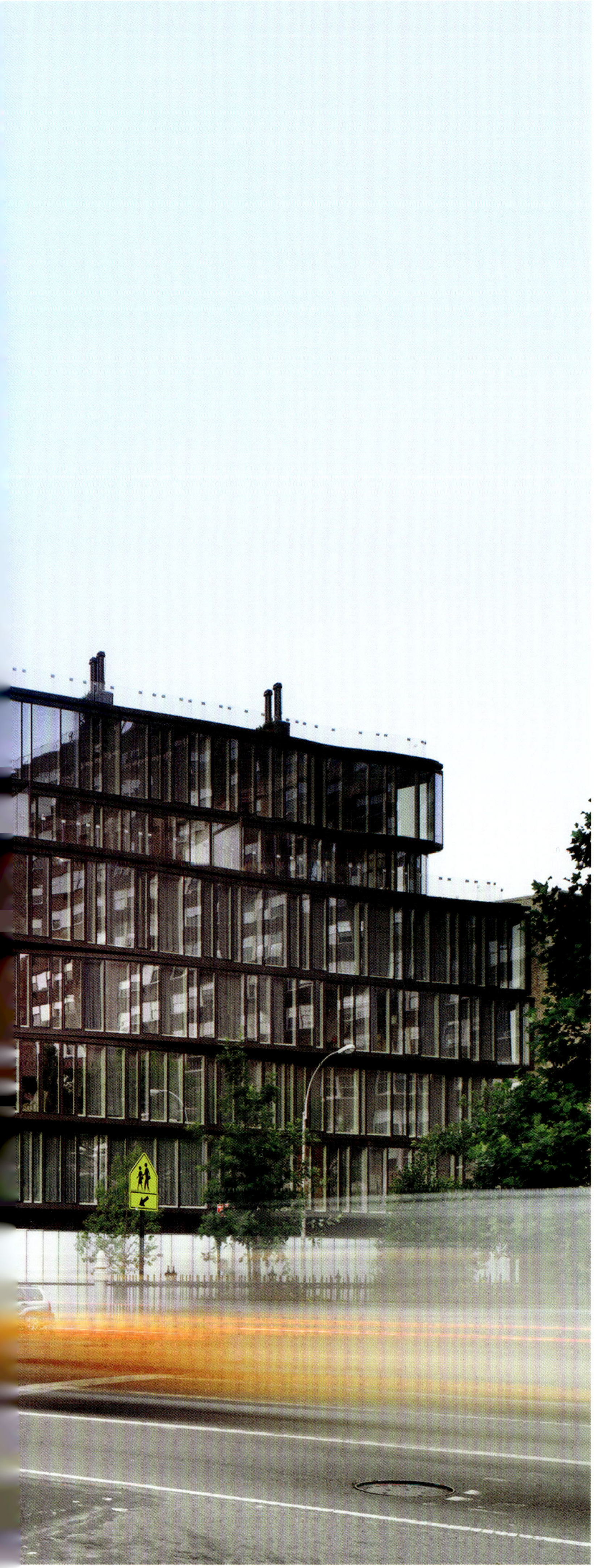

Lower Level Section:
1. Roof terrace
2. Terrace
3. Duplex level 6
4. Apartment level 5
5. Apartment level 4
6. Apartment level 3
7. Apartment level 2
8. Retail
9. Basement
Jackson Square Park
Greenwich Avenue
Eighth Avenue Subway

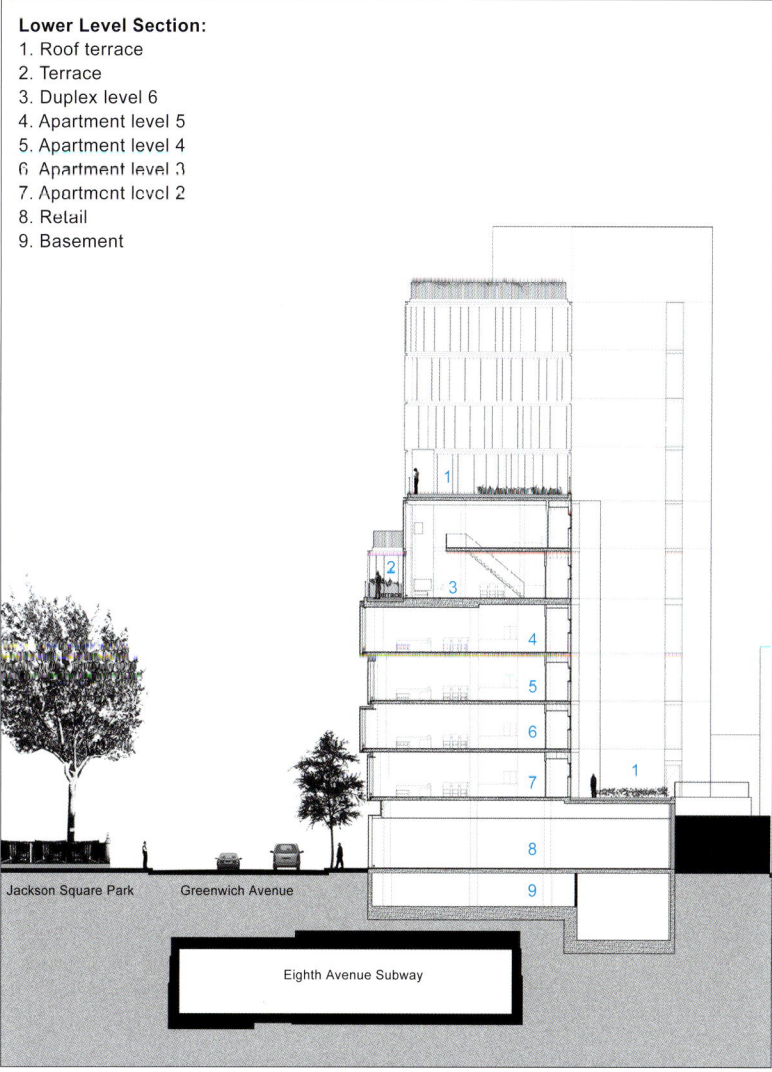

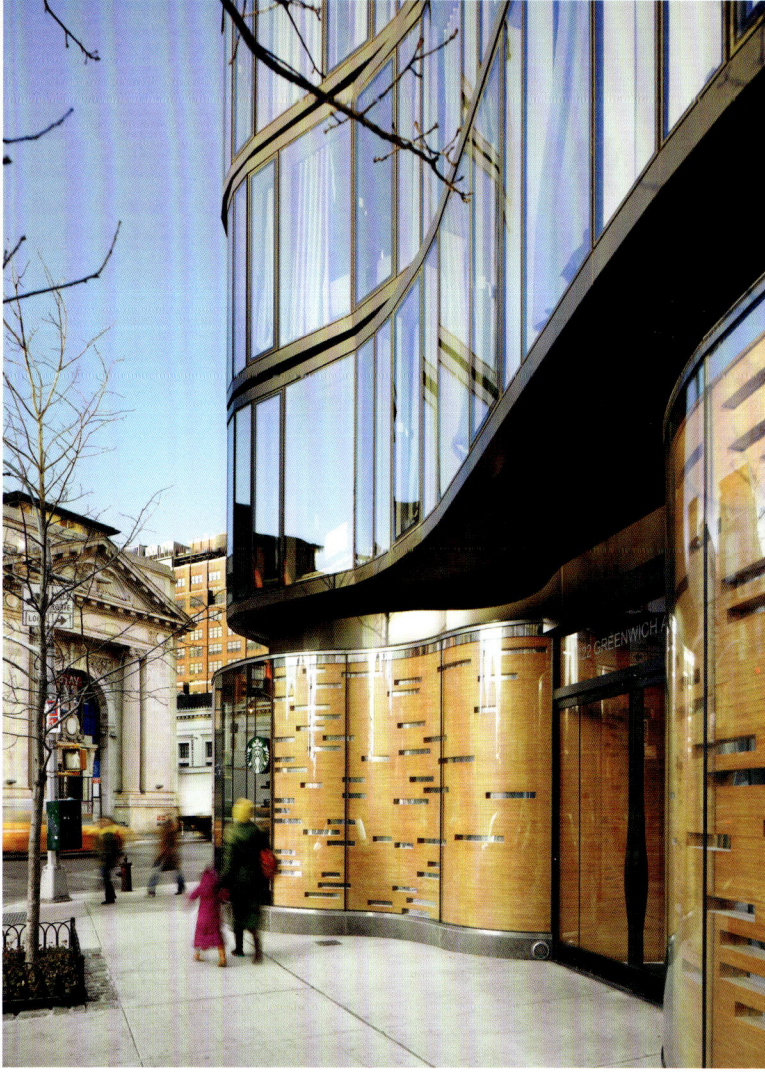

San Francisco Museum of Modern Art Rooftop Garden

Jury Comments:
The notion of fitting this unique series of spaces together at a rooftop level and creating an interesting and exciting venue for the museum to sponsor is the hallmark of this project.
It is its own space and environment but aware of the city surrounding it.
This is a model of how we can enrich the urban fabric via a pavilion rooftop and the safety of a cloistered area.

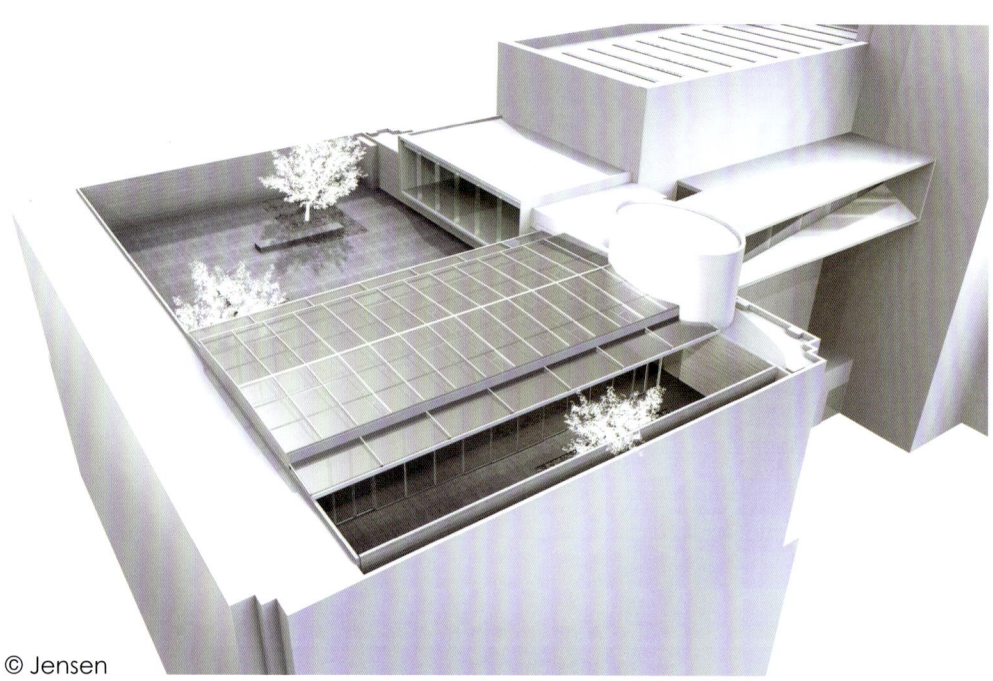
© Jensen

Notes of Interest
The San Francisco Museum of Modern Art Rooftop Garden was conceived as a gallery without a ceiling, defined by the intersection of sculpture, space and light, serving as a quiet, contemplative space for viewing art and hosting the museum's special events.

The garden spaces are accessed via a glass-enclosed bridge that affords sweeping views of downtown and the city's skyline. The new bridge provides circulation down its sloping floor towards the awaiting Pavilion, simultaneously adding an additional 1,500 square feet for art display.

In order to further integrate the Rooftop Garden within the sequence of existing galleries a 3,000-square-foot extension of the fifth floor gallery, suitably named the Overlook, was designed between the rear of the museum and the new garden. The entire back wall of the Overlook is glazed with a large panoramic window, allowing visual connection between gallery and garden.

Consultant: Charles M. Salter Associates, Shenyang Yuanda Aluminum Industry Engineering Co., Ltd
Engineer: Guttmann & Blaevoet Consulting Engineers, Forell / Elsesser Engineers, Inc.
General Contractor: Pdfdfdf
Lighting: Horton Lees Brogden Lighting Design
Owner: San Francisco Museum of Modern Art

Architect
Jensen Architects/Jensen & Macy Architects

Location
San Francisco, California

Photo Credit
© Bernard Andre Photography,
© Richard Barnes Photography,
© Henrik Kam Photography

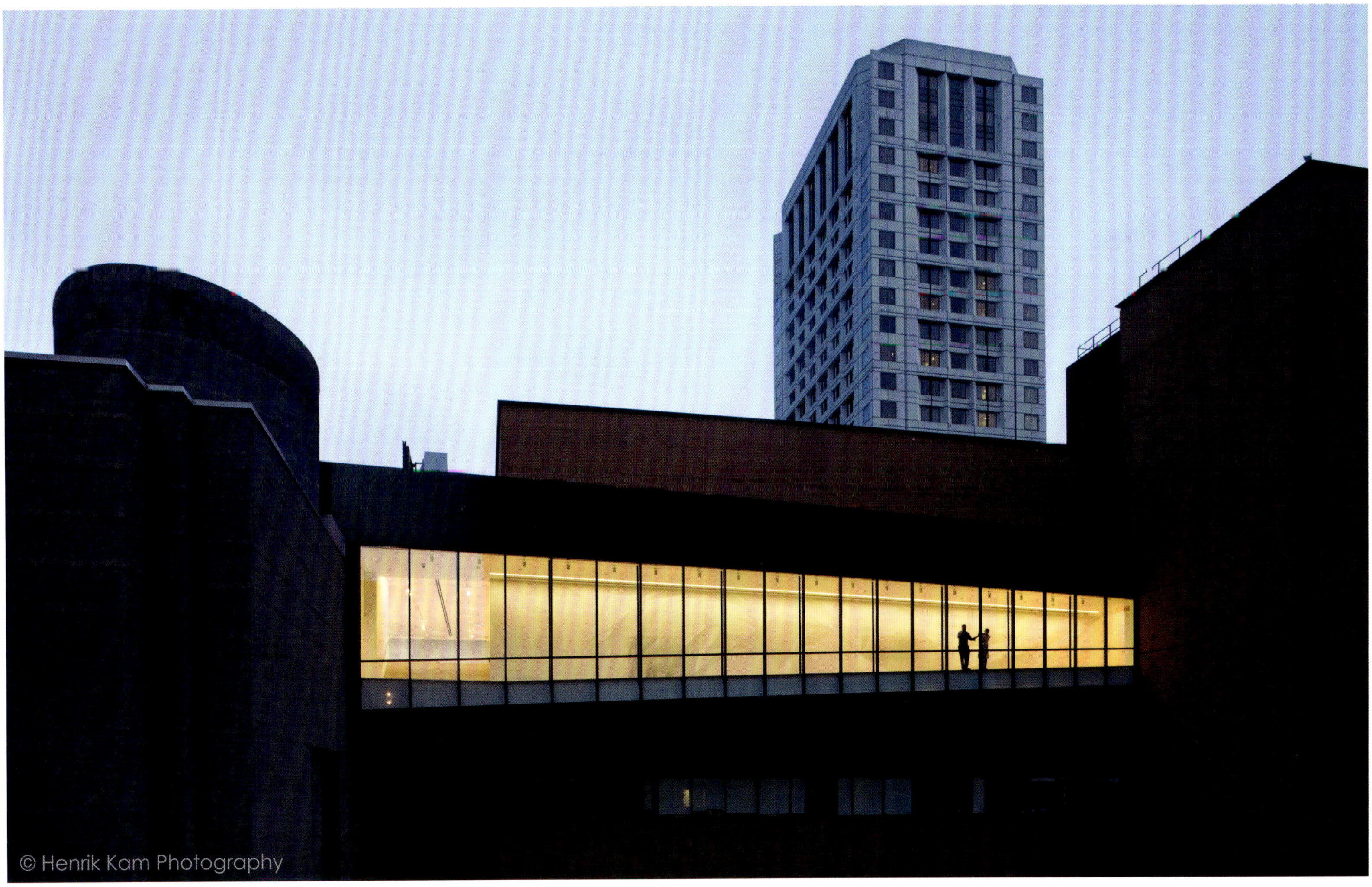
© Henrik Kam Photography

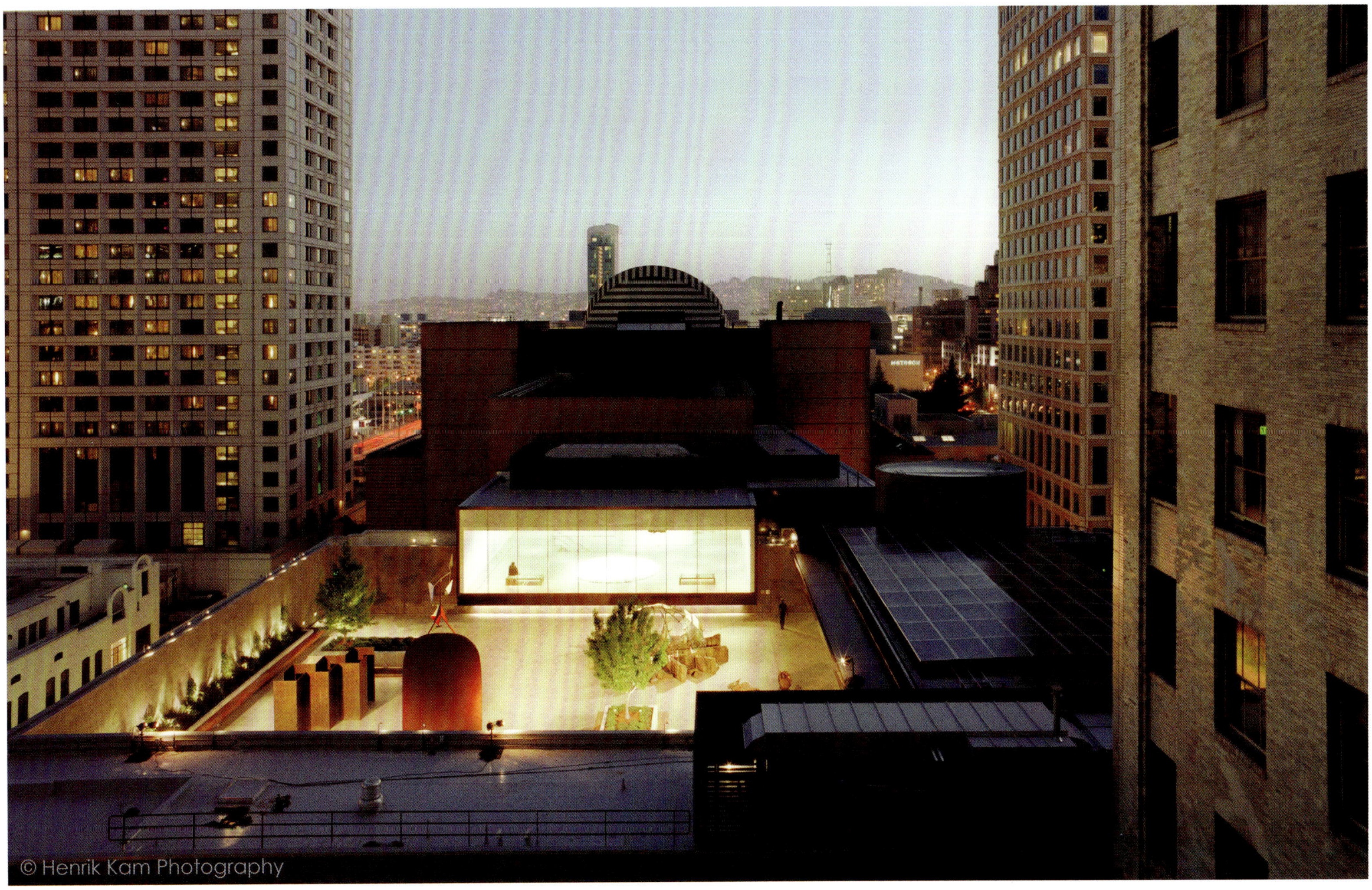
© Henrik Kam Photography

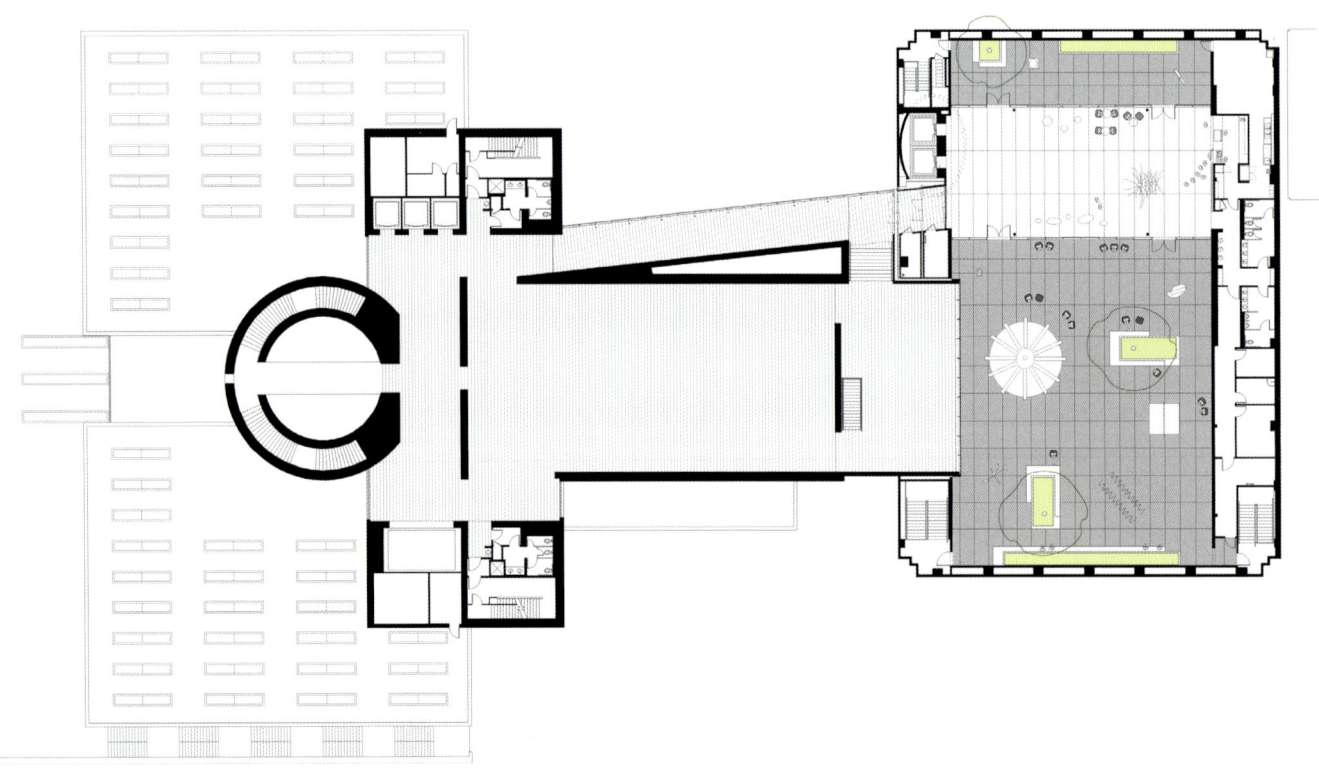

196

© Richard Barnes Photography

© Richard Barnes Photography

197

The Barnard College Diana Center

Jury Comments:
This project is elegant and inviting. The integration of the landscape and architecture is the hallmark of this project and the heart of a good campus building. It still gives a sense of solidity to the wall between the enclosed campus and the outside world, but allows some transparency from the building out to Broadway and back in from the street.

Section:
1. Academic departments
2. Conf/mto/semiar
3. Anth lab
4. Ta/conf
5. Arch studio
6. Senior proj/painting
7. Computer lab
8. Arch adj
9. Breakout
10. Students conf
11. Wac
12. Workroom
13. Office
14. Servery
15. Servery support
16. Storage
17. Control room
18. Events
19. Prefunction
20. Toilet
21. Mech

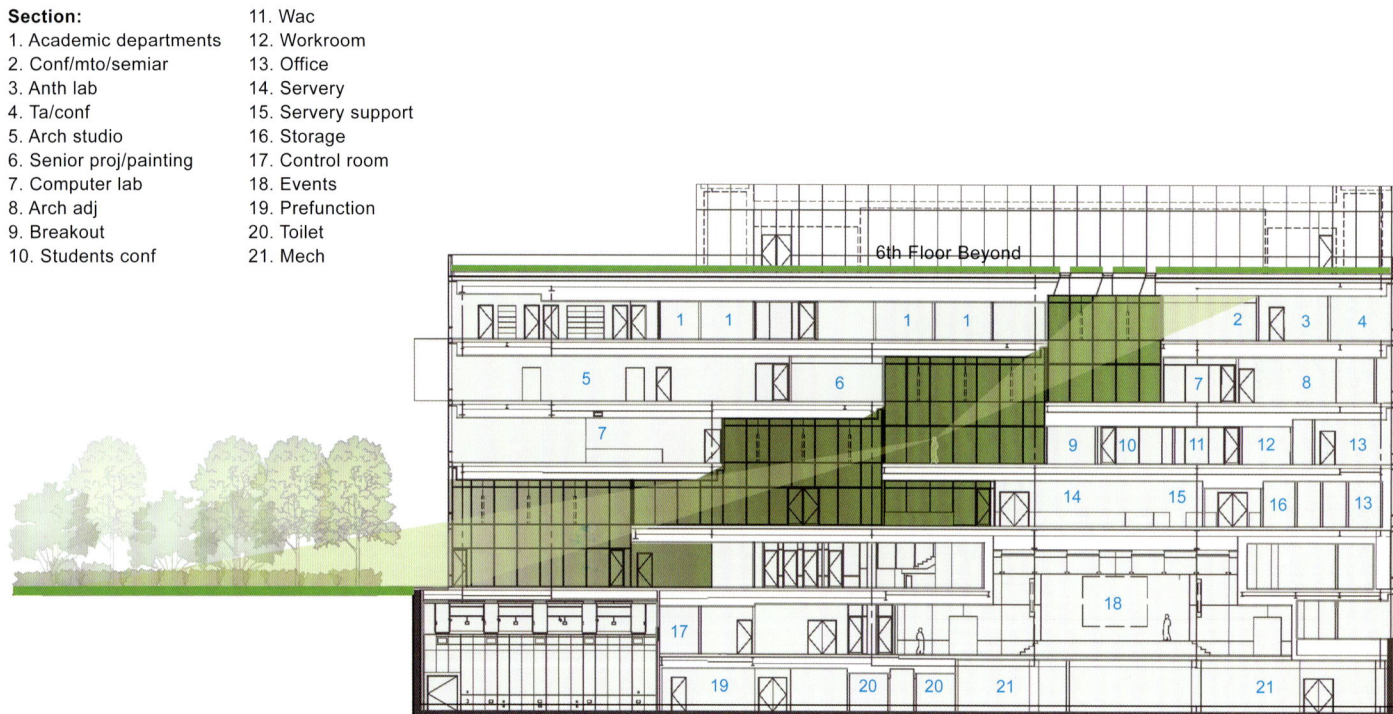

Notes of Interest

The Barnard College Diana Center's site is set within an intimate campus compressed within the dense, urban environment of Manhattan. Located between the Lehman Lawn and Broadway, the Diana Center unites landscape and architecture, as well as interior and exterior spaces, presenting a window onto the College and the city. The 98,000-square-foot multi-use building establishes an innovative nexus for artistic, social, and intellectual life on the campus. The facility brings together spaces for art, architecture, theater, and art history, as well as faculty offices, a dining room, and a Café.

From the historic entrance gate at Broadway, the wedge-shaped design frames a clear sightline linking the central campus at Lehman Lawn to the lower level historic core of the campus. The Diana Center extends Lehman Lawn horizontally and vertically; descending planted terraces cascade north to Milbank Hall, previously isolated by a 14 foot-high retaining wall plaza, and ascending double-height atria bring natural light and views into the seven story structure.

Consultant: Fisher Dachs, Jaffe Holden Acoustics
Engineer: Langan, Jaros, Baum & Bolles Consulting Engineers, Severud Engineers
Lighting: Brandston Partners, Inc.
Owner: Barnard College

Architect
Weiss/Manfredi Architecture/Landscape/Urbanism

Location
New York City, New York

Photo Credit
© Albert Vecerka/Esto, © Paul Warchol Photography

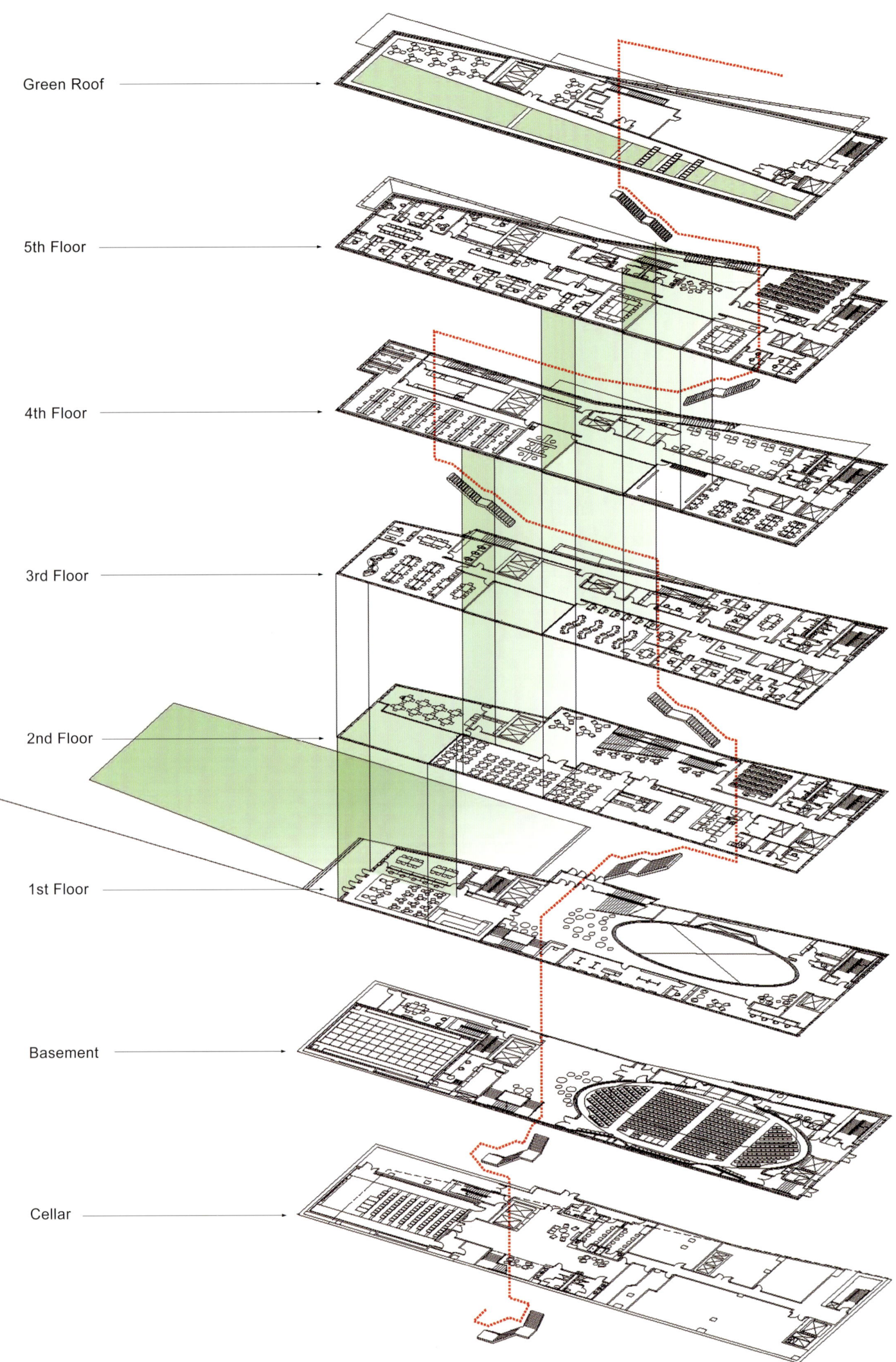

© Albert Vecerka/Esto

© Albert Vecerka/Esto

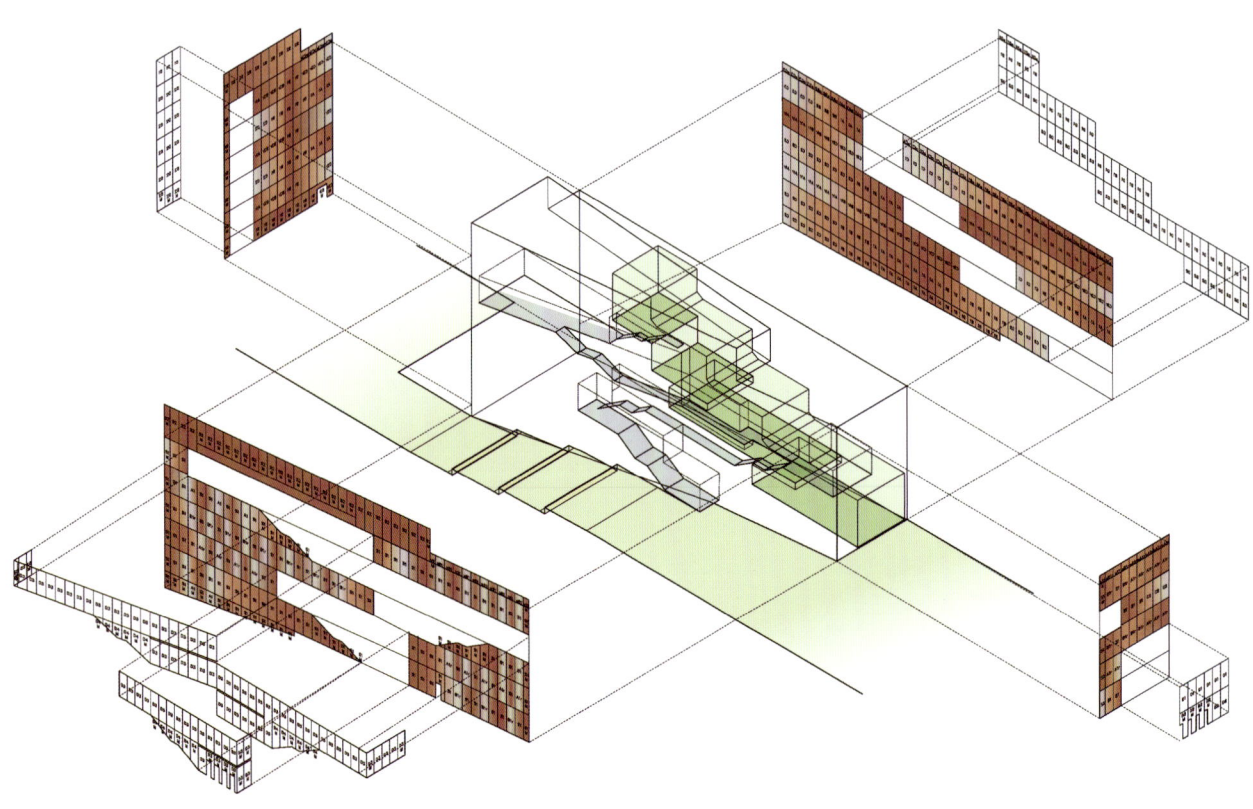

202

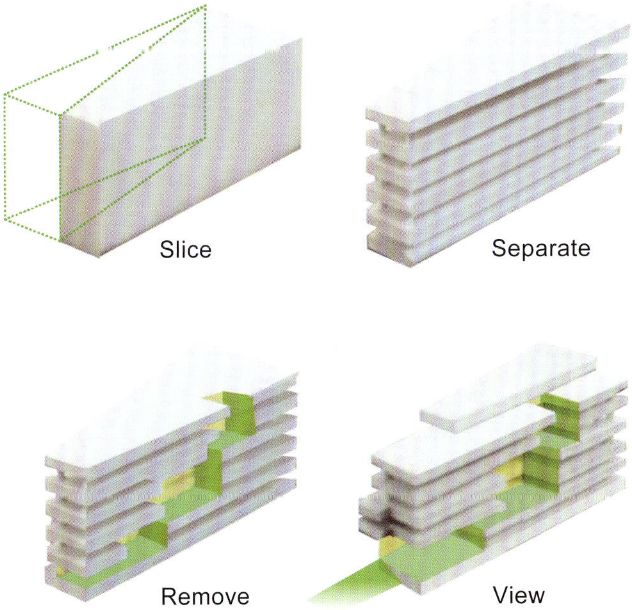

Slice

Separate

Remove

View

Connecting Landscapes:
1. Milbank Courtyard
2. New Stepped Terraces
3. Reconfigured Footprint
4. Lehman Lawn

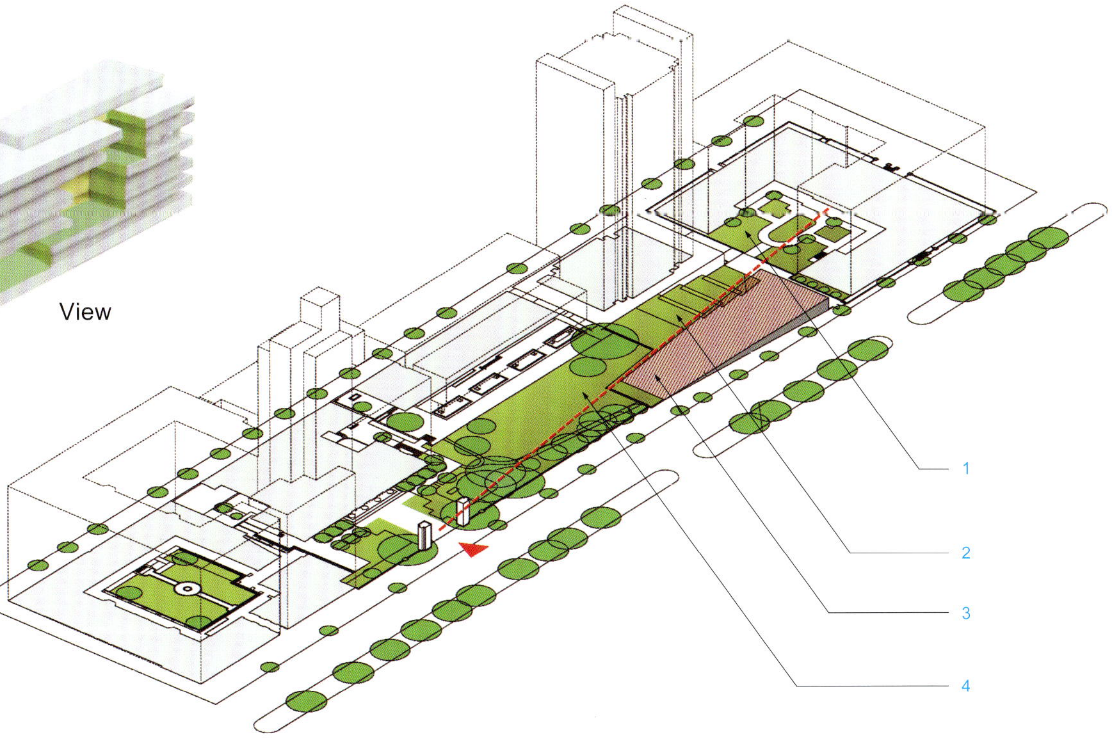

University of Michigan Museum of Art

Jury Comments:
The prominence of the site and juxtaposition of the older bold with new bold is a strong symbol for the university protecting their past and looking towards the future.
A new addition to an existing historic building reads as a new building and true to itself.

Notes of Interest

In creating the University of Michigan Museum of Art (UMMA), the purpose was to completely renovate and modernize the existing Alumni Hall and build an additional 53,452 square feet of space in a dramatic new wing. Located at the gateway to the University's main campus and at the physical intersection of the University and local communities, the Museum rests in a location offering the potential for direct engagement between the Museum, the student body and the general public.

As a teaching museum with broad, near universal collections, the institution serves as a forum for the various academic disciplines of the University as well as a cultural portal for the community of Ann Arbor. While the existing building provides an atmosphere of seclusion, the new architecture achieves an immediacy with the surrounding campus – inviting and even provoking engagement with the building and its programs.

Associate Architect: Integrated Design Solutions
Consultant: RA Heintges, SGH
Engineer: Atwell-Hicks, Arup, KPFF
General Contractor: Pdfdfdf
Landscape Architect: HAWA
Owner: University of Michigan

Architect
Allied Works Architecture

Location
Ann Arbor, Michigan

Photo Credit
© Richard Barnes, Interior, © Jeremy Battermann, Exterior

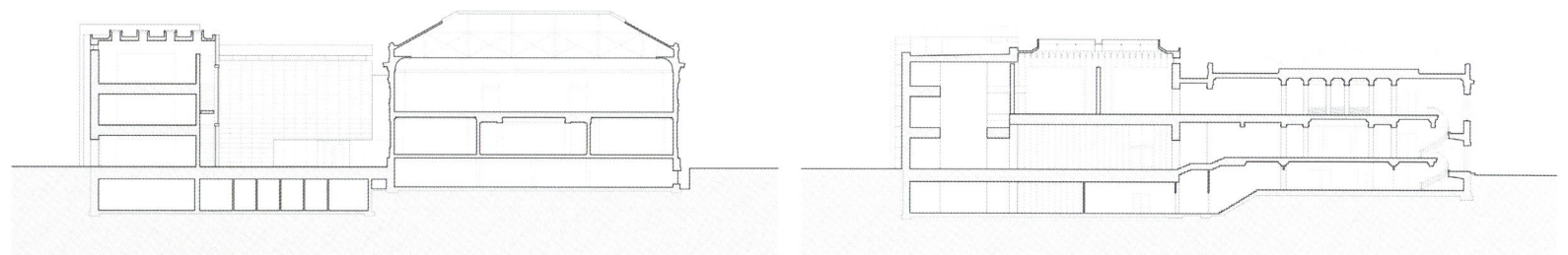

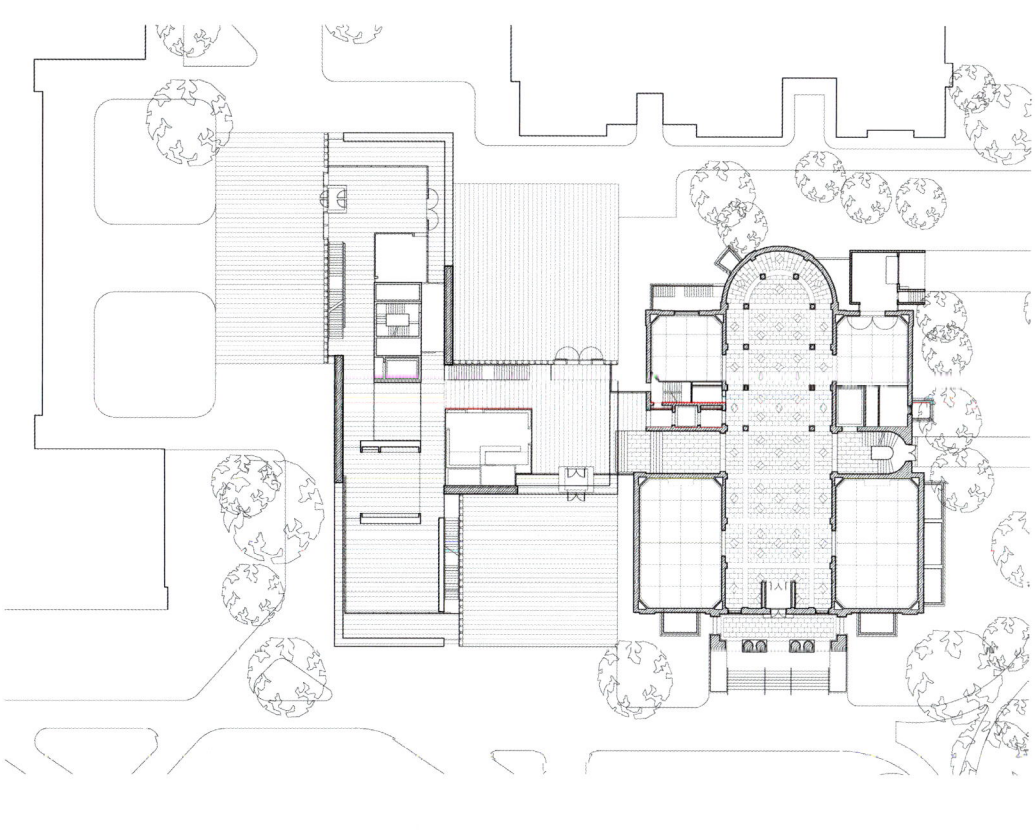
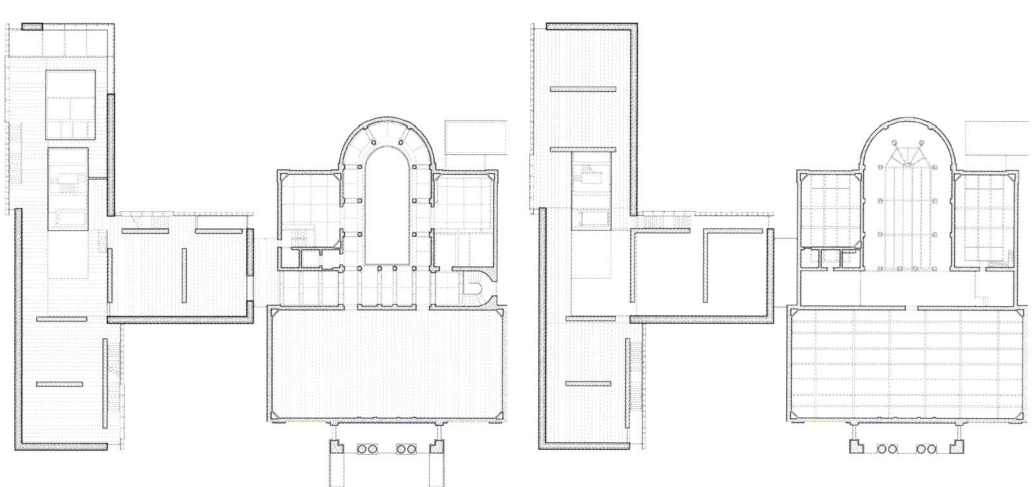

U.S. Land Port of Entry

Jury Comments:
Elegantly premeditated, the building comes out of its function – the conflict between openness and security is pulled off well, while it also feels civic and like it belongs.
It is in a sense a continuation of the regional vocabulary – siding, wood, appropriate for its surrounds – integration of the landscape and public art – with the architecture nicely done.

Notes of Interest

The United States Land Port of Entry supports the mission-driven demands of Customs and Border Protection (CBP), the Department of Homeland Security's agency responsible for securing the nation's borders and promoting legal trade and travel.
Located in Warroad, Minnesota, this 43,000-square-foot facility is composed of three separate enclosed areas linked together with a continuous canopy. The port design manages a complex set of operational issues: the main building houses the officer work area and holding cells; the secondary building houses the vehicular inspection garages, laboratory space and firing range; and the commercial building is used for unloading and inspecting commercial vehicles. The port seamlessly integrates the latest technologies for securing the border into the facility and meets the demands of an energy-efficient and sustainable building.
In addition to meeting these programmatic and operational issues, the port also stands as a gateway to our nation, representing our open and democratic values of transparency, dignity, fairness and humaneness of our federal government.

Engineer: Jacobs, Sebesta Blomberg & Associates, Inc., Meyer Borgman and Johnson, Inc.
General Contractor: Pdfdfdf
Landscape Architect: Coen + Partners
Owner: GSA, Land Port of Entry Division

Architect
Julie Snow Architects, Inc.

Location
Warroad, Minnesota

Photo Credit
© Paul Crosby

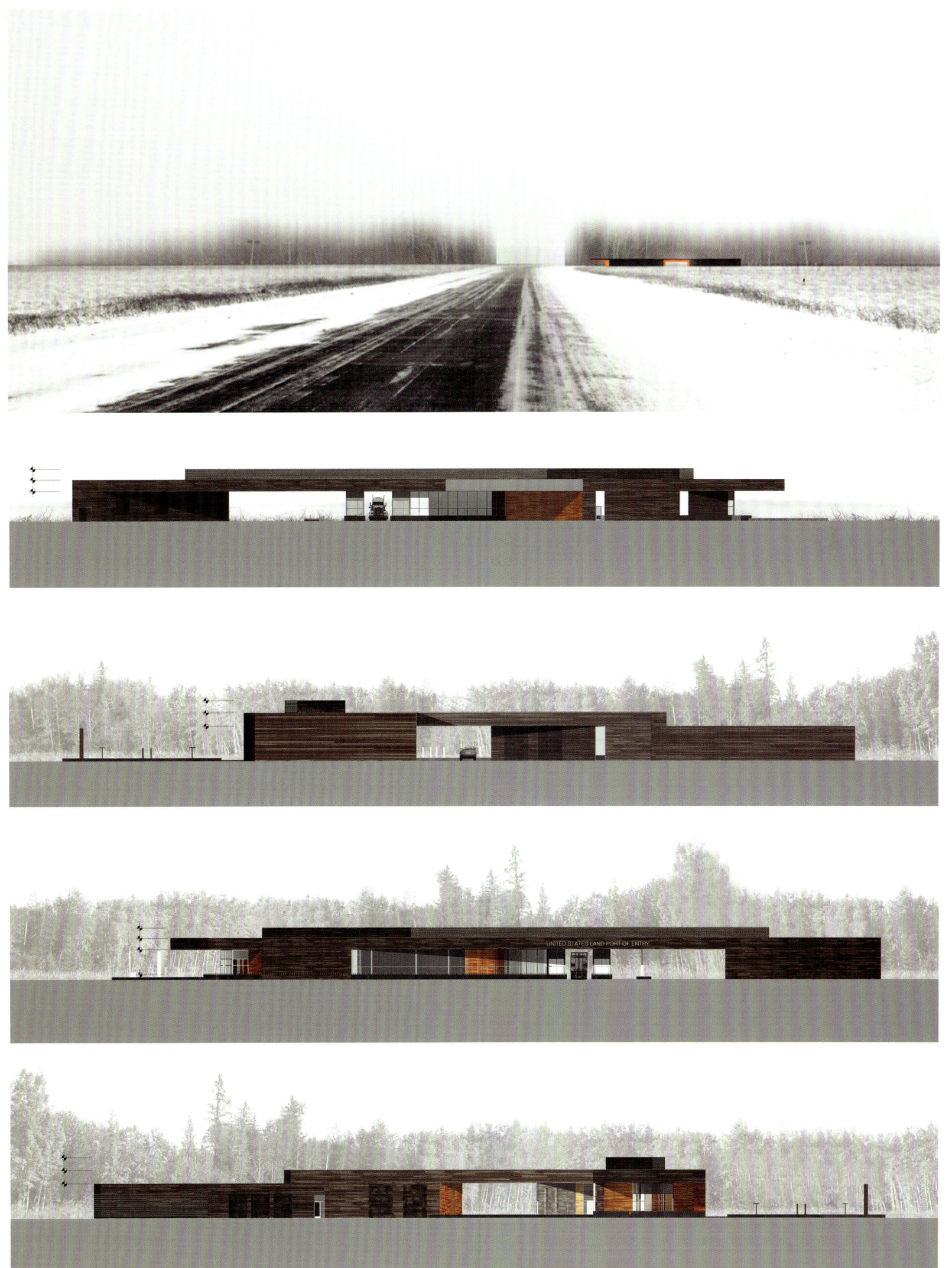

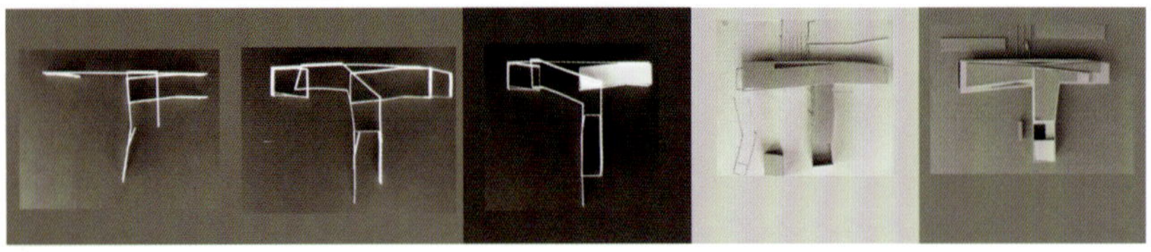

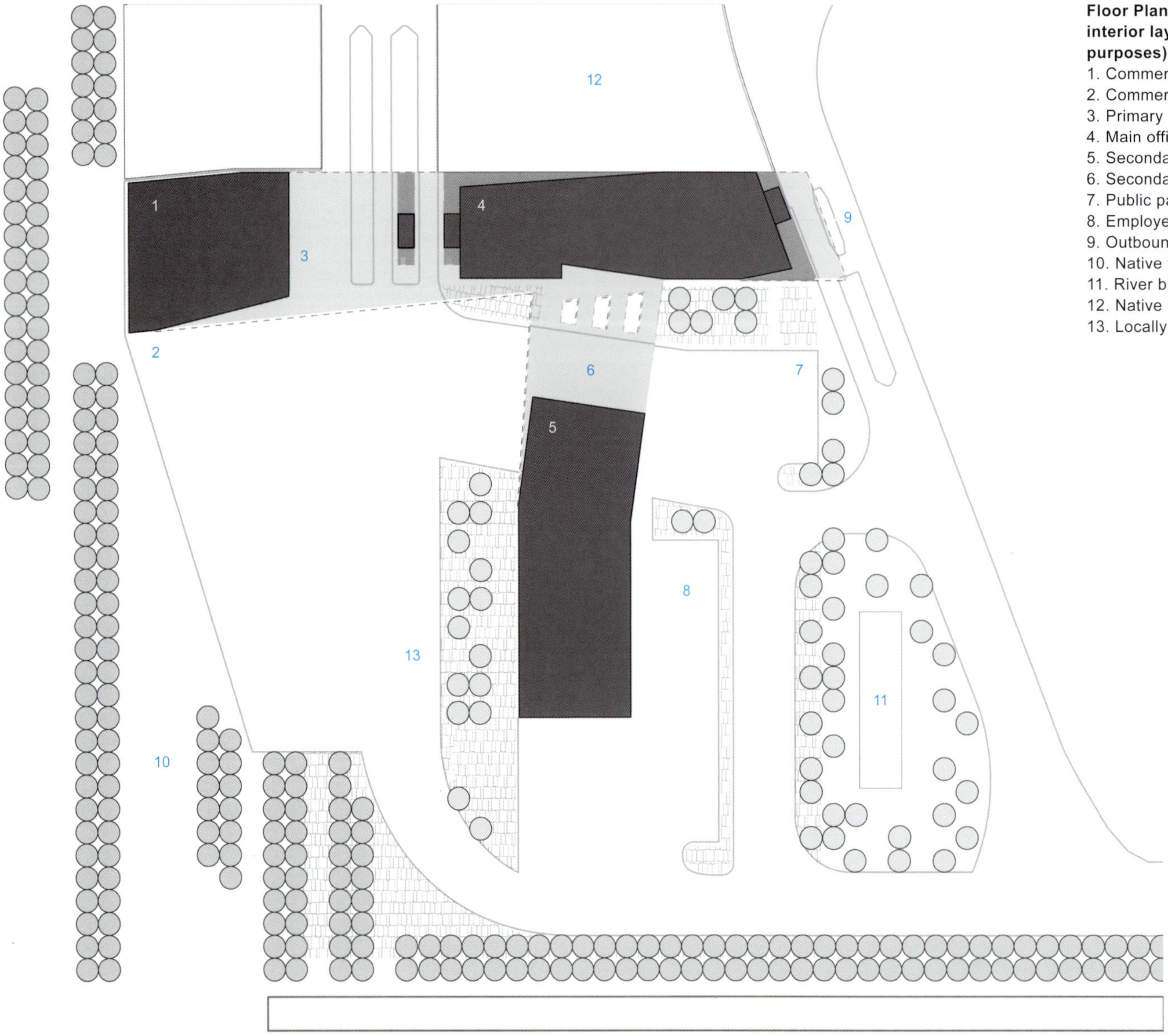

Floor Plan and Landscape Plan (note: interior layout not shown for security purposes):
1. Commercial building
2. Commercial queueing
3. Primary inspections canopy
4. Main office area
5. Secondary inspection area
6. Secondary inspection canopy
7. Public parking
8. Employee parking
9. Outbound inspection canopy
10. Native tamarak wind rows
11. River birch and bioswale
12. Native prairie grasses
13. Locally sourced slate

Alchemist

Jury Comments:
The design is respectful of the site's architecture but manages to shed the trappings of the conventional store by making its presence known in a subtly elegant and sophisticated manner.

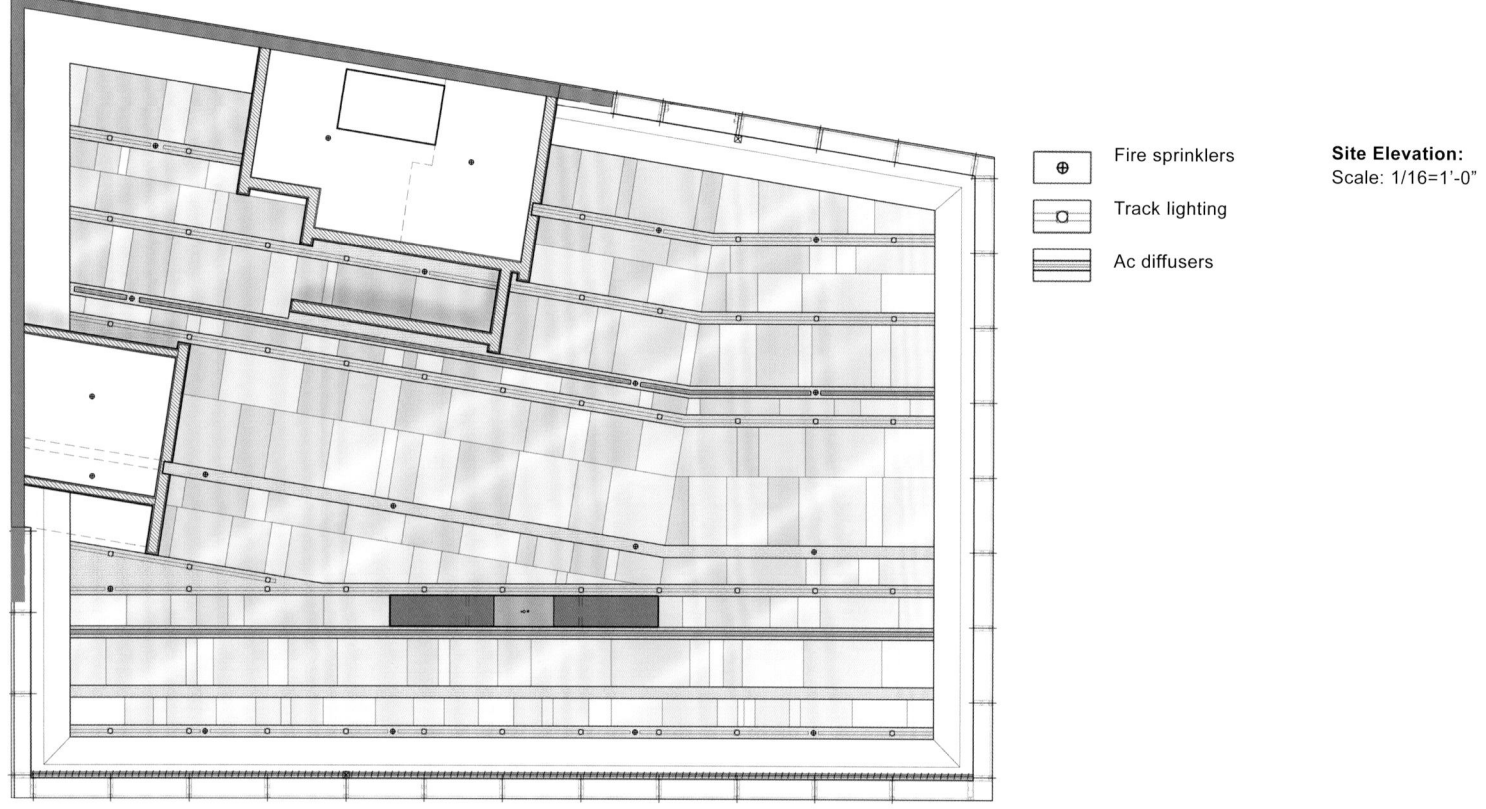

Site Elevation:
Scale: 1/16=1'-0"

⊕ Fire sprinklers
○ Track lighting
▭ Ac diffusers

Notes of Interest
This sparkling glass box of retail is situated on the fifth-floor edge of a parking garage, yet somehow conquers impossible challenges: integrating the shop into the aesthetic of the parking structure and establishing connection and dialogue with the pedestrian environment below.

Notable is this project's ability to captivate both the store patrons and those meandering the streets of Miami Beach. It is composed of twenty-two foot high Starphire Glass which allows for expansive, crystal clear views into the space, allowing the play of light both inwardly and outwardly. The haunting transparency gives the project the appearance of being perched calmly like jewel box above the city. The choice of unobtrusive materials also provides a peaceful, fitting relationship between the shop and the larger parking structure.

In addition to this transparent glass, a complex system of mirrored walls and ceilings provide a dialogue of reflection between the store's goings on and the street below. They are interactive mirrors, operated on sensors which ripple in sync with the occupants' actions within the shop, generated by motion sensors and preset animations.

Engineer: Vidal & Associates, Optimus Engineering
General Contractor: Aaron Builders & Development
Lighting: Brand Lighting
Owner: Roma Cohen

Architect
Rene Gonzalez Architect

Location
Miami Beach

Photo Credit
© Michael Stavaridis

Site Plan+Location Image (Below):
Scale: 3/32"=1'-0"
Location: Miami Beach
Climate Type: Humid Subtropical

Elevation (Below):
1. Project level
Elevation: 58'-4"
2. Ground level
Elevation: 0'-0"

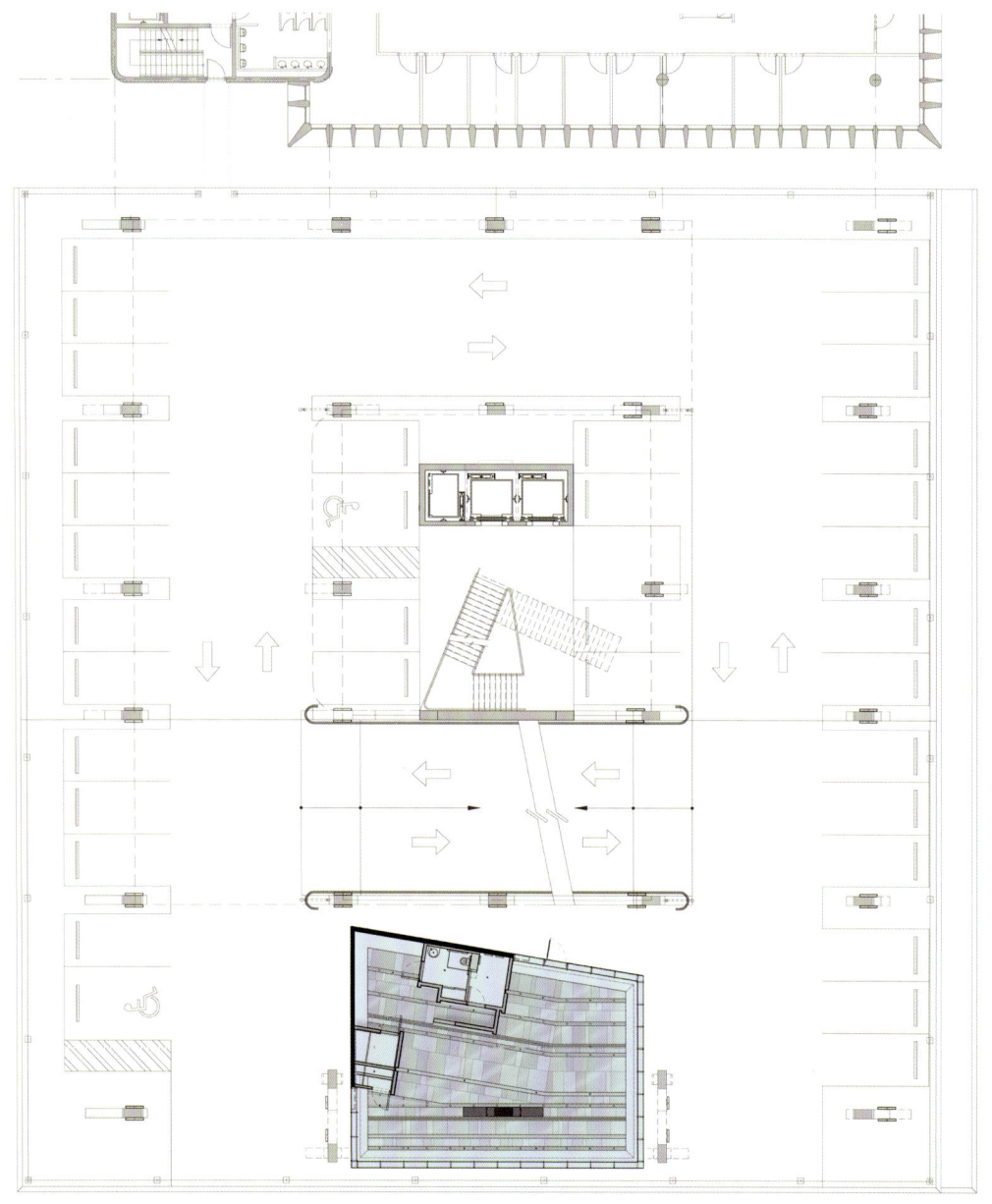
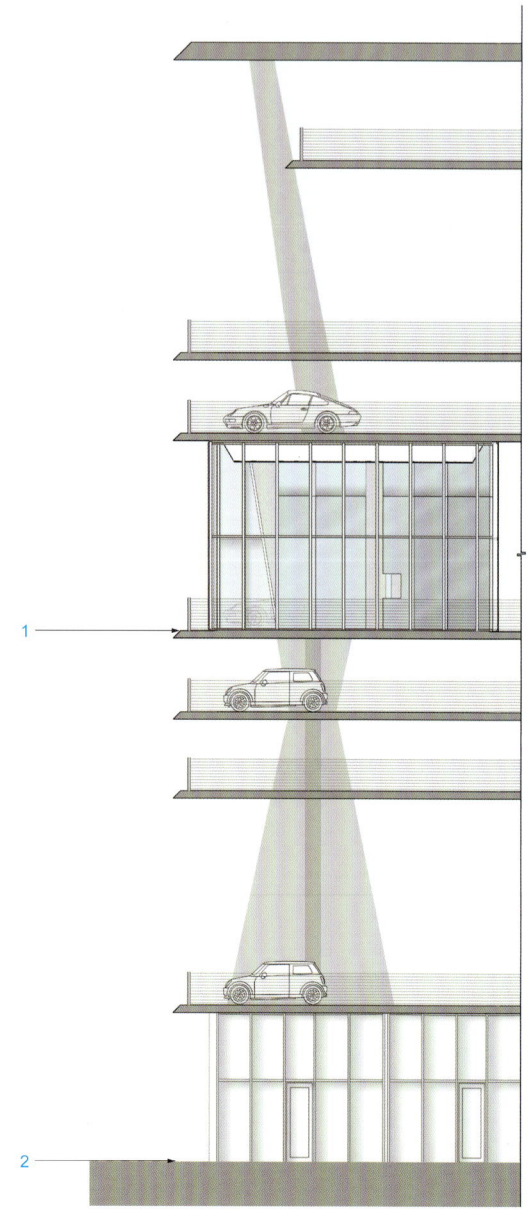

Armstrong Oil and Gas

Jury Comments:
Here, understated materials achieve elegance through superior detailing and craftsmanship.
This design stands out for its thoughtful space-making and through its handling of materials thoughtfully-chosen to respond to the character of the original building.
This project's expression of the best of what the original machine shop building had to offer is superbly celebrated with the architecturally honest palate of brick, steel, concrete and glass.

First floor plan — Blake Street

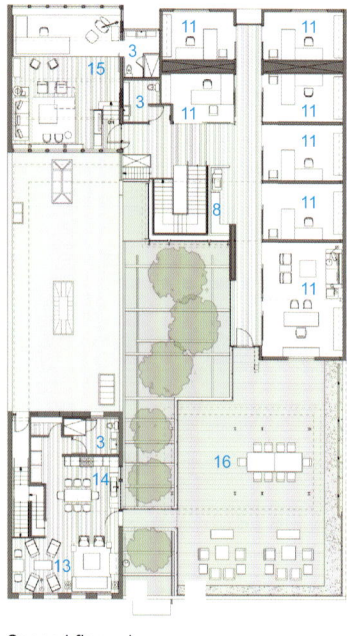

Second floor plan

Site Plan (Left):
1. Entry Court
2. Reception
3. Restroom
4. Seismic Room
5. War Room
6. Catwalk
7. Fitness Lounge
8. Copy Room
9. Courtyard
10. Conference Room
11. Private Office
12. Garage
13. Lounge
14. Kitchen
15. Penthouse Office
16. Roof Terrace

Notes of Interest

This adaptive re-use of an early-1900's industrial machine shop launches a new identity for an established local business in lower downtown Denver. Charged with bringing new life to an underutilized building, the design team planned the enclosed program around existing elements in place and created generous, sophisticated spaces filled with daylight, natural ventilation and views to the Denver skyline.

In keeping with the historic manufacturing roots of the building, the structural steel is architecturally expressed throughout the building. Tipping a hat to the original materials, a firm contrast was maintained between their rustic, shell-blasted feel and the sharper, painted look of the newer elements.

To bring life to the space, the renovation brings new levels of circulation and transparency. The introduction of an interior courtyard sends daylight throughout the entire space, and translucent materials separating many of the workspaces capitalize on this natural light while balancing an element of privacy. The new office building consists of two main volumes and includes a breezeway, a conference room, a waiting area, an employee lounge, an open-air bridge, a roof terrace, outdoor meeting spaces, entertaining spaces and a beautifully redone penthouse office.

Architect of Record: Bothwell Davis George Architects, Inc.
Engineer: McGlamery Structural Group, M.E. Group
General Contractor: Sprung Consultant
Lighting: Fisher Marantz Stone
Owner: Armstrong Oil and Gas

Architect	Location	Photo Credit
Lake | Flato Architects	Denver	© Frank Ooms Photography

Building section through war room looking east:
1. Reception
2. Seismic Room
3. War Room
4. Fitness Lounge
5. Copy Room
6. Private Office
7. Garage
8. Lounge
9. Kitchen
10. Penthouse Office
11. Roof Terrace

Building section through war room looking east

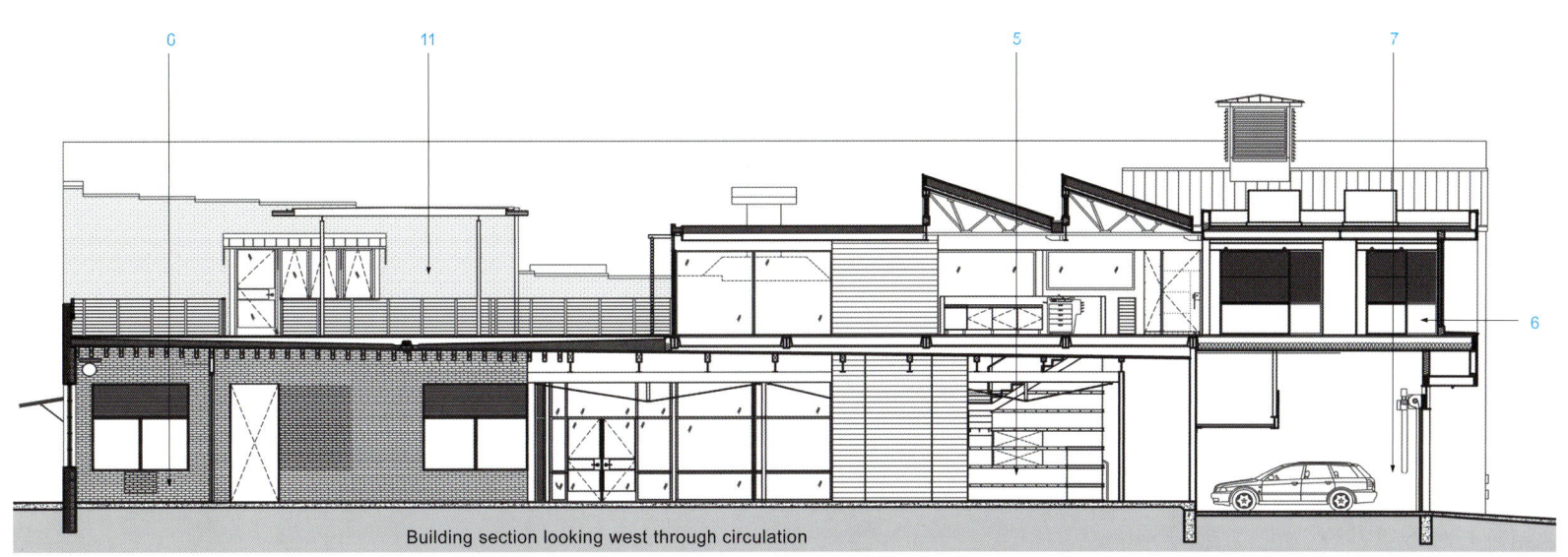

Building section looking west through circulation

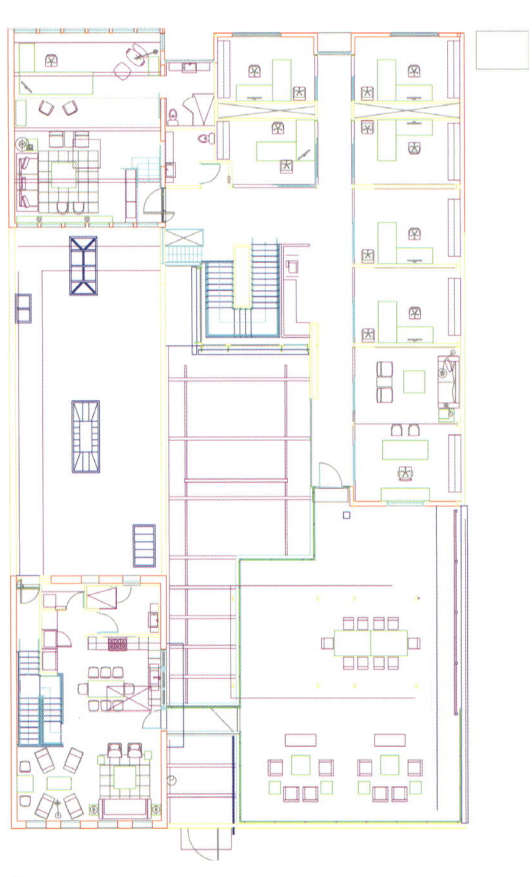
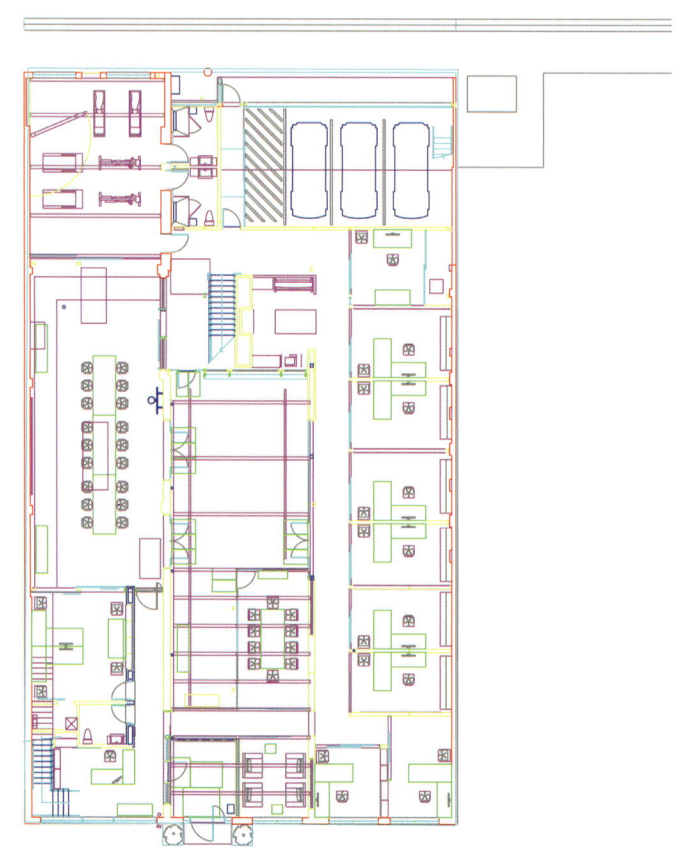

Conga Room

Jury Comments:
The exploration of dance concepts, modular shapes, acoustics and bold colorful form exhibited in this project are combined in a way that one would never expect.
The innovation is full of analogy, sensuality, and technical directness that is just remarkable.

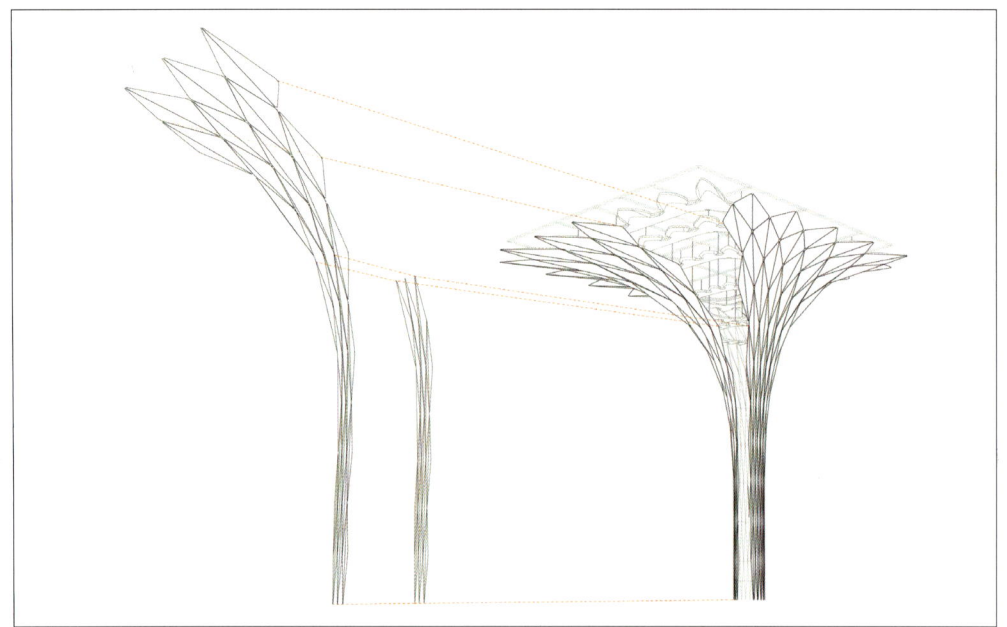 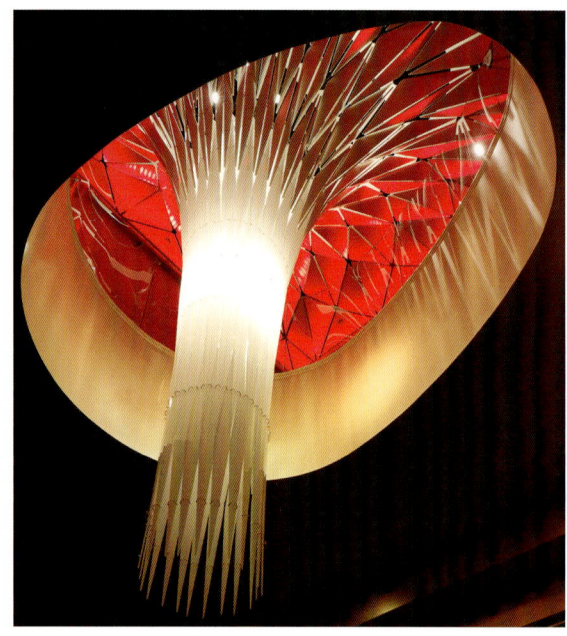

Notes of Interest

This newly constructed Los Angeles Latin live music venue is the premier location for Salsa and Rumba dancing in the area, and it was crucial that the space provide the advanced sound capabilities necessary to respond accordingly for its performers and patrons. But the challenge went even further: the dance hall had to be acoustically absorptive and isolated from the rest of the office building tenants while delivering this rewarding musical experience.

While facing these acoustical issues, the design solution also involves a dramatic visual experience, floating above a sea of dancers, a ceiling that acts as a very present character and that morphs in shape throughout the space while employing acoustical isolation and prescribed sound absorption. Additionally, in an effort to meet the client's aesthetic desires for a ceiling that reflected the vibrancy and dynamism of the Latin culture, a pattern made of diamonds was developed, inspired by the very dance step of Rumba itself!

One last notable flourish was the installation of a twenty-foot-tall lit "Tocado" – or headdress – draped from the ceiling of the primary entranceway. This captivating light display serves as a literal beacon of light, drawing attention from the plaza to the club.

Consultant: John Martin & Associate, John Dorius & Associate, A & F Consulting Engineers
General Contractor: Winters-Schram Associates

Architect
Belzberg Architects

Location
Los Angeles, California

Photo Credit
© Benny Chan/Fotoworks

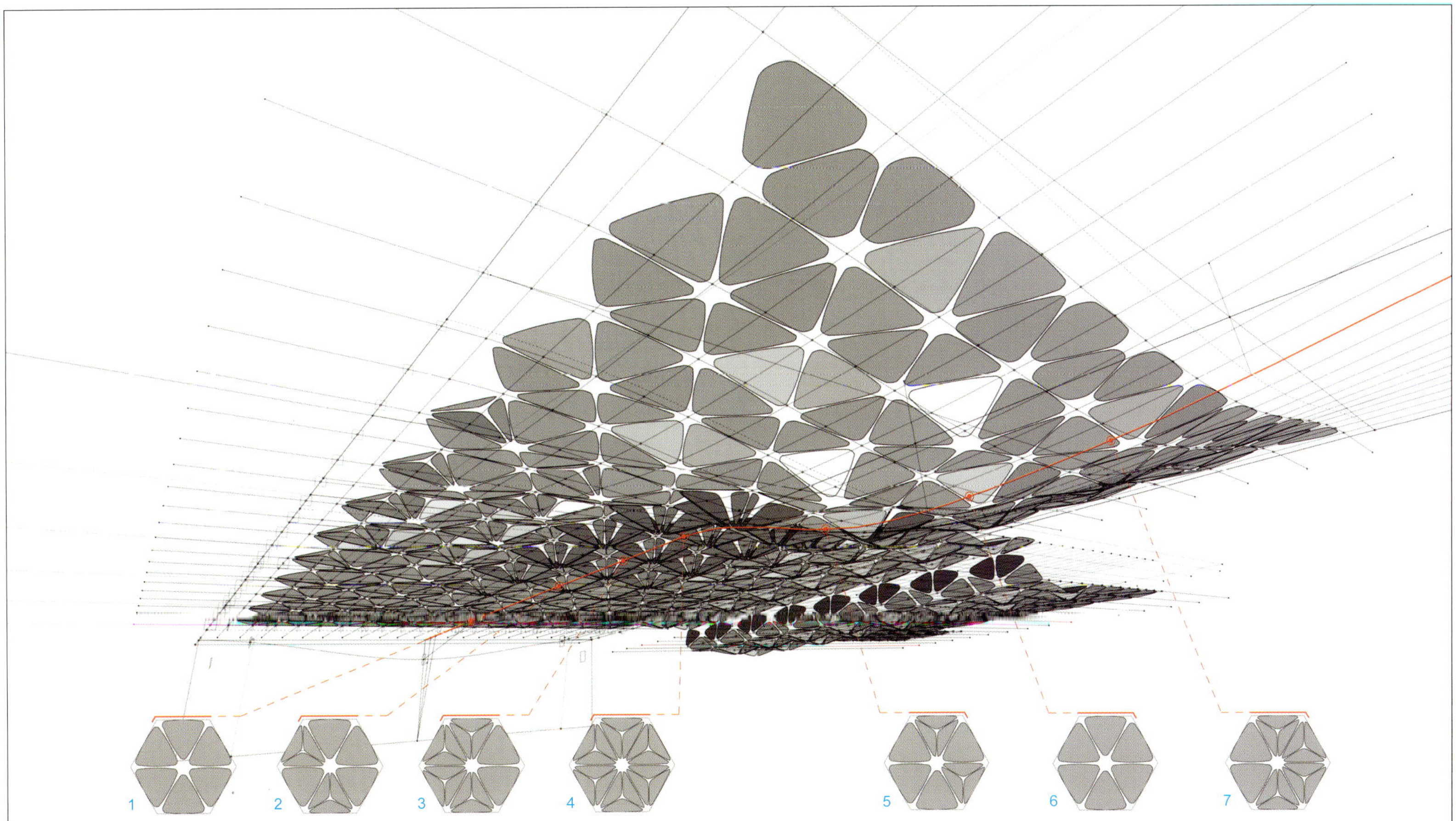

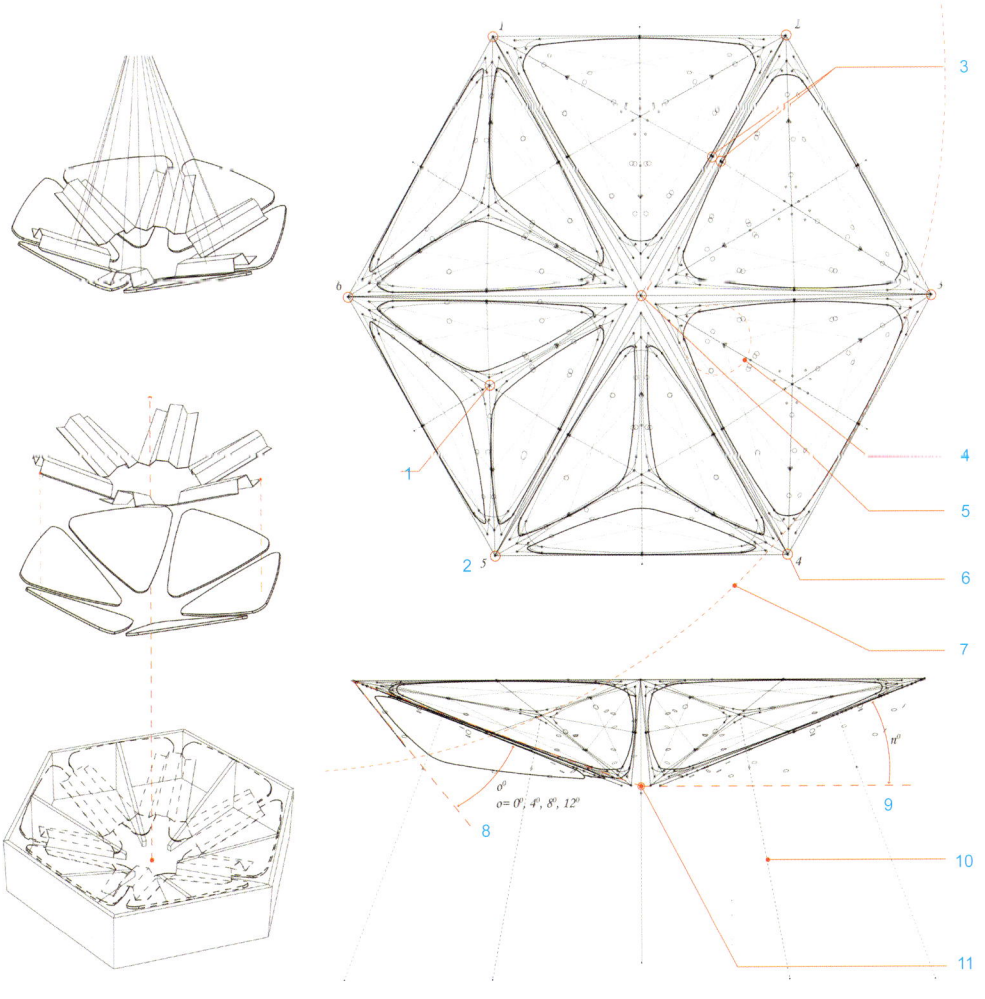

1. Petal angle(n)=0
2. Petal angle(n)=10
3. Petal angle(n)=24
4. Petal angle(n)=31
5. Petal angle(n)=17
6. Petal angle(n)=10
7. Petal angle(n)=17

Elevation of Flower (Left):
1. Petal Radius(0) see below
2. Plan View Flower
3. Panel Offset Point
4. Petal Radius 1
5. Flower Radius(n) see below
6. Instantiation Points (1-7)
7. Petal Radius 1
8. o=0°, 4°, 8°, 12°
9. n=0°,10°,17°, 24°, 31°
10. Petal Surface Normals
11. Angle(n) controls the porosity of a flower based on acoustic

229

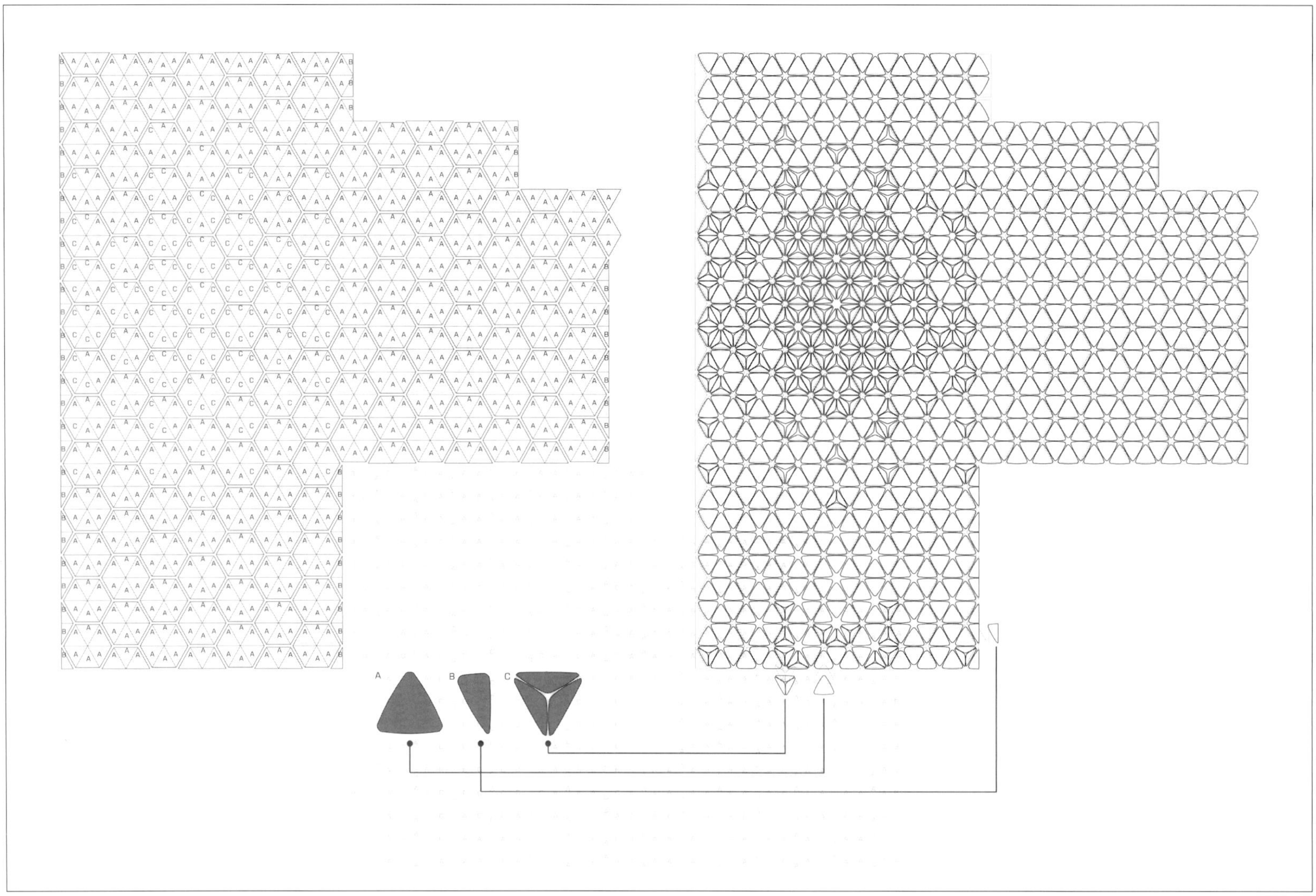

230

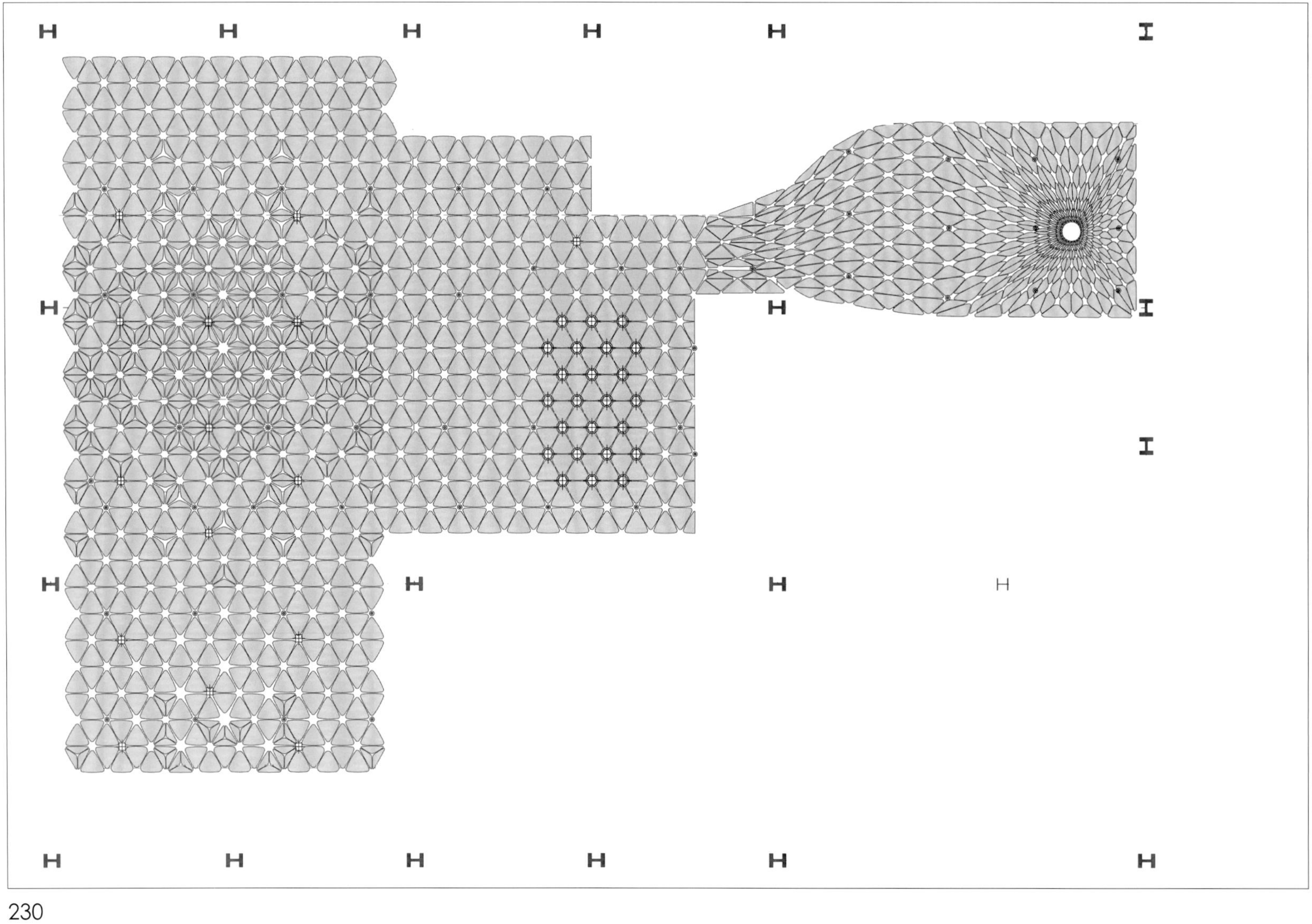

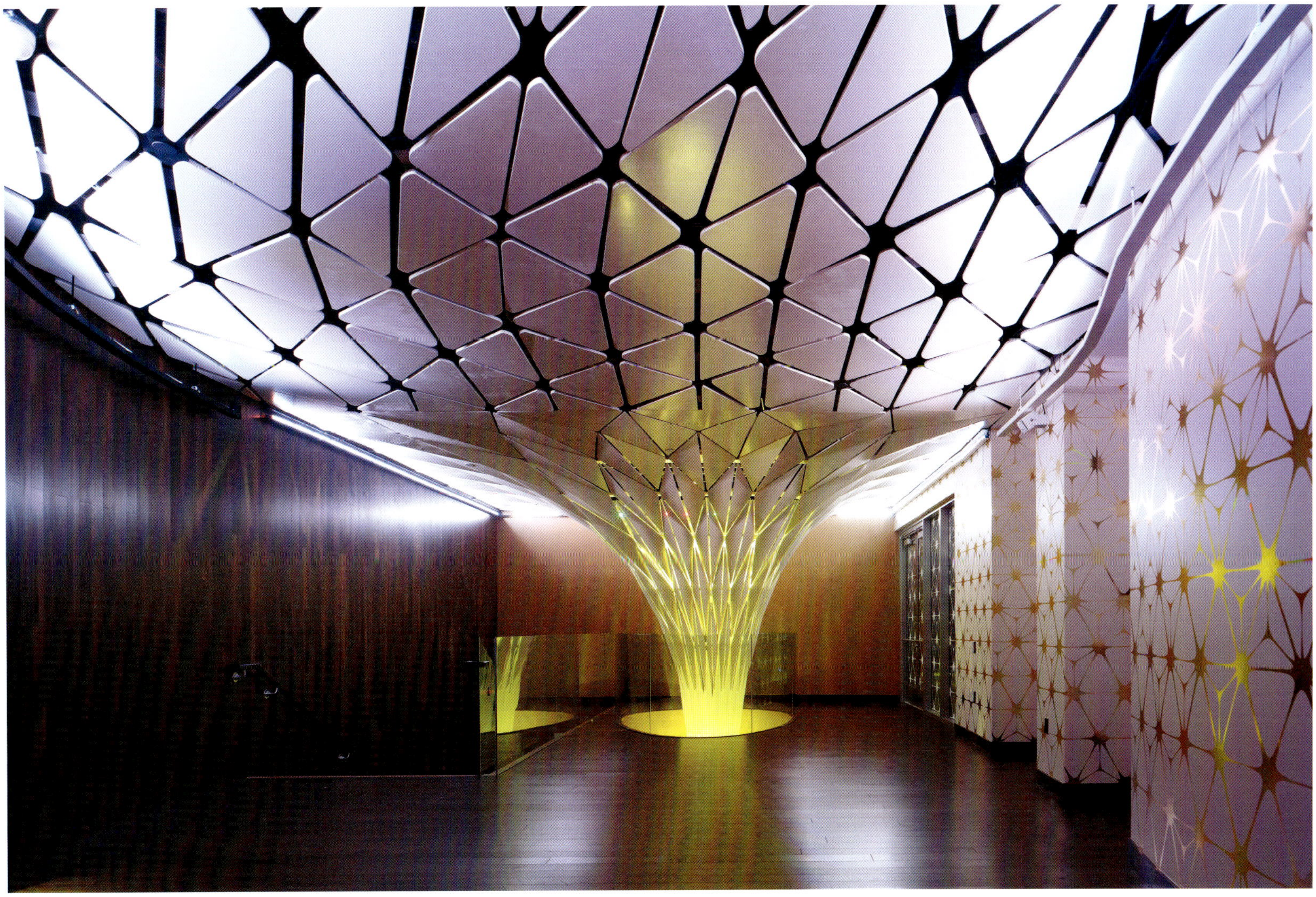

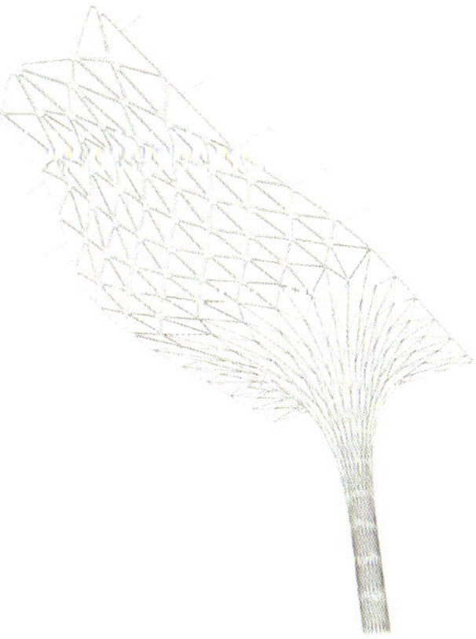

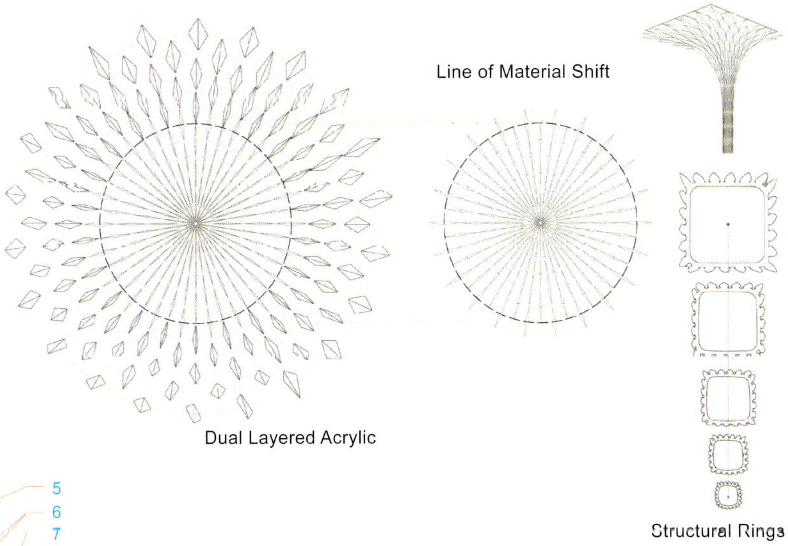

Line of Material Shift

Dual Layered Acrylic

Structural Rings

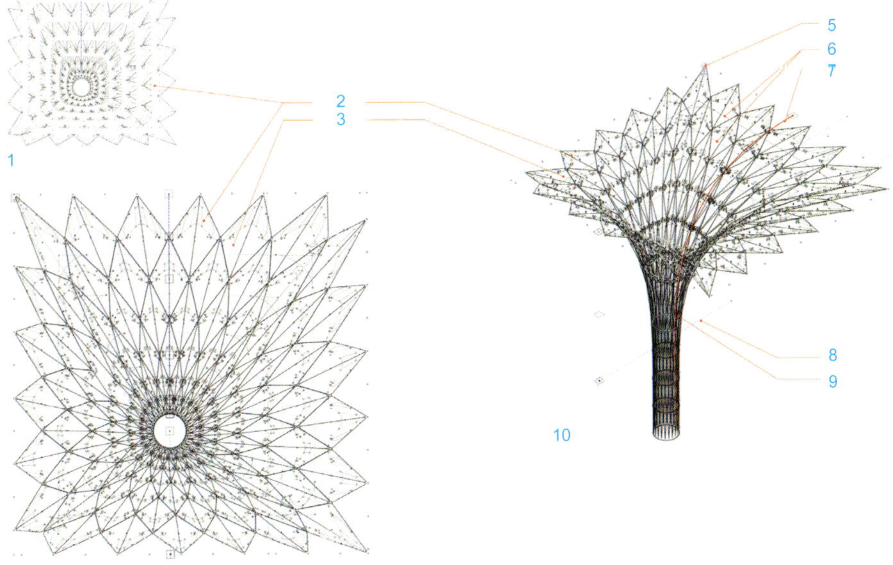

1. Plan View of Tornado showing structural ribs
2. CNC milled structural ribs
3. CNC milled plywood petals
4. Plan View of Tornado
5. Instantiation points
6. Instantiation guides
7. Instantiation control curve
8. Instantiation control curve
9. CNC milled acrylic double sided panels
10. Isometric View of Tornado

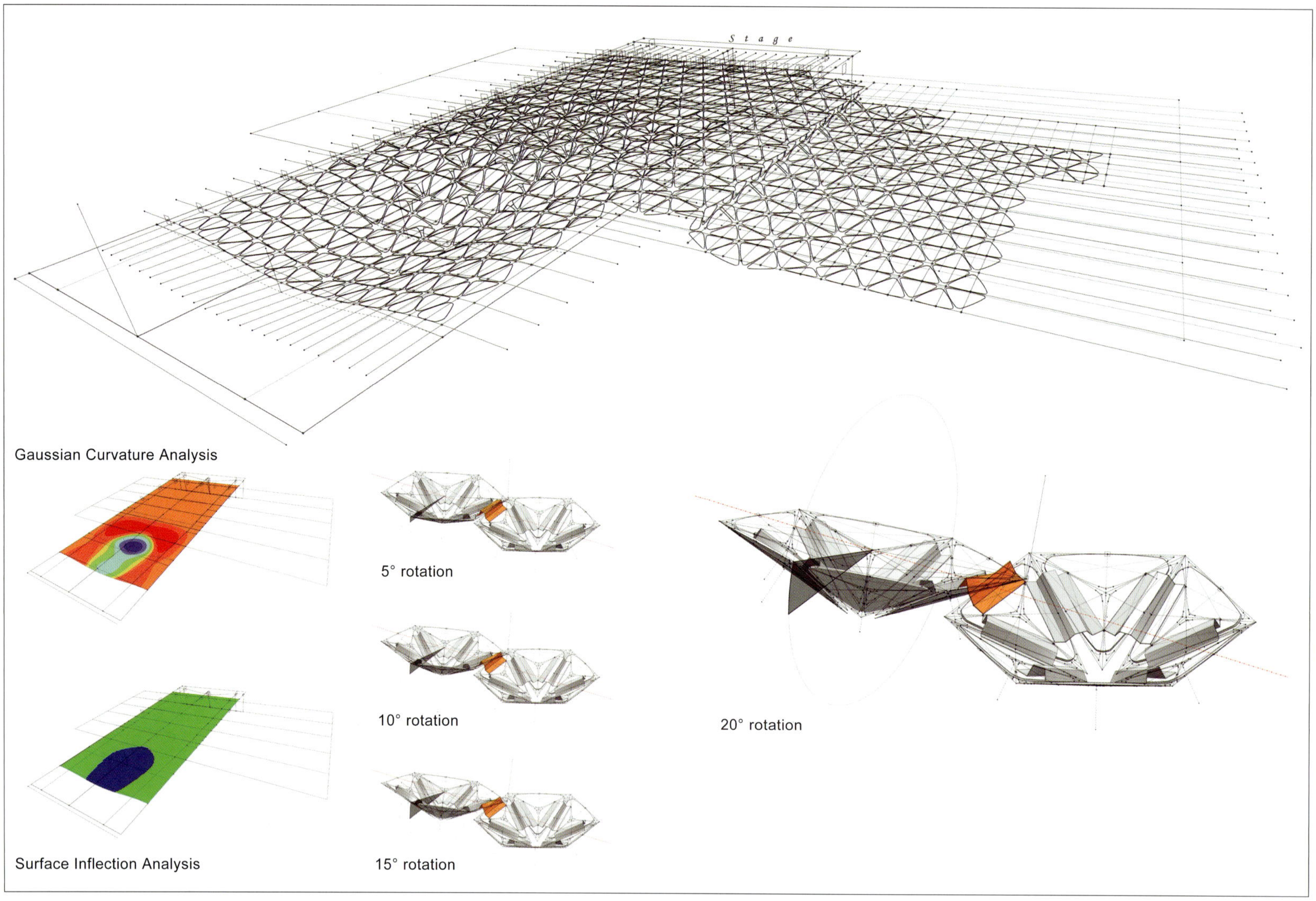
Stage
Gaussian Curvature Analysis
5° rotation
10° rotation
15° rotation
20° rotation
Surface Inflection Analysis

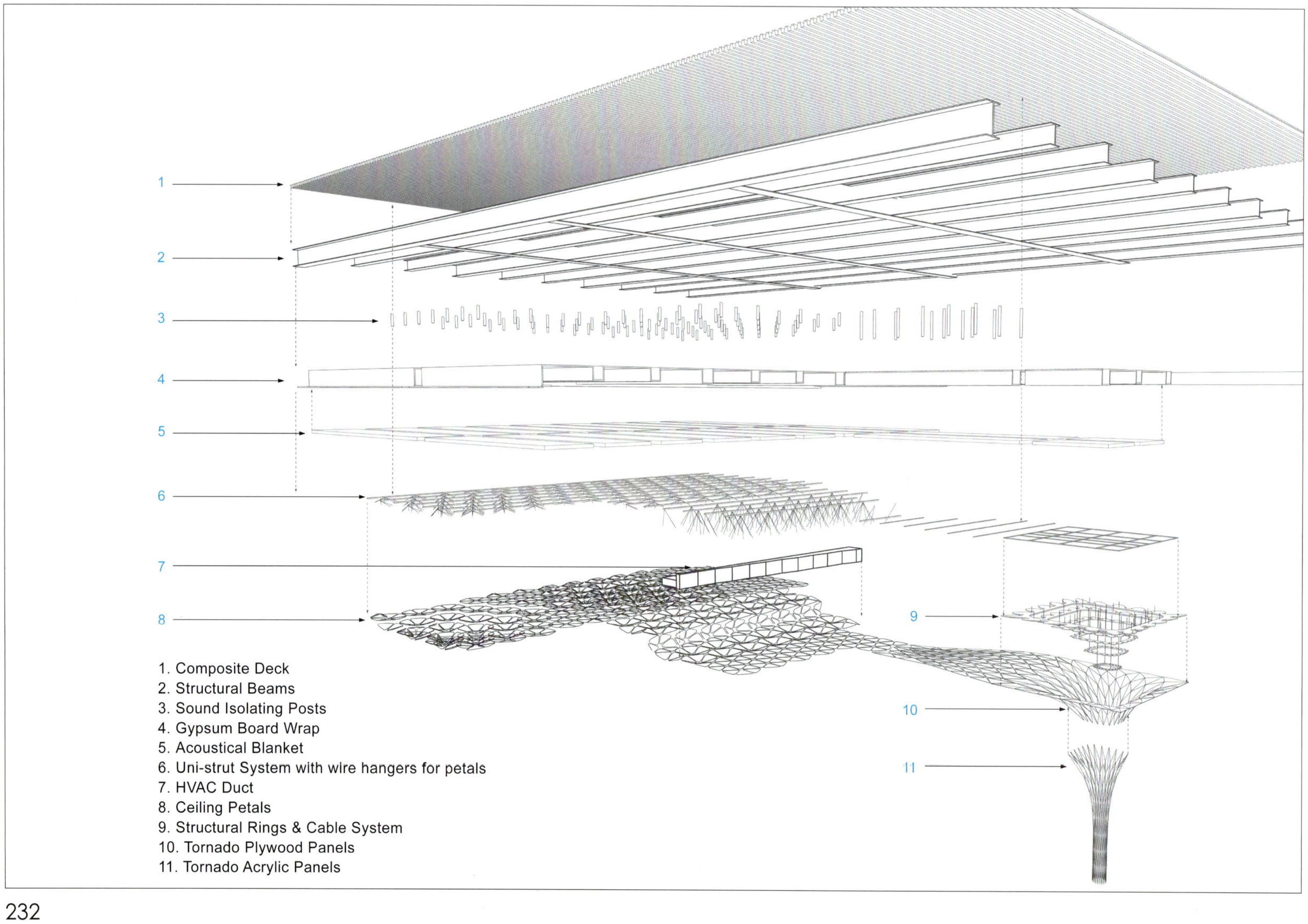
1
2
3
4
5
6
7
8
9
10
11
1. Composite Deck
2. Structural Beams
3. Sound Isolating Posts
4. Gypsum Board Wrap
5. Acoustical Blanket
6. Uni-strut System with wire hangers for petals
7. HVAC Duct
8. Ceiling Petals
9. Structural Rings & Cable System
10. Tornado Plywood Panels
11. Tornado Acrylic Panels

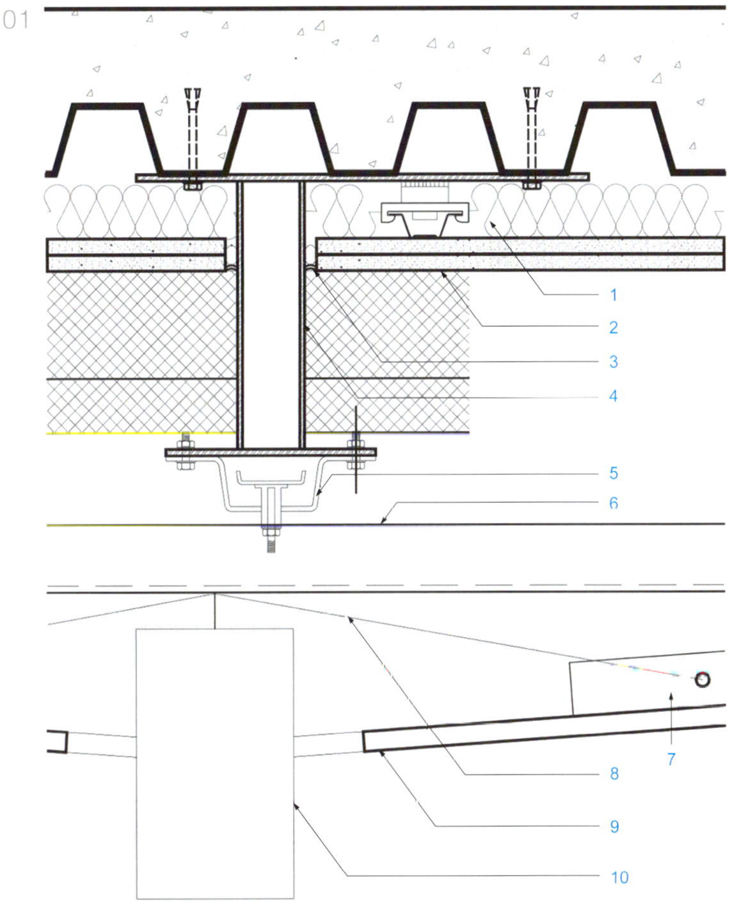

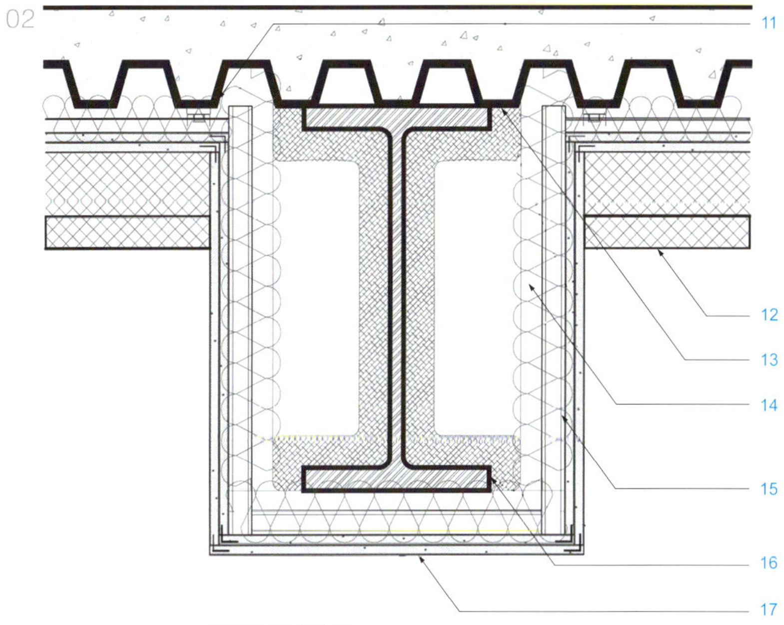

1. R11 batt insulation
2. 2 Layers 5/8" gyp.Bd.On rsic clips & 7/8" furring channels
3. Acoustic sealant and backer rod
4. Steel tube and plate
5. Mason industries hangers type rca -60 typical
6. Uni strut grid
7. Metal bracket
8. Metal hanging wire
9. Plywood ceiling panel
10. Light fixture
11. 12" O.C, on each side of beams rsic-1sound isolation clip mounted to metal plate attached to structural deck (pac international inc.)
12. 4"Johns manville insul-shield i/s 300
3Pcf fiberglass and 2" coated black
Insul-shield i/s150 1,5pcf typical
13. Existing composite deck
14. R-11 batt insulation
15. 1 1/2" Metal studs
16. Existing structural beam
17. 2 Layers 5/8" gyp.Board

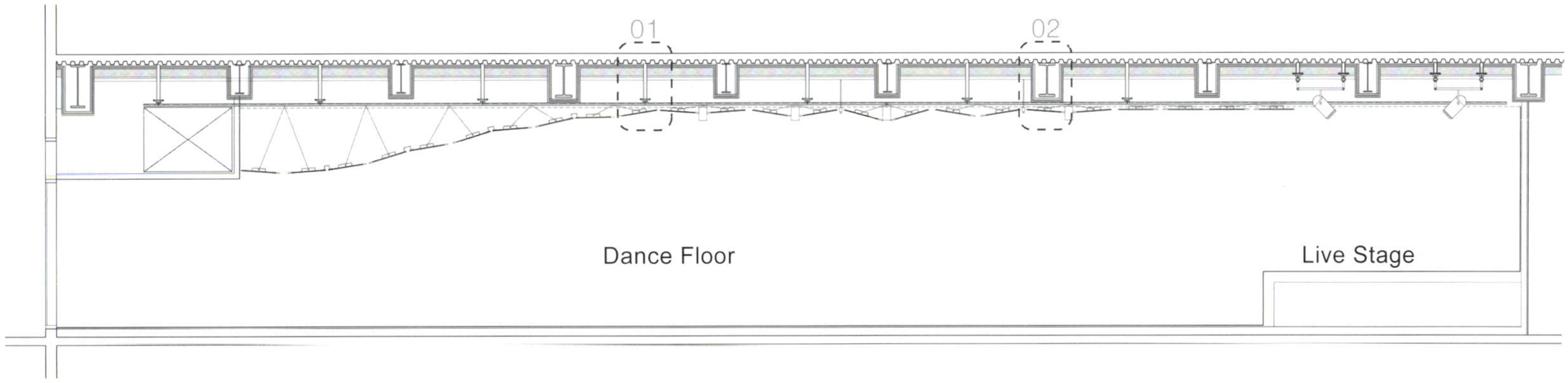

FIDM San Diego Campus

Jury Comments:
A playful, inspiring environment is created through skillful use of color and scale.
What might otherwise be a repetitious or simple environment is differentiated by unique spatial moments and interesting use of materials.
There is a cohesion to the space—despite the use of a wide variety of materials—due to the way the design interlocks the elements: the use of space defining space, no corridors, pockets of color keyed to a function, and lots of transparency moving light around the events, creates a learning environment that is what it espouses... design.

Notes of Interest

The Fashion Institute of Design and Merchandising (FIDM) is a private college with a thirty-five-year history of offering degrees directed at placing students in fashion, design and business. The college requested that its San Diego campus represent the school's progressive attitude towards education. The result is a space that is both non-traditional and tangibly centered around the value of design, appropriate enough for a school with just such a focus.

The project occupies the entire third floor of a high-rise office building. Comprising approximately 30,000 square feet, the space needed to accommodate all of the elements of the school's main campus within the smaller footprint of a regional campus. To achieve this, the school is designed as a sequence of zones: a public entry zone; an educational zone housing classrooms, the library, and technology resources; and an administration zone for the school's staff.

A looped circulation path encircles the floor plan, and generous public areas and hallway lounge settings create opportunities for spontaneous interaction. A strong color palette drawn from the area's native vegetation appears throughout the space. Additionally, a comprehensive graphic program that is integrated with the architecture connotes the function of spaces and leads users through the floor. While each area is self-defined through its color and form, integration between the spaces is very strong throughout.

Engineer: KPFF Consulting Engineers, Walsh Engineers
General Contractor: Steiner Construction
Owner: Fashion Institute of Design & Merchandising

Architect
Clive Wilkinson Architects

Location
San Diego, California

Photo Credit
© Benny Chan/Fotoworks

Moving Picture Company

Jury Comments:
The space is deftly crafted to be appropriate to the program and users it serves. The spatial sequence is cinematic – frame by frame, incorporating the various moods, lighting environments, theatrical clues, and subtle suggestion of movement through a process.
Thought and investigation went into this space that truly embodies themes of the user's business. Movement, drama, and light give this space a fun and dynamic feel.

Notes of Interest

This 8,200-square-foot visual effects post-production facility is located within a generic office building in downtown Santa Monica, California. The Moving Picture Company is a United Kingdom-based visual effects post-production company, a forerunner in the visual effects and animation fields for the feature film, advertising, music and television industries. The facility serves as the United States Headquarters. Without the option of expanding in space further into the office building, the project needed to house grading rooms, edit bays, conference rooms, open and closed offices, client areas, production spaces, entertaining areas, tape vaults, mechanical rooms, machine rooms and support spaces.

An organic, sinuous spine weaves its way through the suite. An appendaged soffit grows from the serpentine walls and serves as an armature for cable trays, mechanical and electrical systems. Light portals pierce the organic forms and are equipped with programmable LED lighting. In addition to the provision of light, structure, and motion, the building itself serves as a reminder and homage to the professional field it aids.

Owner: The Moving Picture Company (MPC)

Architect
Patrick Tighe Architecture

Location
Santa Monica, California

Photo Credit
© Art Gray Photography

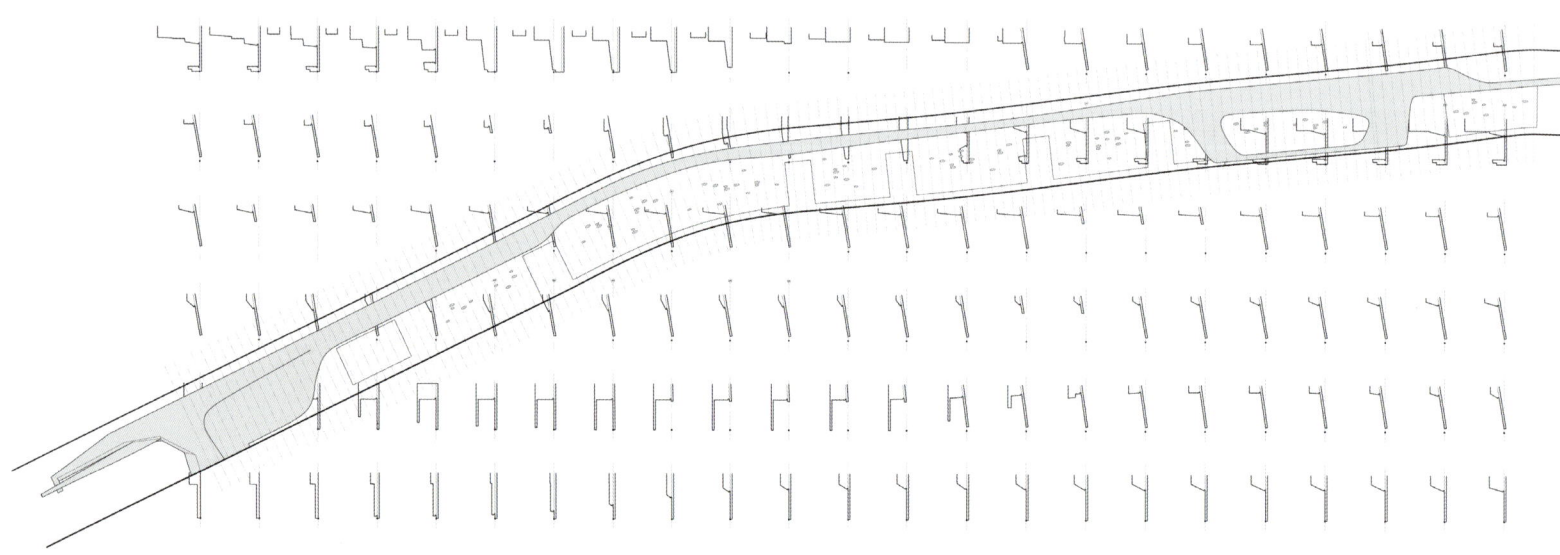

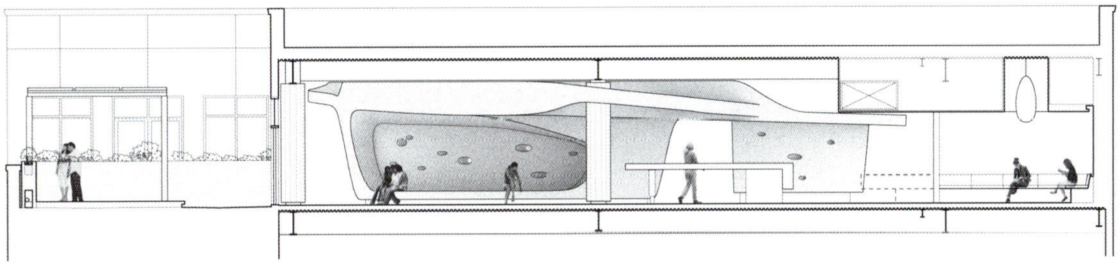

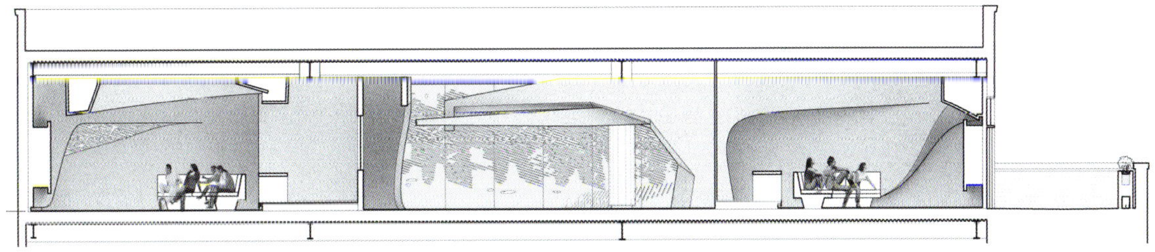

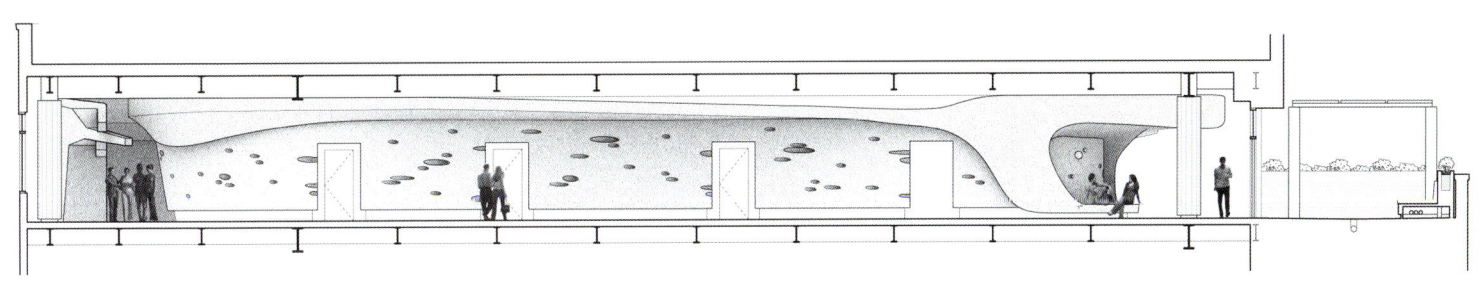

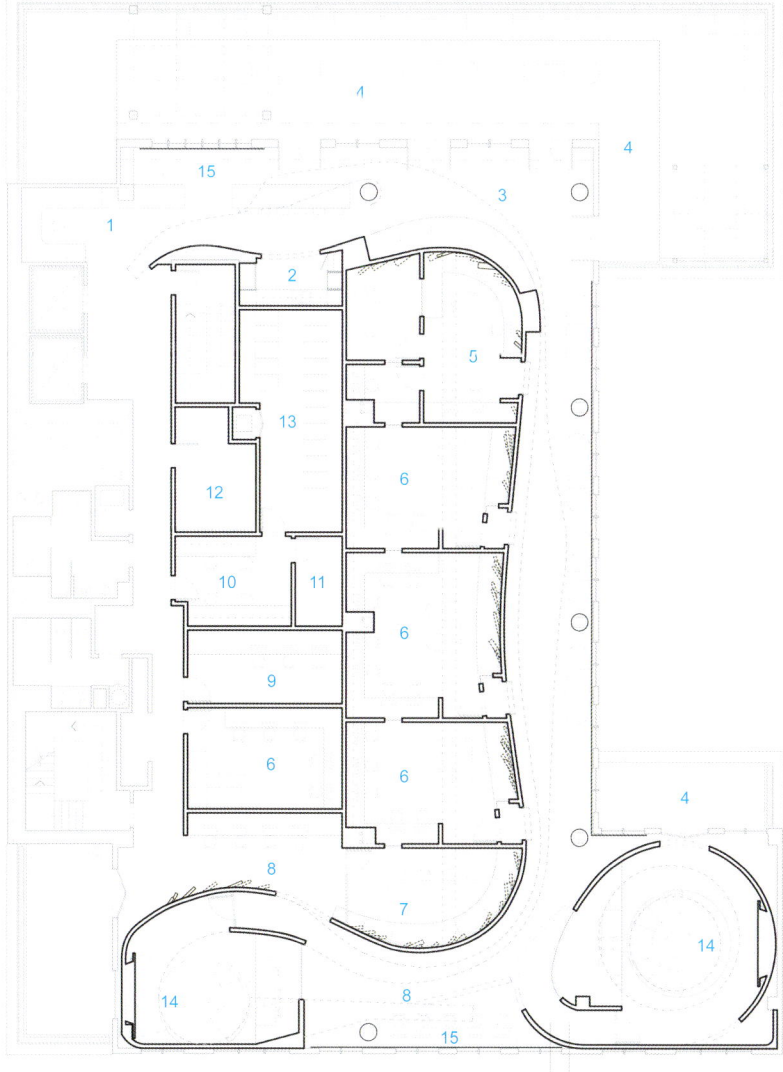

Plan:
1. Lobby
2. Kitchen
3. Common area
4. Terrace
5. Office
6. Project room
7. Conference room
8. Open office
9. Edit room
10. Tape op room
11. Scan
12. Film/tape vault
13. Machine room
14. Garding room
15. Aluminum laser-cut panels

Registrar Recorder County Clerk Elections Operations Center

Jury Comments:
Graphic strength at its best – this design dramatically transforms a mundane warehouse into an energetic, highly functional, and aesthetically pleasing place of work.
Working with a modest budget and minimal means, the designer turned this space into a celebration through a skillful use of color, scale and graphics. The collaborative effort between the architect, client and artist is very successful and commendable.

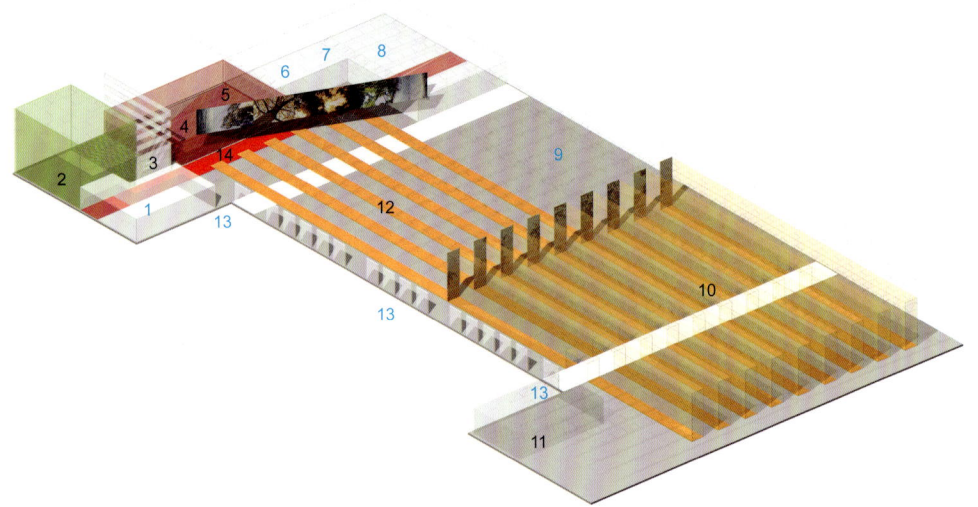

Diagram:
1. Call Center
2. Office
3. Café
4. Restrooms
5. Fire Rated Vault
6. Machine Shop
7. Ballot Inspection Room
8. Ballot Assembly Room
9. Operations Area
10. High Pile Storage Area
11. Equipment Storage Area
12. Staging Area
13. Loading Docks
14. Red "Hall"

Notes of Interest

Registrar Recorder County Clerk Elections Operations Center is a 110,000-square-foot office and warehouse facility that organizes, distributes, collects and processes all of the voting materials of Los Angeles' 5,000 voting precincts for every election. The facility is housed in an existing tilt-up concrete warehouse, a structure of overwhelming size that houses all worker office space, voting pallet storage, digital voting units and personal records.

Designed and built-out in approximately 11 months, the project was brought in – all amenities included – under budget and on schedule. A robust palette of design tools were used to create a place of economy, utility and delight. The architect envisioned large-scale mega-banners that could achieve significant architectural impact. This new technology affordably provides scale and intimacy to this huge warehouse. In a matter of creative funding, the architect/owner team worked with the County Arts Program to commission a local artist. Color was used strategically on vertical and horizontal surfaces with paint and fabric, as well as through mega-banner technology. This use of color and imagery energizes the entire warehouse.

It was the intimate collaboration of architect, owner, user, builder and artist that allowed the success this project achieves. The result is a place of utility and delight, honoring an important institution of democracy as well as the citizens of Los Angeles County.

Owner: Los Angeles County

Architect
Lehrer Architects

Location
Santa Fe Springs, California

Photo Credit
© Michael B. Lehrer

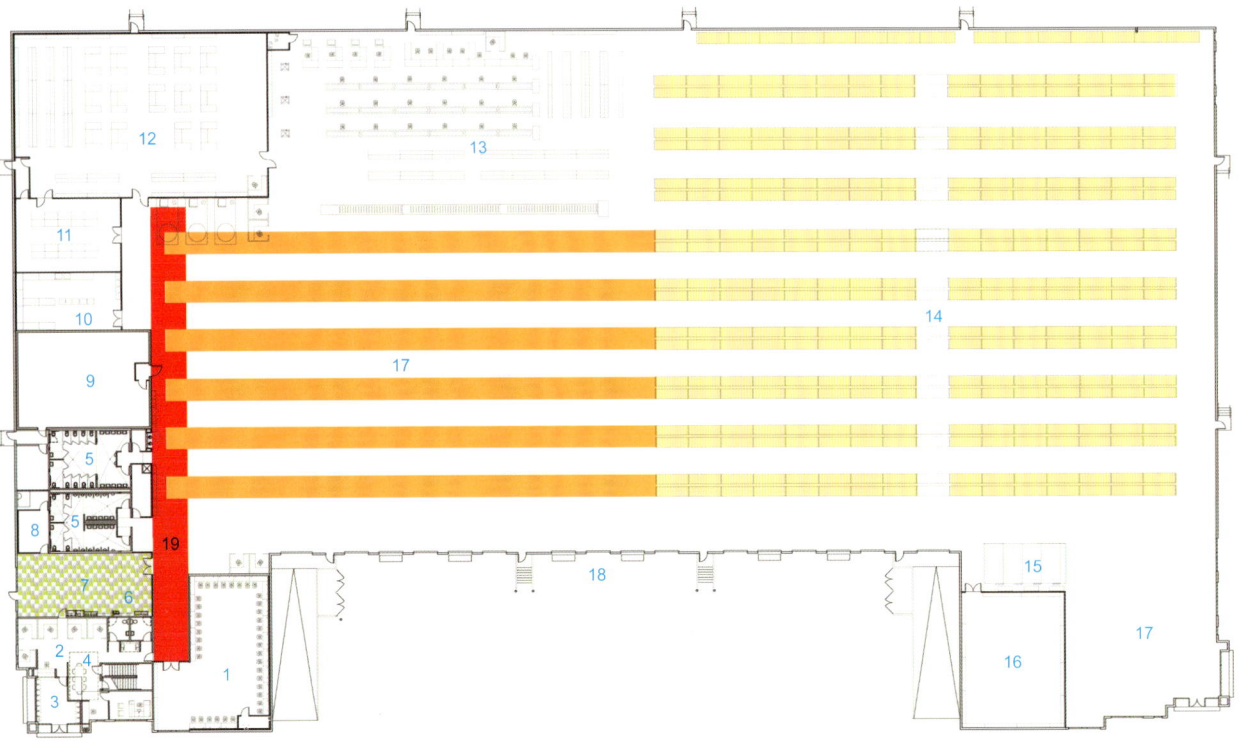

1. Call Center
2. Office
3. Waiting Area
4. Conference Area
5. Restroom
6. Kitchen
7. Café
8. Server Room
9. Fire Rated Vault
10. Machine Shop
11. Ballot Inspection Room
12. Ballot Assembly Room
13. Operations Area
14. High Pile Storage Area
15. Fork Lift Recharge Stations
16. Equipment Storage Area
17. Staging Area
18. Loading Docks
19. Red "Hall"

The Academy of Music

Jury Comments:
Beautiful execution of historic preservation. The fact that this entry was so well documented and expertly executed, down to every faithful detail, makes us proud to revere the past and keep it ever present.
A thoughtful, meticulous restoration in which technical improvements are ingeniously concealed, and lighting is carefully placed to draw attention to the proportions, color and detailing that reawakens the space's unique character.
Sensitive and masterful.

Notes of Interest

The Academy of Music is the oldest continuously operating concert hall in the United States. The first performance occurred on January 26, 1857, but by 2007, years of continuous use had taken its toll on the Academy's Ballroom. The 40' x 80' Ballroom is spatially unchanged from 1857, but unfortunately many other historic features of the room were changed over time.

Through the generosity of Lee Annenberg and the Academy's ongoing restoration fundraising efforts, the Academy was in a position to undo 152 years of alterations. Hundreds of hours of design research went into reconstructing the original design intent for the room, using the Academy's substantial archives, as well as resources from The Philadelphia Historical Commission, The Pennsylvania Historical Society, and The Athenaeum of Philadelphia.

Lengthy efforts to repair the original room went into play, including the reintroduction of the chandeliers and gas light fixtures; the restoration of the glass windows, which had since been walled over and covered with mirrors; months of work reestablishing the paint scheme; and reparation of all water damage, hand in hand with steps taken to prevent future damage.

Engineer: Keast & Hood, PHY Engineers Inc.
General Contractor: L.F. Driscoll Company
Lighting: Horton Lees Brogden Lighting Design
Owner: The Philadelphia Orchestra

Architect
KlingStubbins

Location
Philadelphia, Pennsylvania

Photo Credit
© Tom Crane Photography

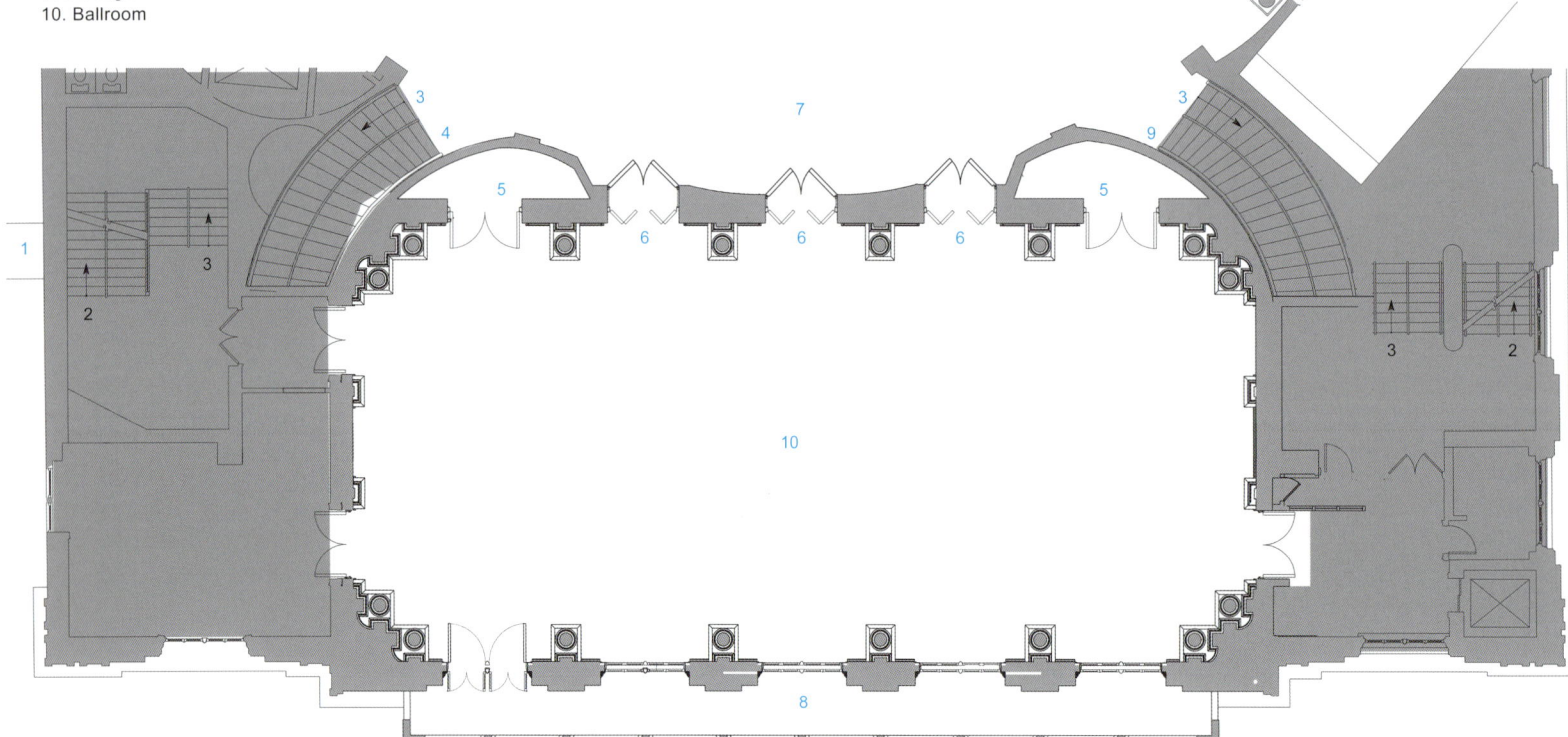

Ballroom:
1. Roof below
2. Up
3. Dn
4. South grand stair
5. Storage
6. Sound & light locks
7. Ambulatory
8. Exterior balcony
9. North grand stair
10. Ballroom

The Power House, Restoration/Renovation

Jury Comments:
An interesting dialogue between present and past...The project maintains, preserves and reestablishes the integrity of the existing, historic building while creating modern, attractive, and energy efficient interior spaces that accommodate user needs.
A balanced and pleasing chiaroscuro effect is produced between new materials reflecting light and the existing materiality of the project that absorbs light.

Notes of Interest

These offices for the design architects' firm occupy a long-abandoned power house, constructed in 1928, part of the Municipal Service Building complex that still occupies an entire block of downtown St. Louis. The Power House component of the complex, designated as a landmark by the National Historic Register, had confounded developers over the years who struggled with its tall volume but relatively small footprint.

The design challenge was to accommodate 32,000 square feet of office, conference and support space for approximately 120 employees in a building with 19,000 square feet of floor area, but over 400,000 cubic feet of volume. New floors needed to be added within the building's massive volume to accommodate the firm's program, but somehow this introduction of multiple stories had to avoid compromising the spatial integrity of its interior space, and most importantly, the 26-foot-tall, arched, revival-style windows. At the same time, the design needed to preserve each individual's connection to the exterior from the workspace. Lastly, it needed to meet and reflect the firm's desire for a new way of working: one that was intuitive, flexible and open.

The second and third levels were added to massive existing steel plate columns – no vertical structure was added. Crisp, modern workspace is juxtaposed against rusted columns and glazed brick. The new floors are held away from the north and east elevations, which contain the dramatic Romanesque windows facing out to the city. The windows afford a significant amount of daylight and views to the surrounding neighborhood. The gallery space is programmed as an event space and a way to engage the community as never before possible.

Engineer: Ruofei Sun, Ph.D., PE
General Contractor: R.G. Ross
Owner: Cannon Design

Architect
Cannon Design

Location
St. Louis, Missouri

Photo Credit
© Gayle Babcock/Architectural Imageworks, LLC, © Patti Gabriel Photography

Second Floor Plan

First Floor Plan

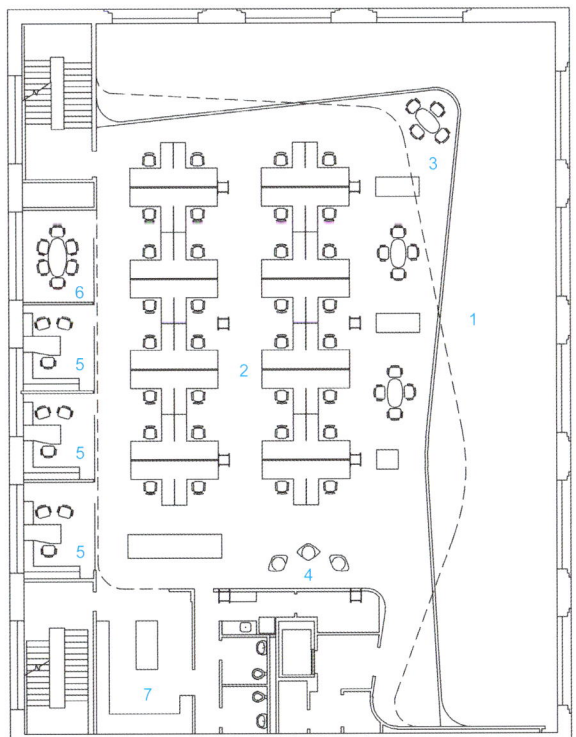

Plans:
1. Reception
2. Gallery
3. Open Office
4. Open Team Space
5. Crit Space
6. Office
7. Conference
8. Work Room
9. Open to Gallery Below

257

Vancouver Convention Center West

Jury Comments:
An amazingly inviting, warm public circulation is achieved through the use of daylighting, building landforms, and local materials that both reference the area's industry and provide richly detailed surfaces.
Unlike the typical convention center, this public space has a well chosen vocabulary of materials and spatial proportions that commits to the connection between interior and exterior, bringing the outdoors in to its interior spaces in a compelling and eloquent manner.

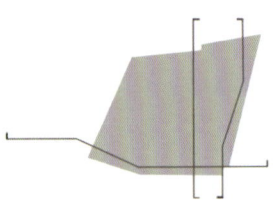

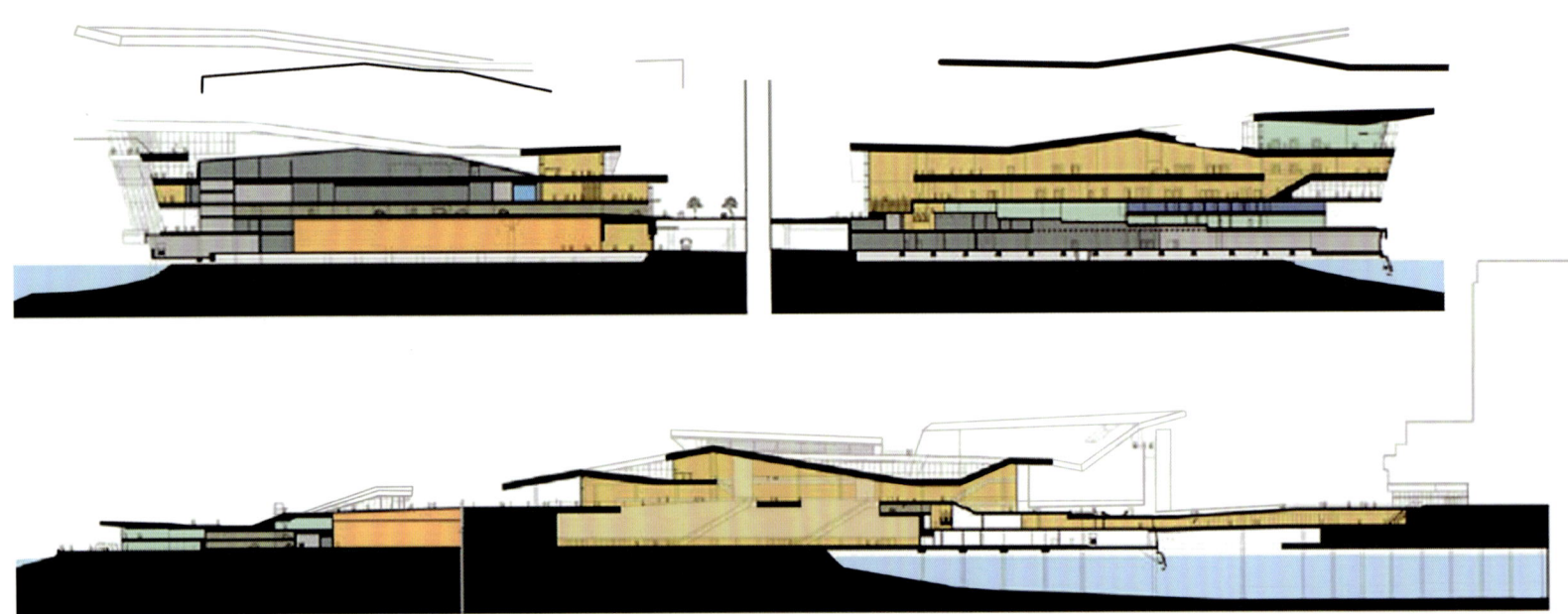

Notes of Interest

The design of the new Vancouver Convention Center West presented an opportunity to fully engage the urban ecosystem at the intersection of a vibrant downtown core and one of the most spectacular natural ecosystems in North America. Certified LEED® Canada Platinum, the project weaves together architecture, interior architecture, and urban design in a unified whole that functions literally as a living part of both the city and the harbor.

Addressing the human environment, the architectural approach creates a community experience that is simultaneously a building, an urban place, a park and an ecosystem. The convention center program emphasizes spaces for both public and private events, gatherings and circulation.

The primary interior expression is the use of naturally occurring materials indigenous to British Columbia, with extensive use of sustainably harvested Douglas fir. The ballroom and meeting room programs that form the core of the building's interior mass are enclosed by a wood cladding system that simulates the texture and directionality of a stack of lumber. Wood ceiling slats oriented in long, dramatic parallel lines combine with the orthogonal massing of the interior spaces to create contrast against the organic geometry of the roof and exterior shell. The strong wood expression takes on an arresting public presence at night as the building glows through its transparent skin.

Engineer: Glotman Simpson Consulting Engineers, EarthTech (Canada) Inc., Stantec Consulting, Schenke/Bawol Engineering Ltd., Sandwell Engineering Inc.
General Contractor: PCL Construction Enterprises
Owner: BC Pavilion Corporation (PavCo)

Architect	Location	Photo Credit
LMN + DA/MCM	Vancouver, Canada	© Nic Lehoux

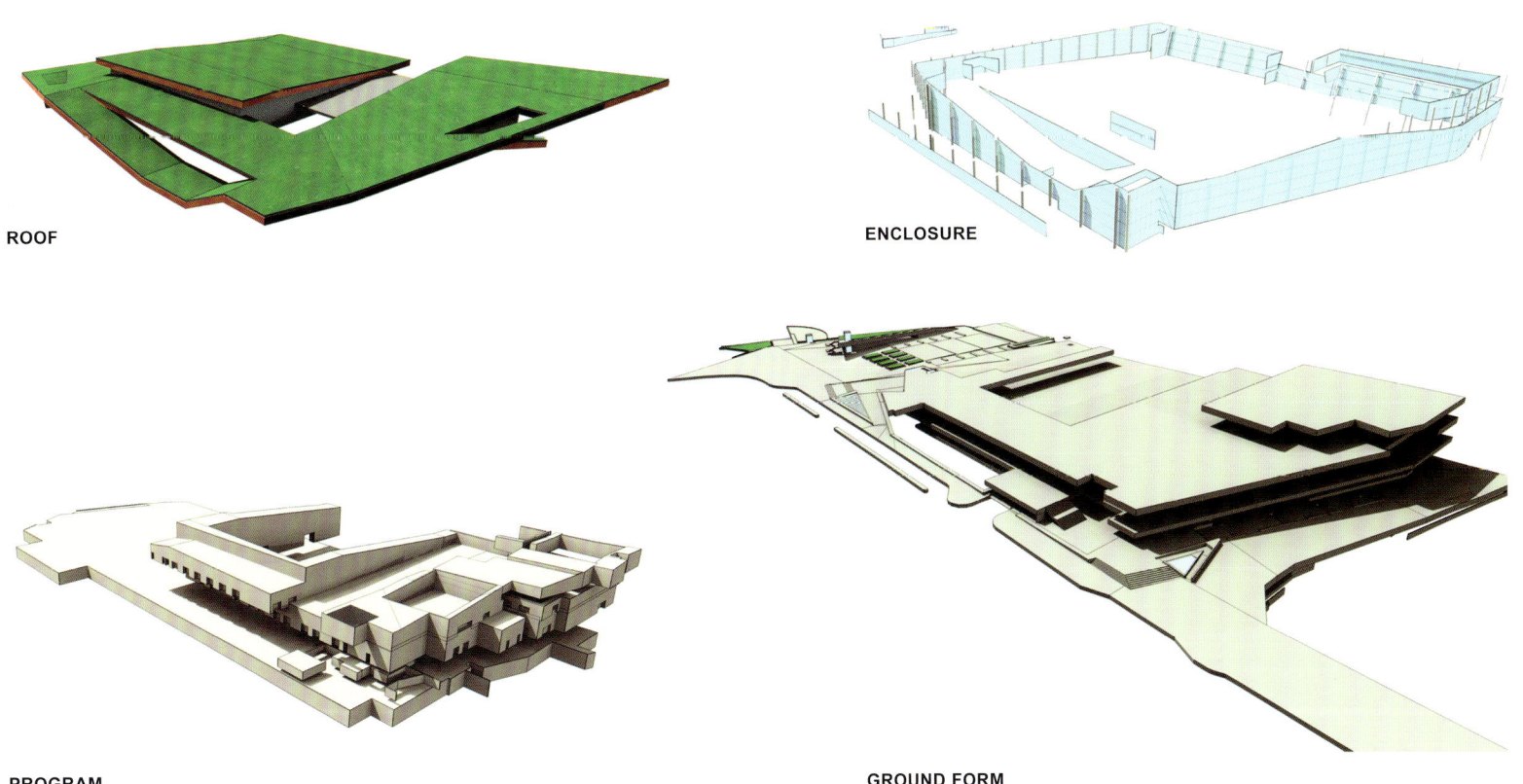

ROOF

ENCLOSURE

PROGRAM

GROUND FORM

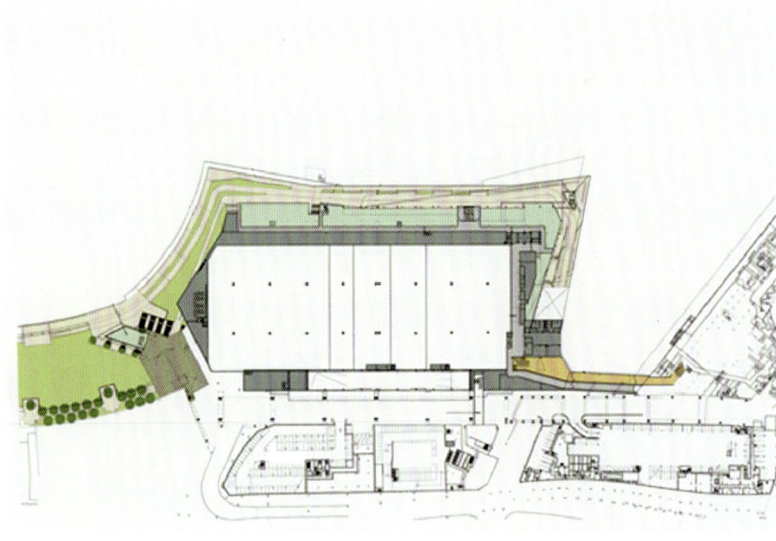
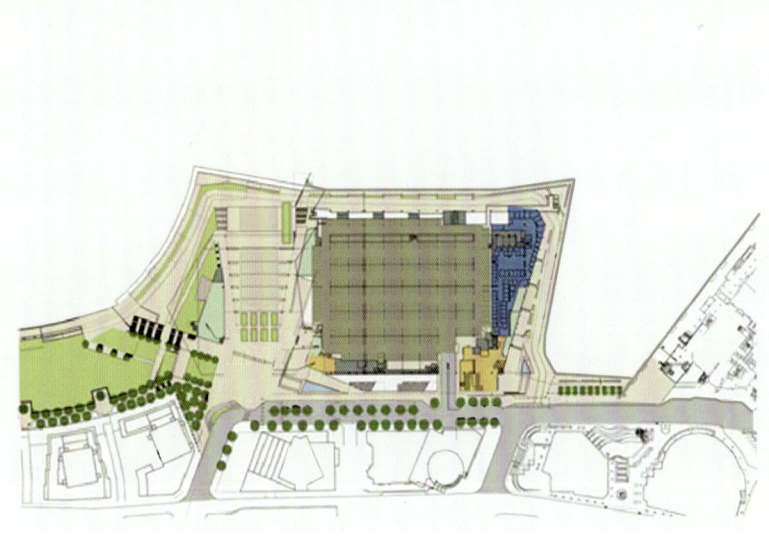

263

Washington Square Park Dental

Jury Comments:
Clever details and ideas are all over this skinny-budget project. It delightfully shows what you can do with a small space through a design that is visually very interesting and highly functional.
The use of serene glowing material, soothing color, simple planes of form, and a clear, open, yet structured, plan calms the nerves and sets a stage like no other dentist office.

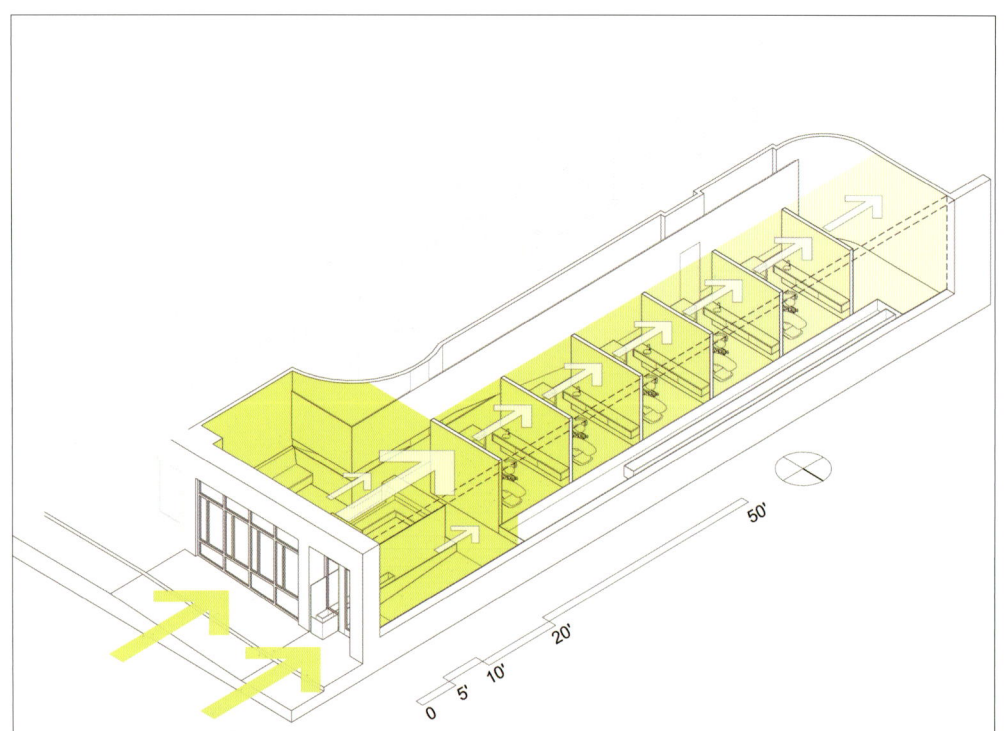

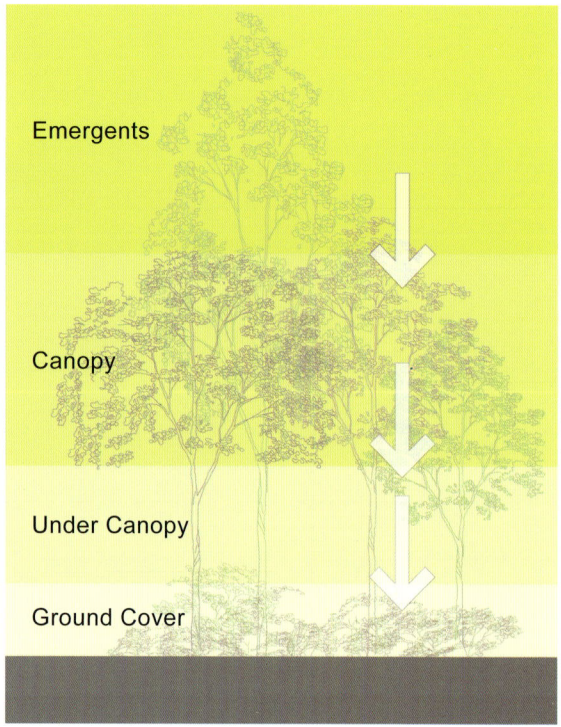

Permeating Natural Light

Notes of Interest
For this dentistry office located on the west edge of Washington Square Park in San Francisco, the main design goals involved maximizing the impression of space and length in the 1900-square-foot building and seamlessly bringing in elements of light and aesthetics from the exterior park all the way throughout the space.

Natural light floods into the space from the front windows all the way through to the back of the office space, despite the office's linear composition that includes five private patient operatory rooms. This is accomplished through the use of "floss" walls.

To extend the spatial depth of the relatively small space and establish a connection to the outside environment, aesthetic elements of the park were drawn into the interior. Low-irrigation interior landscaping is arranged in a beautiful steel perimeter separating polished river rocks from recycled glass. The long, interior entry ramp is framed by this linear garden, and it continues all the way from the exterior of the building down the length of the space to create a series of individual gardens for each of the patient operatories. This view down the entire length of the office is immediately available to the patient upon entrance.

Engineer: Julia Y. Chen Design, Inc., Acies Engineering
General Contractor: Norcal Construction Management Services
Lighting: John Brubaker Architectural Lighting Consultants
Owner: Washington Square Park Dental

Architect
Montalba Architects, Inc.

Location
San Francisco, California

Photo Credit
© Mitch Tobias

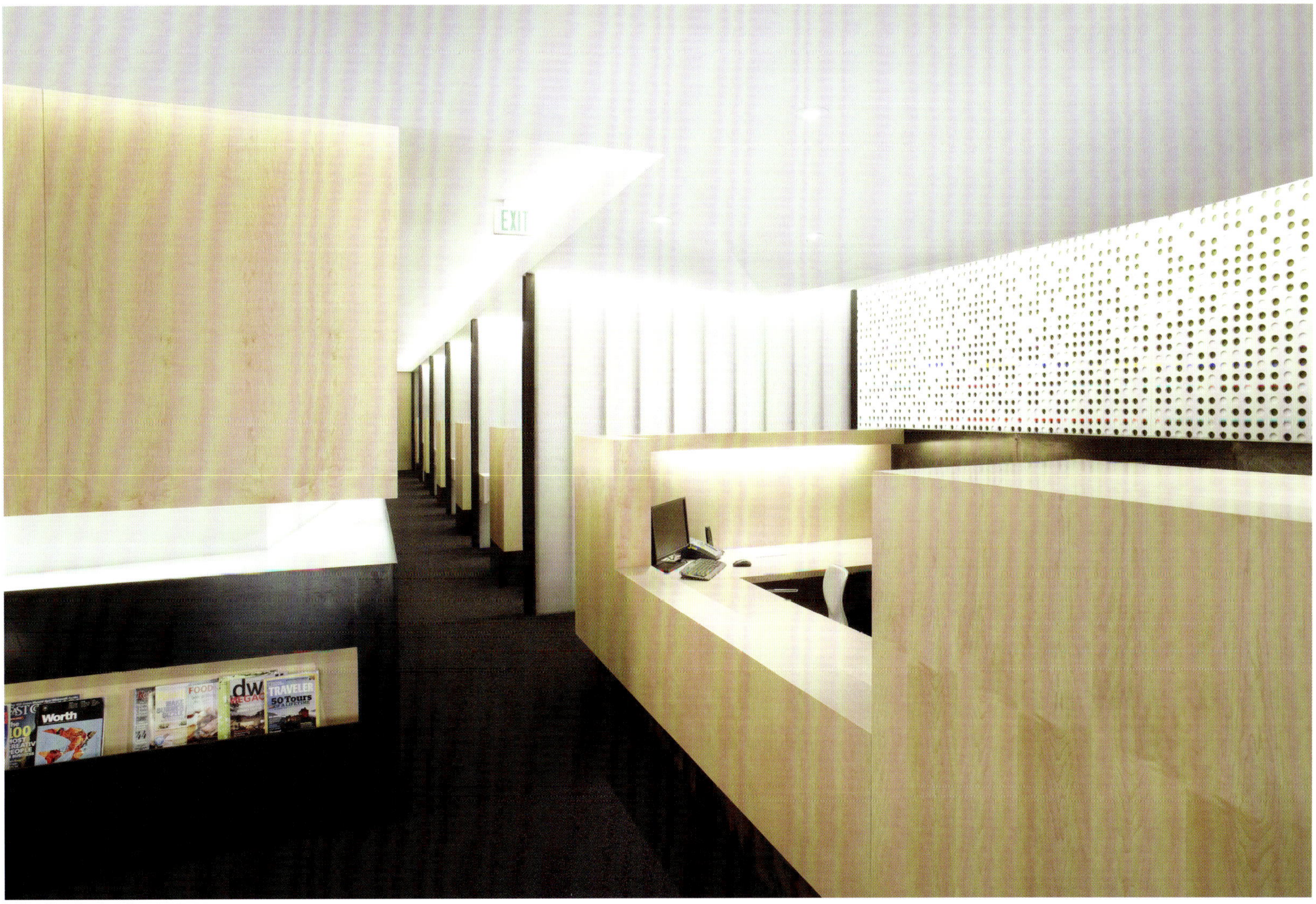
EXIT
Worth
TRAVELER
50 Tours

0'
5'
15'
30'

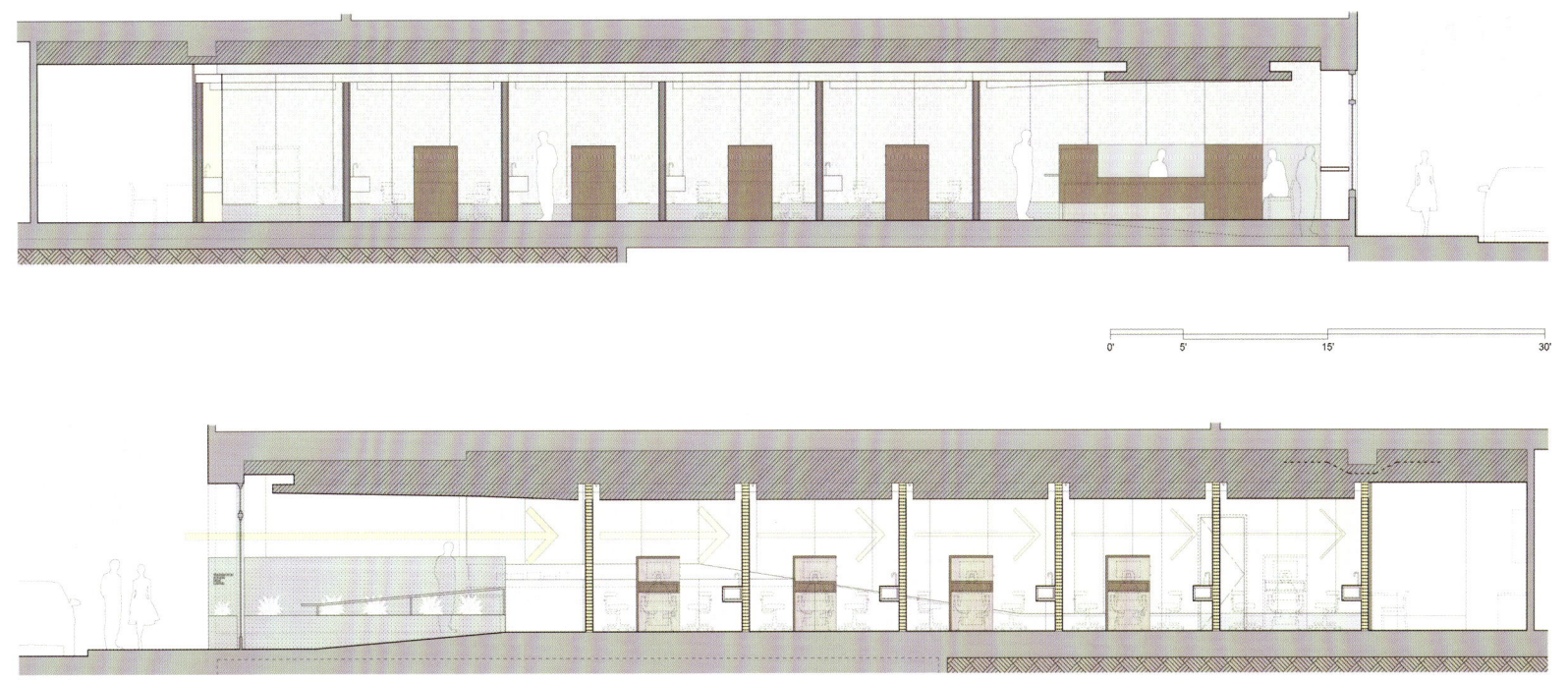

Sustainable Strategies – Exploded Axonometric:
1. High albedo folded celing plane
2. Translucent acrylic panels
3. Enkadrain mats
4. Steel stud construction
5. Fsc certidied wood
6. Recycled hot-rolled steel panels
7. Transparent floss wall assembly
8. Refurbished detail chairs
9. No voc paint
10. Low irrigation interior landscape with recycled glass
11. Carpet tiles from renewable and recycled sources
12. Perforated sound absorbing wall using fsc certified wood

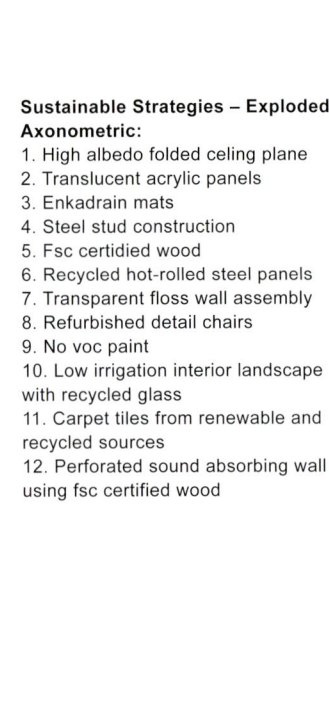

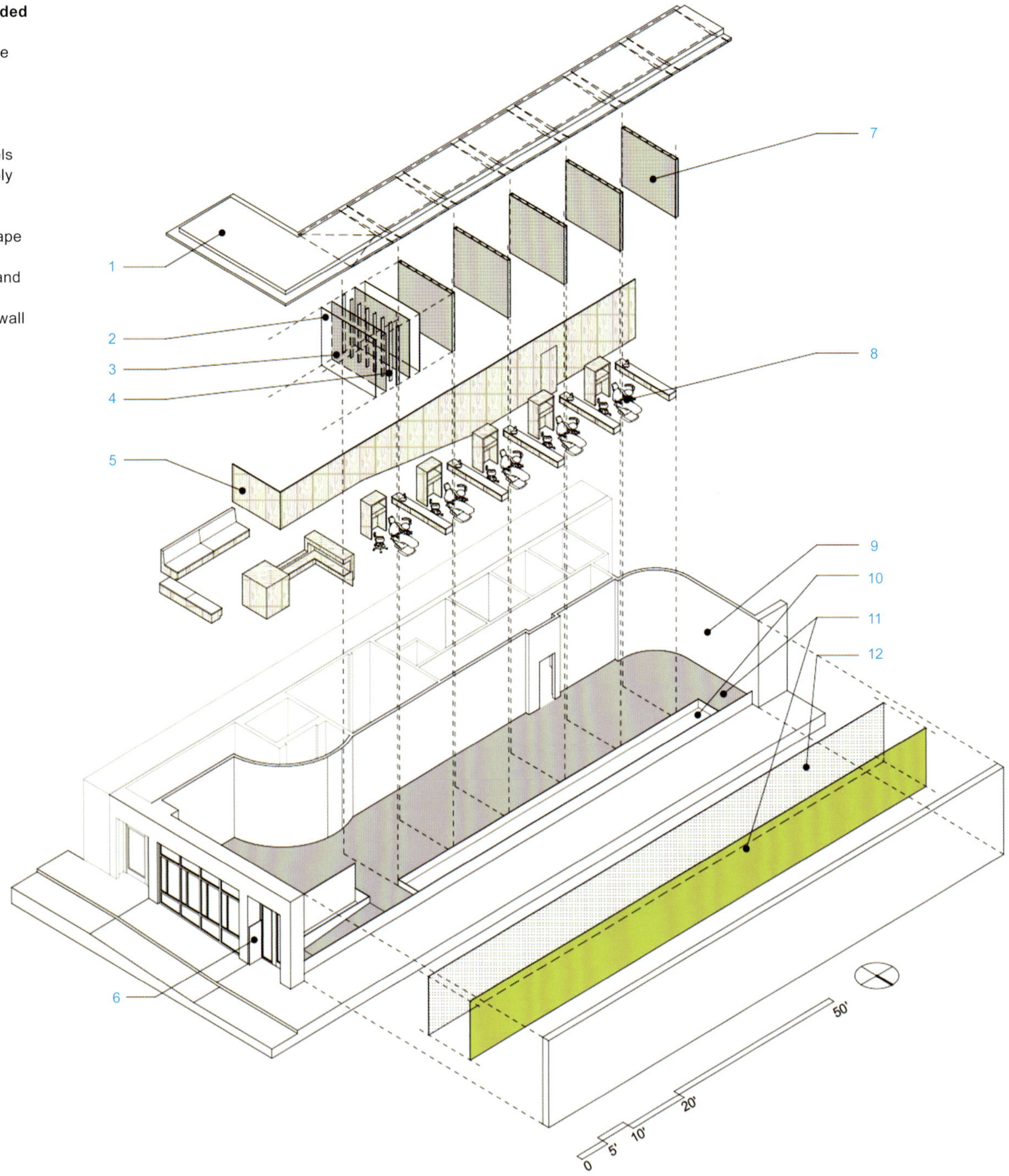

Floor Plan (Below):
1. Entry
2. Reception
3. Waiting area
4. Built-in seating
5. Custom perforated acoustic wall
6. Operatory
7. Custom translucent floss wall
8. Built-in storage
9. Landscape
10. Office

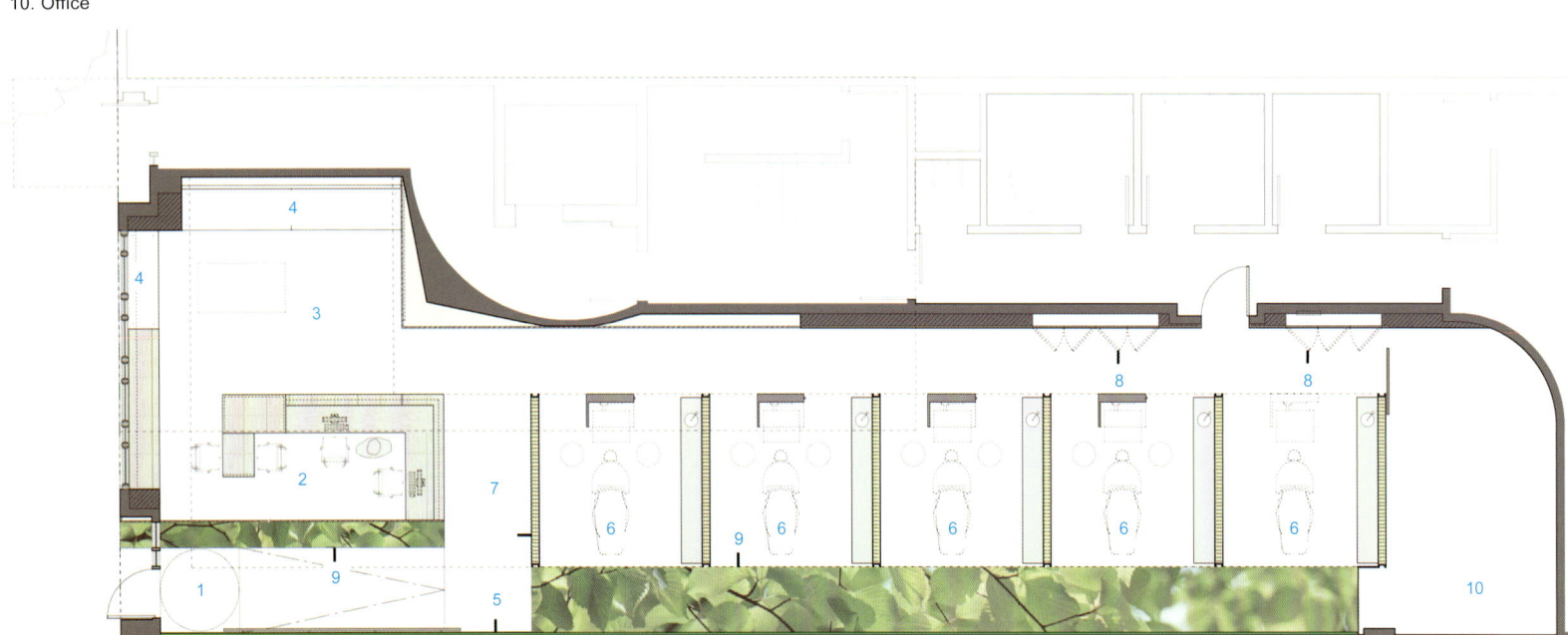

Transverse Building Section Through Typical Patient Operatory:
1. Fixed fsc wood paneling
2. White acrylic lens
Continuous flour. Light fixture
1/4" Thick hot-rolled steel panel
3. Recycled carpet tile
Existing slab on grad or wood
Framing (depending on location)
4. Opening for television in framing
5. 1/4" Frosted acrylic panels
Nylon enkadrain mat
Mc6x12 steel channel
6. Perforated acoustical panel
3/4" Air gap
Recycled carpet tile
Existing demising wall
7. Interior landscape planter

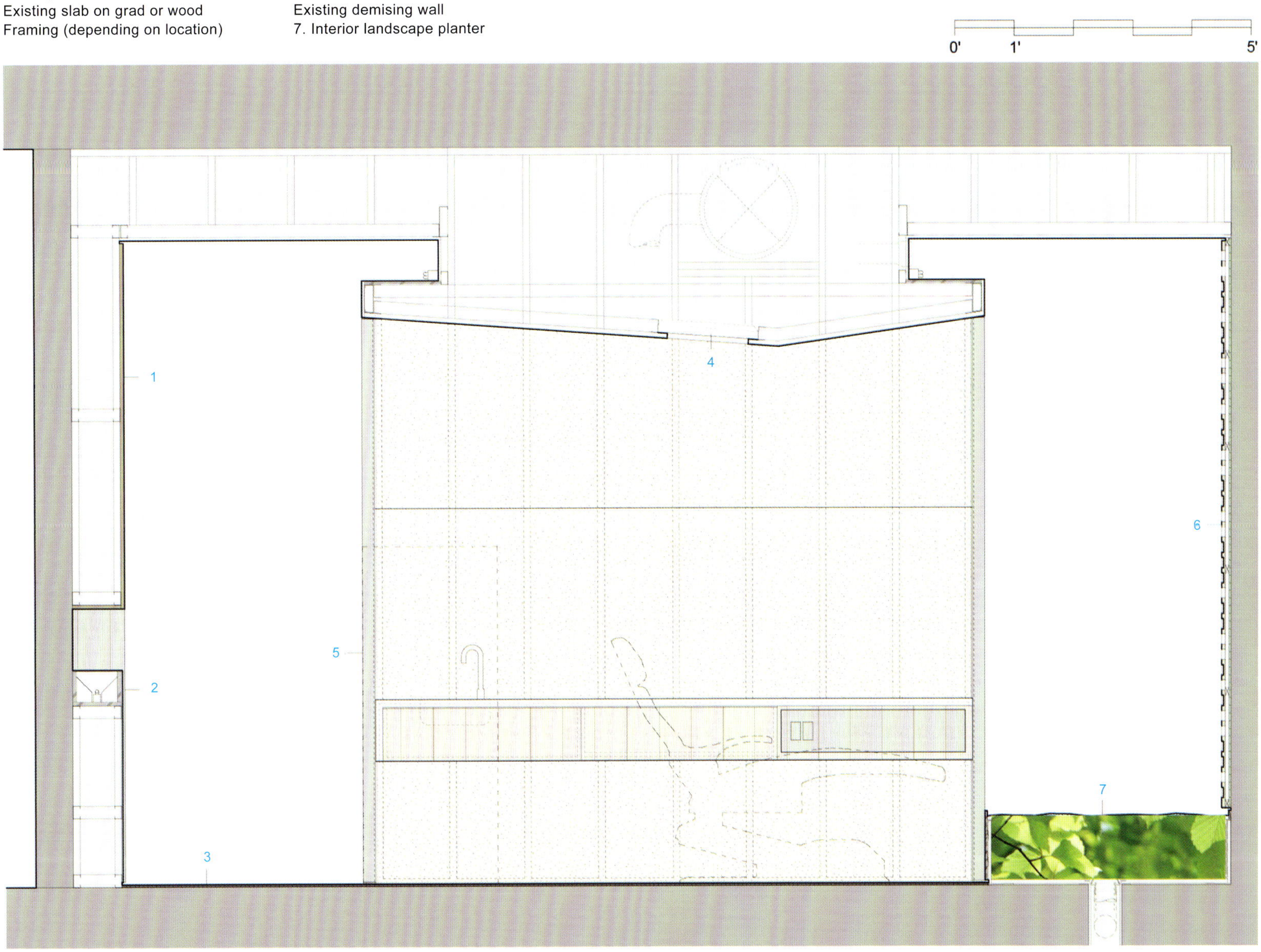

John E. Jaqua Center for Student Athletes

Jury Comments:
Beautifully detailed throughout...Remarkable introduction of color and management of natural light. The atmosphere is comfortable yet stimulating, with furnishings that are highly functional yet inviting and uniquely designed.
Athletics and Education are purely stated here. This facility's integration of diverse and defined spaces, of glass and daylight for engaging learning, of wood for warmth and strength, and with effective graphics celebrating its graduates' post-graduate achievements creates a design whose goals are transparent.

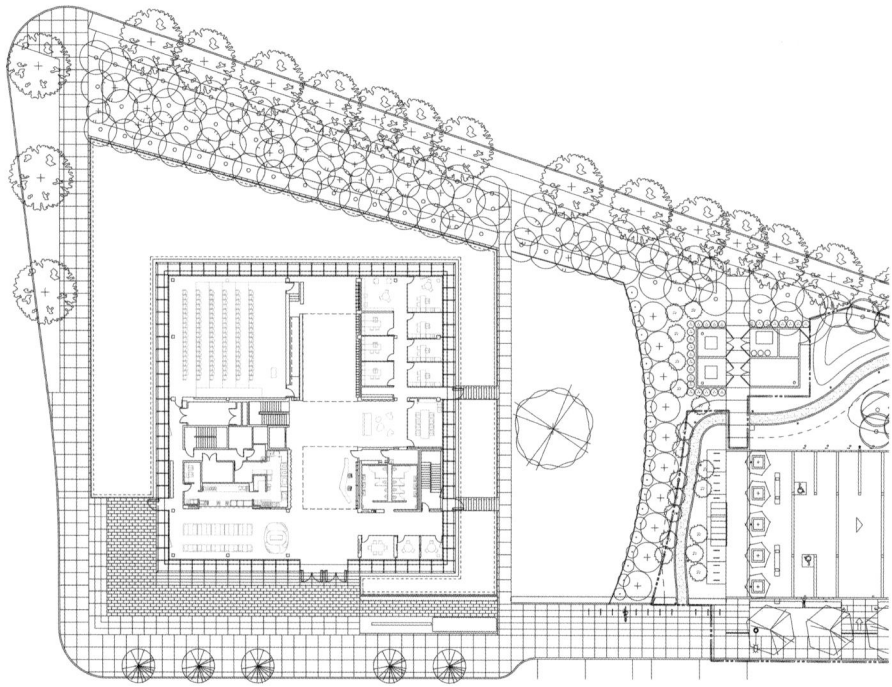

Notes of Interest

The John E. Jaqua Center for Student Athletes at the University of Oregon is a bright space that emphasizes the value of academic and professional achievements to its athletic audience through design. This new 40,000-square-foot, state-of-the-art, academic learning center accommodates the NCAA-mandated academic services for the tutoring of 520 student athletes.

The challenging project site's visual prominence led to the building being designed with four public façades and no "back door", which has reinforced its importance within the landscape as an iconic element.

The notion of a fertile, natural environment to invigorate and inspire learning was the premise on which the design concept was based. The glass structure rests on a "table of water". A "double wall" façade addresses acoustic isolation, thermal insulation, and control of available daylight within the building. A prismatic, vertical stainless steel screen within this façade provides shading, thermal comfort, and ability for heat harvesting as well as visual privacy for the inhabitants. The glazed façade and interior spaces are composed on a rigorous module to achieve an uninterrupted visual connection between internal rooms and the larger garden beyond.

Also present in the project is the university's signature yellow and "O", as well as various achievement-centered art installations, all of which help the facility to serve as a pantheon of student athletic achievements.

Engineer: KPFF Consulting Engineers, Inc., Interface Engineering, Arup, Harper Houf Peterson Righellis, Inc.
General Contractor: Hoffman Construction Company
Owner: The University of Oregon

Architect
ZGF Architects LLP

Location
Eugene, Oregon

Photo Credit
© Basil Childers

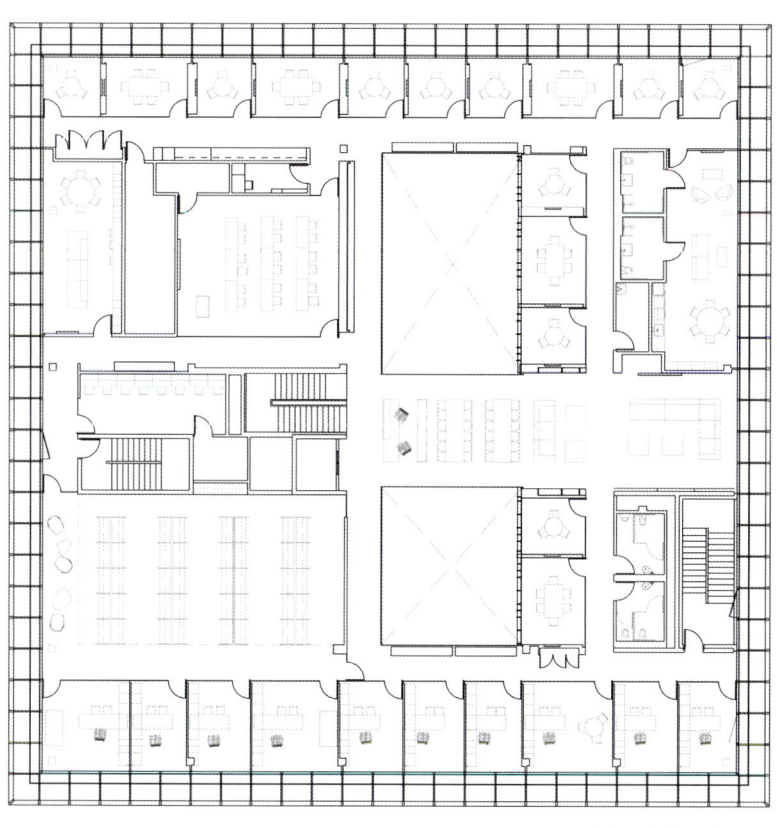

Second Level

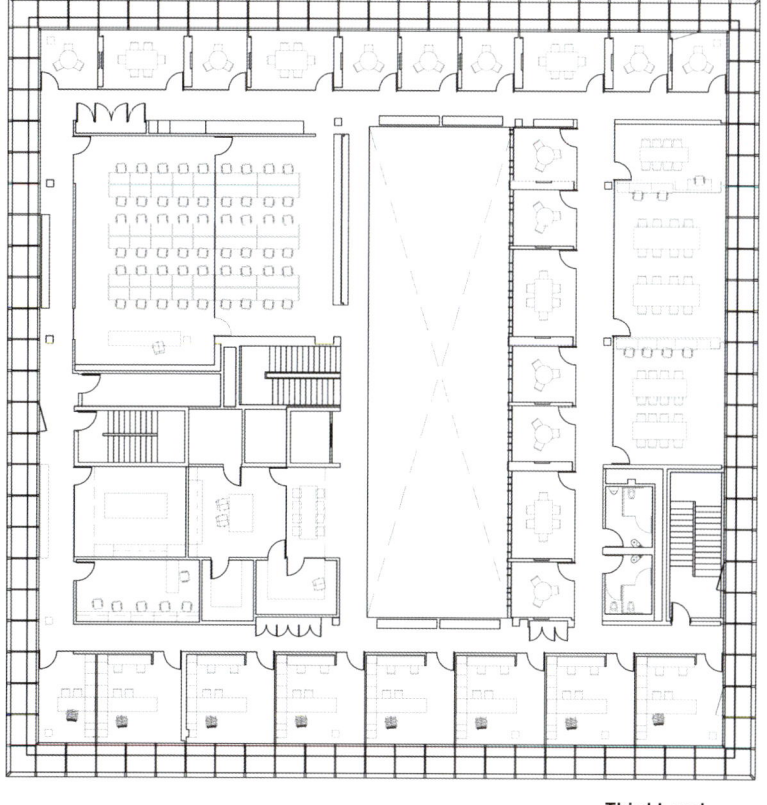

Third Level

Beijing CBD East Expansion

Jury Comments:
A compelling vision for an expanded dense city core that is environmentally sound, with intertwined linear parks creating a variety of pedestrian opportunities, and believably defining and linking multiple districts into a livable city.
In the midst of great density, Beijing has found a sensitive way to incorporate environmental sustainability into its expanded business district. This project shows how planning for a cohesive central business district is the best strategy for truly sustainable development.

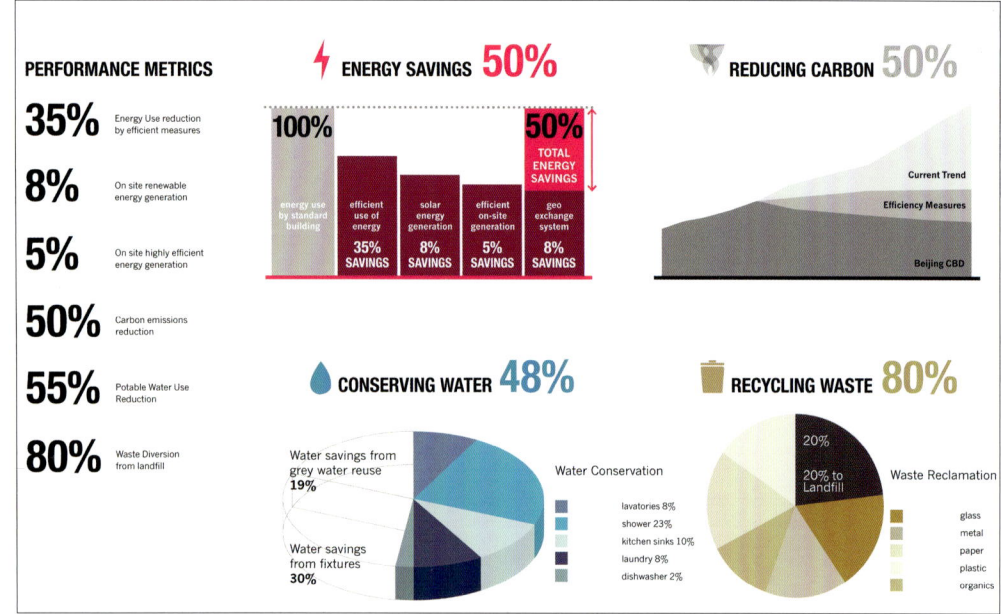 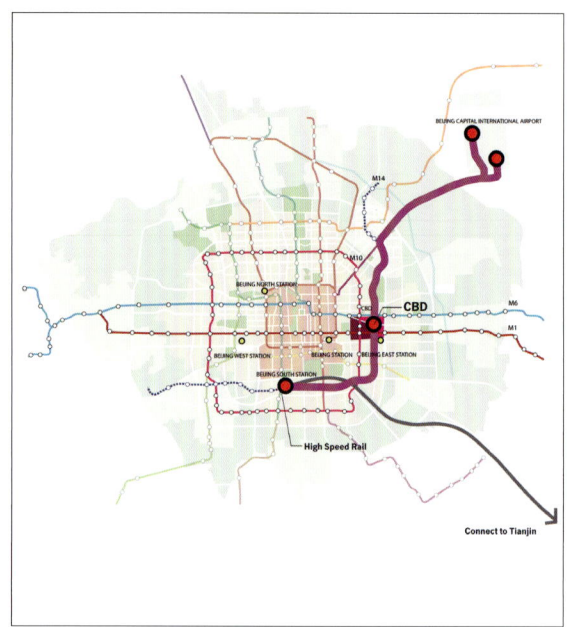

Notes of Interest
Located in the heart of Beijing, the Central Business District (CBD) has emerged over the past decade as China's primary global business address and is now poised for an eastward expansion that will almost double its size. The CBD Eastern Expansion Plan defines opportunities for the growth of commerce, industry, culture and the arts by establishing a flexible framework for growth and an environmentally sustainable approach to 21st Century city design.

Accommodating up to 7 million square meters of new development over a 3-square-kilometer site, the plan calls for a restored commitment to public open space and a heightened focus on connectivity and mobility through advanced public transportation systems. A district-wide intelligent infrastructure system, composed of integrated utilities and controlled by smart technology, enables the CBD to function at optimum efficiencies and creates a model for large-scale, low-carbon, urban development.

With public open space largely absent in the existing CBD, or at best scattered and disconnected, the plan calls for signature parks as the center of new urban districts. Green boulevards connect the parks to provide a comprehensive open space network.

Landscape Architect: The Office of James Burnett
Owner: Beijing CBD Administrative Committee

Architect
Skidmore, Owings & Merrill LLP

Location
Beijing, China

Photo Credit
© Skidmore, Owings & Merrill LLP

Chicago Central Area DeCarbonization Plan

Jury Comments:
An innovative way of looking at long existing urban fabrics that uses common sense approaches to creatively solve common problems.
Kudos to Chicago for being one of the leading U.S. cities working on climate action.
This ambitious proposal shows how a dense urban area can effectively continue to reduce greenhouse gas emissions and lessen the carbon footprint of its business district.

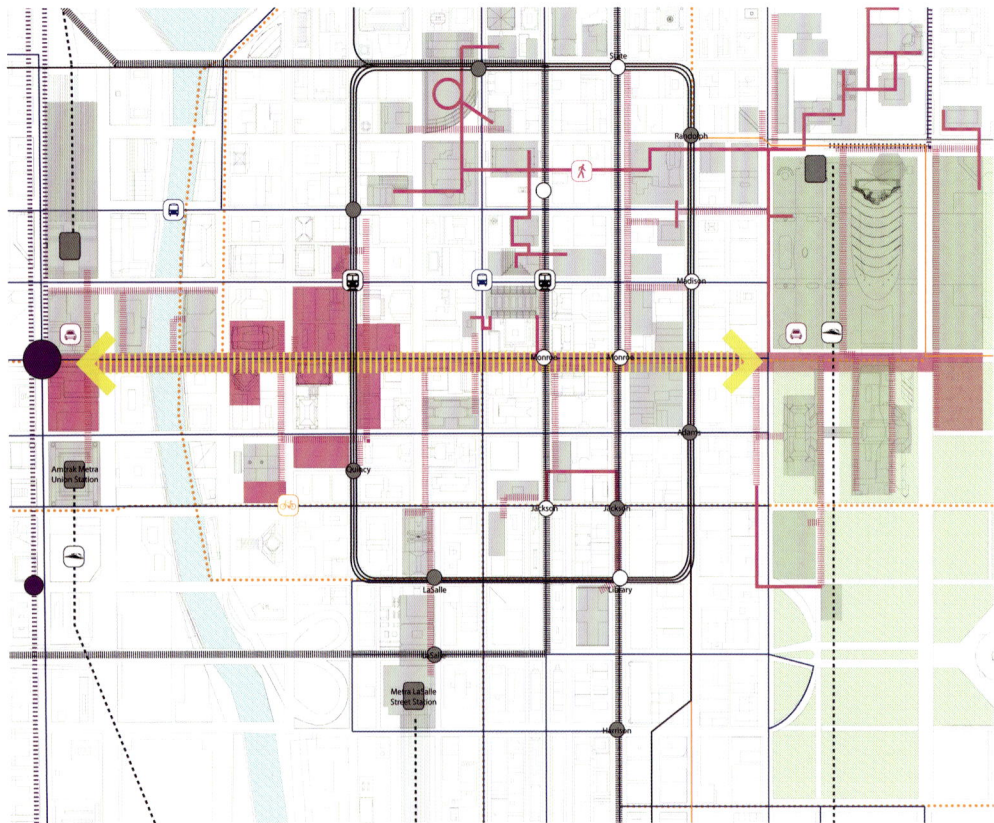

Notes of Interest

The Chicago Central Area DeCarbonization Plan is a comprehensive vision for helping the City of Chicago reach the goals of the Chicago Climate Action Plan and the 2030 Challenge in the downtown Loop. The project team developed a database (energy use, size, age, use, and estimated carbon footprint) of more than 550 buildings. The team used that database, tied to a 3-D model, to develop the DeCarbonization Plan, which interweaves energy engineering, architecture, and urban design.

In the DeCarbonization Plan's synergistic approach, eight key strategies work together with a parametric model. The first strategy, "Buildings", investigates how existing structures can be upgraded to improve efficiency, increase the value of aging building stock and tap into the potential to transfer excess energy back to the grid, all while offsetting the need for new construction. Second is "Urban Matrix", which envisions increasing the residential density of the Loop by enhancing amenities, adding schools and services and converting aging office buildings to residential.

Others strategies include "Smart Infrastructure", a look at how energy can be generated, stored, distributed and shared; "Mobility", assessing DeTransit and connectivity; "Water", examining how this critical resource is used and conserved; "Waste", examining systems for reducing, recycling and disposing of waste; "Community Engagement", involving citizens in the green agenda; and "Energy", an examination of existing and new energy sources.

Consultant: Bryan Cave LLP,
City of Chicago - Mayor's Green Team,
Environmental Systems Design, Inc.
Owner: City of Chicago Department of the Environment

Architect
Adrian Smith + Gordon Gill Architecture

Location
Chicago, Illinois

Photo Credit
© Adrian Smith + Gordon Gill Architecture

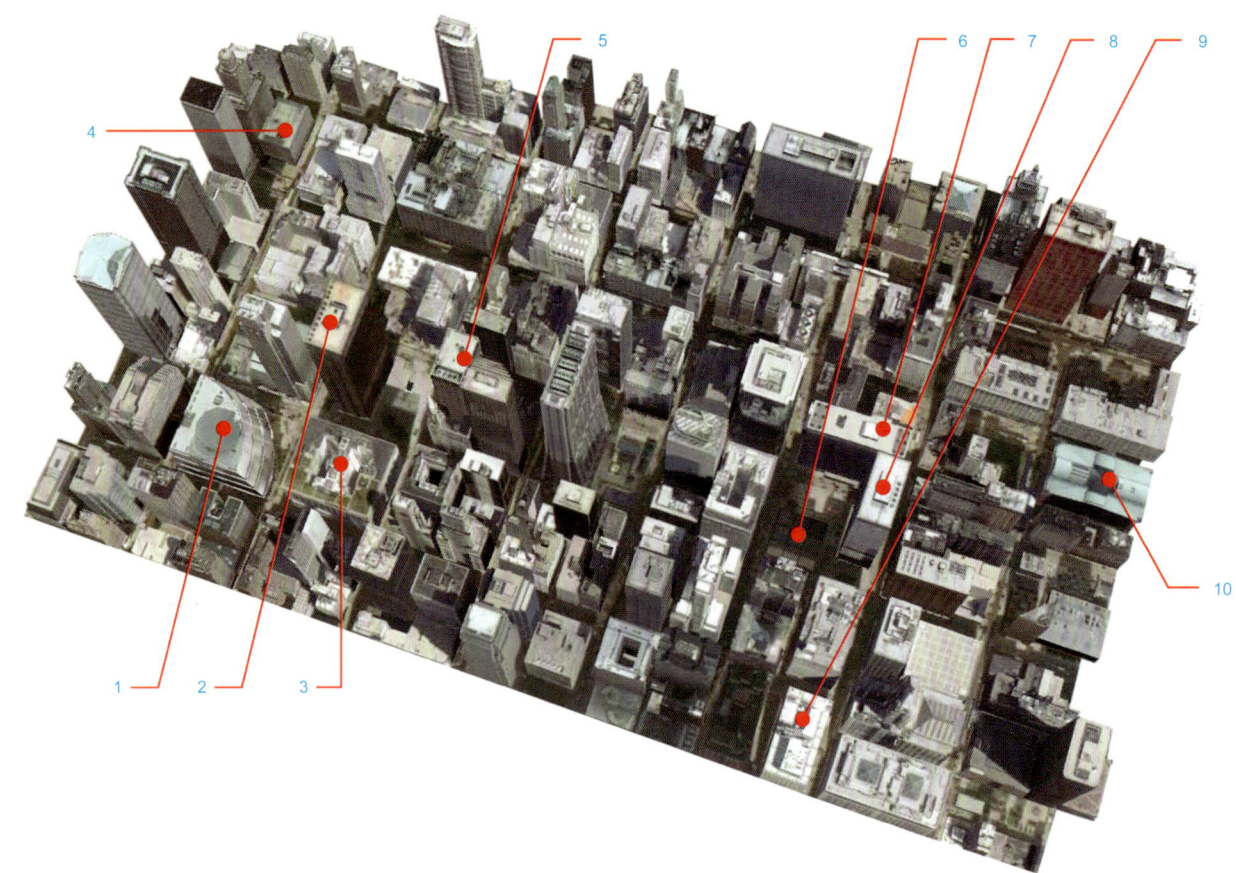

1  **Thompson Center** 100W.Randolph 1985 Helmut Jahn 19 Stories Office/**Retail** 1,557,654GSF	2  **Daley Center** 50W.Washington 1965 Murphy & Naess 32 Stories Office 1,234,848GSF	3  **Daley Center** 48N.Clark 1911 Holabird & Roche 12 Stories Office 1,352,946GSF	4  **Daley Center** 30E.Lake 1962 11 Stories School	
5  **Cook County Admin.** 69W.Washington 1965 Jacques Brownson 35 Stories Office 1,044,938GSF	6  **Fed. Plaza Post Office** 230S.Dearborn 1975 Mies van der Rohe 1 Story Post Office	7  **Federal Plaza Bldg.1** 219S.Dearborn 1969 Mies van der Rohe 39 Stories Office 1,243,980GSF	8  **Federal Plaza Bldg.2** 230S.Dearborn 1975 Mies van der Rohe 45 Stories Office 1,333,800GSF	
9  **Federal Plaza Bldg.** 230S.LaSalle 1922/1960/1986 Graham, A, P& White 14 Stories Office 985,000GSF	10  **H.Washington Library** 400S.State 1991 Hammond, Beeby & Babka 8 Stories Library 756,640GSF			

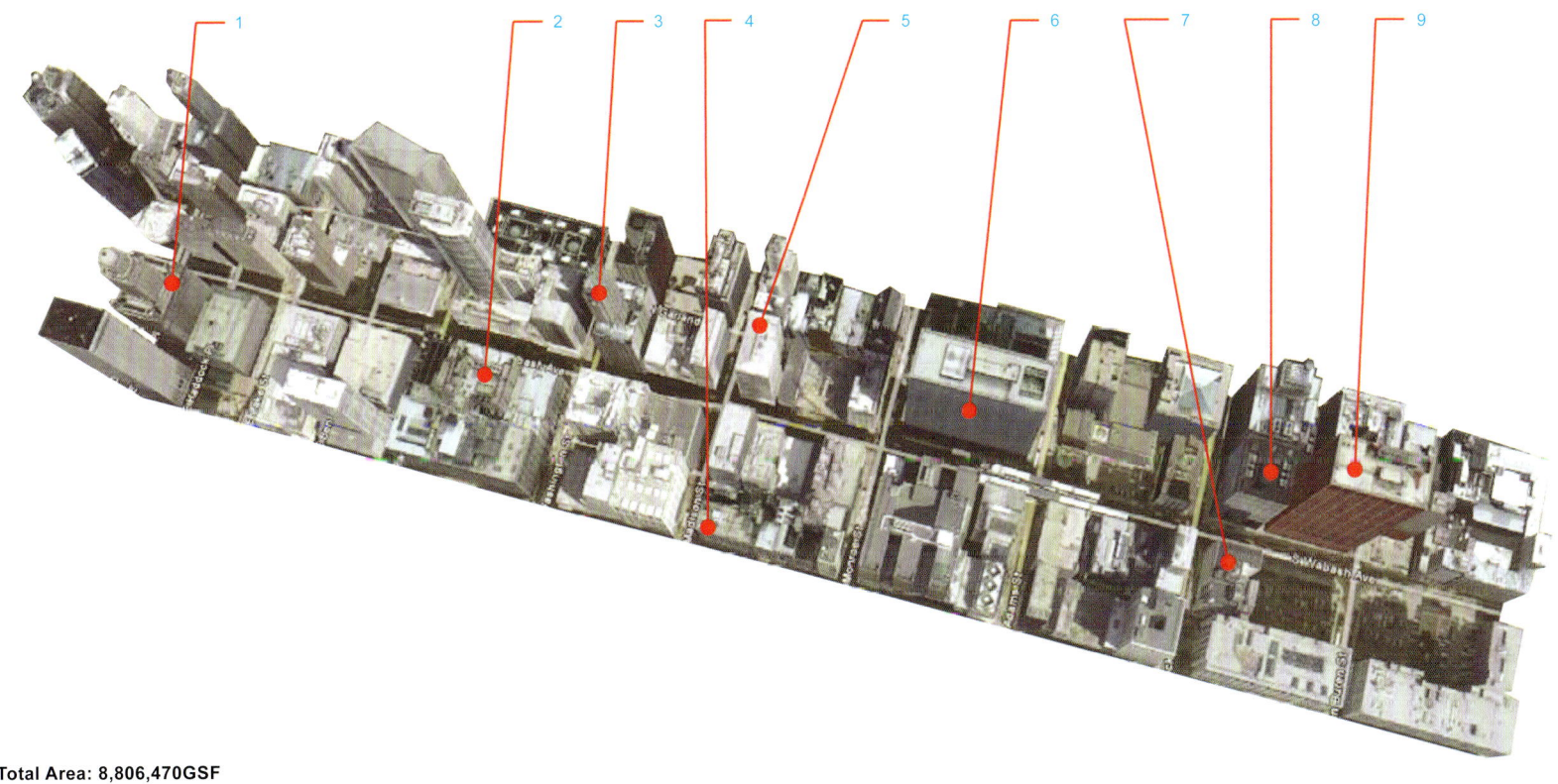

Total Area: 8,806,470GSF

1
Jewelers Building
35E..Wacker
1927
Thielbar & Frugard
40 Stories
Office
966,720GSF

2
Marshall Fields
122N.Wabash
1914
Graham,Burnham&Co.
12 Stories
Department Store
1,600,000GSF

3
Pittsfield Building
55E.Washington
1956-1927
Graham,Anderson,
Probst,and White
38 Stories
Office
515,280GSF

4
Carson Pirie Scott:
5S.Wabash
1899-1961
O'Sullivan,Burnham
12 Stories
Office/Dept.Store
110,640GSF

5
Mallers Building
5S.Wabash
1910
Christian Eckstrom
21 Stories
Office
352,296GSF

6
Mid Continental Plaza
55E.Monroe
1972
Goettsch Parners Inc.
49 Stories
Office
2,899,394GSF

7
DePaul College of Law
25E.Jackson
1917
Graham, Burnham & Co.
16 Stories
School
540,000GSF

8
Carson Pirie Scott:
55E.Jackon
1962
Naess & Murohy
24 Stories
Office
522,140GSF

9
Mallers Building
333S.Wabash
1973
Graham, Anderson,
Probst, and White
44 Stories
Office
1,300,000GSF

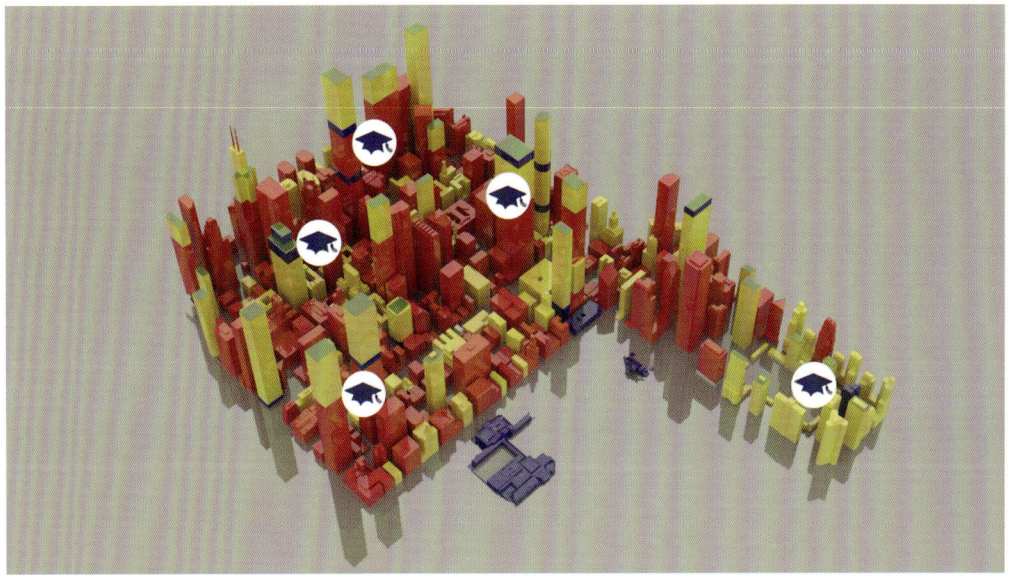

281

"Community | City: Between Building and Landscape Affordable Sustainable Infill for Smoketown, Kentucky"

Jury Comments:
What a thorough analysis of the opportunity for intervention into a typical town that elevates the conversation regarding infill and landscape while respecting history and increasing density. Very applicable to many other places.
This project increases density while sensitively reinforcing the city's historic fabric and reactivates interstitial neighborhood spaces to produce a robust public realm.
The challenges facing Smoketown are found in small and large communities everywhere. Likewise, the plan for Smoketown, with its emphasis on infill development, sustainable landscaping, and sensitivity to cultural and historic components, is a model for communities near and far.

Consultant: Architectural Artisans,
Clarksdale + Smoketown Infill,
K. Norman Berry Associates Architects LLP,
Louis and Henry Group
Project Research: University of Kentucky College of Design, University of Kentucky/University of Louisville Urban Design Center
Research Participants: Bates Memorial Baptist Church/Community Development Corporation,
HOPE VI Development,
The Housing Partnership,
The Kentucky Housing Corporation,
Louisville Metro Housing Authority,
Louisville Metro Parks,
Louisville Metro Planning,
The Olmsted Conservancy,
Smoketown / Shelby Park Residents,
Smoketown Presbyterian Community Center
Owner: City of Chicago Department of the Environment

Notes of Interest
This project remediates existing brownfields and re-activates a long-neglected connection among an historic African American residential neighborhood, an historic Olmsted park, and the Ohio Riverfront. Gaps are filled in an existing neighborhood fabric, increasing density while sensitively reinforcing its historic urban structure. Neighborhood spaces are re-activated to produce a robust public realm.
Full advantage is taken of the project's historic urban location, and its walking-distance proximity to neighborhood amenities. It encourages intense use of the residual spaces between structures as a catalyst, fostering to community identity and a renewed sense of place.

Architect
Marilys R. Nepomechie Architect and
Marta Canaves Interior Design

Location
Smoketown, Kentucky

Photo Credit
© Marta Canaves

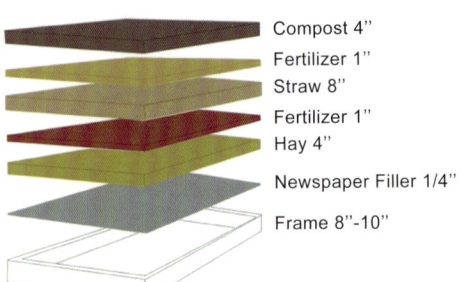

Compost 4"
Fertilizer 1"
Straw 8"
Fertilizer 1"
Hay 4"
Newspaper Filler 1/4"
Frame 8"-10"

LEED ND |

Smart Location and Linkages + Neighborhood Pattern and Design + Green Infrastructure and Buildings

1. Vegetation
2. Growing Medium
3. Drainage, Aeration, Water Storage and Root Barrier
4. Insulation
5. Membrane protection and Root Barrier
6. Roofing Membrane
7. Structural Support

Urban Farming: Roof Terraces

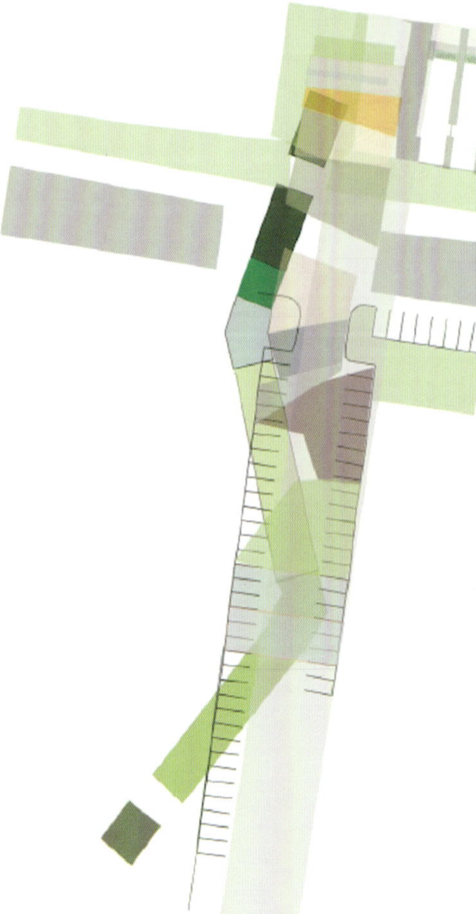

Brownfield Remediation Strategies:
From Parking Lots and Roop Tops to Gardens

Greening Urban Corridors | Re-Connecting to the Riverfront

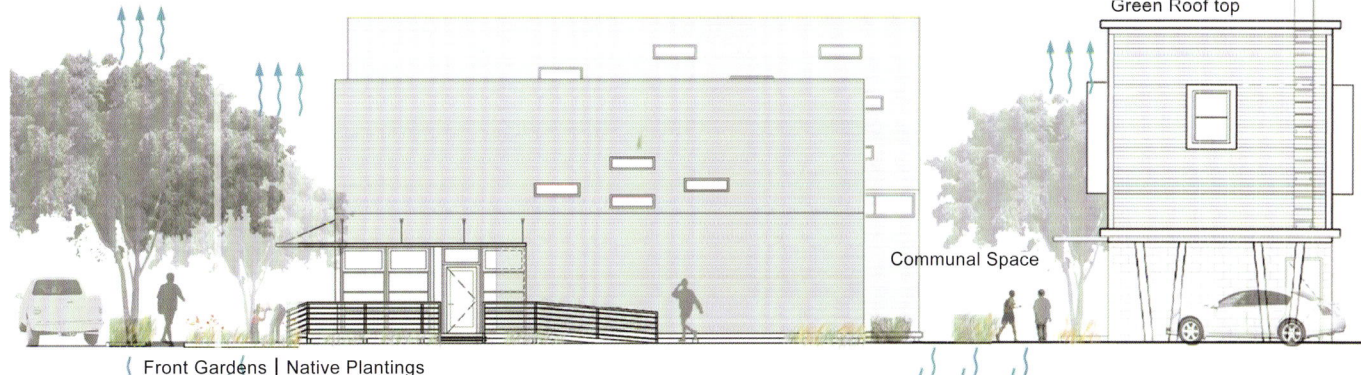

Front Gardens | Native Plantings

Green Roof top

Communal Space

Native Perennials: Little Bluestem; Lobelia; Sea Oats; Butterfly Weed; Copper; Yellow and Blue Iris; Sensitive Fern; Oak leaf Hydrangea
These help to soak up water and filter pollutants that enter with rain water.

LEED ND

Smart location and Linkages + Neighborhood Pattern and Design + Green Infrastructure and Buildings

Permeable Pavers and other Meaterials to:
- Contribute to LEED points
- Capture and treat the first flush
- Reduce runoff by 100% for low intensity storms
- ADA compliant

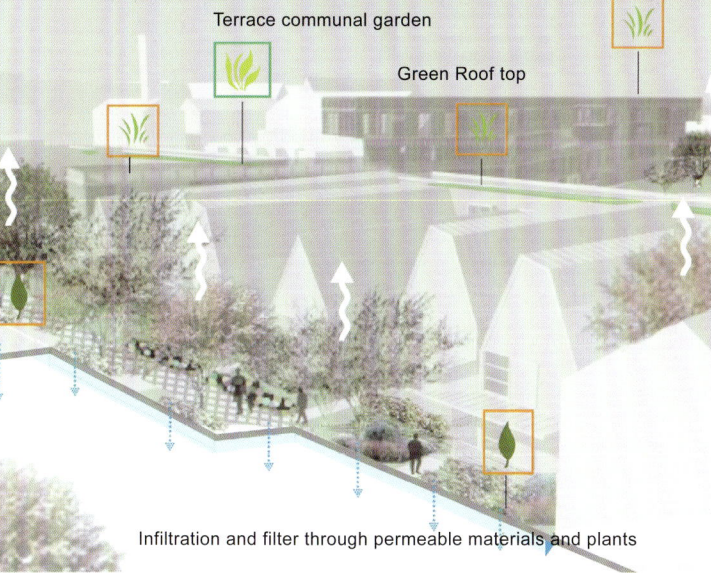

Terrace communal garden

Green Roof top

Infiltration and filter through permeable materials and plants

(RE) BUILDING COMMUNITY:
GREENING the IN-BETWEEN

Community Roof Gardens and Terraces

Gowanus Canal Sponge Park

Jury Comments:
The inspiring approach that can apply to many of our cities' neglected waterfront industrial sites containing a key element in urban transformation and water management.
An inspiring plan that can coexist with its industrial neighbors while redefining the word industrial and waterfront at the same time.
This project addresses a common problem in older cities with a striking way to create valuable urban open spaces as a byproduct.

Notes of Interest

The Gowanus Canal Sponge Park™ is a public open space system that slows, absorbs and filters surface water runoff with the goal of remediating contaminated water, activating the private canal waterfront, and revitalizing the neighborhood. The total proposed area for the Gowanus Canal Sponge Park™ system is 11.4 acres: 7.9 acres of esplanade and recreational open spaces, and 3.5 acres of remediation wetland basins.

The most unique feature of the park is its character as a working landscape: its ability to improve the environment of the canal over time while simultaneously supporting public engagement with the canal ecosystem. New York City has a combined sewer system. Rain that falls within the Gowanus watershed enters the storm drains and mixes with raw sewage in the sanitary sewer system. In a heavy rainfall, the combined sewage and storm water overflow directly into the Gowanus Canal.

The innovative Sponge Park™ plan proposes diverting surface water runoff into a water management system. The storm water management system activates the corridors leading from the adjacent neighborhoods to the park esplanade, while preventing further contamination of the canal. The parks incorporate vegetated landscape buffers to slow, percolate and filter the contaminated water, reducing the input of stormwater into the sewer system while integrating programmed urban outdoor space to create an accessible waterfront.

Funding: The Gowanus Canal Conservancy, The New England Interstate Water Pollution Control Commission, The New York State Council on the Arts
Owner: City of New York, Department of Environmental Protection

Architect
dlandstudio LLC

Location
New York City, New York

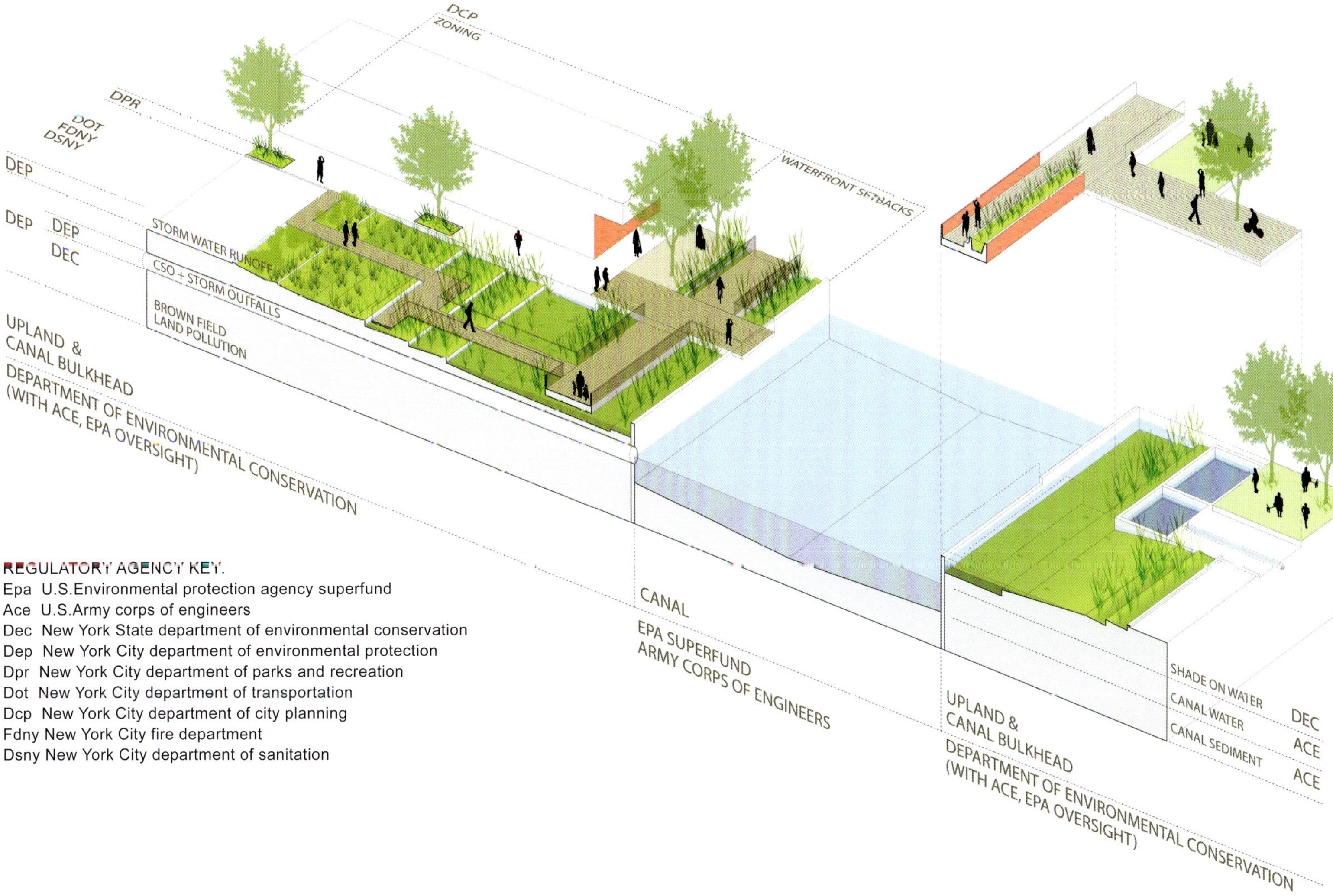

REGULATORY AGENCY KEY:
- Epa U.S. Environmental protection agency superfund
- Ace U.S. Army corps of engineers
- Dec New York State department of environmental conservation
- Dep New York City department of environmental protection
- Dpr New York City department of parks and recreation
- Dot New York City department of transportation
- Dcp New York City department of city planning
- Fdny New York City fire department
- Dsny New York City department of sanitation

A. Water Remediation Wetlands
B. Active Recreation Open space
C. Park and Community Center
D. Public place Proposed Mixed-use Development
F. Passive Recreation Open space
G. Mta f g line Smith-9th st Station
H. Connection To byrne park
I. Byrne park The old stone house Historical site
J. Mta f&g line Bridge
K. Douglass green park
l. Revolutionary war Monument
M. Renovated Power plant
N. Cultural Open space

- Open space
- Pavilion
- Esplanade
- Street end sponge park
- Boat launch
- Water remediation basin

291

"Low Impact Development: A Design Manual for Urban Areas"

Jury Comments:
What a useful, easy-to-understand tool, not only for architects, but also for community leaders and citizens working to ensure environmentally sustainable development. A very clear manual that should become the primer for creating beautiful and sustainable public streets and spaces. Urban design at a scale that architects can grasp and incorporate into their own projects. It is a project both specifically technical and inspiring all at the same time.

Notes of Interest

"Low Impact Development: a design manual for urban areas" is a 230-page publication designed for use by those involved in urban development-from homeowners, to institutions, developers, designers, cities, and regional authorities. Low Impact Development (LID) is an ecologically-based stormwater management approach favoring soft engineering to manage rainfall on site through a vegetated treatment network. The objective is to sustain a site's pre-development hydrological regime by using techniques that infiltrate, filter, store, and evaporate stormwater runoff close to its source.

The manual presents a graphic argument, using urban design templates and scenarios to illustrate the role of LID technology in regional planning and infrastructural design. It is the first to devise a LID Facilities Menu of the 21 assemblages available, organized from mechanical to biological functioning, and based on increasing level of treatment service (quality) and level of volume reduction service (quantity).

The manual's unique contribution to the topic lies in its advancement of LID from a set of Best Management Practices to a highly distributed treatment network deployed at neighborhood, municipal, and regional scales. It shifts LID from an isolated technology to a planning model based on nestled pattern languages in making places. The goals are to promote implementation of LID technologies in urban areas through adoption of best practices in planning and design, and encourage reform in municipal codes.

Engineer: University of Arkansas Ecological Engineering Group
Funding: The Arkansas Natural Resources Commission (ANRC) through a grant from the United States Environmental Protection Agency (USEPA) Region 6 Section 319(h)
Publication: Made possible by generous support from:
Arkansas Forestry Commission's Urban,
Forestry Program and US Forest Service Beaver Water District,
Community Foundation of the Ozarks and Stewardship Ozarks Initiative,
Ozarks Water Watch with Upper White River Basin Foundation,
National Center for Appropriate Technology Southeast Field Office: Fayetteville, Arkansas,
US Green Building Council Western Branch Arkansas Chapter: Northwest Arkansas,
Illinois River Watershed Partnership

Architect
University of Arkansas Community Design Center

Location
Fayetteville, Arkansas

Photo Credit
© University of Arkansas Community Design Center

LID IS SCALABLE TO BUILDING, PROPERTY, STREET, AND OPEN SPACE SYSTEMS.

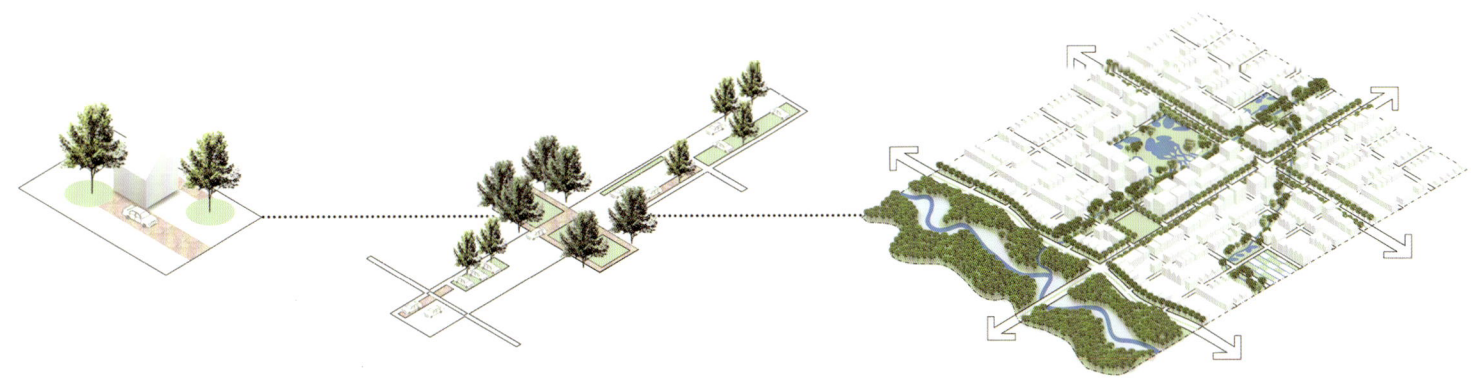

Lots: LID lots infiltrate stormwater through reduction or elimination of impervious surfaces and replacement of turf grass with productive landscapes.

Streets: LID streets are green streets reducing and filtering runoff as it enters public space while enhancing the quality of place.

Networks: LID networks contain treatment facilities connected to regionally scaled systems of stormwater management.

4 underground detention

Optimal level of service:
Detention/infiltration

Location in LID network:
Optimally placed after filtration facilities
To prevent excessive sedimentation

Scale:
Maximum watershed runoff area is 25 acres

Management regime:
Inspection and sediment cleanout

1. Parking
2. Inlet drain
3. Detention cell
4. Outlet pipe

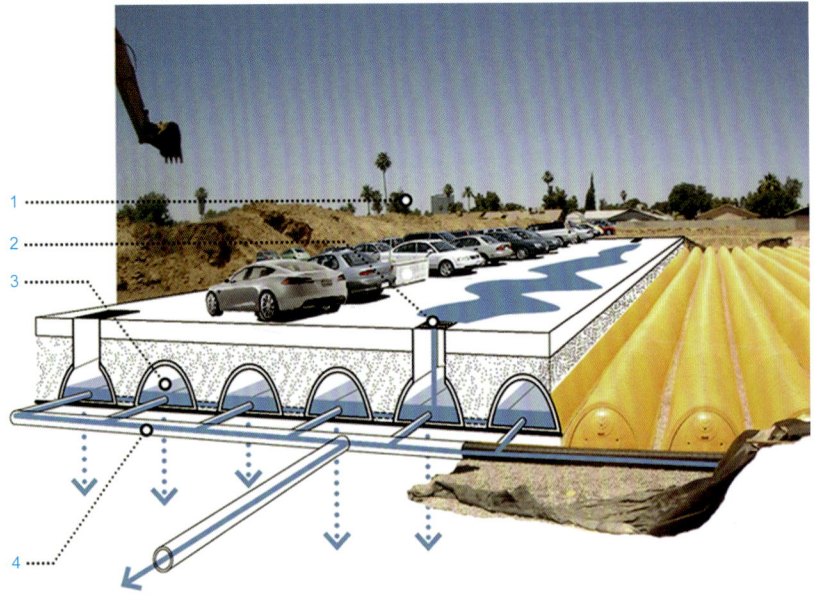

UNDERGROUND DETENTION

Underground detention systems detain stormwater runoff prior to its entrance into a conveyance system.
Underground storage systems store and slowly release runoff into the LID network. Some Systems can infiltrate stormwater if the soil beneath is permeable. Underground storage is employed in places where available surface area for ongrade storage is limited.
Underground storage reduces peak flow rate through metered discharge and has potential for infiltration. Improved water quality is achieved by sedimentation, or the setting of suspended solids. Though at first costly, underground detention systems are easy to access and maintain.

REFERENCES:
Low Impact Development Manual for Michigan
Urban Design Tools – Low Impact Development
Minnesota Urban Small Sites BMP Manual

LID NETWORKS OFFER THE FULL RANGE OF ECOSYSTEM SERVICES

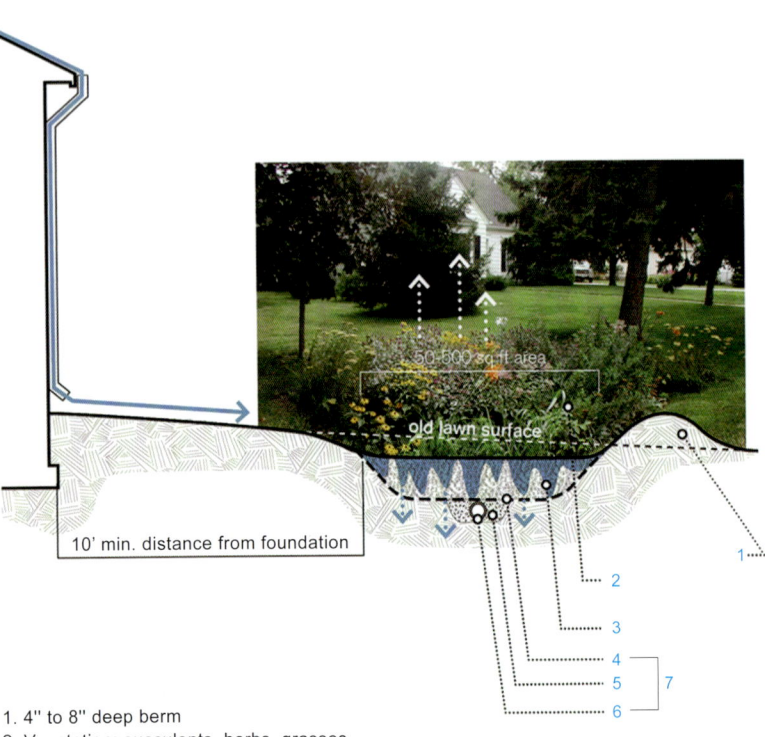

1. 4" to 8" deep berm
2. Vegetation: succulents, herbs, grasses
3. Amended soil mix
4. Filter fabric
5. 3/4" gravel base
6. Perforated underdrain
7. Overflow system for poorly-drained soils or large storm events

REFERENCES:
Low Impact Development Design Strategies – An Integrated Design Approach
Low Impact Development Manual for Michigan
Low Impact Development Technical Guidance Manual for Puget Sound
United States Department of Housing and Urban Development
Minnesota Urban Small Sites BMP Manual

Zone 3: **Runoff Control** – Consists of perennial grasses, with herbaceous and woody vegetation that slow runoff and absorb most contaminants
Zone 2: **Managed Forest** – Consists of slow-growing trees and shrubs that provide wildlife habitat, and mitigate remaining contaminants from zone 3
Zone 1: **Undisturbed Forest** – streamside zone consists of fast-growing, flood-tolerant trees and reedy plants that stabilize banks and cool water through shading

REFERENCES:
Low Impact Development Manual for Michigan
Conservation Buffers: Design Guidelines for Buffers, Corridors, and Greenways

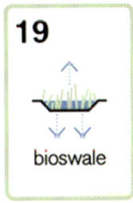

19 bioswale

Optimal level of service:
Filtration/infiltration/treatment

Location in LID network:
Downstream of filtration components, But upstream of larger detention, Retention, or treatment facilities

Scale:
2'-8' wide with 2"-4" optimal water depth

Management regime:
Occasional removal of trash and pruning of vegetation

1. Vegetation: succulents, herbs, grasses
2. Mulch layer, 2"-3" with 1: 3 slope or less
3. Overflow grate
4. Amended soil mix: typically 45% sand, 35% top soil, and 20% compost
5. Filter fabric
6. 3/4" gravel base
7. Perforated underdrain
8. overflow system for poorly-drained soils or large storm events

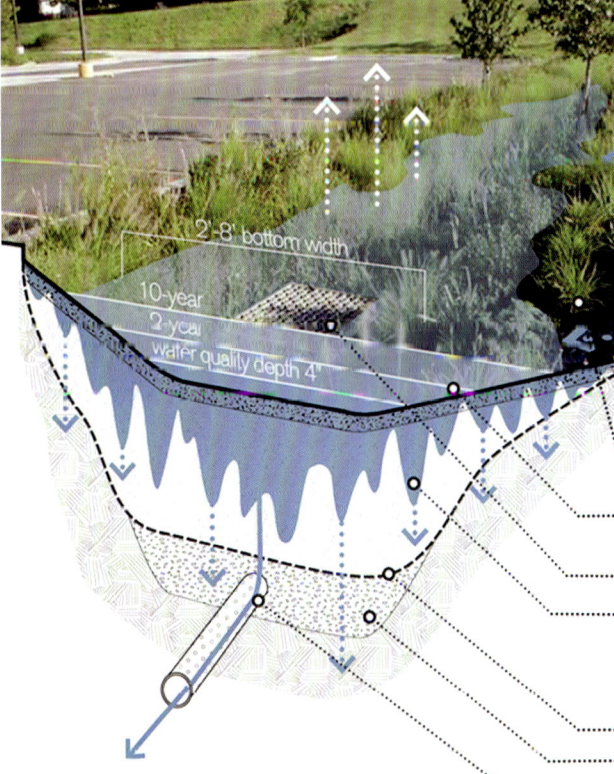

BIOSWALE

A bioswale is an open, gently sloped, vegetated channel designed for treatment and conveyance of stormwater runoff. Bioswales are a bioretention device in which pollutant mitigation occurs through Phytoremediation by facultative vegetation. Bioswales combine treatment and Conveyance services, reducing land development costs by eliminating the need. For costly conventional conveyance systems. The main function of a rain garden is to treat stormwater runoff as it is infiltrated. Bioswales are usually located along roads, drives, or parking lots where the contributing acreage is less than five acres.
Bioswales require curb cuts, gutters or other devices that direct flow to them. They may require an underdrain where soil permeability is limited, as well as an overflow grate for larger storm events.

REFERENCES:
Low Impact Development Design Strategies – An Integrated Design Approach
Low Impact Development Manual for Michigan
Low Impact Development Technical Guidance Manual for Puget Sound
Unite States Department of Housing and Urban Development
Minnesota Urban Small Sites BMP Manual

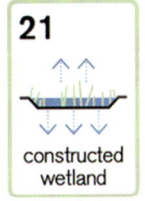

21 constructed wetland

Optimal level of service:
Retention/filtration/infiltration/treatment

Location in LID network:
End-of-line facility, upstream of overflow basins or receiving water bodies

Scale:
From pocket wetlands managing up to 10 acres of drainage to shallow marshes managing more than 25 acres of drainage

Management regime:
System requires removal of trash and sediment between two and ten years, and semiannually during first three years

1. Treatment zone
2. Sedimentation zone
3. Facultative vegetation
4. 12" native topsoil
5. Filter fabric
6. Water table

CONSTRUCTED WETLAND

Constructed wetlands are artificial marshes or swamps with permanent standing water that offer a full range of ecosystem services to treat polluted stormwater.
Considered to be a comprehensive treatment system, constructed wetlands, like infiltration basins, require intrinsic hydrogeologic properties to reproduce natural watershed functioning. As with other infiltration system, resulting in eutrophication or an oxygen deprived system.
Constructed wetlands are land rich biofilters and differ from retention ponds in their shallower depths, greater vegetation coverage, and extensive wildlife habitat. They require relatively large contributing drainage areas to maintain a shallow permanent pool. Minimum contributing drainage area should be at least 10 acres, although pocket wetlands may be appropriate for smaller sites if sufficient water flow is available.

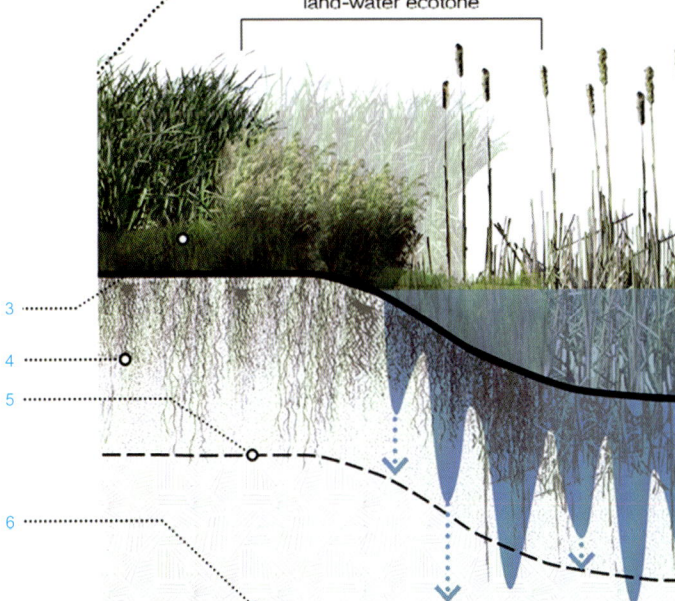

REFERENCES:
Low Impact Development Manual for Michigan
United States Department of Housing and Urban Development
Minnesota Urban Small BMP Manual

THE CITY AS A NATURAL STORMWATER UTILITY

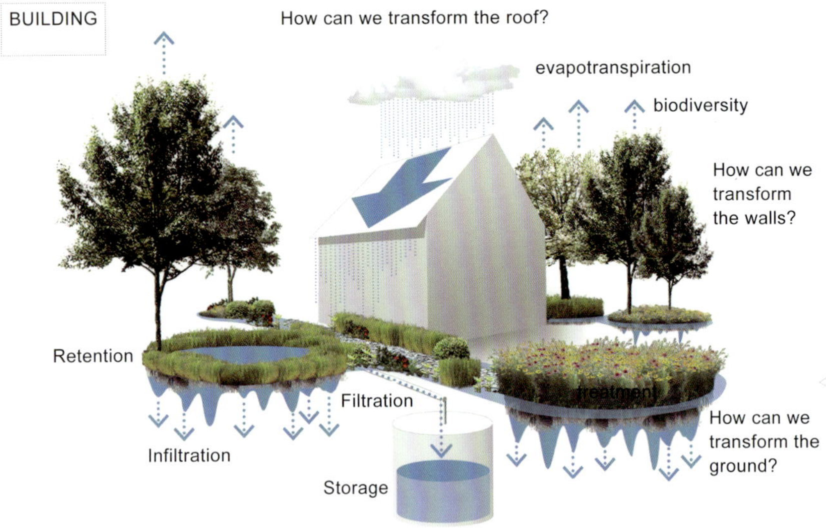

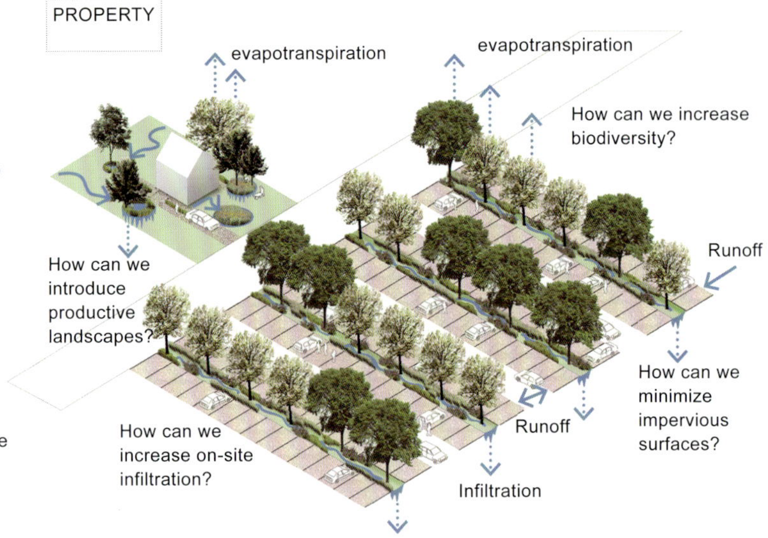

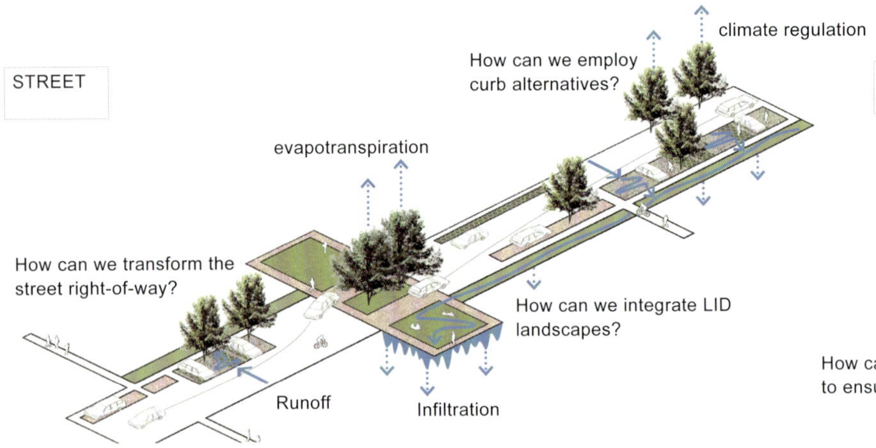

BUILDING — How can we transform the roof?
- evapotranspiration
- biodiversity
- How can we transform the walls?
- How can we transform the ground?
- Retention
- Infiltration
- Filtration
- Storage
- Treatment

PROPERTY
- evapotranspiration
- How can we increase biodiversity?
- How can we introduce productive landscapes?
- How can we increase on-site infiltration?
- Runoff
- Infiltration
- How can we minimize impervious surfaces?

STREET
- How can we transform the street right-of-way?
- evapotranspiration
- climate regulation
- How can we employ curb alternatives?
- How can we integrate LID landscapes?
- Runoff
- Infiltration

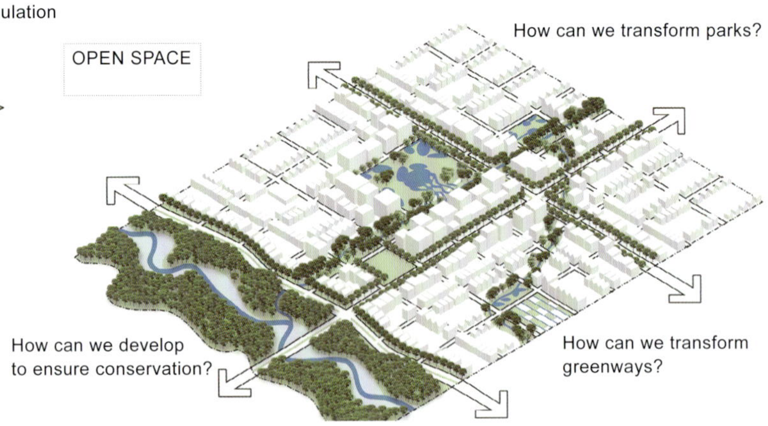

OPEN SPACE
- How can we transform parks?
- How can we develop to ensure conservation?
- How can we transform greenways?

HARD ENGINEERING VS. SOFT ENGINEERING

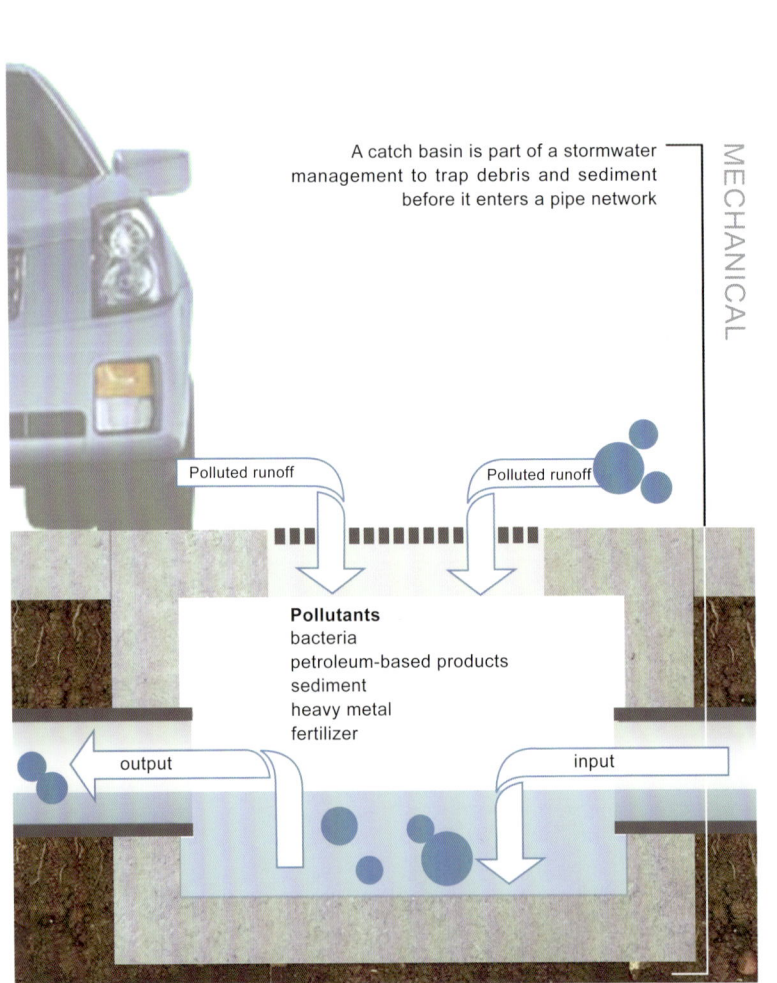

MECHANICAL

A catch basin is part of a stormwater management to trap debris and sediment before it enters a pipe network

Polluted runoff

Pollutants
- bacteria
- petroleum-based products
- sediment
- heavy metal
- fertilizer

output — input

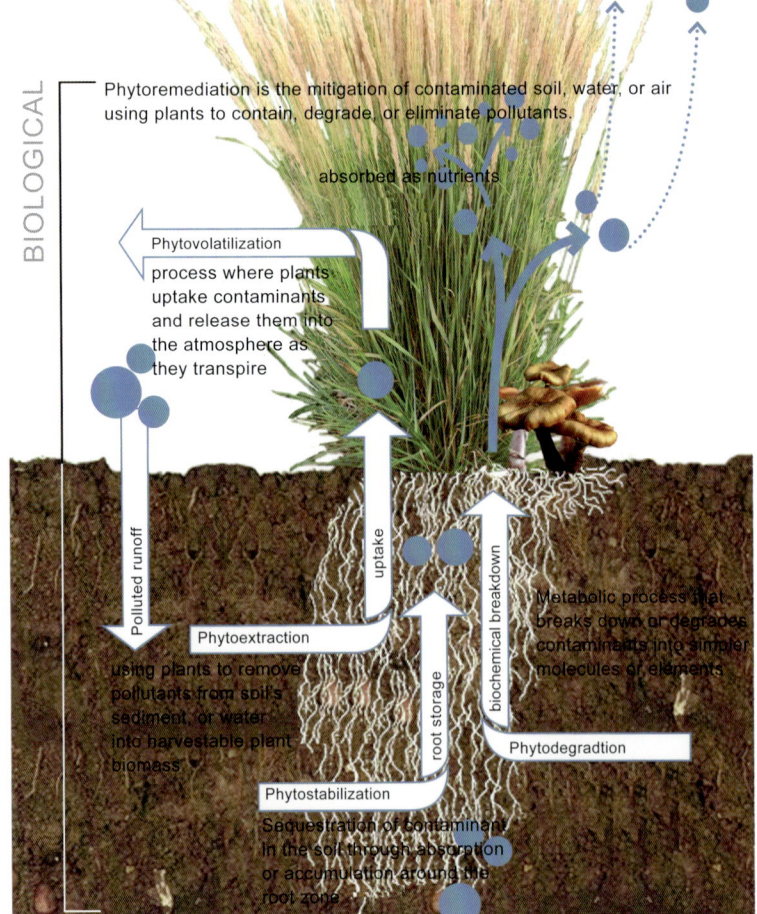

BIOLOGICAL

Phytoremediation is the mitigation of contaminated soil, water, or air using plants to contain, degrade, or eliminate pollutants.

absorbed as nutrients

Phytovolatilization — process where plants uptake contaminants and release them into the atmosphere as they transpire

Polluted runoff — uptake — biochemical breakdown

Phytoextraction — using plants to remove pollutants from soil, sediment, or water into harvestable plant biomass

root storage

Metabolic process that breaks down or degrades contaminants into simpler molecules or elements

Phytodegradtion

Phytostabilization — Sequestration of contaminants in the soil through absorption or accumulation around the root zone

THE SIX WATER TREATMENT TECHNOLOGIES

Mechanical — Biological

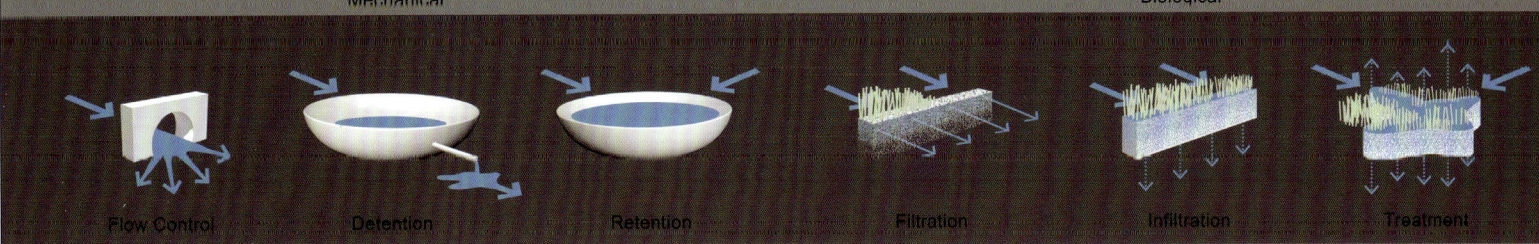

Flow Control — Detention — Retention — Filtration — Infiltration — Treatment

SLOW ———————————————→ SPREAD ———————————————→ SOAK

flow control: The regulation of Stormwater runoff flow rates.

detention: The temporary storage of stormwater runoff in underground areas to allow for metered discharge that reduce peak flow rates.

retention: The storage of stormwater runoff on site to allow for sedimentation of suspended solids.

filtration: The sequestration of sediment from stormwater runoff through a porous media such as sand, a fibrous root system, or a man-made filter.

infiltration: The vertical movement of stormwater runoff through soil recharging groundwater.

treatment: Processes that utilize phytoremediation or bacterial colonies to metabolize contaminants in stormwater Runoff.

THE 21 LID FACILITIES

1. Oversized pipes
2. Flow control devices
3. Dry swale
4. Underground detention
5. Detention pond
6. Wet vault
7. Rainwater harvesting
8. Retention pond
9. Filter strip
10. Underground sand filter
11. Surface sand filter
12. Vegetated wall
13. Vegetated roof
14. Pervious paving
15. Infiltration trench
16. Tree box filter
17. Rain garden
18. Riparian buffer
19. Bioswale
20. Infiltration basin
21. Constructed wetland

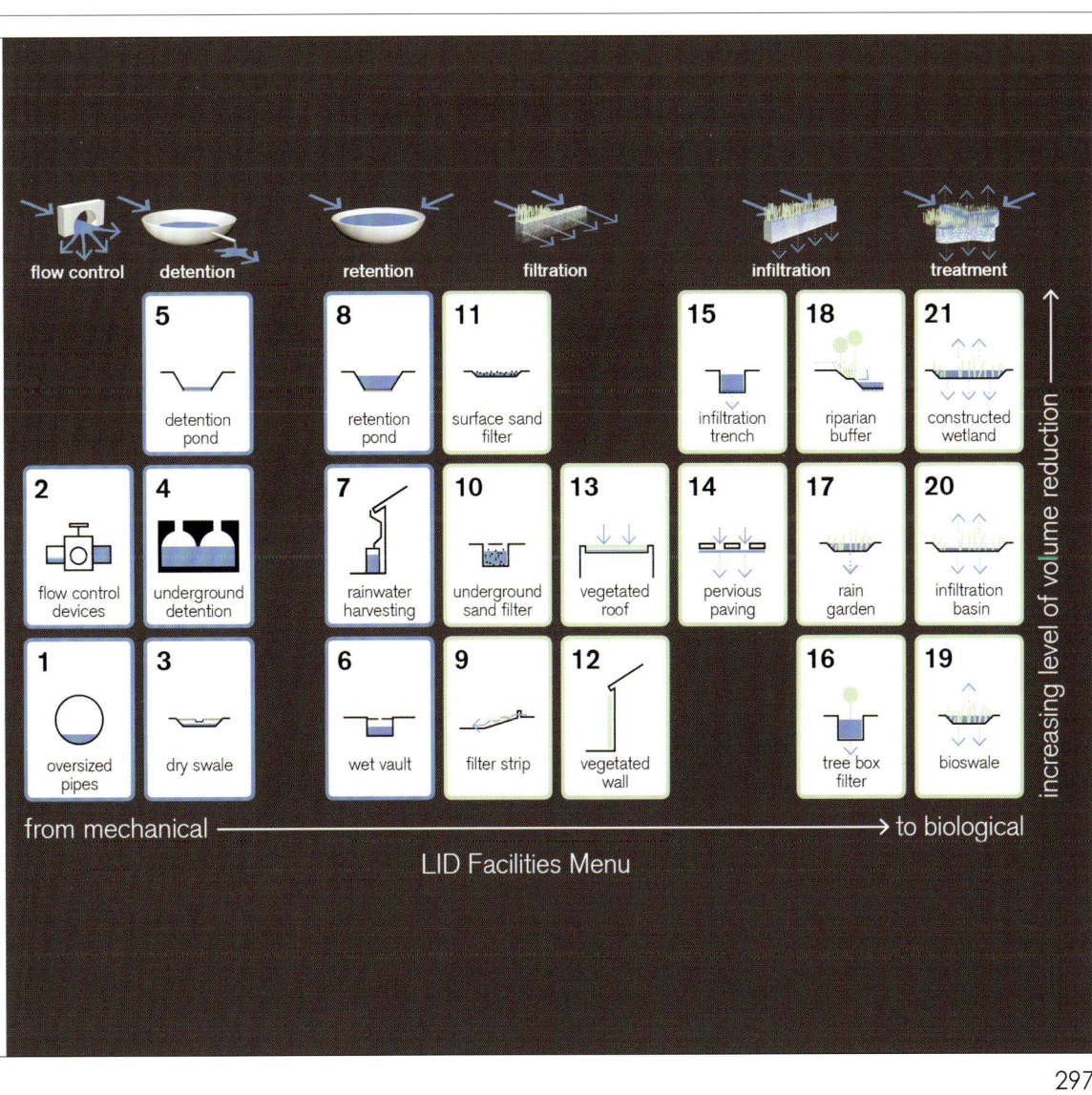

LID Facilities Menu — from mechanical → to biological — increasing level of volume reduction

Townscaping an Automobile-Oriented Fabric

Jury Comments:
There is much that we can learn from smaller communities, and "townscaping" is a creative example of what a small, long-established community can do to transform its 20th century roadway system into a 21st-century amenity. An urban design approach that is both design driven and community oriented simultaneously. This plan proves that a place laid out originally for cars can be adapted to a future where people are connected in other ways. A beautiful model for greening and organizing small town USA.

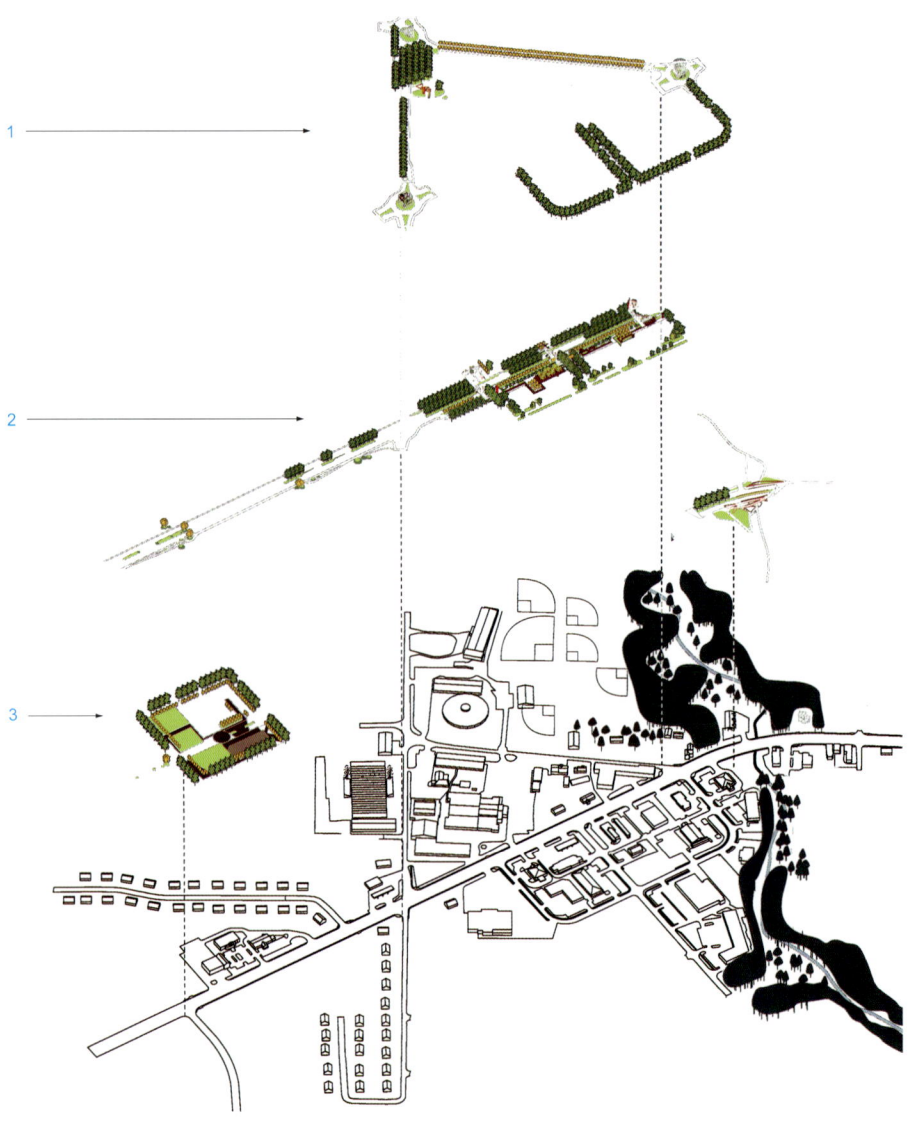

1. STEP3: Accentuate with landmarks
2. STEP2: Frame with landscape and new street geometries
3. STEP1: Bound with gateways

Notes of Interest

The townscape plan for Farmington proposes new public landscapes to restitch a 5,000-person bedroom community fragmented by a five-lane commercial arterial. Once a vibrant farming community, central to one of the nation's largest strawberry and apple-producing regions in the early 1900s, Farmington is now a bedroom community. Unlike the totalizing pattern of a master plan, townscaping employs a serial organization of nodes to create a walkable urban environment within an automobile-oriented fabric.

As a retrofit planning strategy, townscaping offers a model for an incremental urbanization without reliance on capital-intensive architectural investments. The goal is to create a memorable town fabric for anchoring new growth in an otherwise

Funding: The National Endowment for the Arts 2010 Grant Award for Access to Artistic Excellence
Owner: City of Farmington

Architect
University of Arkansas Community Design Center

Location
Farmington, Arkansas

Photo Credit
© University of Arkansas Community Design Center

1. Farmers market
2. Town green
3. Hard fruit trees
4. Espalier
5. Hard fruit trees
6. Soft fruit trees
7. Soft fruit orchard
8. Air filtration
9. Hard fruit allee
10. Soft fruit allee
11. Arboretum
12. Pedestrian
13. Arcade
14. Roosting Tower
15. Foraging riparian
16. Viticetum Gateway

fragmented and anonymous landscape. Working within the context of Farmington's limited resources, townscaping creates "articulated environments" through sleuth planning techniques.

Beginning with the ordinary components commonly budgeted in urban infrastructure, the townscape plan condenses these elements into a series of nodes that galvanize a sense of place. The townscape plan for Farmington integrates multiple placemaking strategies in: 1) context-sensitive highway design, 2) public art planning, and 3) agricultural urbanism. Placemaking in the townscape vocabulary offers a strategic pedestrianization of automobile-oriented patterns without denying the automobile's fundamental role in servicing contemporary development.

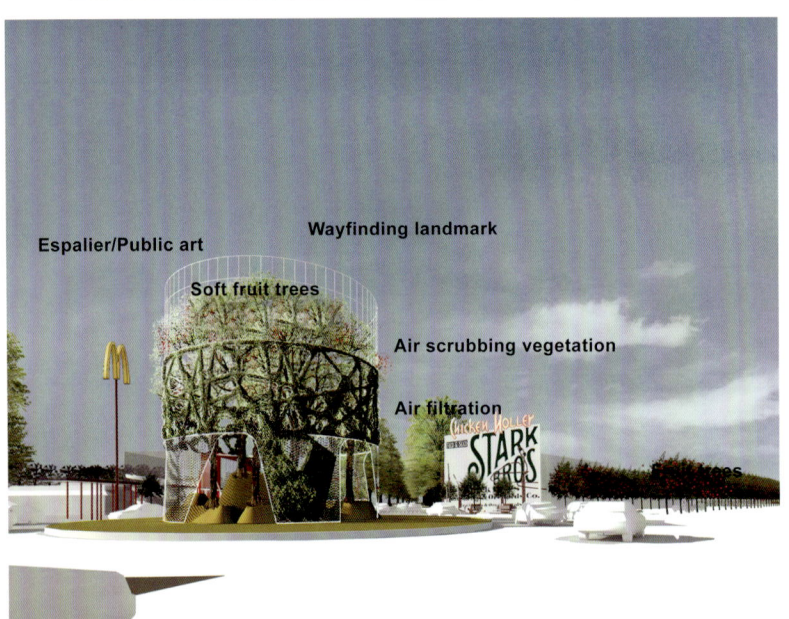
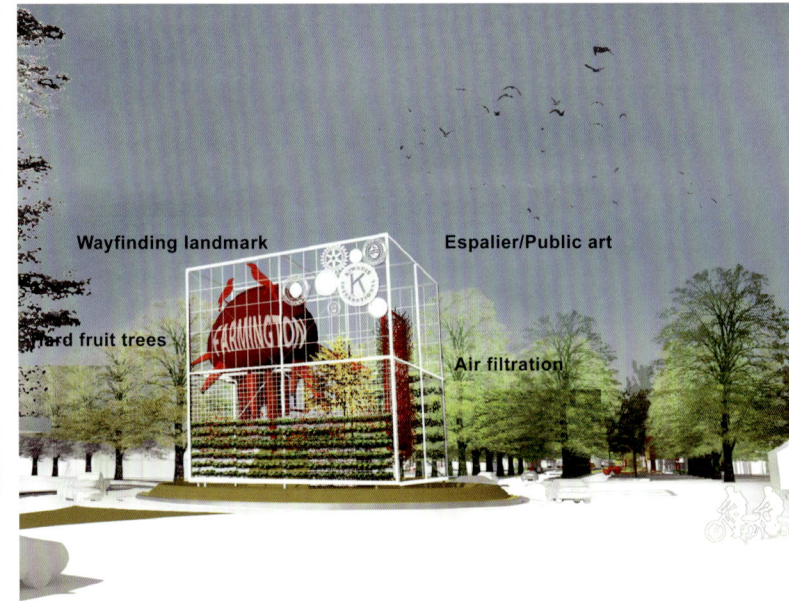

NEW MULTI-WAY BOULEVARD AND PEDESTRIAN INTERFACE

The new multi-way boulevard can accommodate existing land uses while incentiving new urban mixed-use development.

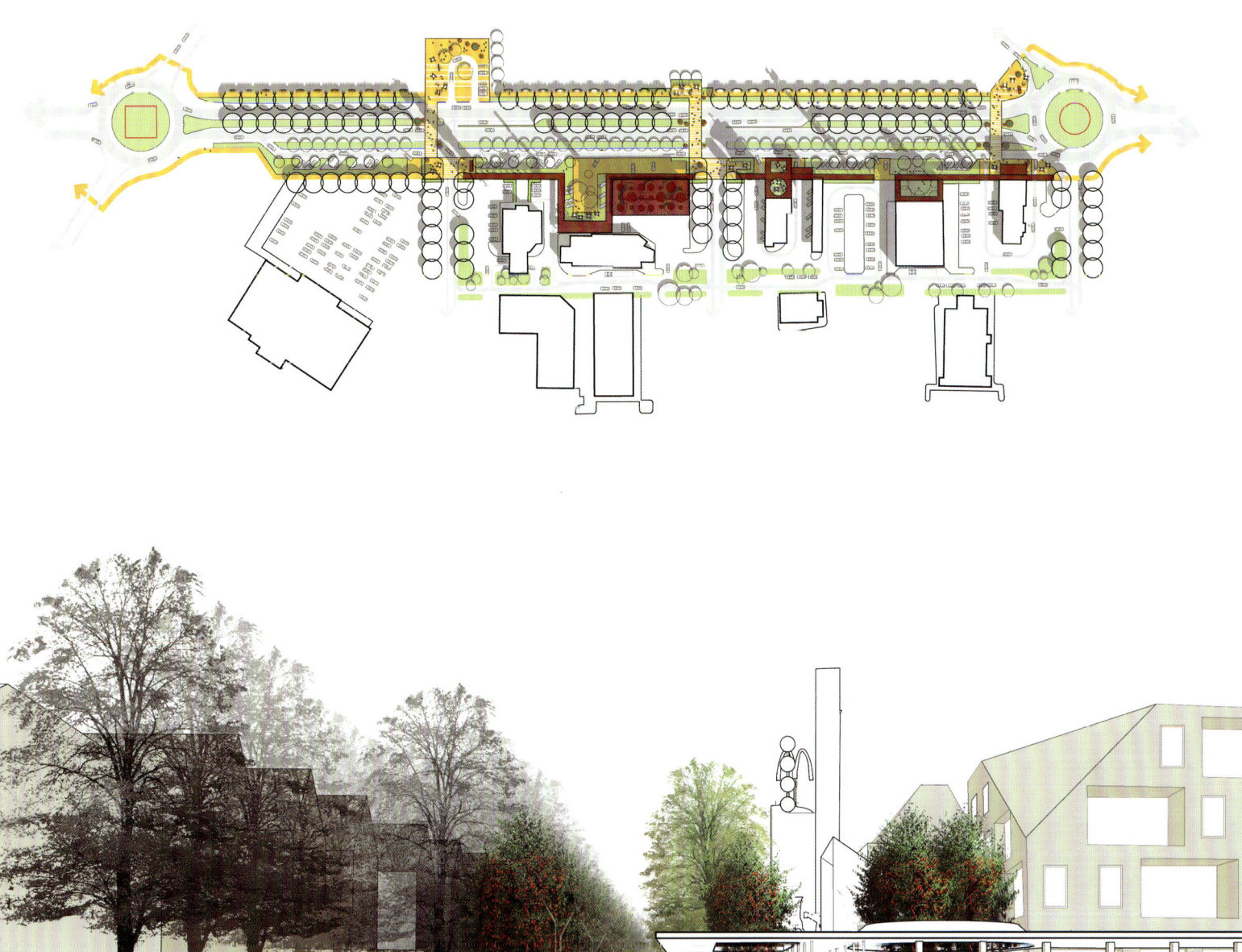

John Hancock Tower

Notes of Interest

The John Hancock Tower is an office building commissioned by the John Hancock Mutual Life Insurance Company principally for its own use, with a few floors occupied by other tenants. The building contains a gross floor area of 2,060,000 square feet on sixty-two floors above grade and two below. The architect was I. M. Pei & Partners (now Pei Cobb Freed & Partners), with Henry N. Cobb, FAIA, as design partner. Construction was completed in 1976.

The site's adjacent architectural landmarks – in particular Trinity Church and the Boston Public Library – were what made Cobb's mission exceptionally difficult. It became apparent that it would be a great challenge to adhere to the firm's trademark rationalism and insert such a tall building into the site without fatally rupturing Copley Square's sense of scale and proportion.

The solution was single-minded and rested in the minimalism of the design: a smooth, reflective, glass tower with no spandrel panels and minimal mullions – essentially a very large mirror. To minimize its intrusion on the adjacent landscape, the building is rhomboid in shape and placed diagonally on the site, so its shorter, slightest side faces the church and plaza.

The John Hancock Tower recently achieved LEED Gold Existing Building certification for energy use, lighting, water, and material use as well as a variety of other sustainable strategies. Some of these involve equipment upgrades, while others were integral to the original design. For example, the building's glass façade and narrow floor plate allow natural light to reach 86 percent of all work areas.

In awarding it the 1983 Harleston Parker Medal, the Boston Society of Architects jury unanimously agreed that the John Hancock Tower met its criterion: to be the city's "most beautiful piece of architecture". Paul Goldberger, Hon. AIA, architecture critic for the The New Yorker, went even further when he wrote recently, "the John Hancock Tower remains one of the most beautiful skyscrapers ever built."

Architect
I.M. Pei & Partners (now Pei Cobb Freed & Partners)

Location
Boston

Photo Credit
© Gorchev & Gorchev; Peter Vanderwarker (Detail)

2012 INSTITUTE HONOR AWARDS FOR ARCHITECTURE JURY

Rod Kruse, FAIA, Chair
BNIM Architects

Barbara White Bryson, FAIA
Rice University

Annie Chu, AIA
Chu & Gooding Architects

Dima Daimi, Assoc. AIA
Rossetti

Harry J. Hunderman, FAIA
Wiss, Janney, Elstner Associates, Inc.

Scott Lindenau, FAIA
Studio B Architects

Kirsten R. Murray, AIA
Olson Kundig Architects

Thomas M. Phifer, FAIA
Thomas Phifer & Partners

Seth H. Wentz, AIA
LSC Design, Inc.

2012 Institute Honor Awards

2012 INSTITUTE HONOR AWARDS FOR INTERIOR ARCHITECTURE JURY

Elizabeth Corbin Murphy,
FAIA, Chair
CMB Architects

Robert Allen, Jr., AIA
Metalhouse

Mark Jensen, AIA
Jensen Architects

David Lenox, AIA
University Architect/Dir. Campus Planning
Stanford University

Erick S. Ragni, AIA
MaRS Architects

2012 INSTITUTE HONOR AWARDS FOR REGIONAL AND URBAN DESIGN JURY

Bruce Lindsey, AIA, Chair
Washington University in St. Louis

Catherine Seavitt Nordenson, AIA
Catherine Seavitt Studio

Martha Welborne, FAIA
Los Angeles County Metropolitan Transportation Authority

Rod Kruse, FAIA, LEED AP
2012 Chair,
Institute Honor Awards for Architecture

Elizabeth Corbin Murphy, FAIA
2012 Chair,
Institute Honor Awards for Interior Architecture

© Mary S. Watkins

© Studio Martone

Rod Kruse, Principal | BNIM has built a reputation as one of the Central States Region's strongest design talents. He has gained recognition on national, regional and local levels for his projects, including a 2002 National AIA Award for Design Excellence for Architecture for the Newton Road Parking and Chilled Water Facility at the University of Iowa and a 2000 National AIA Award for Design Excellence for Architecture for the Center Street Park and Ride Facility. In the role of Principal, he is uniquely honored by having received two AIA National Firm Awards, for BNIM in 2011 and for Herbert Lewis Kruse Blunck Architecture in 2001.

Well-established as a leader in design, Rod's work has been included in several traveling exhibitions, and he has lectured widely. Rod's work and writings have also been featured in numerous national and regional periodicals including Architecture, Architectural Record, I.D. Magazine and Iowa Architect. Rod has chaired or served on numerous Design Excellence Awards juries and also chaired the AIA College of Fellows jury.

Recognizing Rod's Design Excellence and Leadership, the American Institute of Architects named him a Fellow 1996.

Chambers, Murphy & Burge will recycle old historic structures for new uses or restore unique landmarks to strict conservation standards. The firm of which Ms. Murphy is principal was founded as Chambers & Chambers Architects almost fifty years ago, and is dedicated solely to preservation and restoration technology and design. Elizabeth and her business partner consult with other architects on projects like the Dallas County Courthouse, the Supreme Court Building in Columbus, and the Minnesota State Capitol. The firm assists architects and building owners with the state and federal rehabilitation tax credits, design related to old or historic structures, detailed restoration specifications, and historic interiors. Elizabeth has developed with Edsel & Eleanor Ford House a Cyclical Maintenance Plan for the care of the six Albert Kahn structures at Gaukler Point. The Cyclical Maintenance Plan (interior and exterior materials) for the Henry Ford Estate in Dearborn incorporates 13 structures, in a Jens Jensen landscape.

Elizabeth Corbin Murphy, FAIA is past chair of the Advisory Group for the American Institute of Architects National Committee on Historic Resources. Ms. Murphy is a Professional Peer for the GSA Design Excellence and First Impressions Programs. She has served on several design awards juries including the AIA National Honor Awards, the GSA National Design Excellence Awards, the AIA Ohio Gold Medal Award, the AIA Cleveland Honor Awards, and the Charles E. Peterson Prize Awards. Having served for nine years with the Board of Regents for the American Architectural Foundation and serving on the Octagon Committee, Ms. Murphy now serves on the Executive Board for AIA Ohio and the Board of Advocates for the Preservation Institutes of Nantucket (PI:N) and Saint Augustine (PI:SA), both programs of the University of Florida College of Design Construction and Planning.

With her professional degree from the University of Notre Dame, Elizabeth completed the Masters of Architecture program at Kent State University to allow herself more research time in preservation of the built environment. Elizabeth is a Professor of Practice at Kent State University where the students she teaches have won eleven national awards in the fifteen entries made to the Charles E. Peterson Prize Competition. Ms. Murphy's students have more "first place" awards than any other professor. Ms. Murphy is registered with NCARB and with NCIDQ.

Bruce Lindsey, AIA
2012 Chair,
Institute Honor Awards for Regional & Urban Design

© Stan Strembooki

As Dean, E. Desmond Lee Professor for Community Collaboration, College of Architecture and Graduate School of Architecture & Urban Design, Washington University in St. Louis, Bruce Lindsey, AIA, has made significant contributions to beginning design education, sustainable design education, and community design education. He began his tenure as Dean of Architecture at Washington University in November 2006, and since then has led the Master of Landscape Architecture initiative, strengthened community design programs, and enhanced environmental education at all levels. Design Intelligence named him one of the Most Admired Educators of 2009.

Lindsey serves on the steering committees of the International Center for Advanced Renewable Energy and Sustainability and the Institute for Public Health, and the Gephardt Institute for Public Service. He also serves on the boards of the Downtown Partnership and the St. Louis chapter of the United States Green Building Council.

Lindsey's research has long focused on the application of digital tools to design and construction practice. In 1992, his work in digital-aided manufacturing was cited by Engineering News Record as one of the year's 10 most significant contributions to the construction industry. His book Digital Gehry: Material Resistance Digital Construction (2001) explores the use of technology in the design process of architect Frank Gehry. A practicing architect, Lindsey worked with Davis + Gannon Architects to design the Pittsburgh Glass Center, which earned a gold rating under LEED guidelines. The project also received an AIA Design Honor Award and was chosen as one of 2005's top 10 green buildings by the AIA's Committee on the Environment.

Lindsey earned an M. Arch degree at Yale University and an MFA in Sculpture & Photography and a BFA in Art from University of Utah.

8 House

Jury Comments:
The 8 House masterfully recreates the horizontal social connectivity and interaction of the streets of a village neighborhood through a series of delightful accessible ramps in a mixed use, multifamily housing project. The skillful shaping of the mass of the facility provides an invigorating sculptural form while creating the ramped "pedestrian" street system and providing full depth dwelling units which are filled with light and views.
People really "live" in this newly created neighborhood with shopping, restaurants, an art gallery, office facilities, childcare, educational facilities and the sound of children playing. This is a complex and exemplary project of a new typology.

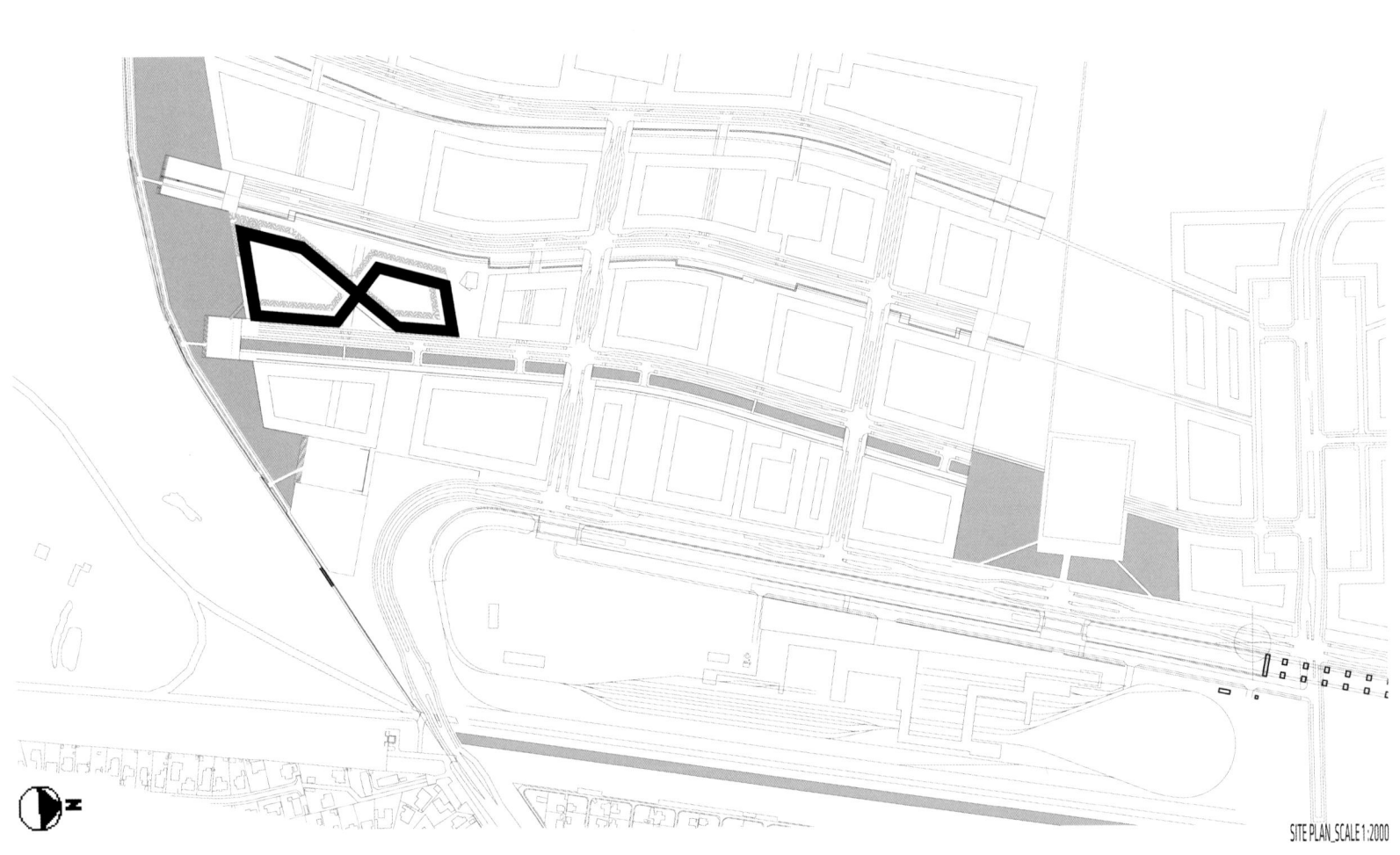

SITE PLAN_SCALE 1:2000

Notes of Interest

The 8 House is located in Ørestad South on the edge of a canal with a view of the open spaces of Kalvebrod Fælled in Copenhagen. With 475 units in a variety of sizes and layouts, the building meets the needs of people in all of life's stages: young and old; nuclear families and single people; families that grow and families that become smaller.

The bow-shaped building creates two distinct spaces, separated by the center of the bow which host the communal facilities of 5,300 sf. At the very same spot the building is penetrated by a 30-foot-wide passage that connects the two surrounding city spaces: the park area to the west and the channel area to the east. Instead of dividing the different functions of the building — for both habitation and trades — in separate blocks, they have been spread out horizontally.

The apartments are placed at the top, while the commercial program unfolds at the base of the building. As a result the apartments benefit from sunlight, fresh air and

Engineer: Moe & Brødsgaard
Owner: Høpfner A/S, Danish Oil Company, St. Frederikslund

Architect
BIG

Location
Copenhagen, Denmark

Photo Credit
© Dragor Luftfoto, © Jens Lindhe, © Julien Lanoo, © Jan Magasanik, © Ty Stange, © Ulrik Reeh

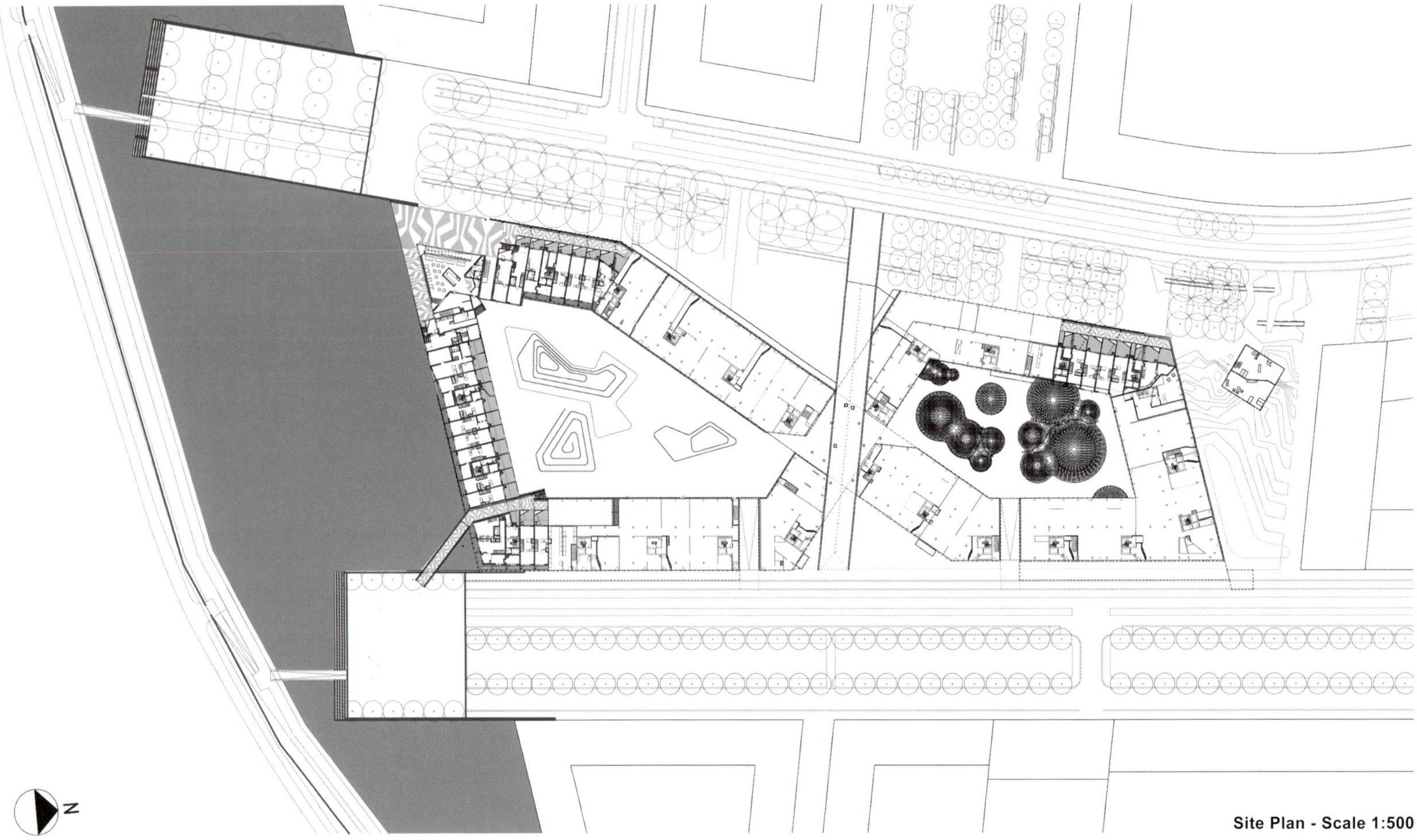

Site Plan - Scale 1:500

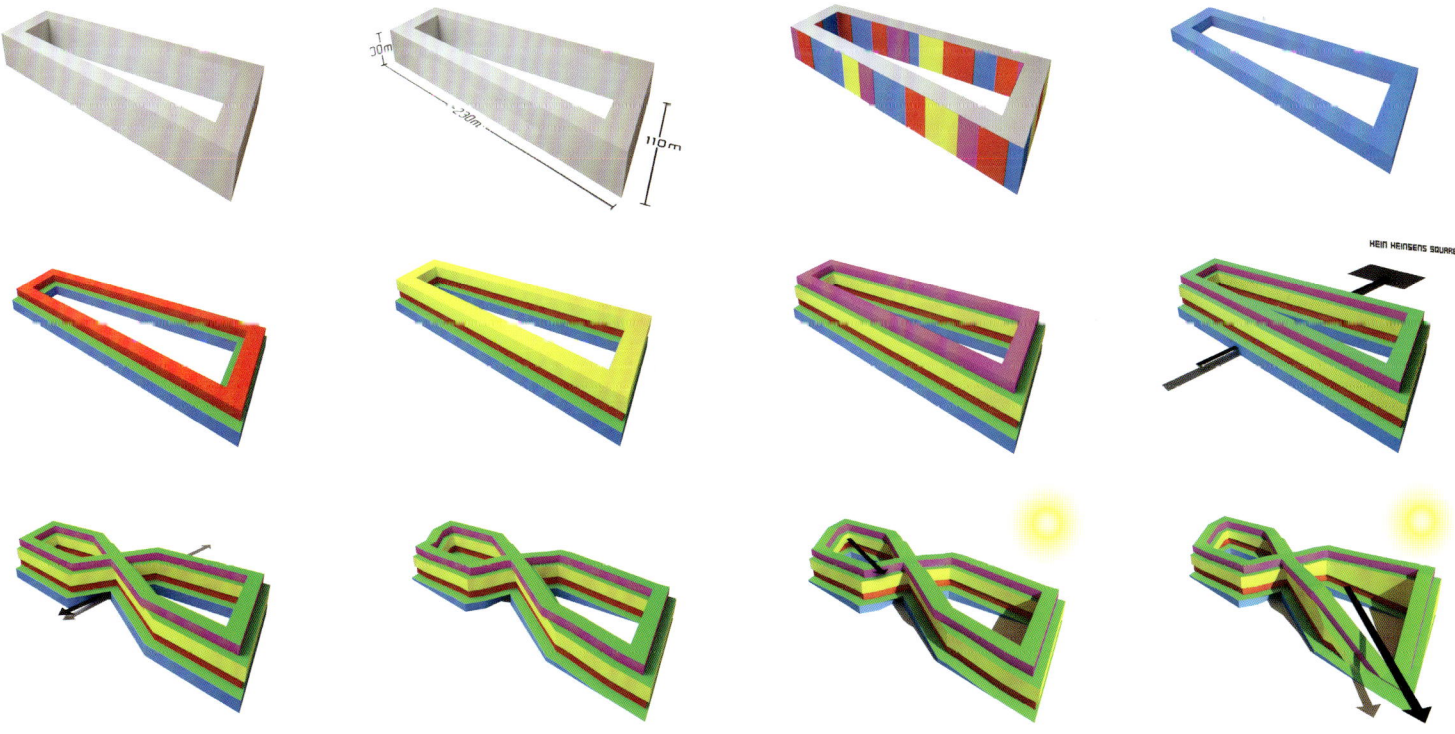

the view, while the commercial spaces merge with life on the street. The 8 House has two sloping green roofs totaling over 1,700 m², which are strategically placed to reduce the urban heat island effect as well as to visually tie it back to the adjacent farmlands towards the south.

The shape of the building allows for daylighting and natural ventilation for all units. In addition, rainwater is collected and repurposed through a stormwater management system.

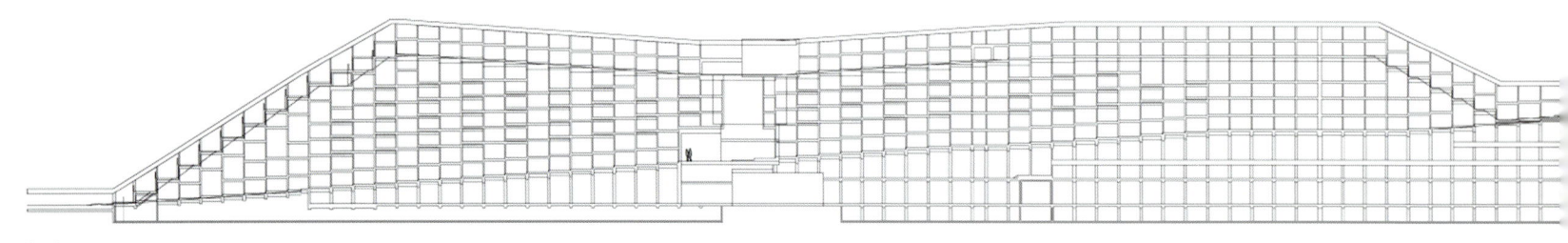

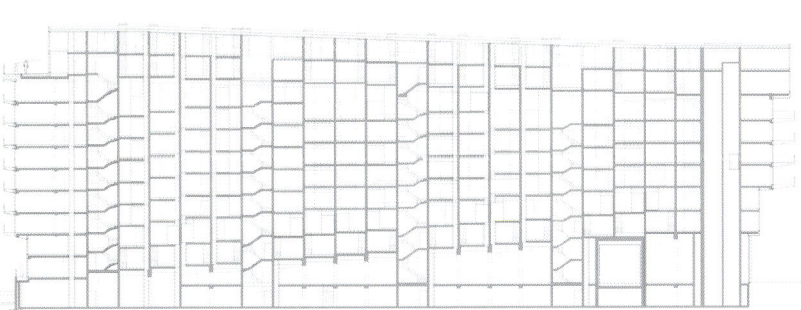
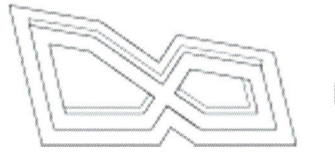

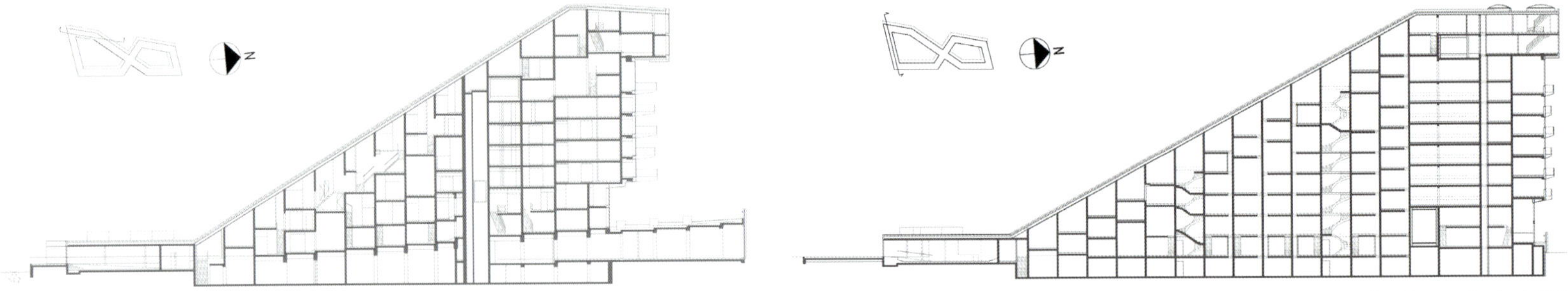

Sections - Scale 1:200

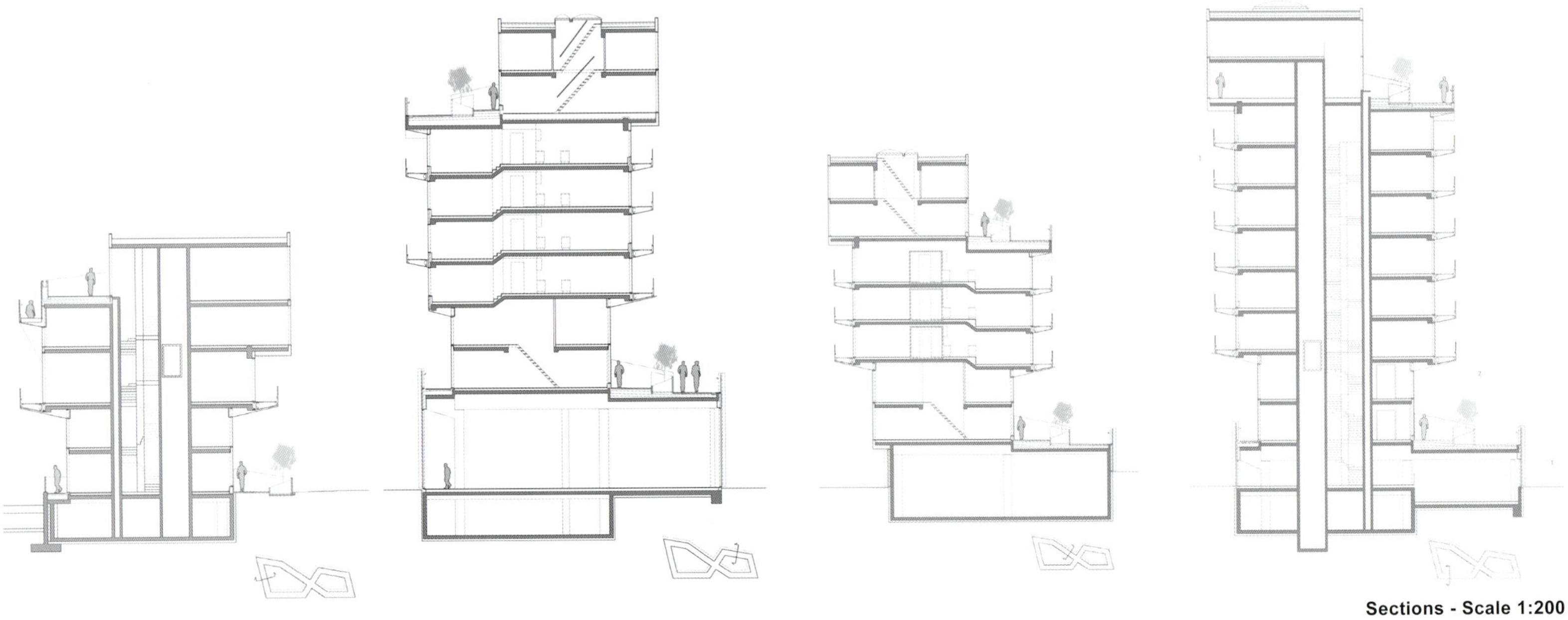

Sections - Scale 1:200

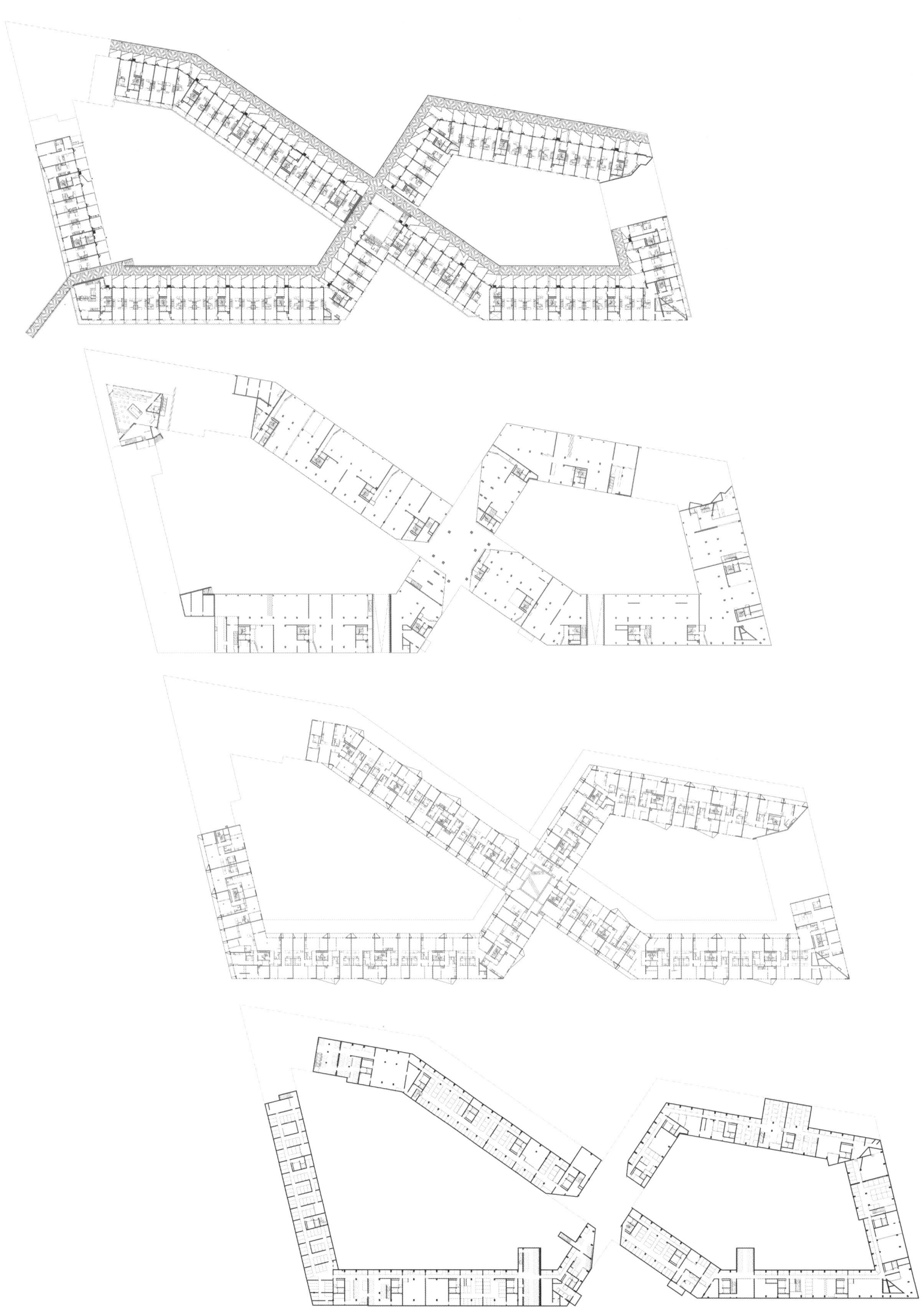

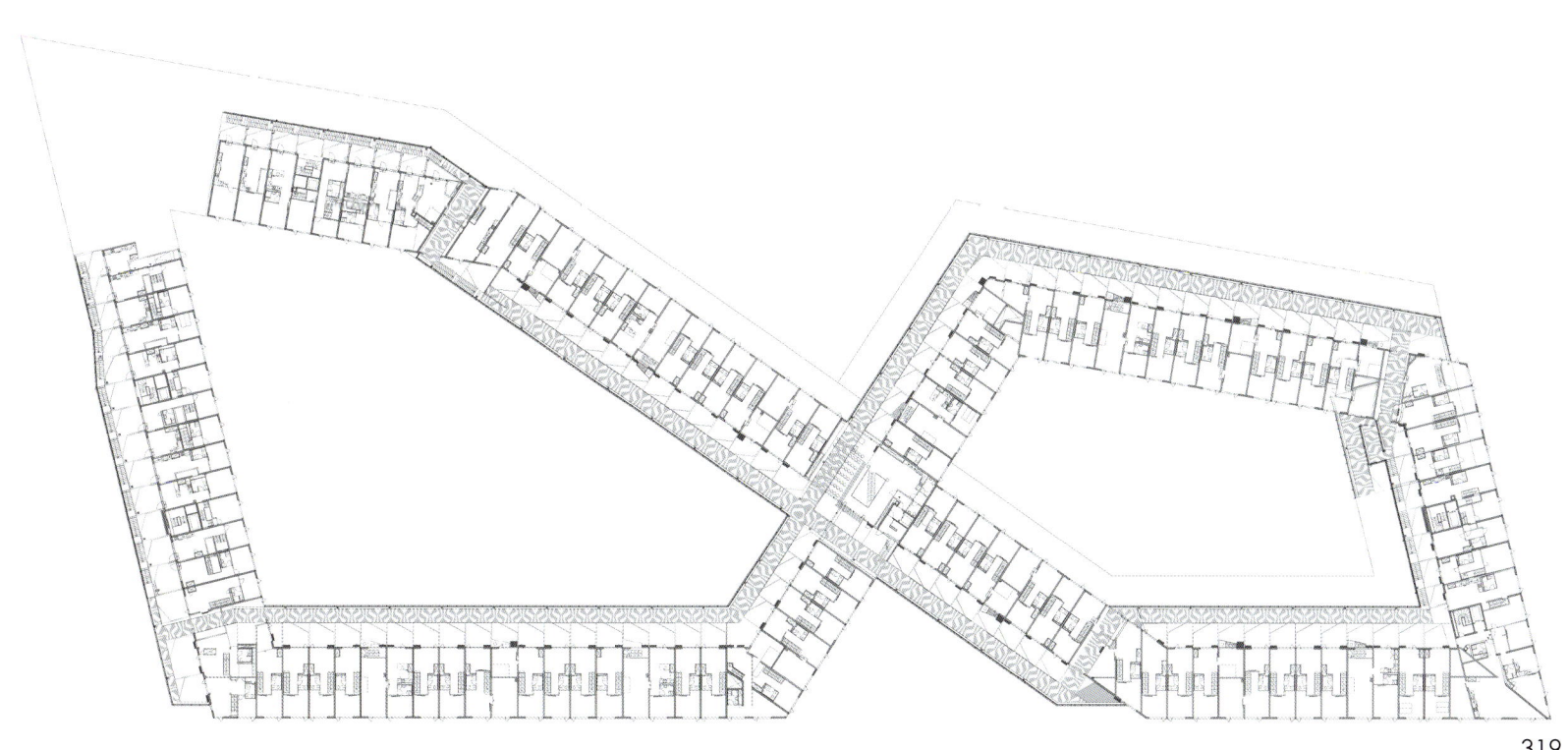

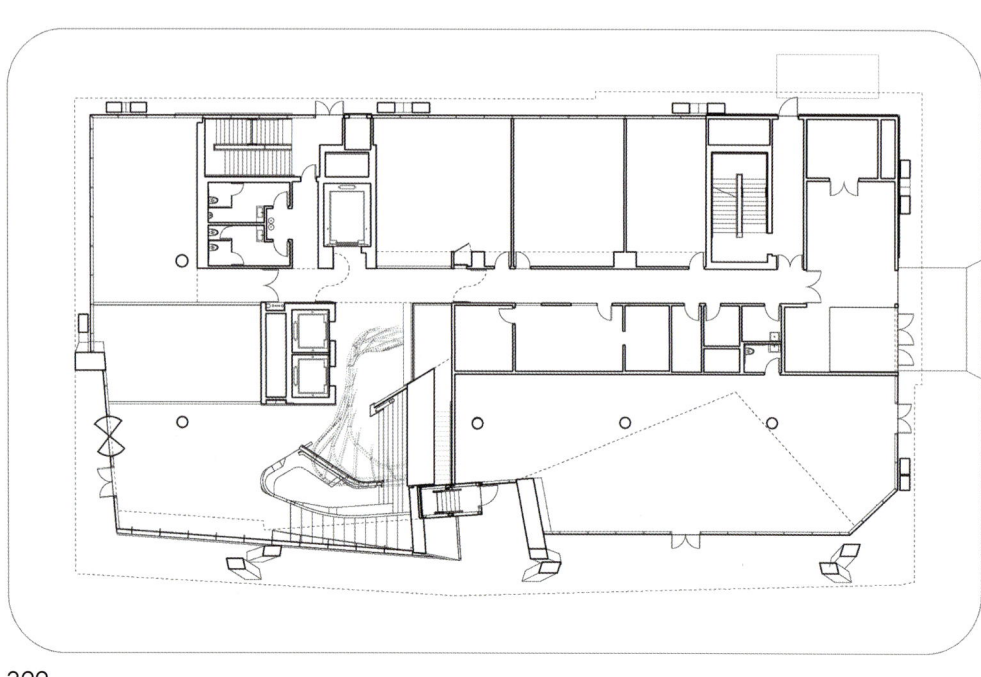

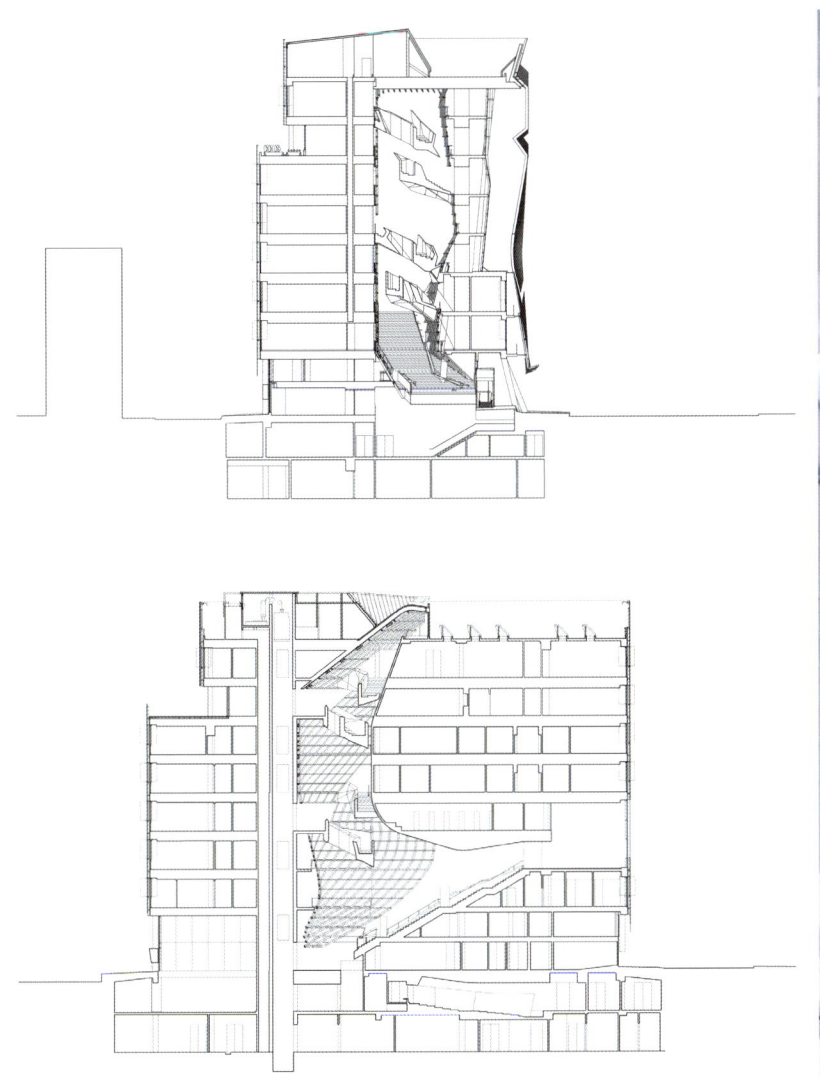

The Gates and Hillman Centers for Computer Science

Jury Comments:
This project is scaled perfectly within an urban campus and within a uniquely difficult site. The building not only matches the culture and aspirations of the school but also provides campus connections that had been clearly missing before. The fenestration and zinc exterior skin surprisingly relate beautifully to the campus fabric without being literal. Perhaps the most wonderful aspect of the project is a set of views and visual connections created by transparent interior glazing, non-reflective exterior glazing as well as carefully placed and angled floor plates.

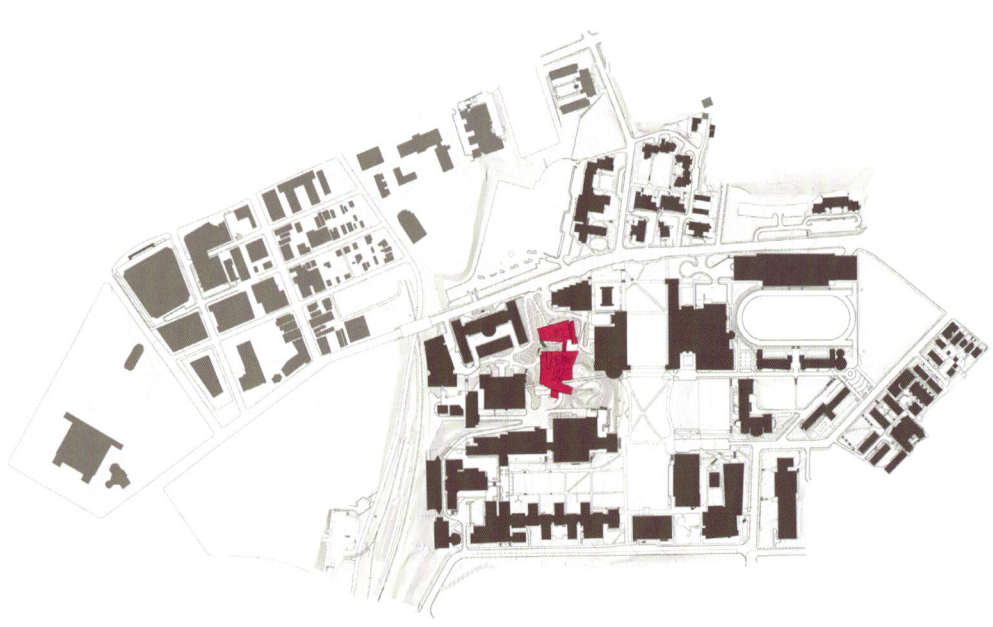

Notes of Interest

The Gates and Hillman Centers for Computer Science completes a computer science complex on Carnegie Mellon University's west campus. The building houses four departments of the School of Computer Science providing offices, conference rooms, open collaborative spaces, closed project rooms and a reading room for more than 120 faculty, 350 graduate students, 100 researchers or postdoctoral fellows and 50 administrative staff members along with a more public component of 10 university classrooms, a 250-seat auditorium, a Café and 2 university computer clusters.

The design of the Gates and Hillman Centers required negotiating a series of complex existing site conditions and programmatic pre-requisites. Site challenges included demolition of existing buildings, a large zone of subsurface rock, existing sewer lines that limited the constructable area, and an existing campus spacial hierarchy that had to be respected.

Programmatic pre-requisites included the need for a single building that could be treated as two separate buildings, the need for a variety of campus connections, both for pedestrians and for service purposes across a terrain that included variations of up to 75 feet in elevation.

Associate Architect: Gensler
Local Architect: EDGE Studio
Owner: Carnegie Mellon University

Architect
Mack Scogin Merrill Elam Architects

Location
Pittsburgh, Pennsylvania

Photo Credit
© Timothy Hursley, © Nic Lehoux

© Timothy Hursley

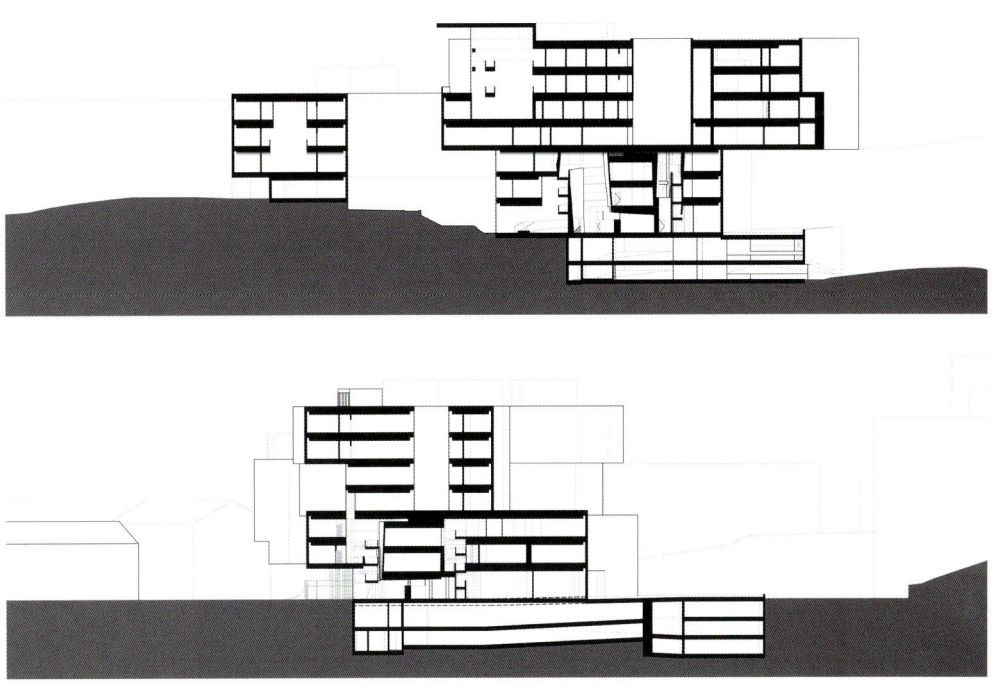

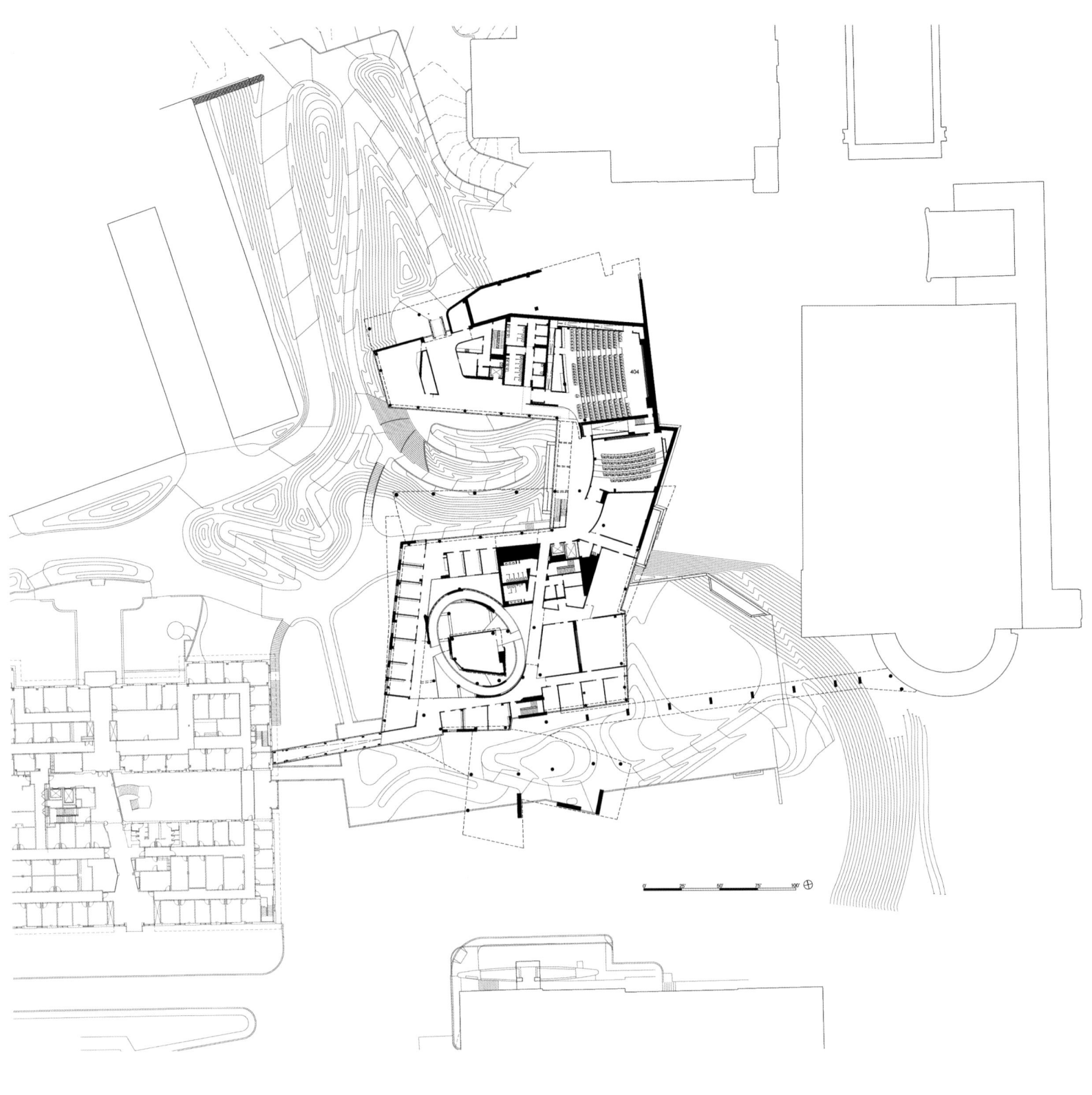

© Timothy Hursley

© Nic Lehoux

Ghost Architectural Laboratory

Jury Comments:
This project reveals itself as more than just a grouping of buildings; it is a physical experiment in education as well as an act of will to preserve the serene beauty in the landscape. As a teaching tool the students find themselves immersed in an environment where they are challenged to produce high quality designs they can self construct.
This project is truly more than the sum of its parts; it is a wonderful resolution of materials, details, landscape, and learning.

Notes of Interest

The Ghost Laboratory is sited at the LaHave River estuary on Nova Scotia's Atlantic coast, where Samuel de Champlain made his first landfall in the new world in 1604. This landscape was re-cleared from forest by the architect over the past 25 years, revealing its historic ruins and its 400 years of agrarian history.

The Ghost Lab is an architectural education center in the tradition of Frank Lloyd Wright's Taliesin or Samuel Mockbee's Rural Studio. The permanent structures which now occupy the site among the ruins – tower, studio, cabins, barns and boathouse – are, in part, products of the design/build curriculum itself. They provide accommodation for the program and a venue for community events.

Each component started as a two-week project; from design, to foundation, to framing, to sheathing. The tower, which marks the south corner of the courtyard, and the barn, are sited just outside the fence and are built on wood post foundations. The studio and four cabins inside the fence are heated structures on concrete foundations. Each of the cabins is a prototypical and modest, 700-square-foot, two-bedroom structure comprised of a "servant" box and a "served" shed, clad in eastern cedar shingles. The 90 foot long, metal clad studio is dominated by a 40-foot worktable and a 72-foot totemic cedar cabinet. The 72-foot Ghost 9 barn contains an equipment shed and free stalls for horses, while creating a second working courtyard. The historic octagonal Troop barn, which has been moved 200 miles and redesigned to fit its new home, contains a community gathering hall on top and sheep stables below.

Engineer: Campbell Comeau Engineering Ltd.
Building: Gordon MacLean Builders

Architect
Mackay-Lyons Sweetapple Architects Limited

Location
Upper Kingsburg, Nova Scotia

Photo Credit
© Manuel Schnell, © Brian MacKay-Lyons, © James Steeves

© Manuel Schnell

LumenHAUS

Jury Comments:
The creative use of materials and the flexibility of its components quickly respond to changes in the environment through automated systems that optimize energy consumption. The plan and section are orchestrated by light and materials to enhance the perception of a small footprint.
The interior is cleverly designed with comfortable if compact spaces, compatible materials, and a rationale and clear layout.

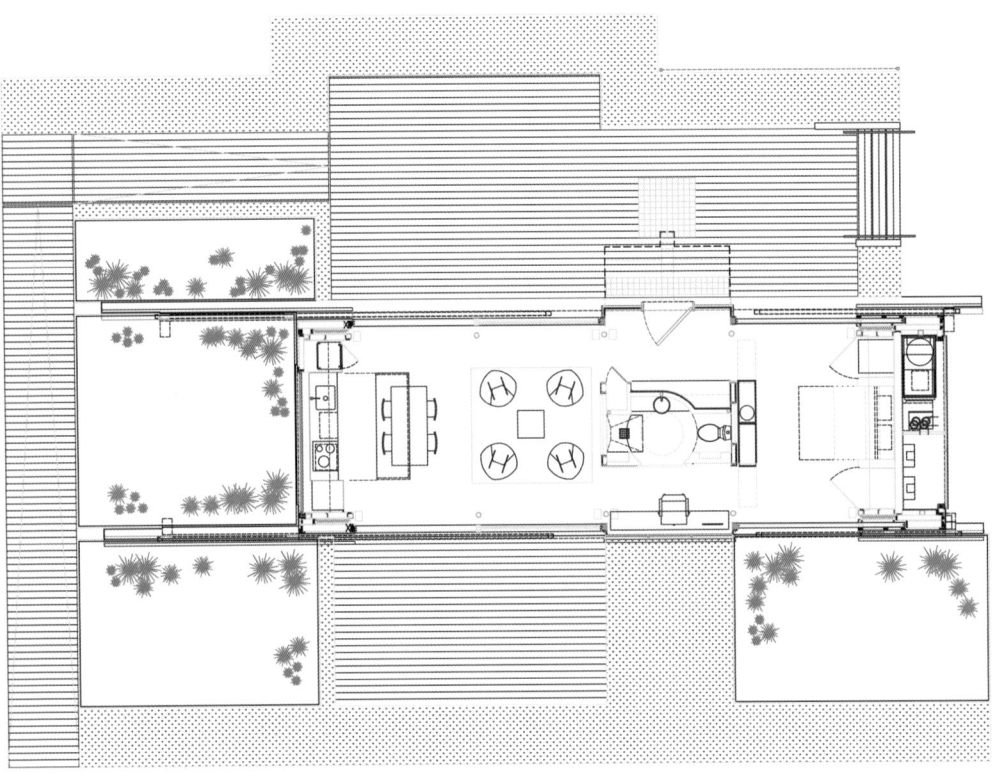

Notes of Interest

The house is both a dwelling and an exhibition informing the public about issues of alternative energy and sustainability. It has been exhibited in Washington D.C., Times Square, Madrid, Spain, Millennium Park, and at the Farnsworth House in Plano Ill.

This is a grid-tied solar powered house based on the concept of "Responsive Architecture". It adjusts to climactic changes and user requirements through automated systems that optimize energy consumption while offering an architecture of delight.

As a net-zero energy house employing active and passive systems, it generates more power than it uses over the course of a year. It achieves its positive energy balance by incorporating a contemporary reinterpretation of the architectural shutter and screen with innovative technology.

Built and operated using industrialized processes, the Eclipsis System optimizes energy use, makes building more efficient, and improves the quality of architectural space. The Eclipsis System is made of two exterior layers – laser cut stainless steel shutter screens and aerogel filled polycarbonate insulation panels – both of which integrate the house's technical and architectural identities. Rich and divergent qualities of light fill the house from sunrise to sunset, and sliding panel systems automatically respond to climactic conditions, providing a full range of protection from the elements and a rich architectural experience.

Structural Engineer: ARUP
Cladding/Material Fabrication: Zahner and Associates, Inc.
Control Systems: Siemens
Geothermal Materials: Mechanical Equipment Sales
Hardware: Hafele America Co.
Photovoltaics: Solar Connexions; Baseline Solar, AltEnergy, SMB Solar, RTKL
Owner: School of Architecture + Design, Virginia Tech

Architect
Center for Design Research, School of Architecture + Design, Virginia Tech

Location
Blacksburg, Virginia

Photo Credit
© Virginia Tech Solar Team

337

Pittman Dowell Residence

Jury Comments:
The house acts like an optical instrument with staged views of the surrounding landscape including spectacular views of the valley below and the hills above.
The clear concise presentation of details and the theatrically arranged spaces constitute a sublime and poetic expression and push the boundaries of what a house can be.

Notes of Interest
North of Los Angeles at the edge of Angeles National Forest, the residence is sited on 6 acres originally planned as a Richard Neutra designed development. Although three pads were cleared, only one home was built. The current owners, who own the original Neutra home, have developed a desert garden on one of the clearings. The new home sits on the last clearing.

Five decades after the original house was constructed, the site's visual and physical context has changed dramatically. Similarly, the contemporary needs of the artist residents required a new relationship between building and landscape.

Inspired by geometric arrangements of interlocking polygons, the home is a heptagonal figure whose purity is confounded by a series of intersecting slices. Bounded by an introverted exterior, living spaces unfold in a moiré of shifting perspectival frames. Movement and visual relationships expand and contract to respond to the centrifugal nature of the site and context. An irregularly shaped void defined by these intersections creates an outdoor room whose edges blur into the adjoining spaces.

Engineer: B.W. Smith Structural Engineers, Paller-Roberts Engineering, Inc., The J Byer Group
General Contractor: Asterisk Builders
Arborist: Robert W. Wallace
Owner: Lari Pittman and Roy Dowell

Architect
Michael Maltzan Architecture, Inc.

Location
La Crescenta, California

Photo Credit
© Iwan Baan

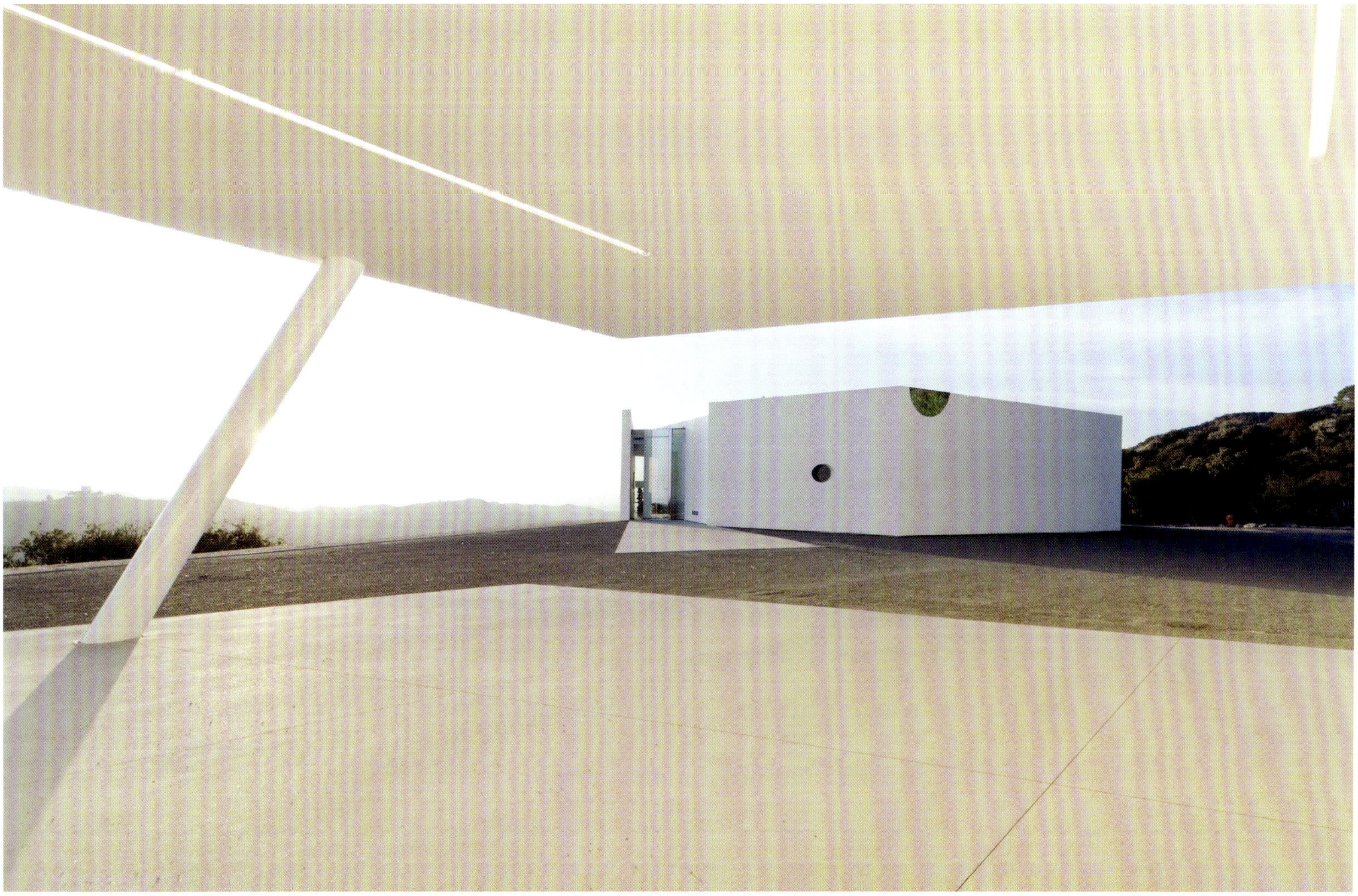

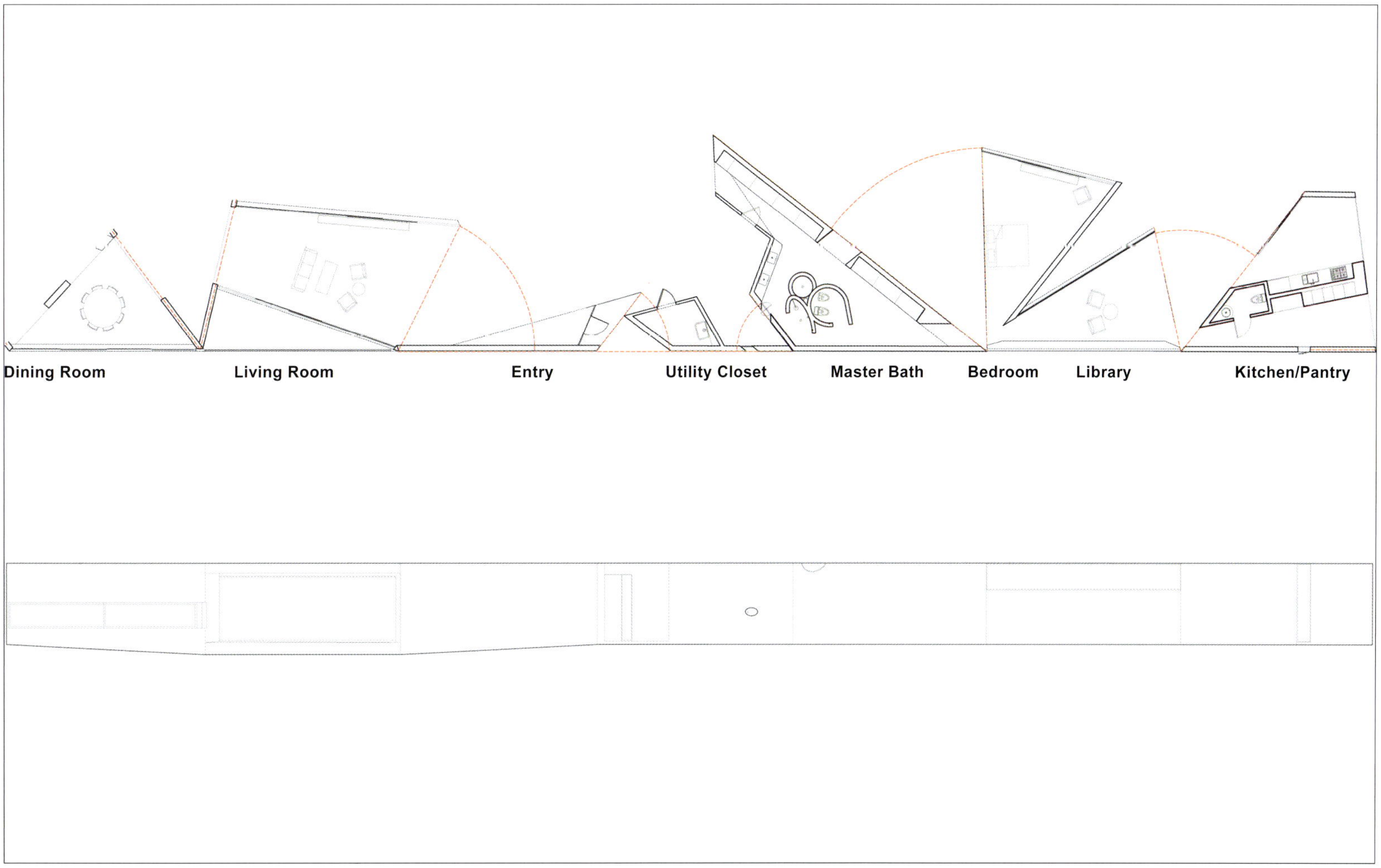

| Dining Room | Living Room | Entry | Utility Closet | Master Bath | Bedroom | Library | Kitchen/Pantry |

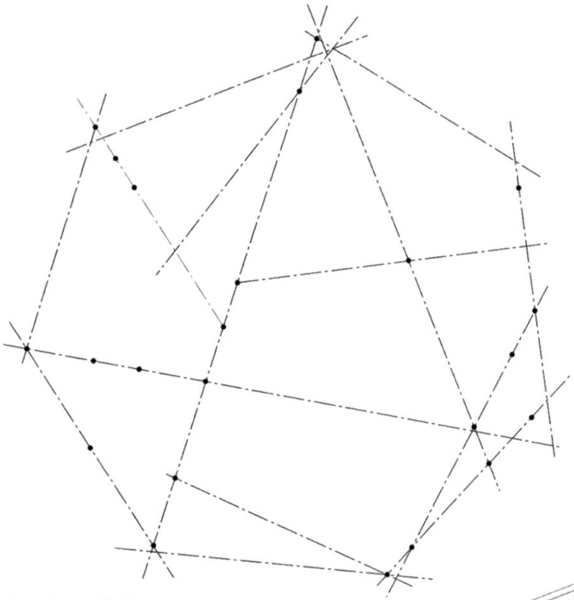

Structural Grid

Floor Plan (Right):
1. Entry
2. Living Room
3. Dinning Room
4. Kitchen
5. Office
6. Powder Room
7. Library
8. Bedroom
9. Master Bath
10. Utility Closet
11. Courtyard
12. Balcony

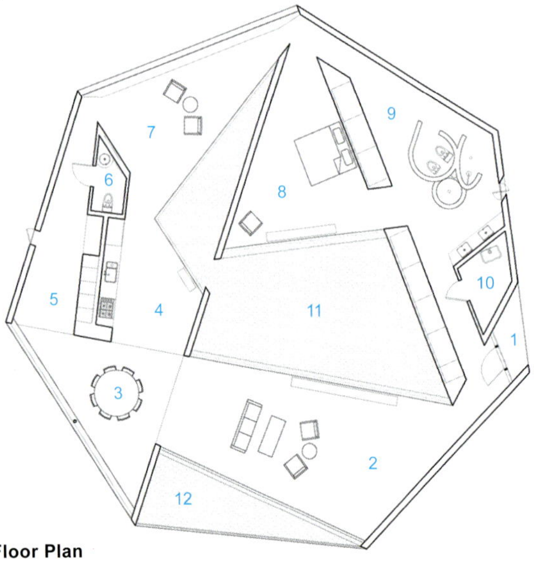

Floor Plan

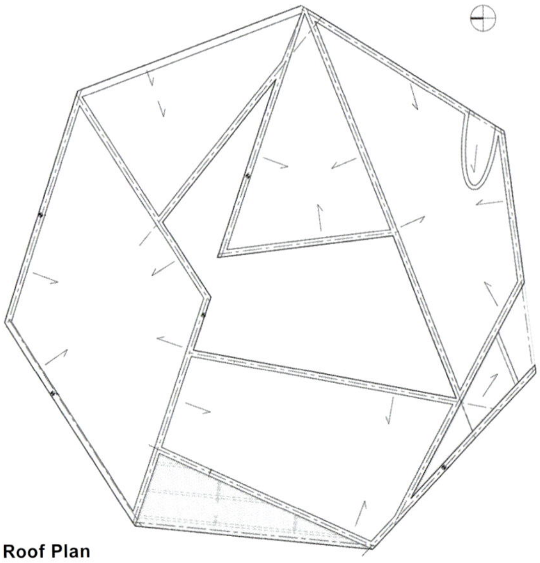

Roof Plan

Poetry Foundation

Jury Comments:
This building unfolds as it is experienced and is sublime in its stillness and detailing.
From the street, one is seduced by is secrecy and upon entering its crafted inner court, the project is revealed much like a poetry reading.
The manipulation of light through sectional explorations and the weaving of its limited material use through its interiors are resolved exceptionally well.

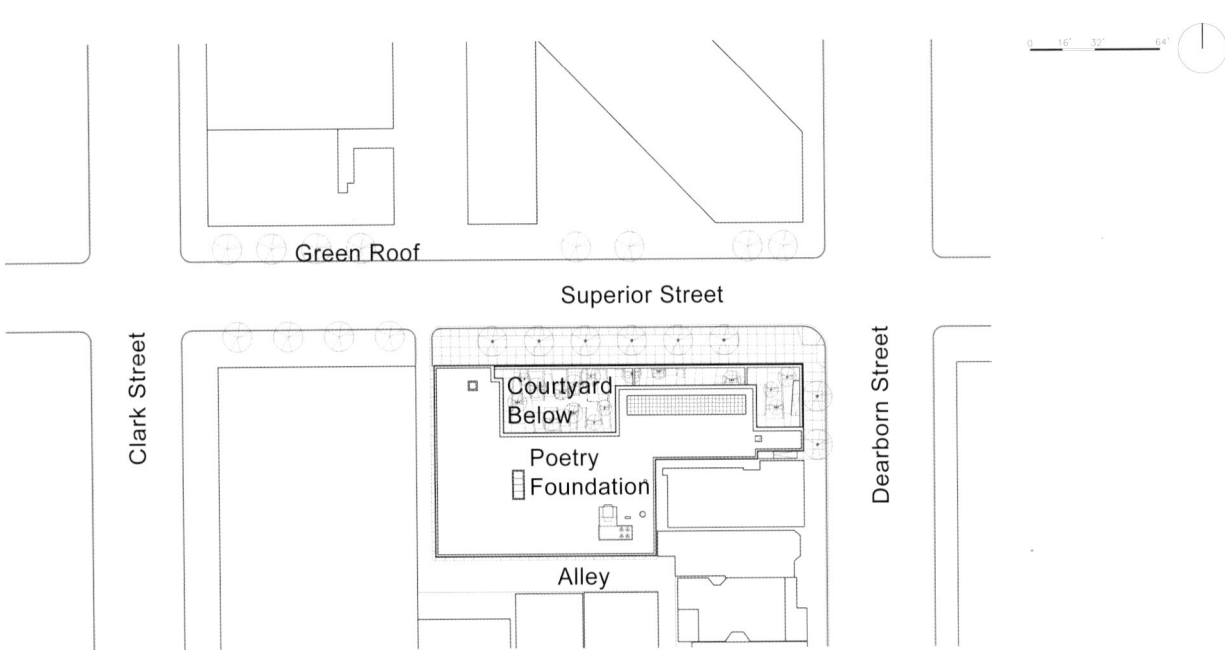

Notes of Interest
The Poetry Foundation is comprised of a building in dialogue with a garden created through erosion of an implied volume as described by the L-shaped property boundary. The garden interlocks with the building and is conceived as another "room", part of the building's slowly-unfolding spatial sequence revealed space by space, not unlike a poem is revealed line by line.

Visitors enter through the garden, an urban sanctuary that mediates between the street and enclosed building. Entering the garden, visitors first encounter the library space, announcing that they are entering into a literary environment. Inside, an exhibition gallery connects the library to the performance space, where visitors listen to poets read their work against the backdrop of the garden.

Public functions (performance space, gallery and library) are located on the ground floor, while office spaces are located on the second level, organized into three areas (Foundation Administration, Poetry magazine/website, and Programs). The building is configured to allow for views from all spaces out onto the garden.

Tectonically, the building is conceived of as a series of layers that visitors move through and between. Layers, of zinc, glass, and wood, peel apart to define the various spaces of the building. The building's outer layer of oxidized zinc becomes perforated where it borders the garden, allowing visual access to the garden from the street to encourage public investigation.

Engineer: ARUP; dbHMS; Terra Engineering
Development: U.S. Equities Realty; Norcon
Landscape Architect: Reed Hilderbrand Associates
Lighting: Charter Sills
Acoustical: Threshold Acoustics
Owner: Poetry Foundation

Architect
John Ronan Architects

Location
Chicago, Illinois

Photo Credit
© Hedrich Blessing

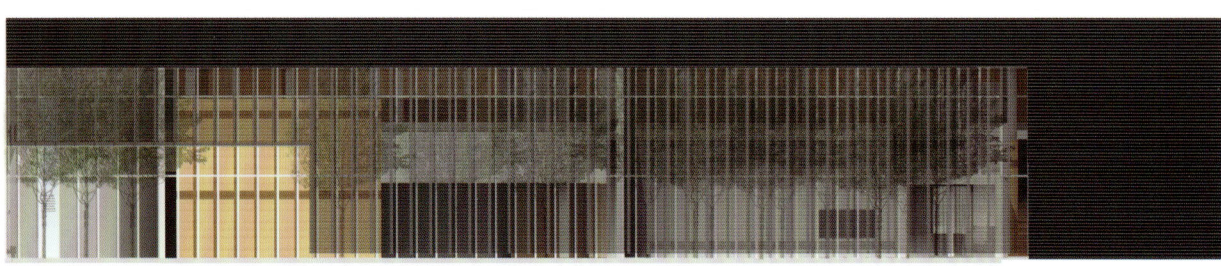

East Elevation **North Elevation**

CONFERENCE
OPEN OFFICE
MAIN STAIR
STORAGE
ALLEY
ENTRY
VESTIBULE
GARDEN
STREET

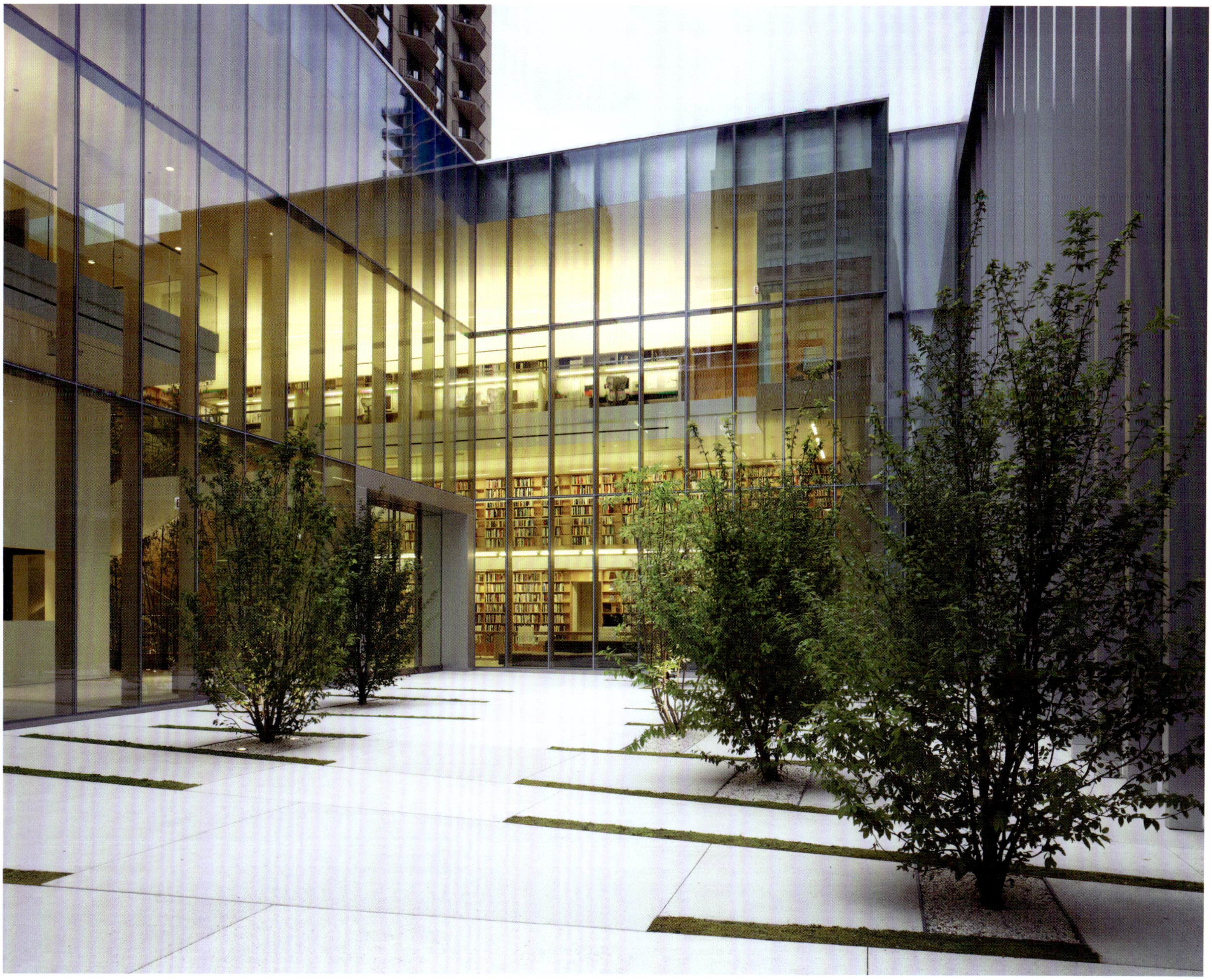

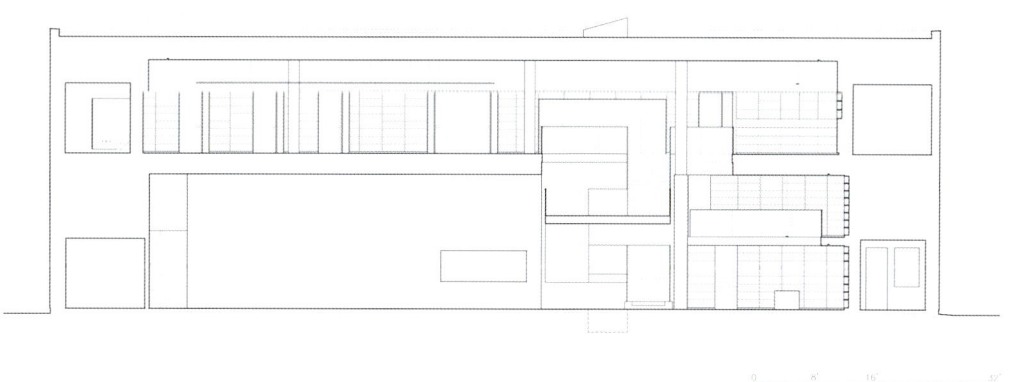

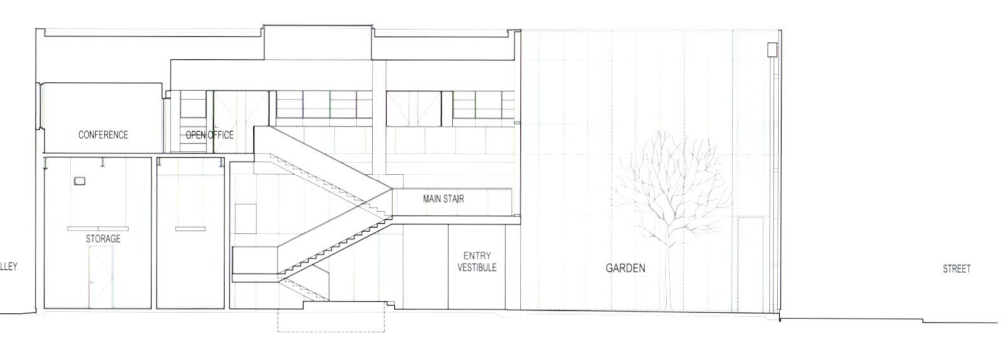

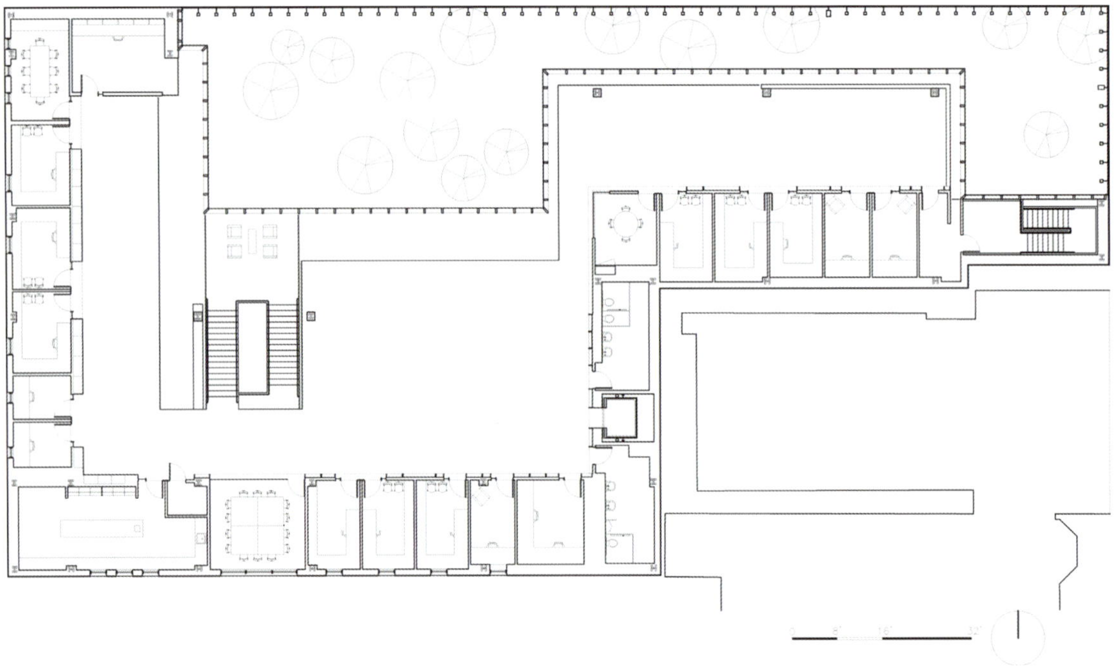

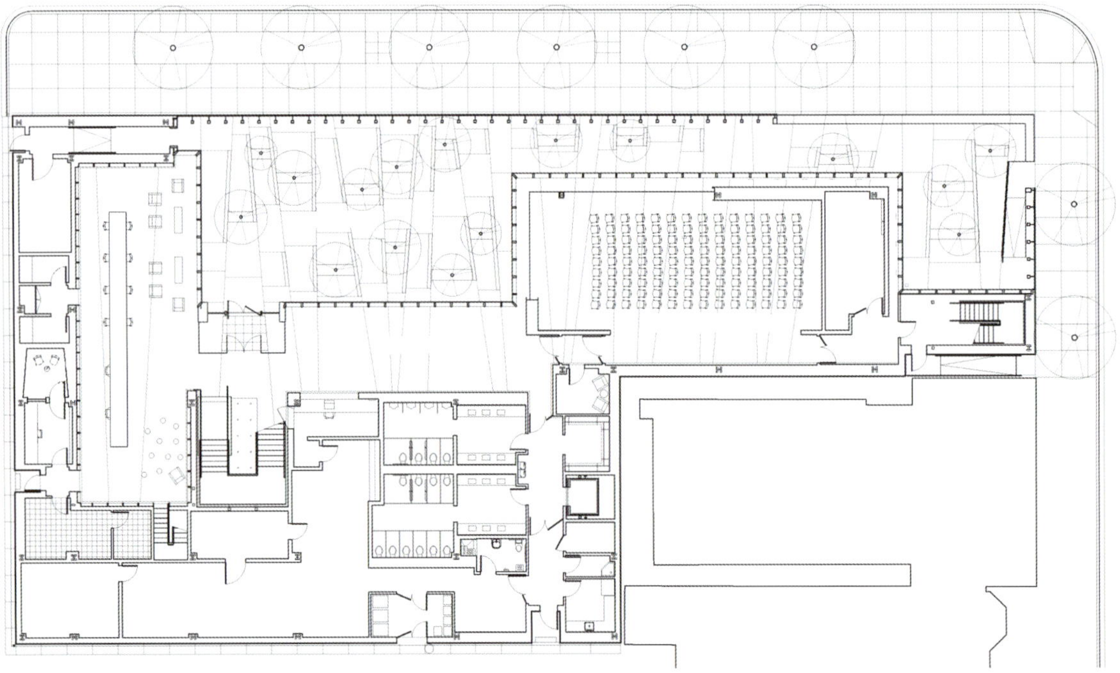

Ruth Lilly Visitors Pavilion

Jury Comments:
This pavilion is artfully cast in the shadows of the adjacent trees, its transparency is enhanced by its latticed canopy which filters light thru its entirety and the floor to ceiling glazing hides no secrets.
Its low posture and horizontal form enhances the encompassing flora and is quite elegant in its lightness while reaching out and inviting nature in.

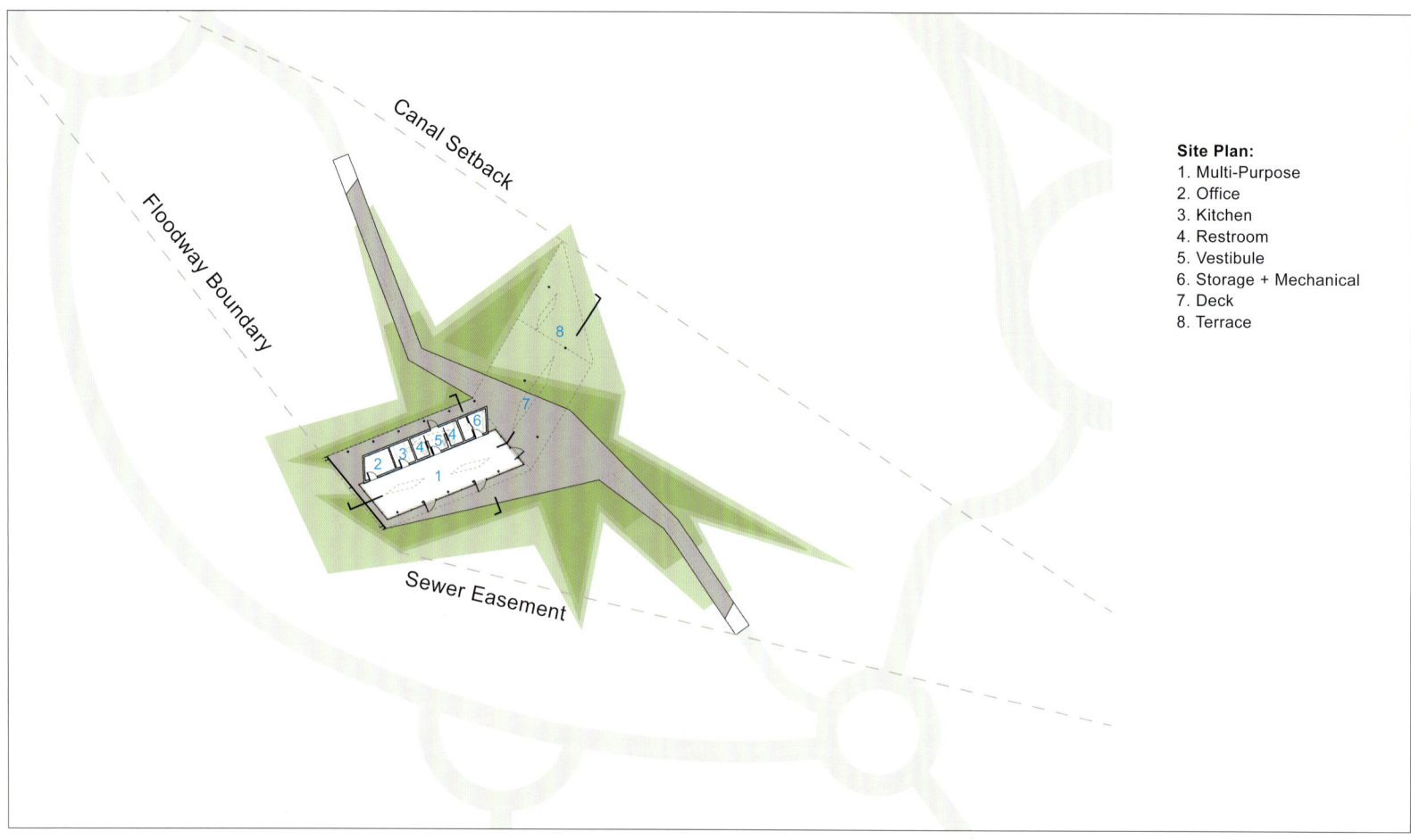

Site Plan:
1. Multi-Purpose
2. Office
3. Kitchen
4. Restroom
5. Vestibule
6. Storage + Mechanical
7. Deck
8. Terrace

Notes of Interest

The Ruth Lilly Visitors Pavilion is the result of a studied relationship between building, land and art, and serves as both a threshold to and a destination within the 100 Acres Art & Nature Park at the Indianapolis Museum of Art.

The goal was to craft a logic of ideas and physical works that reveal the repressed raw power of environment, art, and architecture through a rethinking and re-making of "where we already are". Questions are born from within the found condition, resulting in an immanent response, imbued with conviction, meaning, and significance for the Museum of Art, its patrons and the citizens of Indianapolis.

The Visitors Pavilion is a place of shared resolve where nature and artifice are sensually perceived as one and many; the detail and horizon. The 100 acre park site is born of wildly turbulent natural and cultural phenomena constantly changing the land's structure, and is a place where one becomes conscious of the residual forms that reveal the creative life force at work in our world.

Tinkering with it as cultivated urban wilds proves a sound means of joining Nature and City as a recovered, unpredictably changing but cultivated landscape. Prone to flooding across the entire park by the White River, the park offers less than an acre for the construction of the Ruth Lily Visitors Pavilion.

Engineer: Guy Nordenson & Associates, L'Acquis Consulting Engineers, Cripe Architects & Engineers
General Contractor: Geupel DeMars Hagerman
Landscape Architect: The Landscape Studio; NINebark
Owner: Indianapolis Museum of Art

Architect
Marlon Blackwell Architect

Location
Indianapolis, Indiana

Photo Credit
© Timothy Hursley

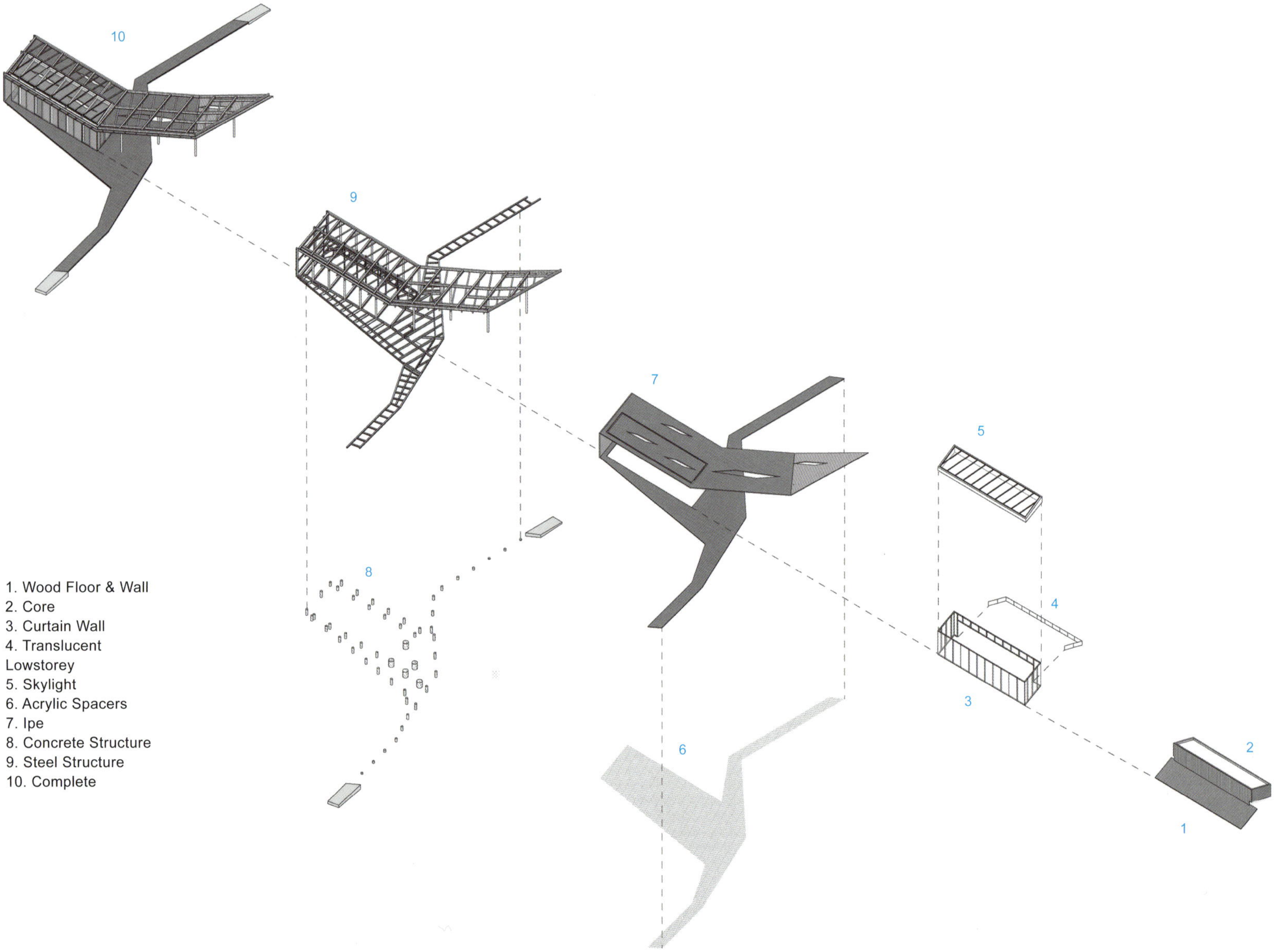

1. Wood Floor & Wall
2. Core
3. Curtain Wall
4. Translucent Lowstorey
5. Skylight
6. Acrylic Spacers
7. Ipe
8. Concrete Structure
9. Steel Structure
10. Complete

The Standard, New York

Jury Comments:
The building addresses the urban scale as a tower relating to highline and river well. It blends seamlessly with the fabric of the surrounding neighborhood.
There is clarity in the choice and articulation of materials and a sense of restraint, though the end result is one of high visual impact.
The goal for transparency and openness successfully drives design and detailing decisions.

Notes of Interest

Located in Manhattan's Hudson riverfront Meatpacking District, the hotel responds to its context through contrast: sculptural piers, whose forms clearly separate the building from the orthogonal street grid, raise the building fifty-seven feet off the street, and allow the horizontally-scaled industrial landscape to pass beneath it and natural light to penetrate to the street.

The 18-story building straddles the High Line, a 75-year-old elevated railroad line recently developed into a new linear, public park. The two slabs of the building are "hinged", angled to further emphasize the building's distinction from the city's grid and its levitation above the neighborhood.

The low-scale environment affords the building unique visibility from all directions, and unobstructed 360° views of the city. The juxtaposition of the building's two materials – concrete and glass – reflects the character of the city: the gritty quality of the concrete contrasts with the refinement of the glass. The concrete grid provides a delicate frame for the exceedingly transparent water-white glass, the two materials unified in the continuous plane of the curtain wall.

The curtain wall breaks with the traditional architecture of hotels, replacing opacity with transparency, privacy with openness and defining a new paradigm.

Engineer: DeSimone; Edwards & Zuck, H.A. Bader, Langan Engineering & Environmental Services
Façade: R.A. Heintges
Interior Design: André Balazs Properties; Shawn Hausman; Roman and Williams
Acoustical: Cerami & Associates
Owner: André Balazs Properties

Architect
Ennead Architects

Location
New York City, New York

Photo Credit
© Alex MacLean/Landslides Aerial Photography
© Jeff Goldberg/Esto, © Aislinn Weidele/Ennead Architects

© Jeff Goldberg/Esto

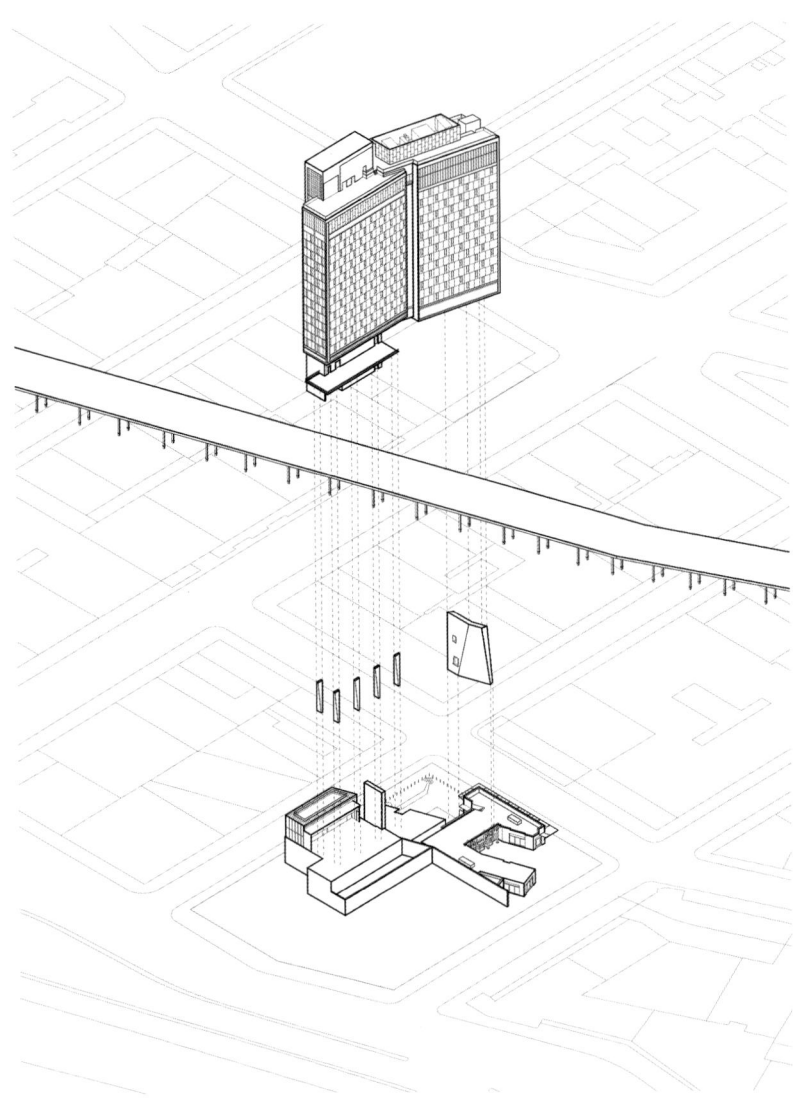

Massing Transformation

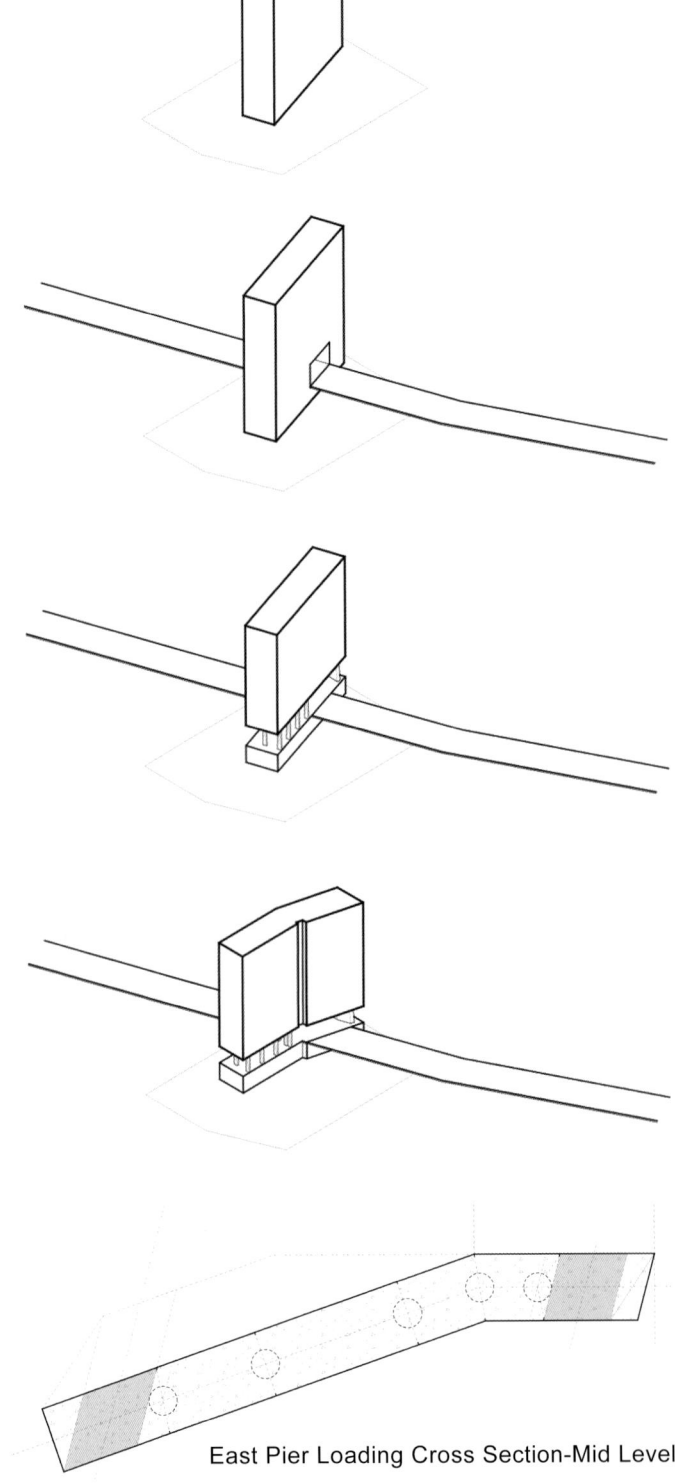

East Pier Geonmetry

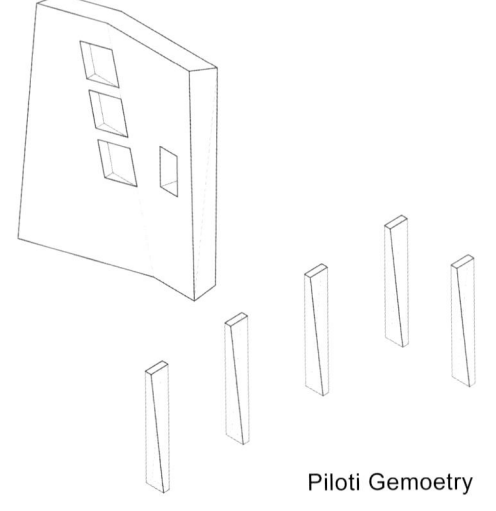

Piloti Gemoetry

East Pier Loading Cross Section-Mid Level

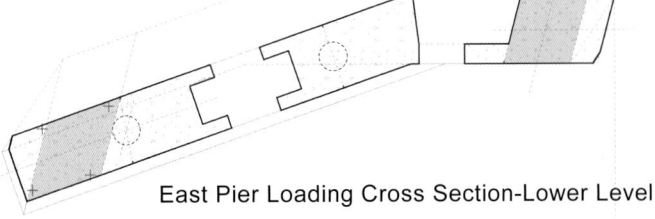
East Pier Loading Cross Section-Lower Level

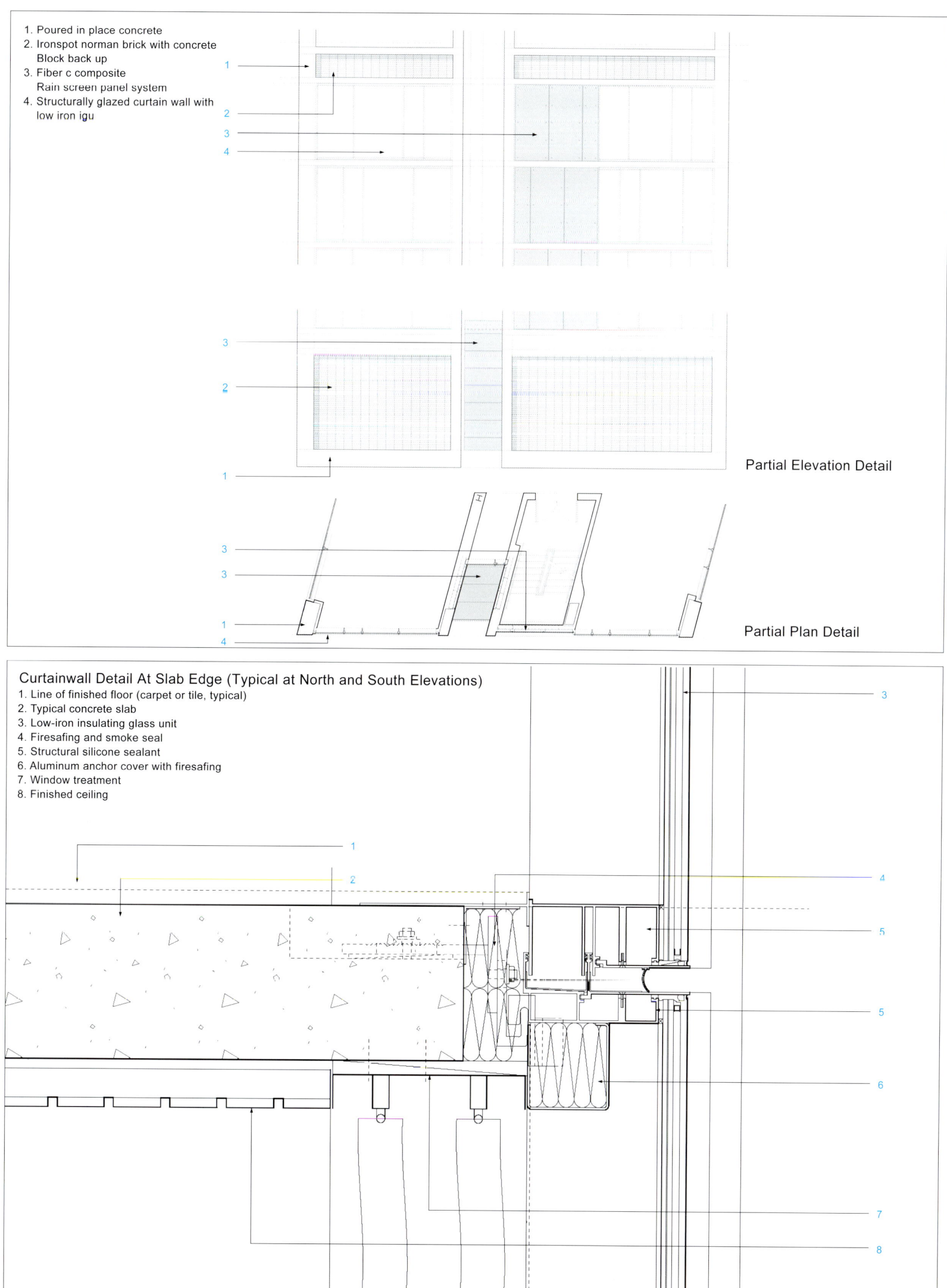

© Jeff Goldberg/Esto

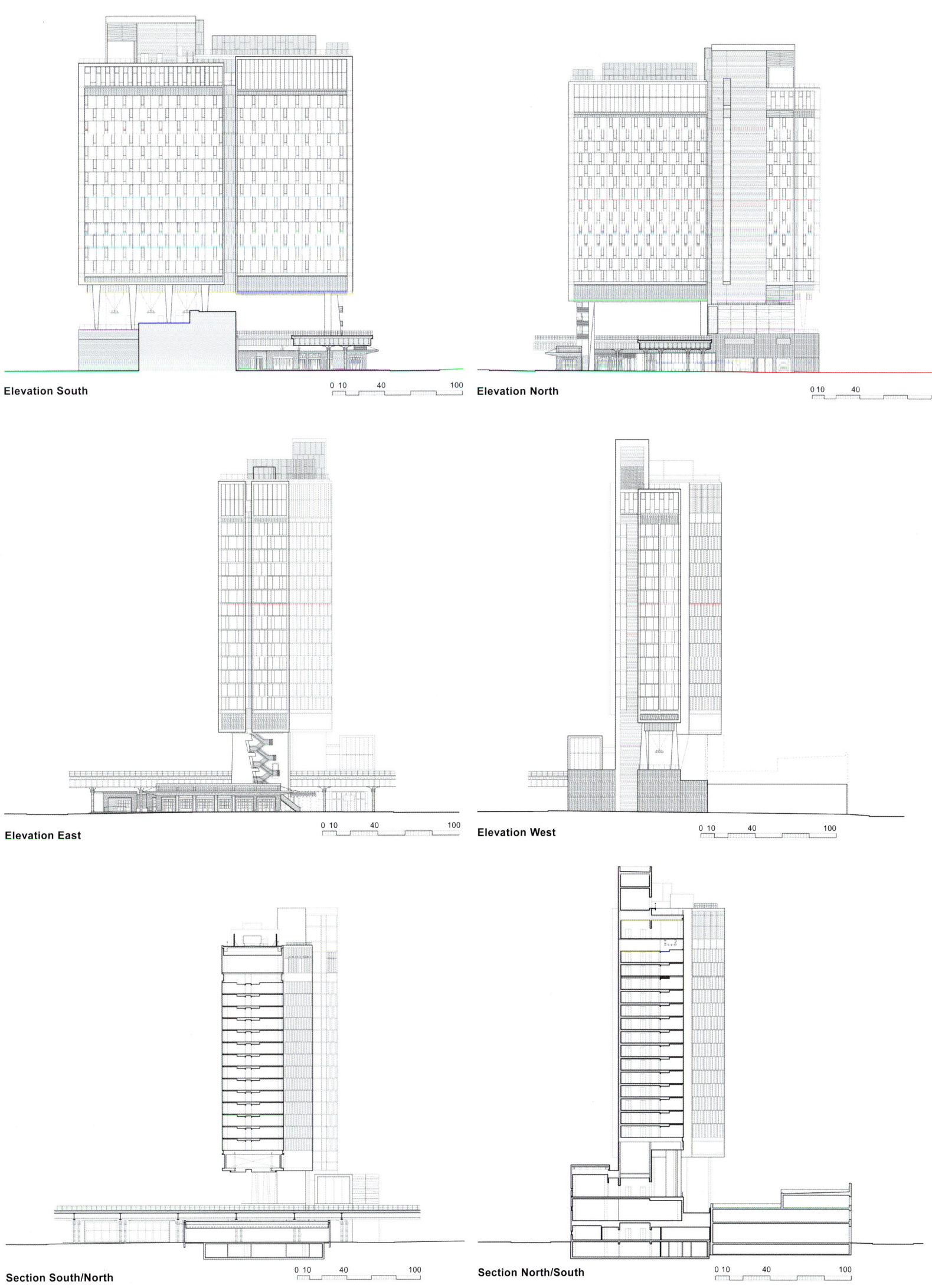

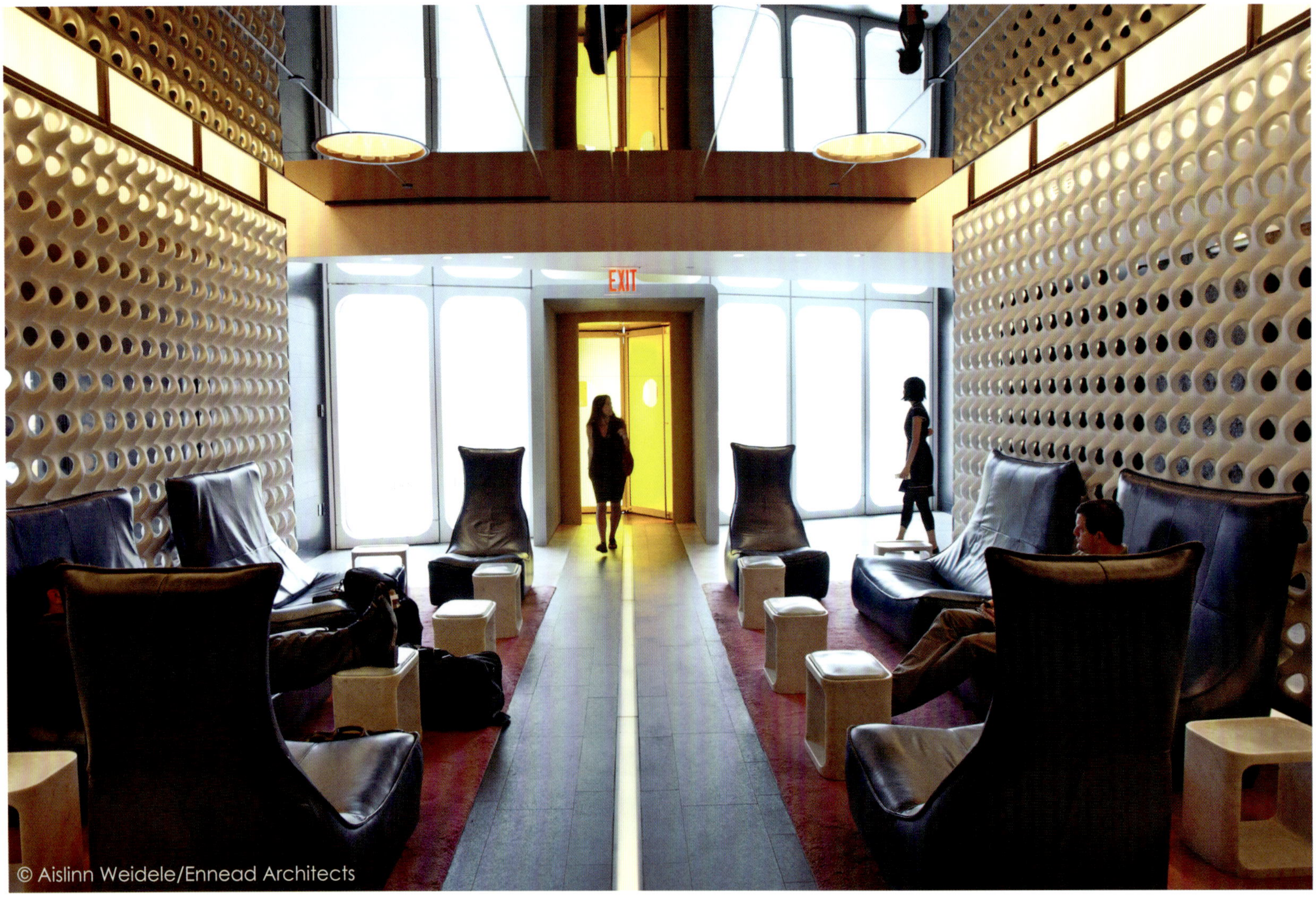

© Aislinn Weidele/Ennead Architects

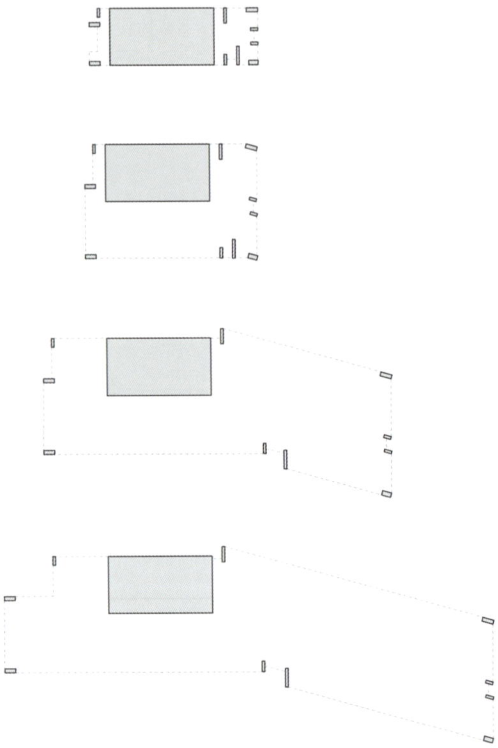

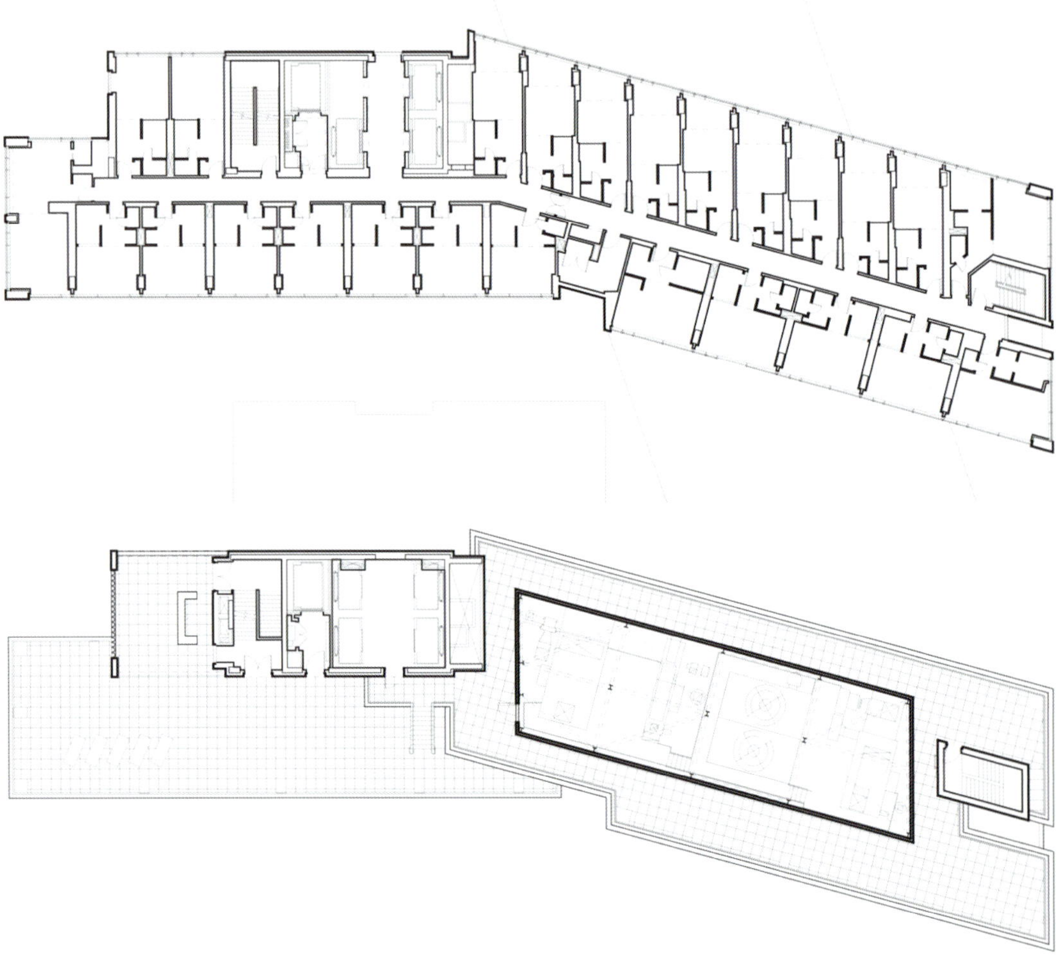

Level 1

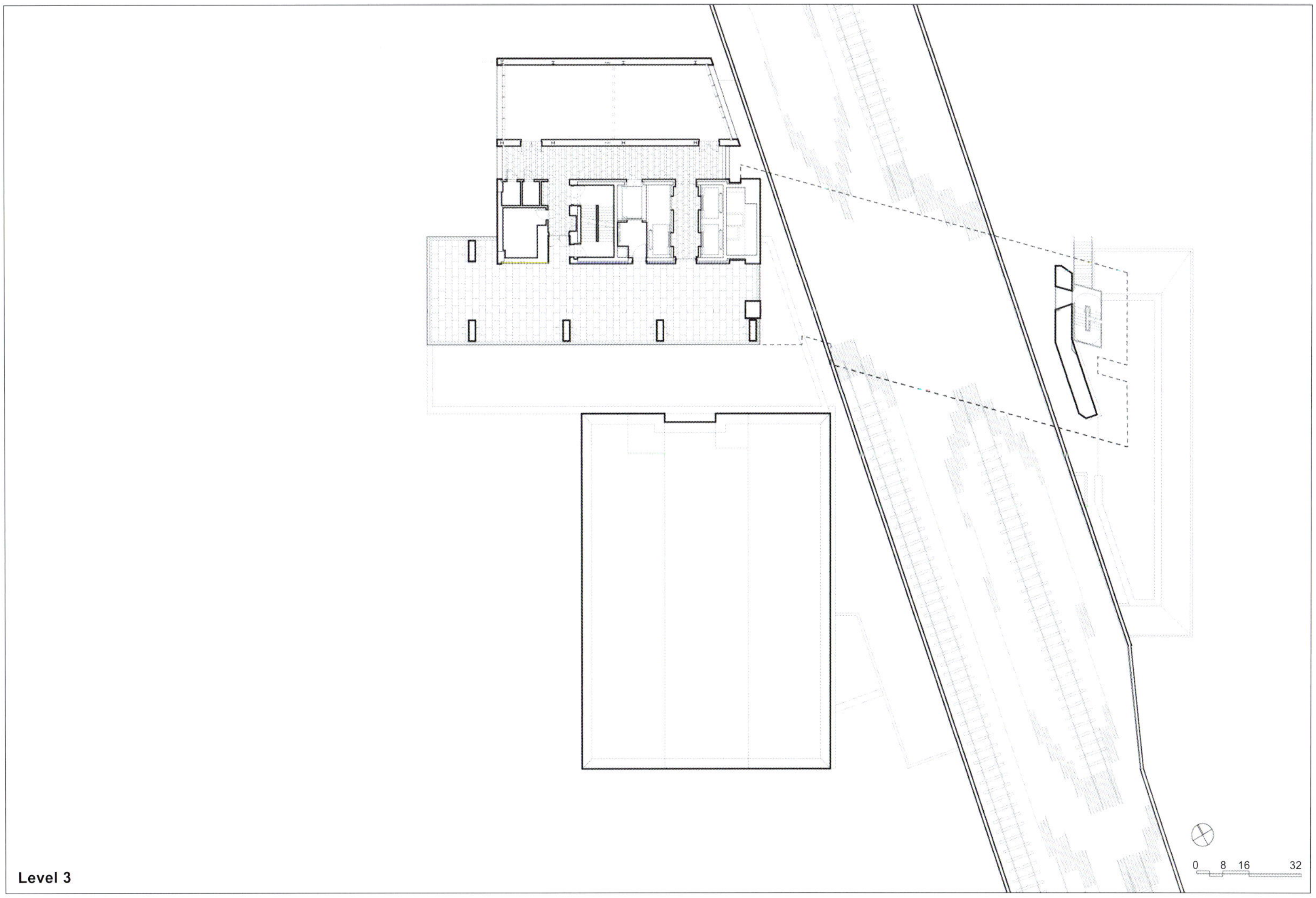

0 10 40 100

Level 3

0 8 16 32

359

ARTifacts

Jury Comments:
An excellent example of what is possible within limited means and unlimited desire. Working within a historical structure, the project sensitively responded to both program and context in a series of deliberate and carefully considered moves, keeping with the spirit of the place and its inspiration.
The solution was both raw and refined.

Notes of Interest
Kent Bellows (1949-2005) was a lifelong Nebraska Artist who has been recognized as one of America's greatest masters of American Realism and was known as a mentor for friends, colleagues and burgeoning artists.

The Kent Bellows Foundation requested a renovation to the artist's work/live building to transform it into a center for art and student mentoring. The Kent Bellows Studio and Center for Visual Arts strives to ignite the creative spark in inner city youth, encouraging them to reach their highest potential through self expression in the visual arts. Artists ages 12-21 attend workshops and receive mentoring from nationally renowned artists through various programs and events put on by the Center.

The artist had worked in the building for twenty years and had built out much of the space with his own hands. Their intention was to identify the artifacts the artist left that had meaning. They identified and preserved 9 artifacts (gallery floor, Kent's parka, glass block transom, moving backdrop wall, books, collages, light fixture pulley, wall mural, and wall installation).

Working with the artifacts, the design focused on minimal interventions to upgrade the building and provide the new spaces for the facility. The storefront intervention was a three dimensional sculpture of steel plates/tubes which creates windows, seating, facility signage, and the main entrance. The staircase/balcony intervention creates a continuous steel plate walkway that connects the entrance, gallery, library, office and the second floor studios. The library intervention is a meeting and reading space hovering above the gallery defined by a folded wood panel wall/ceiling that frames the artist's moving backdrop wall.

Construction: University of Nebraska Architecture Students
Owner: Kent Bellows Studio and Center for Visual Arts

Architect
Randy Brown Architects

Location
Omaha, Nebraska

Photo Credit
© Farshid Assassi

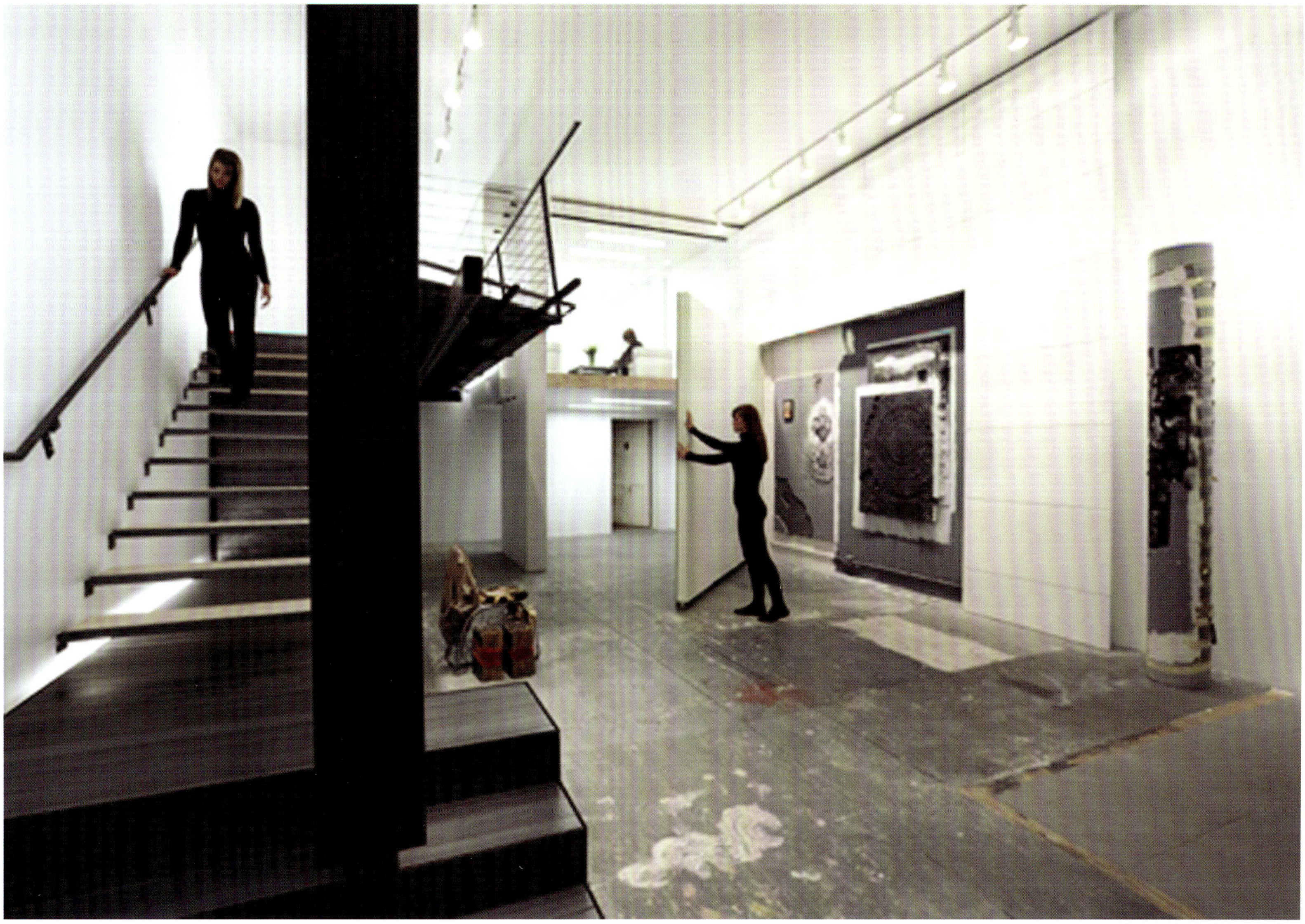

Plan Key:
1. Student Work Space
2. Gallery
3. Bellows' Preserved Studio
4. Library
5. Office
6. Bellows' Preserved Mural Space

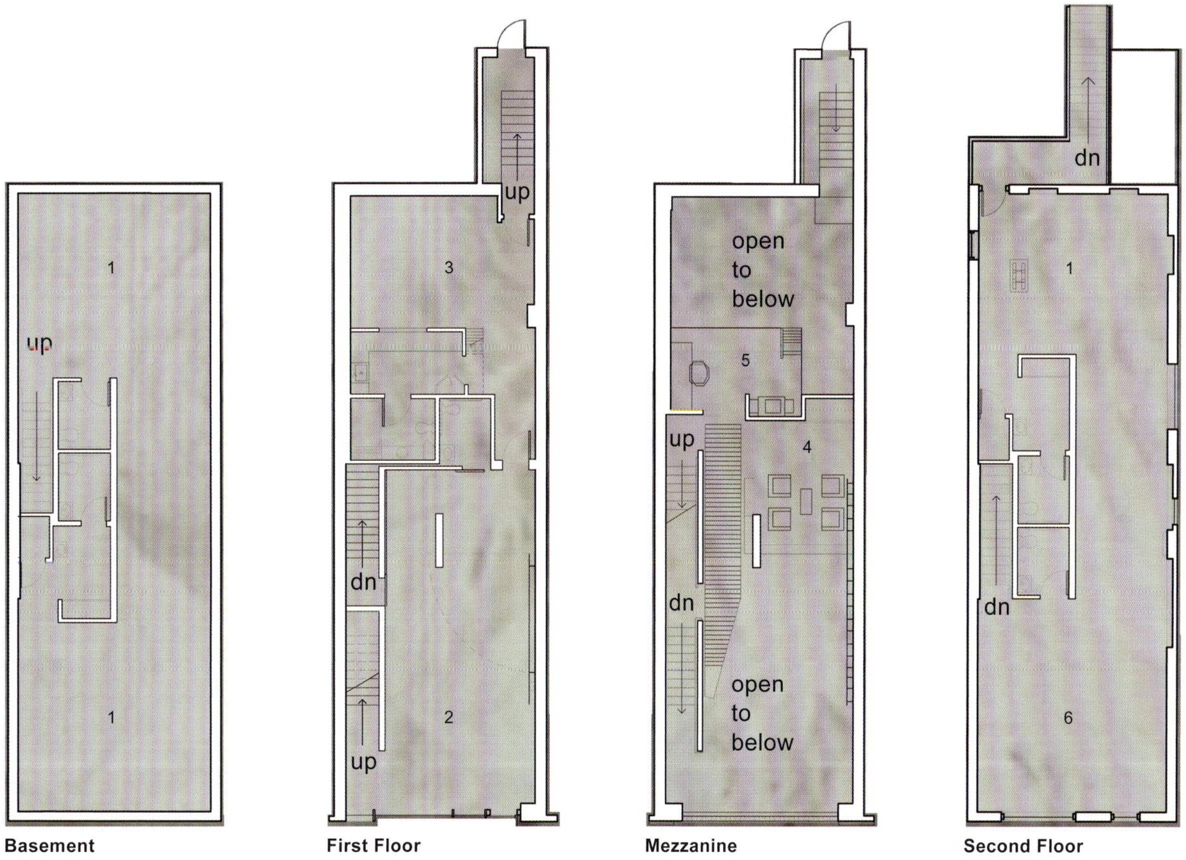

Basement

First Floor

Mezzanine

Second Floor

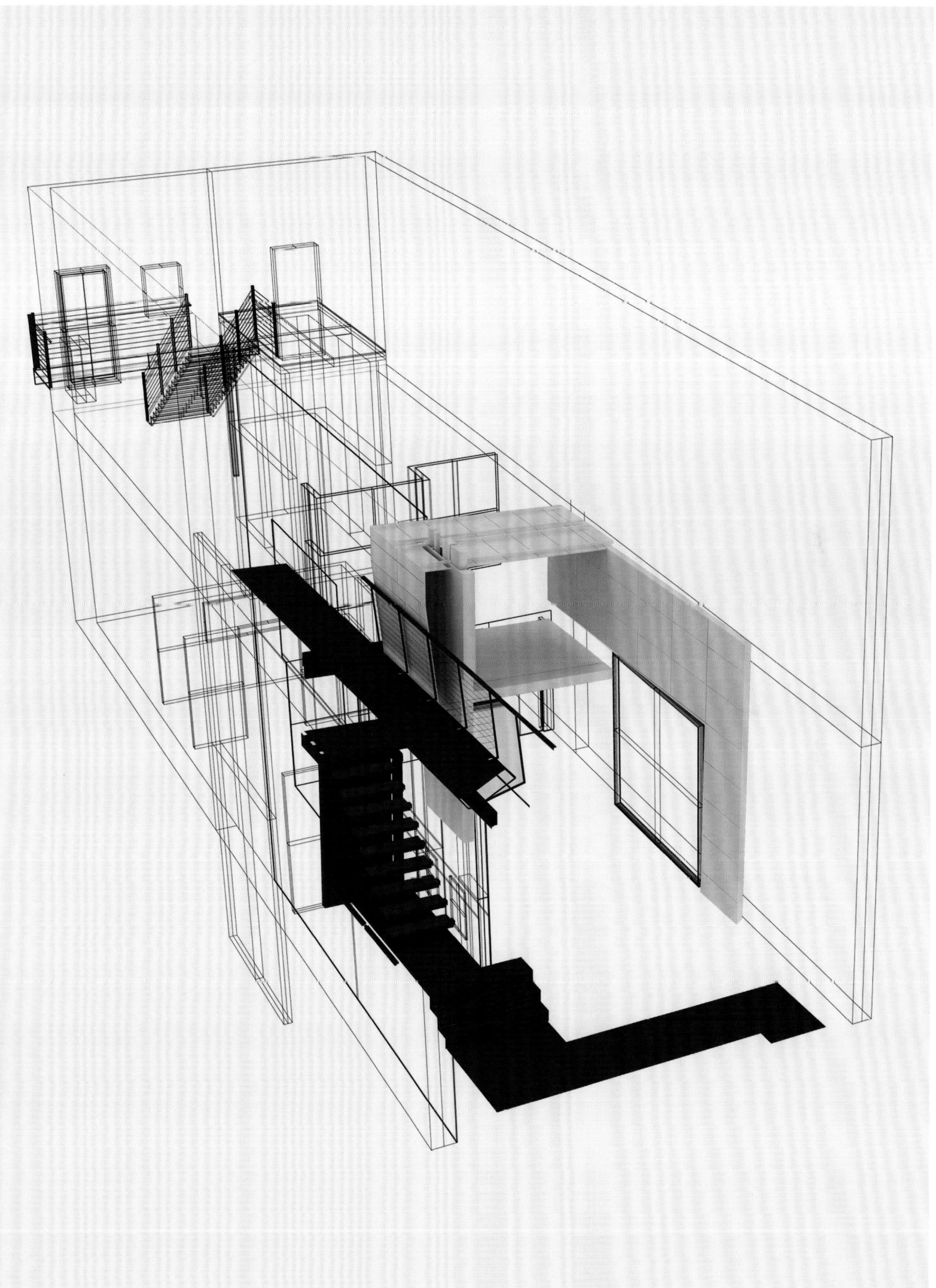

Children's Institute, Inc. Otis Booth Campus

Jury Comments:
An excellent example of adaptive re-use, this project creates a safe place for families exposed to violence.
The spatial zone between the north portion and the southern portion is well considered, effectively serving to open the building to natural light and interactive activities.

Notes of Interest

The adaptive reuse of three industrial buildings created the headquarters for a non-profit organization that assists children and families exposed to violence.

The campus is split by an alley with the north site focusing on preschool and early childhood services and the south site anchored around a community center offering educational programs (art, technology, nutrition, and after-school) as well as counseling services.

Therapy rooms are dispersed around community spaces to make visits an everyday, rather than clinical, experience. This innovative strategy deinstitutionalizes the services' traditional delivery and builds trust in a neighborhood in need of both counseling and community programs.

On a tight budget ($10.5 million), the design provides required amenities that also add a sense of identity and welcome. A key part of the process was re-thinking program organization to reveal opportunities for creative and collaborative community engagement.

Engineer: John A. Martin & Associates, Inc., KMA Consulting, KPFF Consulting Engineers
General Contractor: Swinerton
Environmental Graphics: Newsom Design
Geotechnical: Geotechnologies, Inc.
Hardware: Finish Hardware Technology
Landscaping: Nancy Goslee Power & Associates
Lighting: Horton Lees Brogden Lighting Design
LEED: AECOM
Signage: Newsom Design
Specifications: Specifications West, LLC
Waterproofing: IRC Waterproofing
Owner: Children's Institute, Inc.

Architect
Koning Eizenberg Architecture

Location
Los Angeles, California

Photo Credit
© Eric Staudenmaier

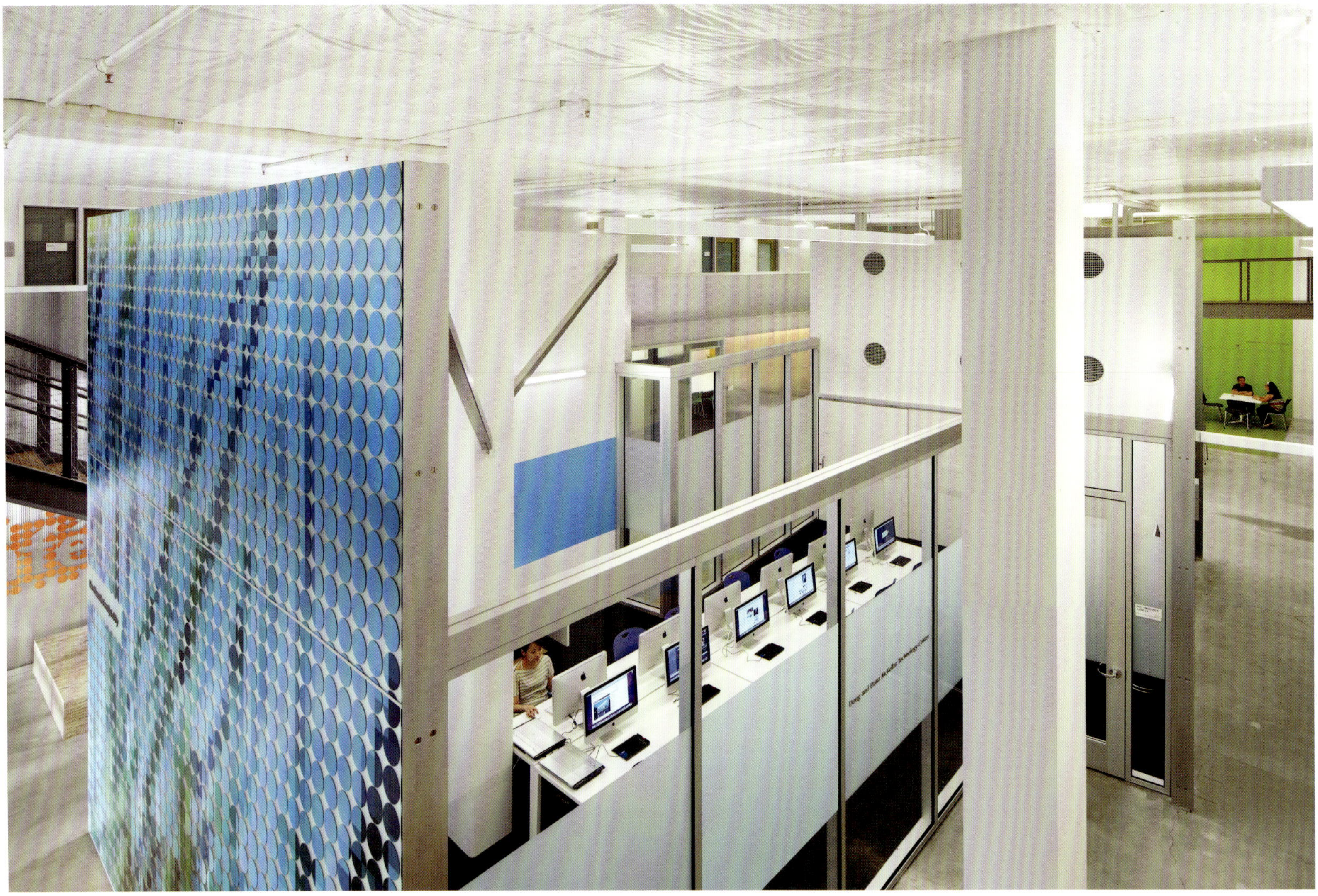

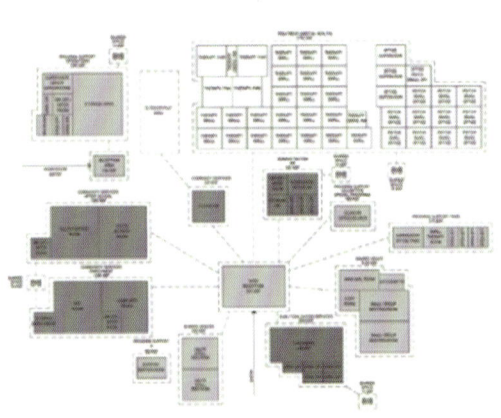
1. Owner's Program

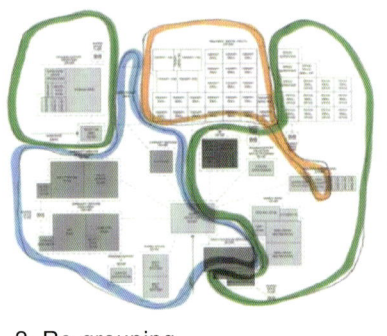
2. Re-grouping

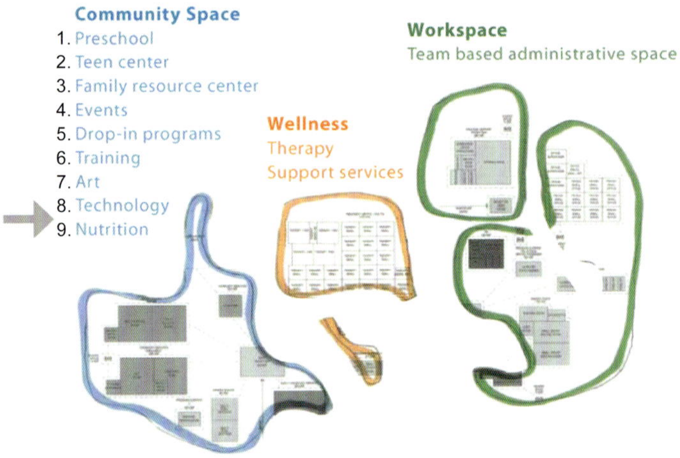

Community Space
1. Preschool
2. Teen center
3. Family resource center
4. Events
5. Drop-in programs
6. Training
7. Art
8. Technology
9. Nutrition

Wellness
Therapy
Support services

Workspace
Team based administrative space

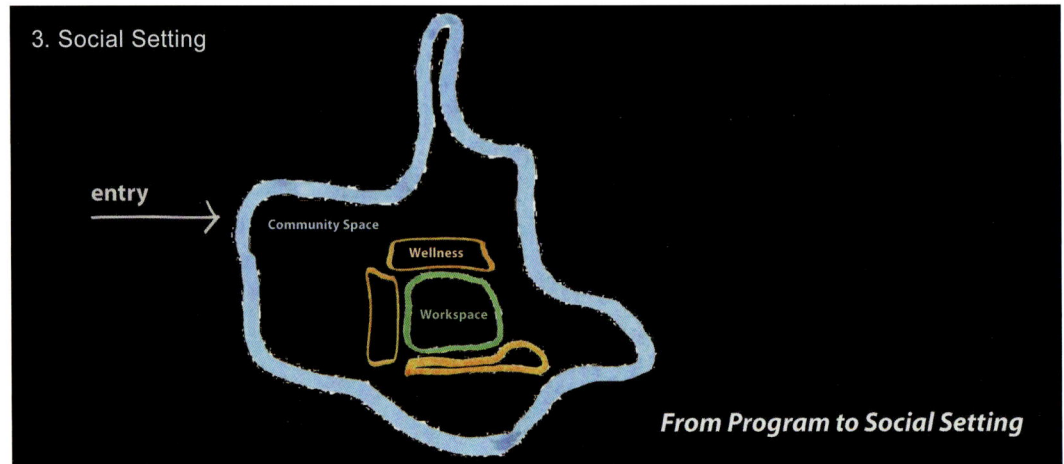

From Program to Social Setting

Key:

🟩 Workplace

🟧 Wellness Program

🟦 Community Space

Second Floor

Ground Floor

1. Entry
2. Curiosity Box Around Tech Center
3. Art Room
4. Big Room/Space
5. Activity Room
6. Café/Nutrition
7. Family Resource Center
8. Deliveries
9. Patio/Garden
10. Orange Grove
11. Edible Garden
12. Preschool
13. Play Yard
14. Workplace Reception
15. Half Court/Parking
16. Teen Center

David Rubenstein Atrium at Lincoln Center

Jury Comments:
This space is sensitively transformed incorporating nature, art, and commercial activity in a carefully modulated manner. The multiple scales created by the ceiling "puddles" and huge custom textile art are brought down to human scale by the inclusion of mural plantings, tables and chairs, reading areas, and well situated vendor stations.
This is an exceptional revitalization of an urban interior space that is both uplifting and considerate.

Notes of Interest

Harmony atrium, a privately owned public space, was a defacto homeless shelter and small rock-climbing business. Lincoln Center sponsored the space with the true intention of creating a place for the public.

Wedged into Manhattan's dense fabric, the 7,000 sf passageway serves as Lincoln Center's public visitor facility, welcoming city newcomers and neighborhood residents. The space, known as The David Rubenstein Atrium at Lincoln Center, offers free performances, information and tickets to events, and a place to have a cup of coffee or a glass of wine.

Cantilevered canopies announce the presence of the atrium. Visitors enter through large glass doors. They are greeted by 20-foot-high plant walls. Green marble benches, as well as moveable chairs and tables, offer places to rest. A fountain in the ceiling drops thin streams of water into a stone basin. Sixteen occuli pierce the golden ceiling to bring natural light into the double height space. In the evening, they are illuminated with colored artificial lights creating an ideal atmosphere for concerts.

Enormous felt paintings hang on two walls. One installation, grey ellipses rolling playfully on a yellow background, relates to the ceiling, and the other surrounds a media wall that serves as a canvas for projected information, images, and film. Transformed by light, color, texture, and thoughtfully chosen materials, the space is now a tranquil and welcoming oasis. In the first five months, more than 250,000 people visited the atrium.

Consultant: Acoustic Dimensions; Axis Group Limited; Dan Euser Waterarchitecture Inc; Fisher Dachs Associates; Pentagram Design, Inc.; Steven Winter Associate, Inc.; Vertical Garden Technology
Engineer: ARUP
General Contractor: RCDolner Construction LLC
Lighting: Fisher Marantz Stone
Owner: Lincoln Center for the Performing Arts

Architect
Tod Williams Billie Tsien Architects

Location
New York City, New York

Photo Credit
© Nic Lehoux, © Tod Williams Billie Tsien Architects

HyundaiCard Air Lounge

Jury Comments:
The project takes an innovative approach to the airline lounge model, effectively establishing a unique relationship between the passenger and the space.
The well-conceived assimilation of technology engages the traveler in both the "black box" and the surrounding walls that integrate the helpful passenger flight status flip-screens.
Extraordinarily clean detailing that does not come at the expense of function or friendliness.

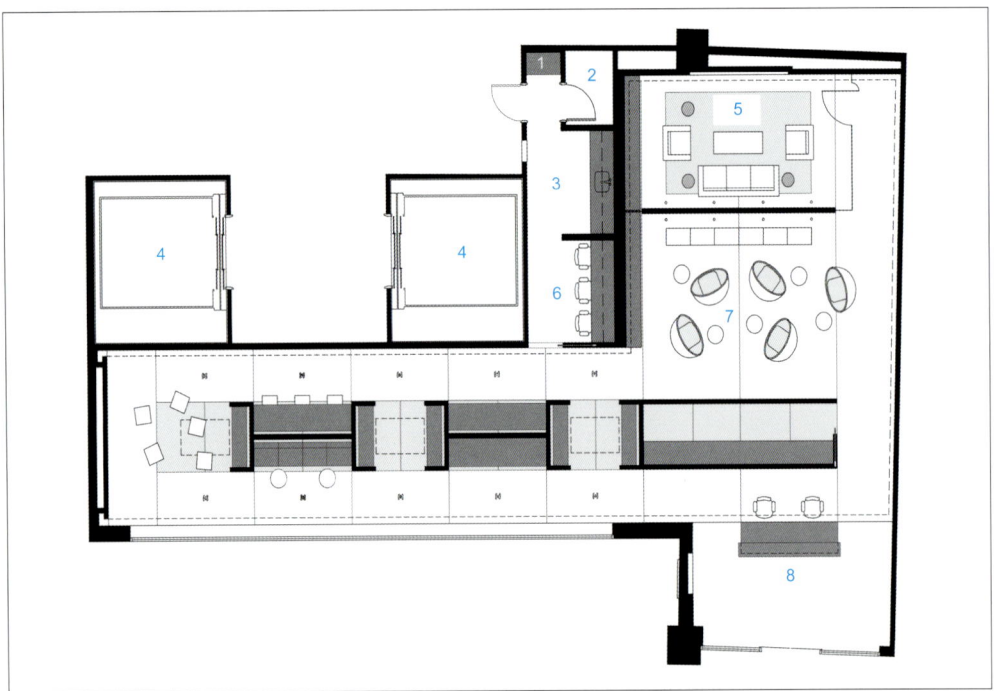

1. Locker
2. Janitor Closet
3. Pantry
4. Freight Elevator
5. Small Vip
6. Office
7. Large Vip
8. Reception

Notes of Interest

Located at Incheon Airport in Korea, this 250 sm project seeks to create an exclusive environment to offer unique travel assistance for HyundaiCard Black members. As a counterpoint to the surrounding visual noise and frenzied airport activity, the proposed parti is deceptively simple, with functions arranged in a freestanding "black box".

Much like a perfectly organized suitcase, this monolithic object contains all the information, accessories, entertainment, and gifts needed for a memorable travel experience. The HyundaiCard space shifts the paradigm of a traditional lounge by combining lounge, retail, and museum programs. Rather than a static place for waiting, it is a dynamic space one passes through to better prepare for the trip ahead. As such, visitors are able to pace their movements through the space according to individual needs, desires, and schedules.

Among the unique features in the lounge are a custom vending machine, fantastic dream-like art movies by Hiraki Sawa, and a personalized flight tracking system. Also, there are two virtual skylights in the black box, both of which move slowly through the color spectrum of the sky. These spaces act as haven-like environments in which travelers become aware of the sky's variations, thus establishing a symbolic, if not poetic relationship with the notion of air travel.

Within the constraint of a small envelope, reflective surfaces provide visual relief while cove lighting plays up the ethereal atmosphere of the space.

Consultant: Laschober + Sovitch
Engineer: Kesson International
Lighting: Kaplan Gehring McCarroll
Owner: HyundaiCard Company

Architect	Location	Photo Credit
Gensler	Incheon, South Korea	© Ryan Gobuty

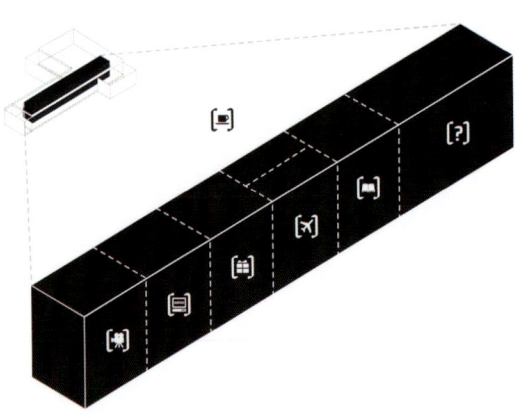

[?] Concierge
[✈] Travel Accessories
[▤] Printed Materials
[▦] Food & Refreshments
[▥] Giveaways
[▩] Business Center
[▶] Entertainment
[▣] VIP Lounge

How much time do you have?

- • • • • 05 Minutes [?]
- • • • • 15 Minutes [?]+[✈]
- • • • • 30 Minutes [?]+[✈]+[▤]
- • • • • 45 Minutes [?]+[▤]+[▦]+[▥]+[▩]
- • • • • 60 Minutes [?]+[▤]+[▦]+[▥]+[▩]+[▶]

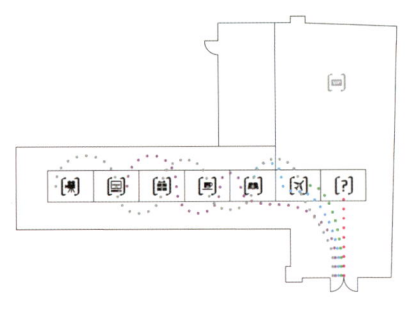

Virtual Skylights
The black boxes act as "skyspaces", i.e. impressively minimal structures with virtual skylights designed to change the way viewers perceive light. Because of the meditative way in which they channel light, the spaces act as haven-like environments in which travelers become aware of the sky's variations, thus establishing a symbolic, if not poetic, relationship with the notion of air travel.

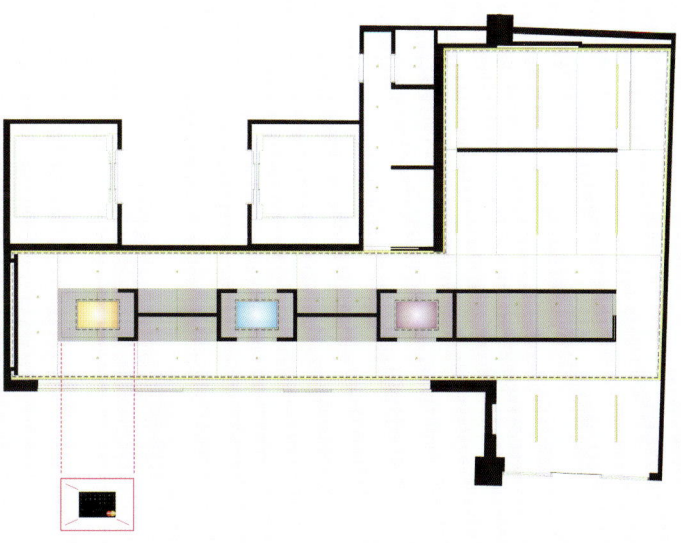

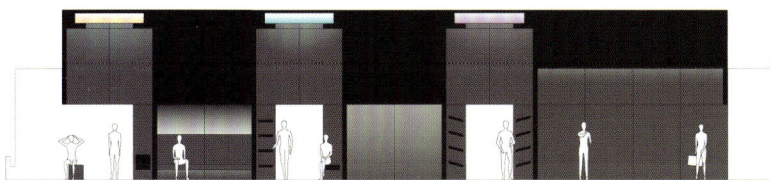

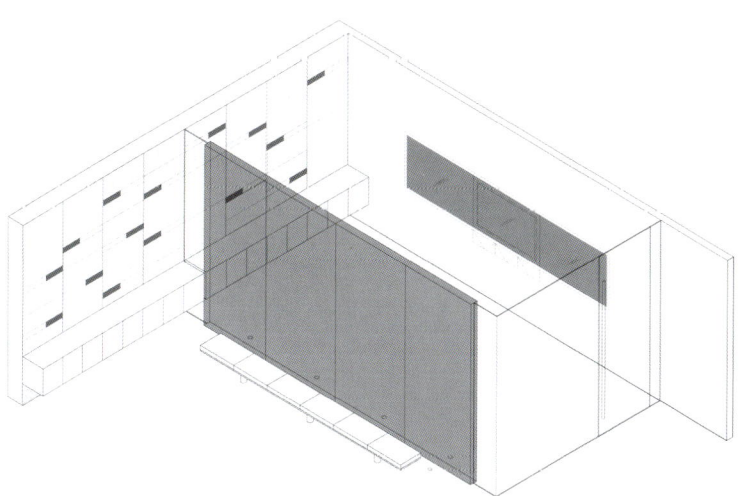

Flip Screens
Wanting to bring some of the excitement and romance associated with departures, we re-imagined the classic flip screen designed by Giorgio Segatto for the Solari di Udine Station in Milan. Upon check-in with the concierge, a traveler's information is relayed to one of fifteen LCD displays. Each LCD display cycles through a series of seven slides (guest name, airline, flight number, destination, gate/terminal, flight status and boarding time), thus creating a dynamic, personalized and artful way to ensure that card members make it on time.

The Integral House

Jury Comments:
The relationship of the home to both its musical program and its surrounding environment was superbly articulated.
The louvered vertical fins modulate the light and views to the exterior surroundings as well as correlate to music theory rooted in strong rhythm and syncopation. The fins added both measure and cadence to the overall movement.
The sensitivity, appropriate application, craft, and execution of detail were well executed.

Notes of Interest

The Integral House creates a place for architecture, music, and performance located at the threshold between Toronto's urban fabric and its extensive natural ravine system. In the project's program brief, the client clearly articulated his dual passion for mathematics and music and his interest in curvilinear shapes resulting in spatially complex volumes.

Viewed from its residential neighborhood, one reads a two story building with a grounded wood base sitting below a translucent gently shaped etched glass skin. The wooden base dissolves into oak clad fins echoing the undulating contour lines of the river valley and the winding pathways of the native forest of oaks, beaches, and maples. The main concert hall/performance space is located a full floor below your entry level and becomes intertwined with the verdant ravine landscape.

The project integrates many sustainable features into the site and building. A field of vertical geothermal pipes supplies heating and cooling for the entire project including the main concert hall/performance space for 150–200 people. A lush green roof is centrally located and a visual feature from many parts of the project. The vertical wooden fins provide sun shading from the exterior as well as contributing to the acoustical performance of the concert hall/performance space. Materials have been carefully selected for their aesthetic contribution as well as their enduring qualities based on life cycle costing calculations.

Engineer: Blackwell Bowick Partnership; DT Prohaska Engineering; Dynamic Designs and Engineering Inc.; Toews Engineering
Fountain Consultant: Waterarchitecture Inc.
General Contractor: Eisner Murray Custom Builders
Interior Design: Decisive Moment
Landscape Architect: NAK Design Group
Lighting: Suzanne Powadiuk Design Inc.
Acoustical: Swallow Consultants
Owner: Dr. James Stewart

Architect
Shim-Sutcliffe Architects

Location
Toronto, Canada

Photo Credit
© James Dow

Joukowsky Institute for Archaeology & the Ancient World

Jury Comments:
This is an extremely intelligent and compelling project on multiple levels.
The design makes a clever reference to its archaeological interests by creating a "found" object that is both beautifully detailed and sophisticated in expression.
The effort directed at dissolving the boundaries between student and teacher is admirable and the overall project renders a fresh, dynamic interior intervention that is both innovative and beautifully resolved.

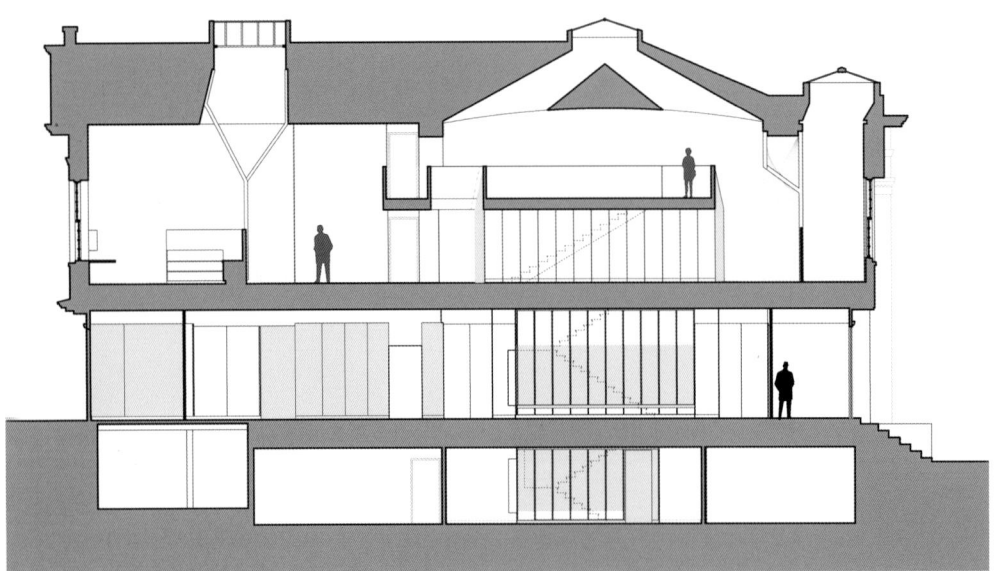

Notes of Interest

The Joukowsky Institute for Archaeology and the Ancient World completely reinvents Rhode Island Hall, a historic Greek Revival building at the center of the Brown University campus. It is an endowed institute, serving the Brown community with teaching, research, fieldwork, and classroom studies for both graduates and undergraduates.

This project restores Rhode Island Hall's exterior, and entirely renovates its interior. The extensive spatial and structural reconfiguration allows us to reconsider the ways that daylight was delivered throughout the project. Translucency of both glass and wood creates varying levels of transparency and daylight between program spaces, encouraging a more interactive dialogue between faculty and student.

The contemporary intervention within this historic shell challenges the notion of archaeology as a conservative and dusty pursuit, and supports the mission of the Joukowsky Institute as a progressive leader in the field of archaeology. The transformation of Rhode Island Hall as the home for the new Joukowsky Institute is a significant part of Brown's new Plan for Academic Enrichment.

The project is a leading example of the University's approach to reanimating its historic building fabric and also demonstrates its commitment to sustainability. Rhode Island Hall is the first building at Brown to be certified LEED Gold for New Construction.

Engineer: RDK Engineers; Richmond So Engineering; GZA GeoEnvironmental Inc.
General Contractor: Shawmut Design & Construction
Landscape Architect: Hines Wasser & Associates
Lighting: LAM Partners, Inc.
Owner: Brown University

Architect
Anmahian Winton Architects

Location
Providence, Rhode Island

Photo Credit
© Peter Vanderwarker

Memory Temple

Jury Comments:
This project presents a remarkable approach to investigating the creation of space.
The idea of generating a form-aesthetic memory of environmental sounds by using a six-axis CNC machine that mills mapped frequencies translated into points and vectors is altogether fascinating.
The ingenious process of fabrication is visible as final product; interior space, in this case, becomes a physical manifestation of another aspect of current culture.

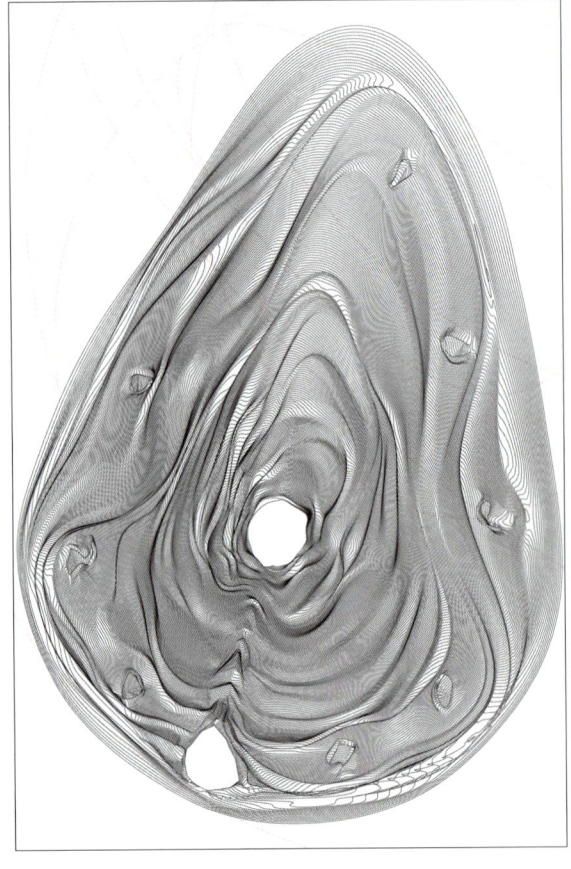

Notes of Interest
Memory Temple is an experience at the convergence of sound, material, light, form, and technology. The installation is accompanied by a site-specific composition by a world-renowned composer. The sound-scape is integral to the experience and used to explore the spatialization of sound within the physical boundaries of the gallery.
The installation proposes a new structural materiality through the use of renewable polyurethane foam. The foam was used as a total building assembly: structure, envelope, and acoustical barrier. Layers of closed cell foam (used structurally) and open cell foam (used acoustically) were combined to make up the wall assembly.
The pure geometry of the parabola provided a natural self-structural form. The musical composition is integral to the experience and provided an ever-changing mobile performed with custom software designed specifically for the installation. Resonance was exploited within the acoustically absorptive space.

Architect
Patrick Tighe Architecture

Location
Los Angeles, California

Photo Credit
© Art Gray Photography

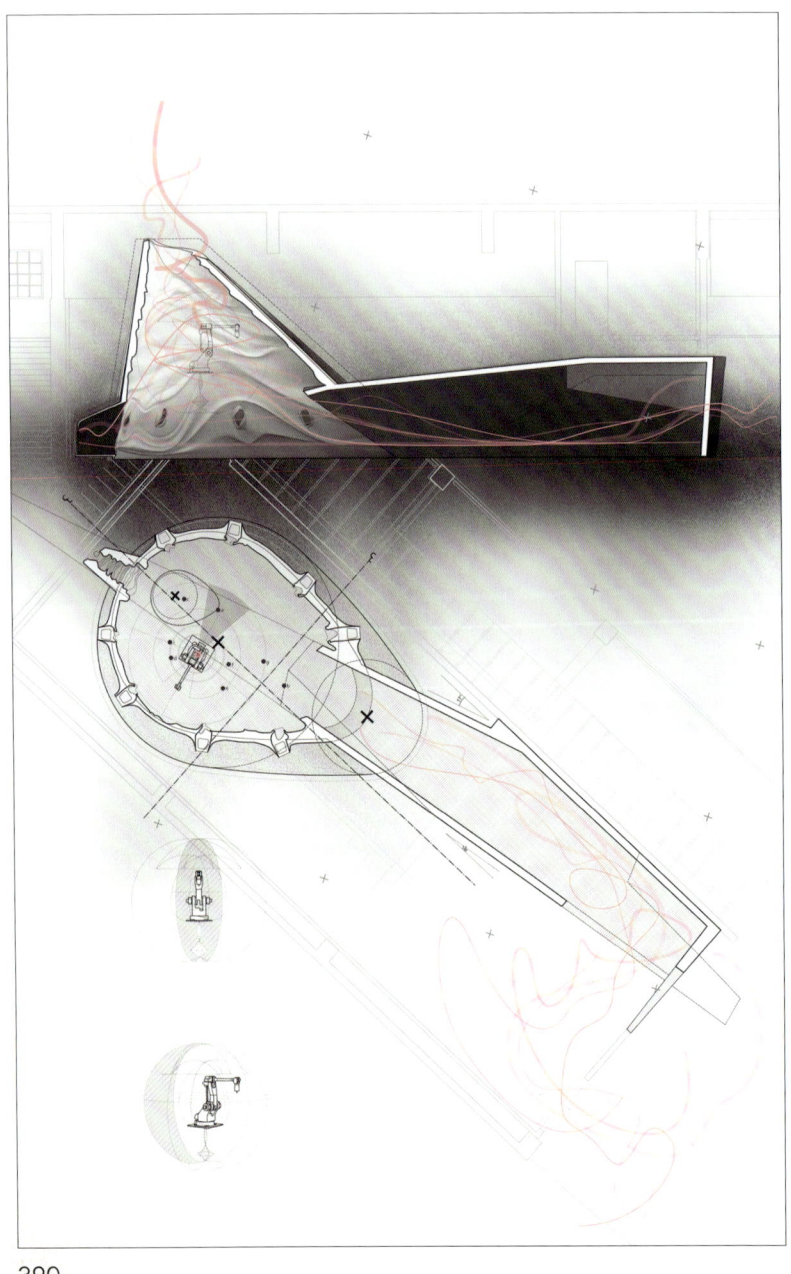

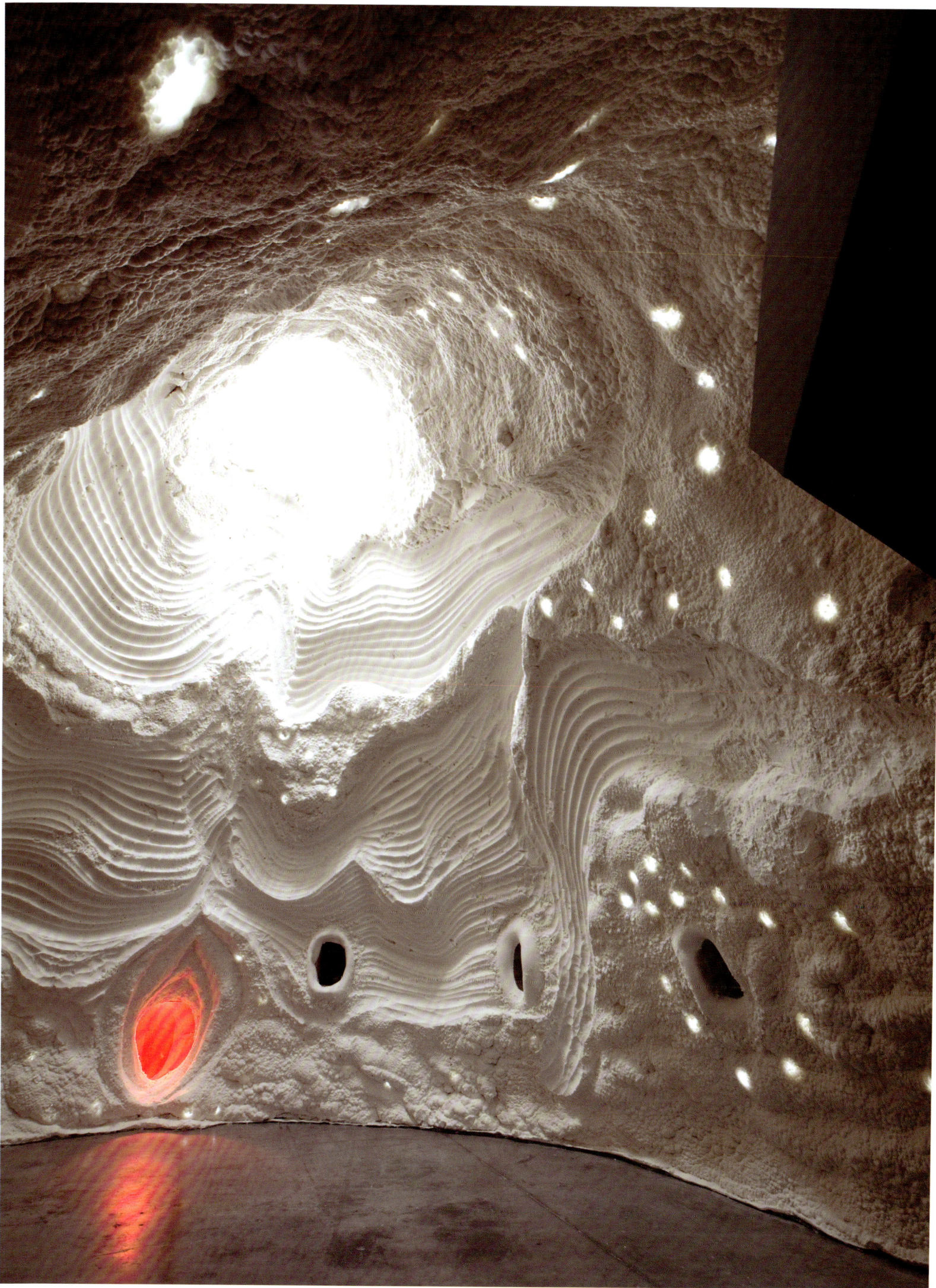

Prairie Management Group

Jury Comments:
Small and well-executed, this project is quiet, restrained, and sophisticated with a straight-forward manner towards both the composition and detail that reinforces the larger concept.
Standing in contrast to the natural prairie grass outside, the design effectively organizes the plan around a central armature inducing the glass screen walls to both modulate the plan and effectively provide light and views to the meadow beyond.

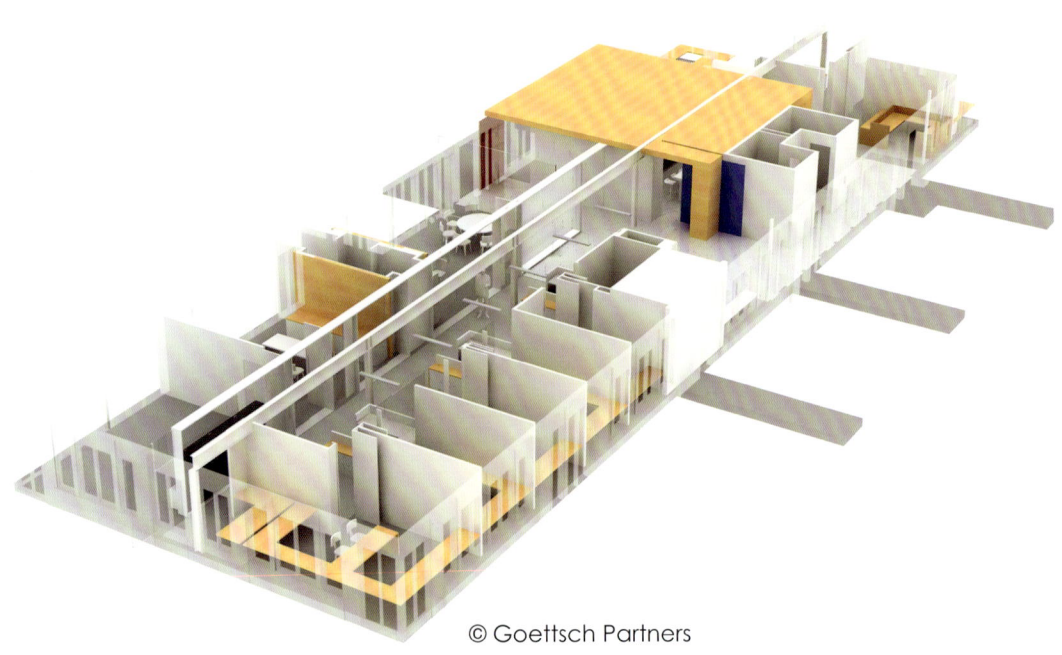

© Goettsch Partners

Notes of Interest

Executive investment offices for a retired design entrepreneur, the founder of a national home furnishings retailer, provided the opportunity to leverage the client's passion for clean, bold modern design into a dramatic, light-filled investment office environment showcasing the client's extensive glass and ceramic art collection.

Inserted into a single-story, speculative office suite, the 7,500 sf facility is organized around three compositional elements: the colonnade, created by the building's exposed structural steel columns and central ridge beam; full-height glass screen walls; and a custom maple "pavilion".

The simple, classic interior composition of thin glass frames and bold, clear millwork forms rendered in a timeless color palette – all awash in natural light – creates a platform in which the appreciation of fine art, design, and nature enables a pioneering entrepreneur to continue his lifelong passion for creating business value through design.

Engineer: Cartland Kraus Engineering, Ltd,
The Structural Group
General Contractor: Pepper Construction
Landscape Architect: Hoerr Schaudt Landscape Architects
Owner: Prairie Management Group

Architect
Goettsch Partners

Location
Northbrook, Illinois

Photo Credit
© Michelle Litvin, © Goettsch Partners

© Michelle Litvin

Record House Revisited

Jury Comments:
An excellent example of new work within a significant mid-century modern structure, the interventions appear to reinforce the original design concept.
Eliminating carefully selected interior walls allows floor-to-ceiling openings, emphasizing the integrity of the two pavilions.
The new work serves to highlight the naturally lit passage and accentuate the overall spirit of the house.

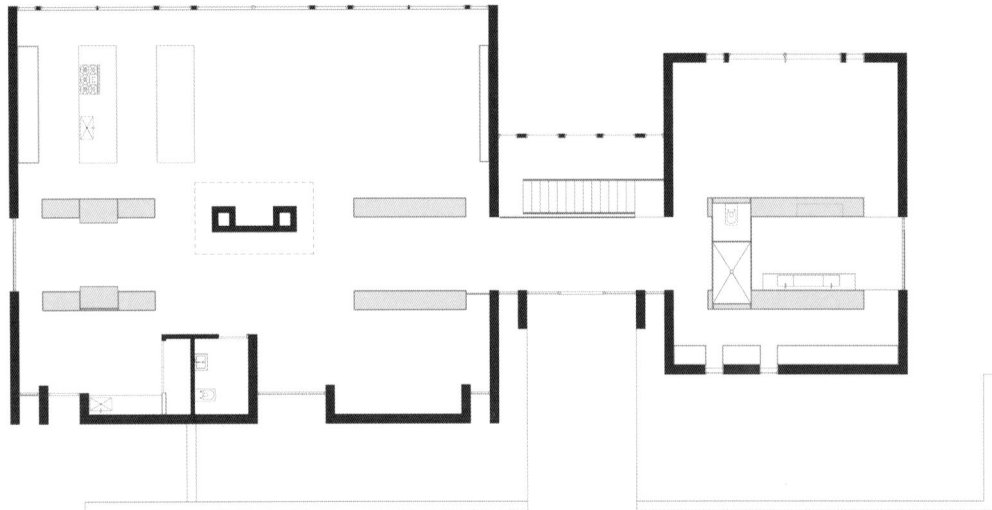

Notes of Interest

Four decades after their project was featured in the 1969 Record Houses issue of Architectural Record, the owners sold the house to a young couple. A condition of the sale was that the new owners would respect the character of the project, yet be able to revisit and alter the contained quality of the interior rooms to create a continuous living space visually connected to the woodland site.

An analysis of the existing structure revealed ordering devices through which the new work could be understood. A truss roof system allowed interior walls to be eradicated, yielding a condition of an unencumbered public and private pavilion linked together by a glass entry node. Floor to ceiling window apertures relating the pavilions could not be experienced within the original floor plan.

Registering the new work to the existing house is a conceptual allee of walnut casework. The casework weaves together and provides clarity to the various living areas. The quarter sawn casework and flat sawn flooring employ walnut in a Chiascuro manner, creating bold contrasts to the existing white painted brick walls and plaster ceiling. Corian casework elements are positioned as kitchen, mudroom, and bath objects, further juxtaposing a smoothness to the textural brick and plaster.

The purity of the original brick fireplace and skylight ring at the center of the house is exposed and left uninterrupted, allowing for additional connection to the site.

General Contractor: Prr

Architect
David Jameson Architect

Location
Owings Mill, Maryland

Photo Credit
© Paul Warchol

The Wright at the Guggenheim Museum

Jury Comments:
This project is sensitively handled and respectful of the essence of the original architecture.
With the confined space and ostensibly modest budget, given those challenging constraints, this project is exceptional. Of special note is the programmatic flexibility.
The design approach was controlled but playful, and complements the nuance of the museum overall movement and dynamic.

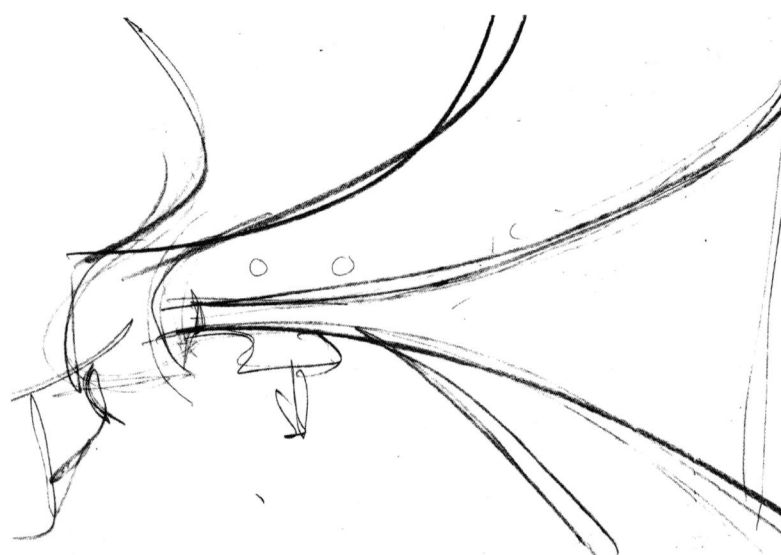

Notes of Interest
It was both an incredible honor and an exhilarating challenge to create The Wright, the new restaurant at the Guggenheim Museum — which is the first addition to the building's iconic interior. The architect sought to create a contemporary response to complement the building with an extremely modest budget and 1,600 square feet in which to work.

The design solution references the building's architecture, what Wright specifically called "the primitive initial", without repeating it. In the process, the architects transform underlying architectural geometries into dynamic spatial effects. The sculptural forms create a flared ceiling. The undulating walls become comfortable seating. The arced bar and communal table animate the space. The playfulness of these forms offers a dynamic experience for visitors.

This project is highly tactile and crafted from innovative, contemporary materials. These include fiber-optic layered walnut, a shimmering skin of innovative custom metalwork, seamless Corian surfaces, illuminated planes of woven grey texture, and a glowing white canopy of layered taut membranes. Together these materials and colors form a perfect complement to the site-specific artwork by Liam Gillick. The surfaces and textures embody movement, creating an ever-changing aesthetic that is enlivened with subtle layers of illumination and glowing tiers of light that envelope the room.

The space achieves an elegant and dynamic setting for dining that both celebrates the museum and transcends it.

Engineer: HHF Design Consulting, Ltd.
General Contractor: James G. Kennedy & Co., Inc.
Lighting: Tillotson Design Associates
Owner: Restaurant Associates

Architect
Andre Kikoski Architect, PLLC

Location
New York City, New York

Photo Credit
© Peter Aaron

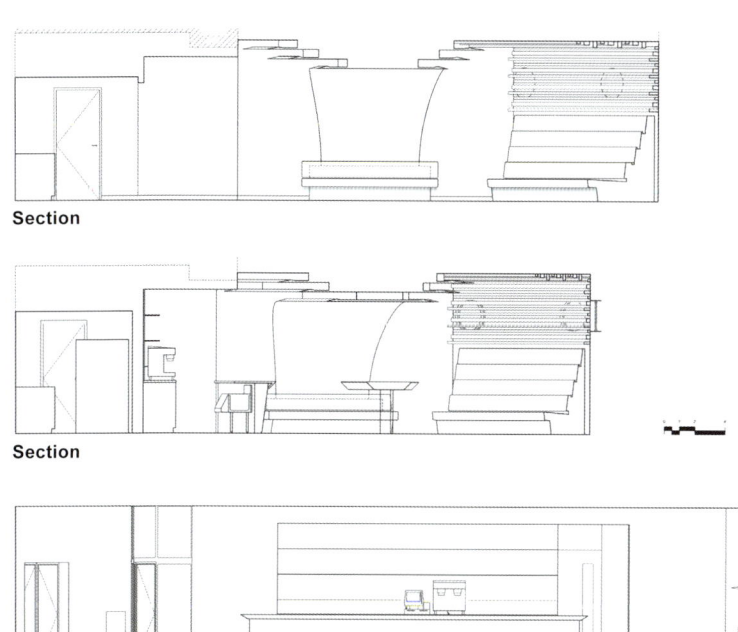

Section

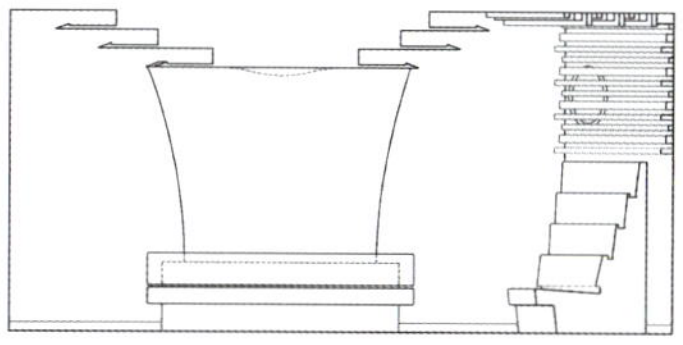

Section

Elevation Northeast

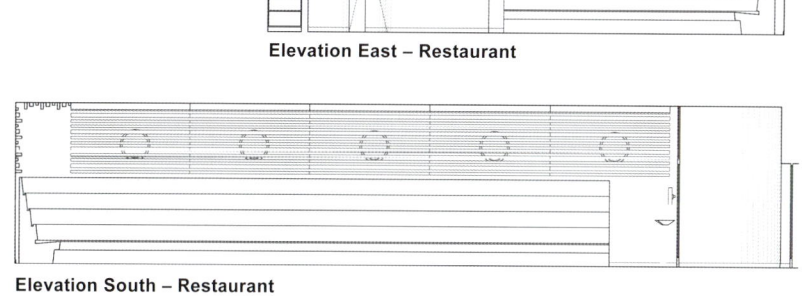

Elevation Northeast - Restaurant

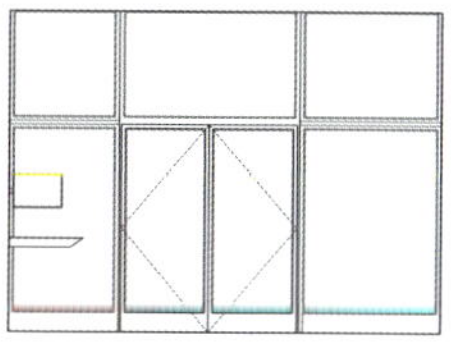

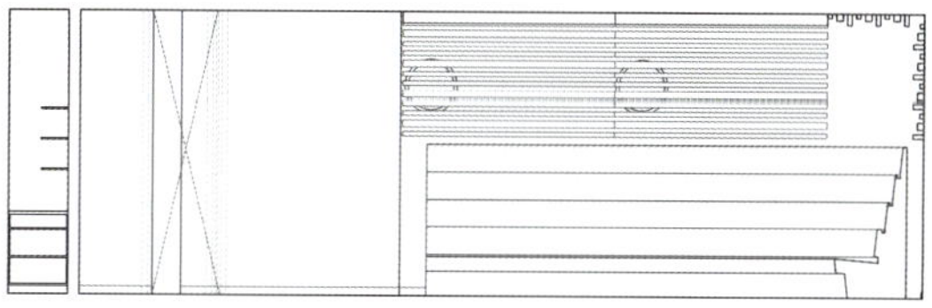

Elevation East – Restaurant

Elevation South – Restaurant

Elevation West- Restaurant

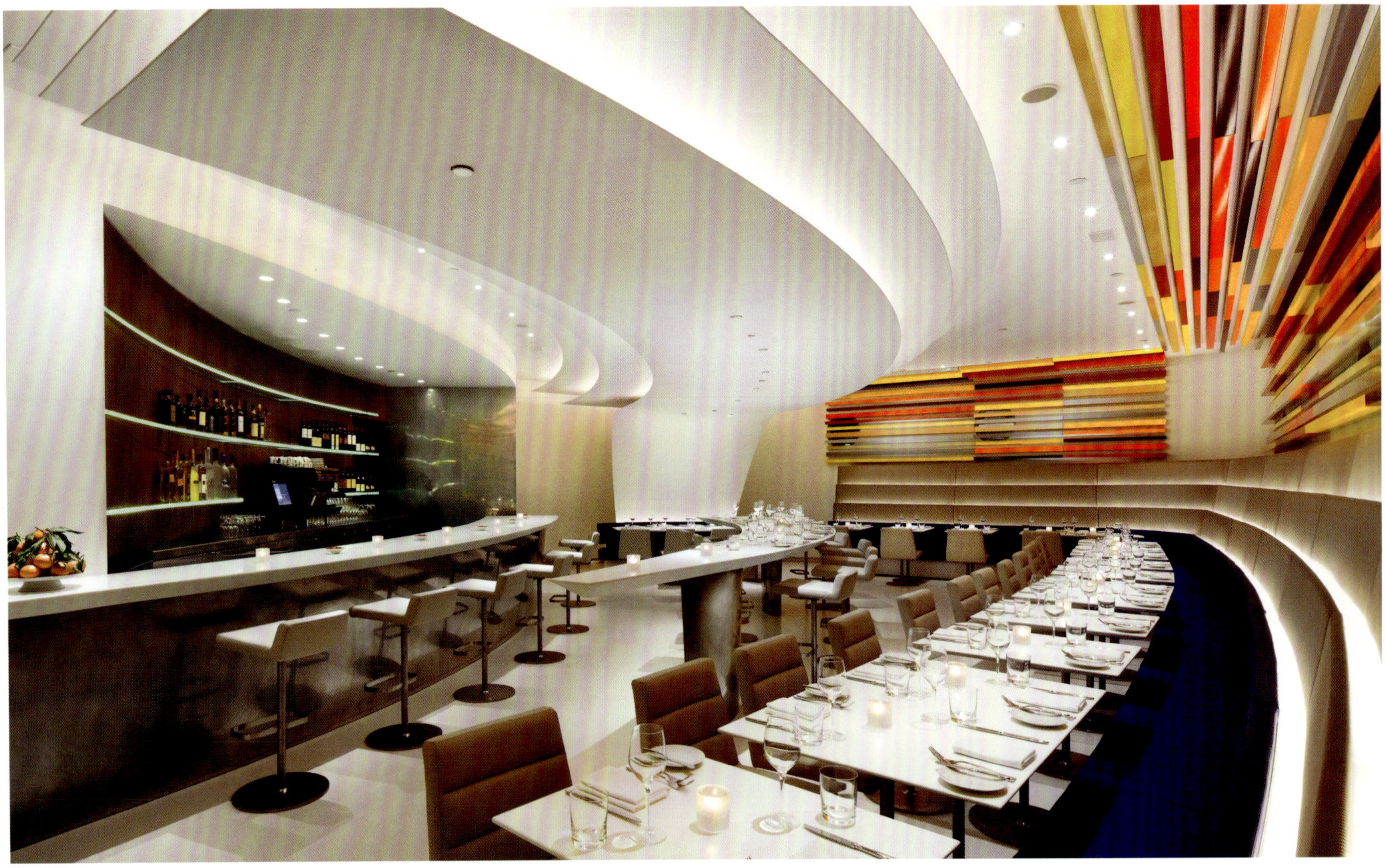

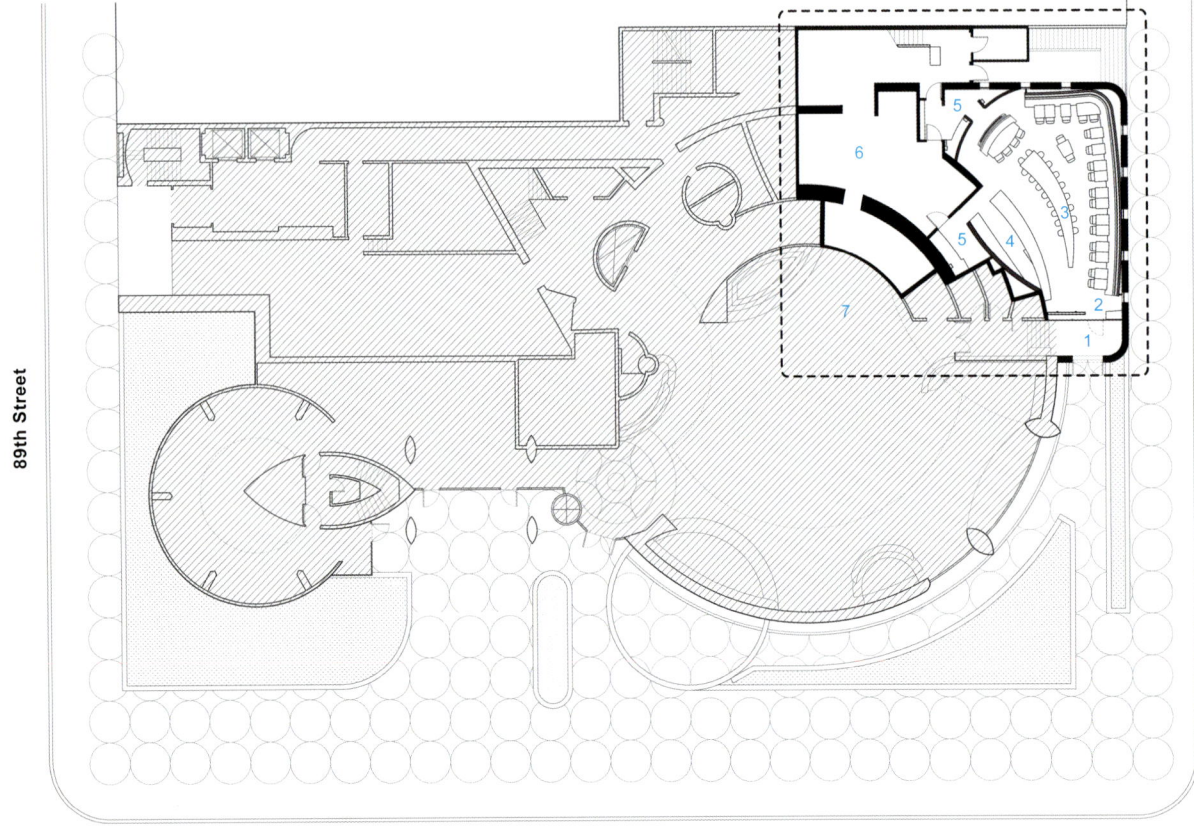

Site Plan:
1. Vestibule
2. Hostess
3. Dining Room
4. Bar
5. Service
6. Kitchen
7. Not In Scope

89th Street

Fifth Avenue

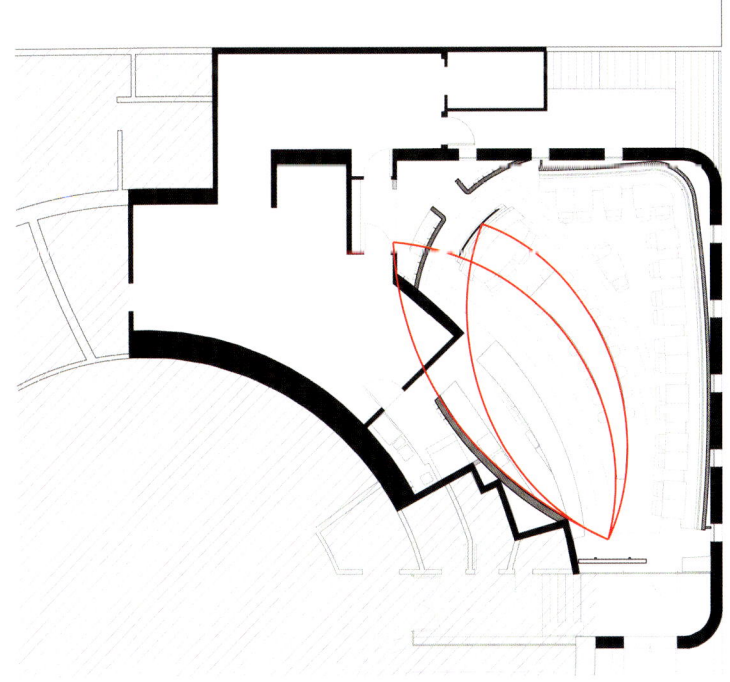
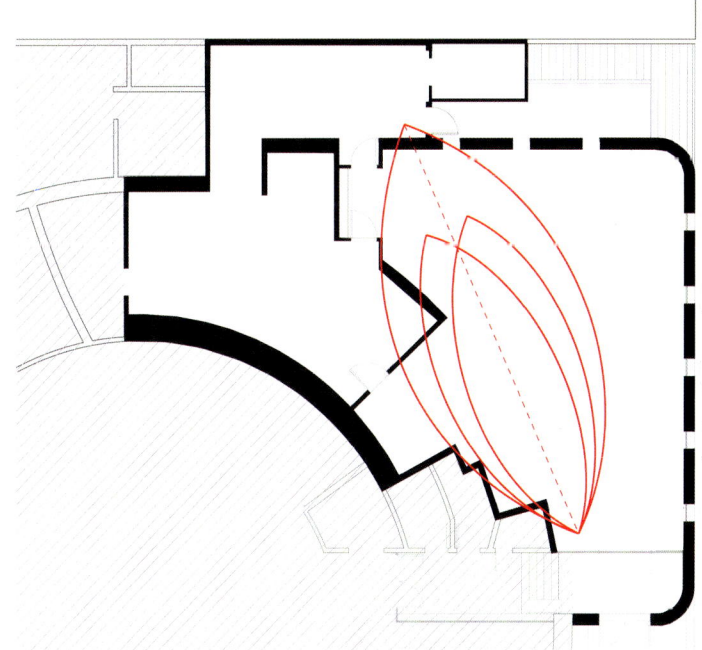

Fayetteville 2030: Transit City Scenario

Jury Comments:
The premise of this project is very forward-thinking.
There is a great appreciation for the comprehensive scope of this project as well as the clear visualization of the character of the public space within the scale of infrastructure.
The preservation of the rural character of the existing town as well as the addition of the more modern elements has been masterfully handled.

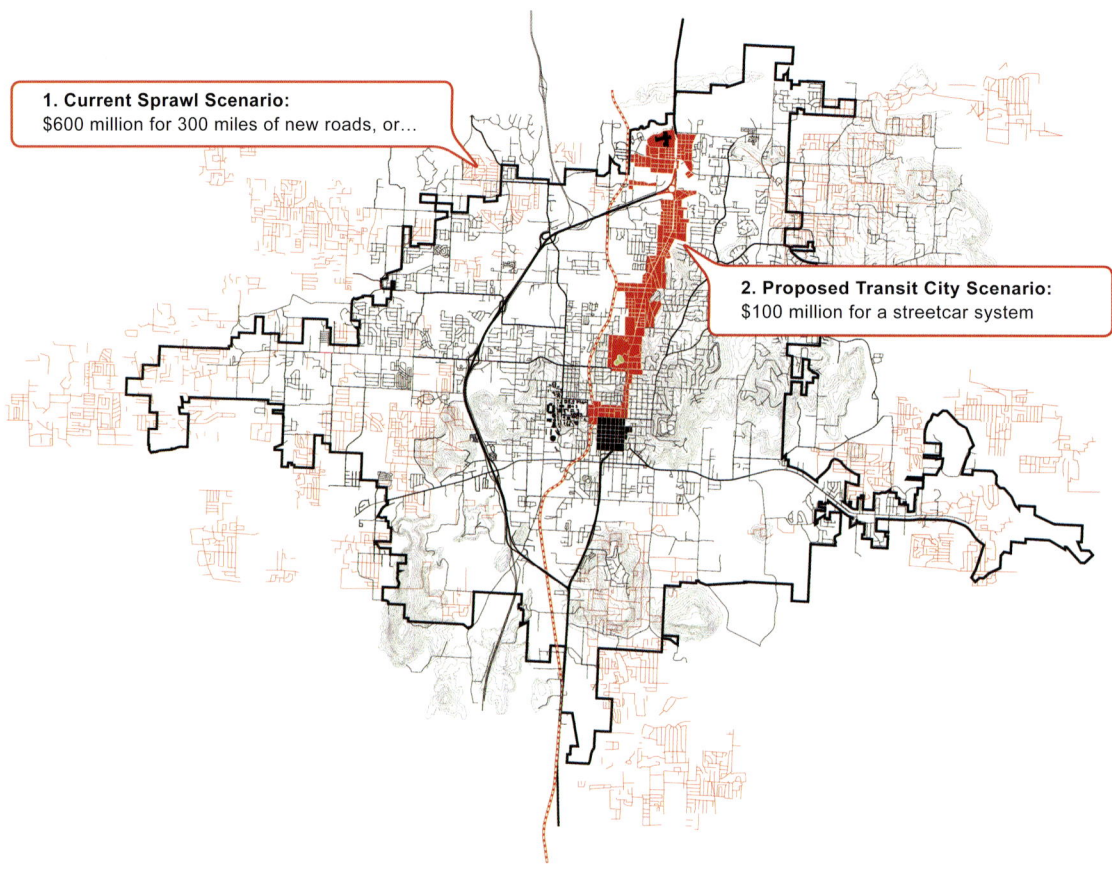

Notes of Interest

As a complement to Fayetteville's 2030 City Plan, a 2030 Transit City Scenario Plan independently models a future based on development of a streetcar system. While city planning is generally future-oriented, scenario planning models specific futures from the insistent exploration of a particular driver through "what if" propositions.

Scenario planning helps the community envision plausible planning possibilities that would not have emerged from charrettes and similar participation processes. They ask: what if 80% of future growth was incented to locate around a street car system proposed for Fayetteville's main urban arterial? The city could create a five-mile signature multi-modal transit boulevard, transforming underperforming development into mixed-use transit-oriented neighborhoods.

The post-carbon sustainable city will be based on multi-modal transportation systems that support passenger rail and walkable neighborhoods in tandem with the automobile, and their objective was to prepare such a model for a five-mile segment between the downtown/university district and the regional shopping mall at the city's edge.

Akin to the early 20th century streetcar cities, built at 7-14 dwelling units per acre, their plan updates the role of rail transit in reforming land uses for small town markets.

Owner: City of Fayetteville, Arkansas

Architect
University of Arkansas Community Design Center

Location
Fayetteville, Arkansas

Photo Credit
© University of Arkansas Community Design Center

In 2000, NWA households spent more on transportation than they did on housing. According to the Center for Neighborhood Technologies, a typical NWA household spent 29% of its annual income on transportation, far above the national average household in rail transit cities spent 16% of its annual income on transportation.

What if 80% of all new growth projected for Fayetteville over the next twenty years were incented to locate around a streetcar system proposed for College Avenue?

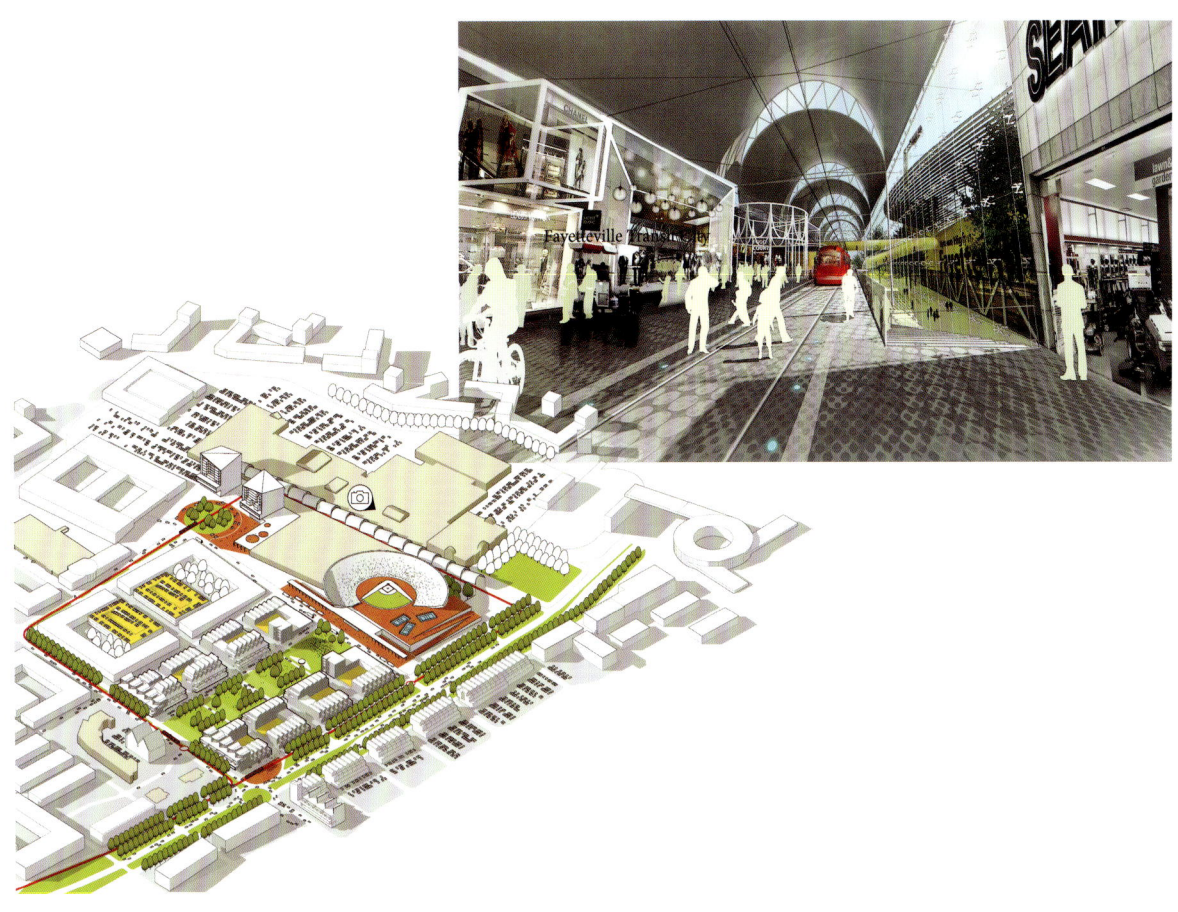

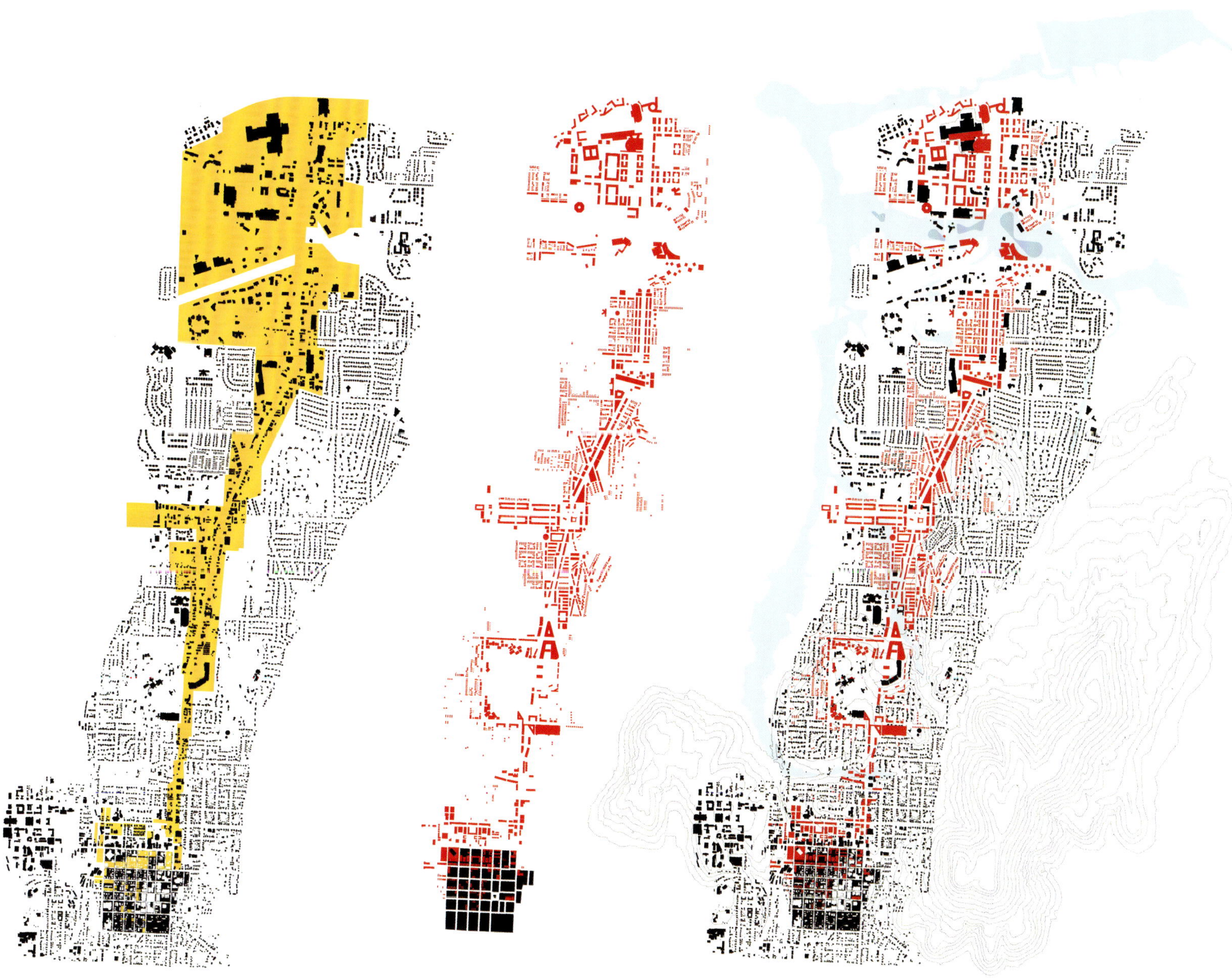

Grangegorman Urban Quarter Master Plan

Jury Comments:
This project presents an impressively comprehensive approach to site planning, with clear and systematic design strategies. The adaptive reuse of the historic existing buildings appears to be very successful.
The sense of transparency both within the new buildings and through the interstitial public space is impressive. The diagrammatic representation of the fundamental design strategies was both clear and compelling.

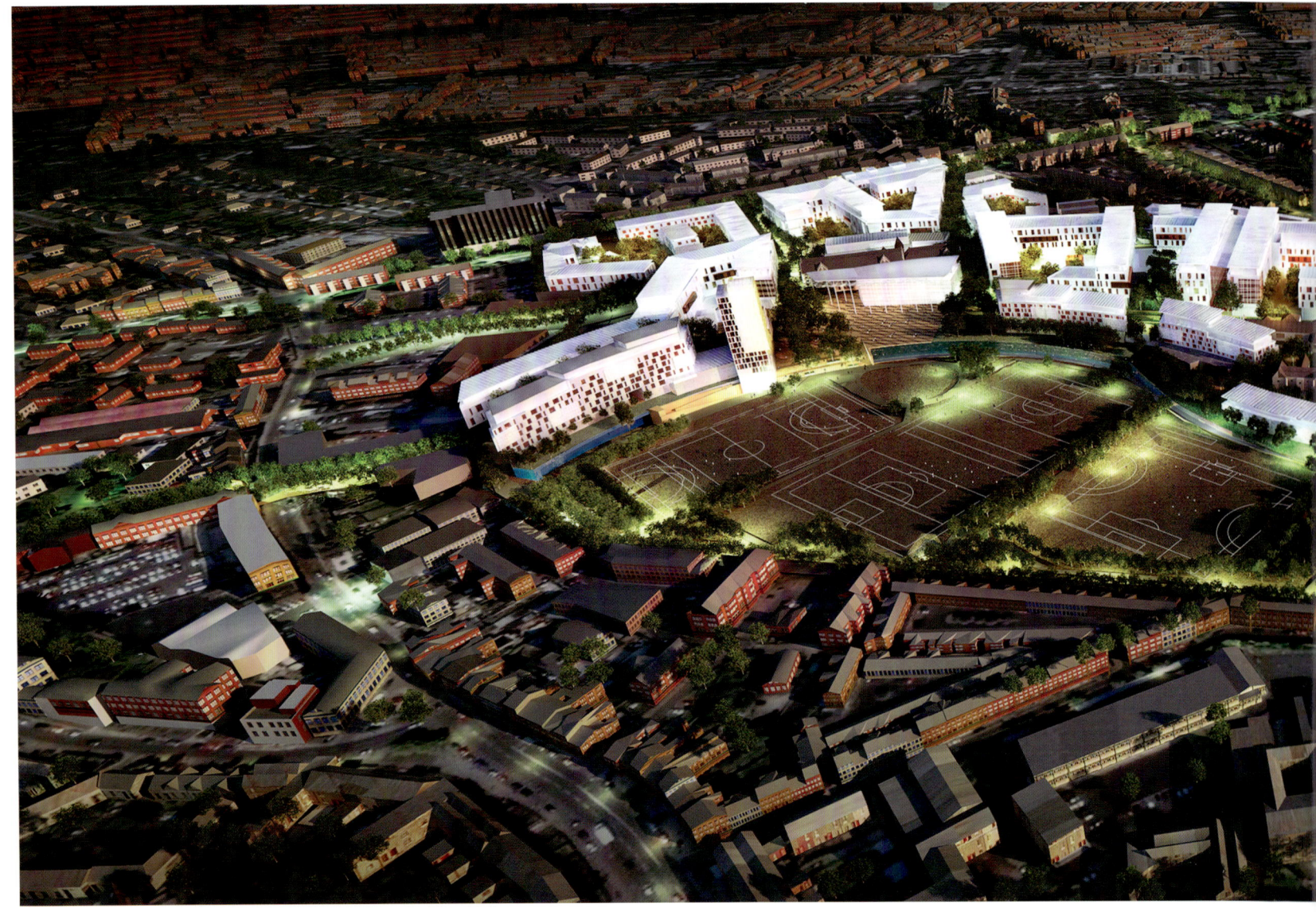

Notes of Interest

The Grangegorman Master Plan represents the largest higher-education campus development ever undertaken in the history of the state of Ireland, creating a vibrant new Urban Quarter for Dublin's north inner city.

It will accommodate 422,300 square meters of academic and residential buildings for the Dublin Institute of Technology (DIT), along with replacement psychiatric facilities and new primary care facilities for Ireland's national health care service, the HSE, and new amenities for the local community Urd the wider surrounding city.

The site is 73 acres which is currently used by the old St. Brendan's Psychiatric Hospital. It has been walled off from the rest of the city of Dublin since the early nineteenth century and is one of the largest undeveloped pieces of land in the city.

Engineer: ARUP
Environmental Sustainability: Battle McCarthy Consulting Engineers
Landscape Architect: Lützow 7
Conservation: Shaffrey Associates
Owner: Dublin Institute of Technology and Health Service Executive

Architect
Moore Ruble Yudell Architects & Planners; DMOD Architects

Location
Dublin, Ireland

Photo Credit
© Moore Ruble Yudell Architects & Planners

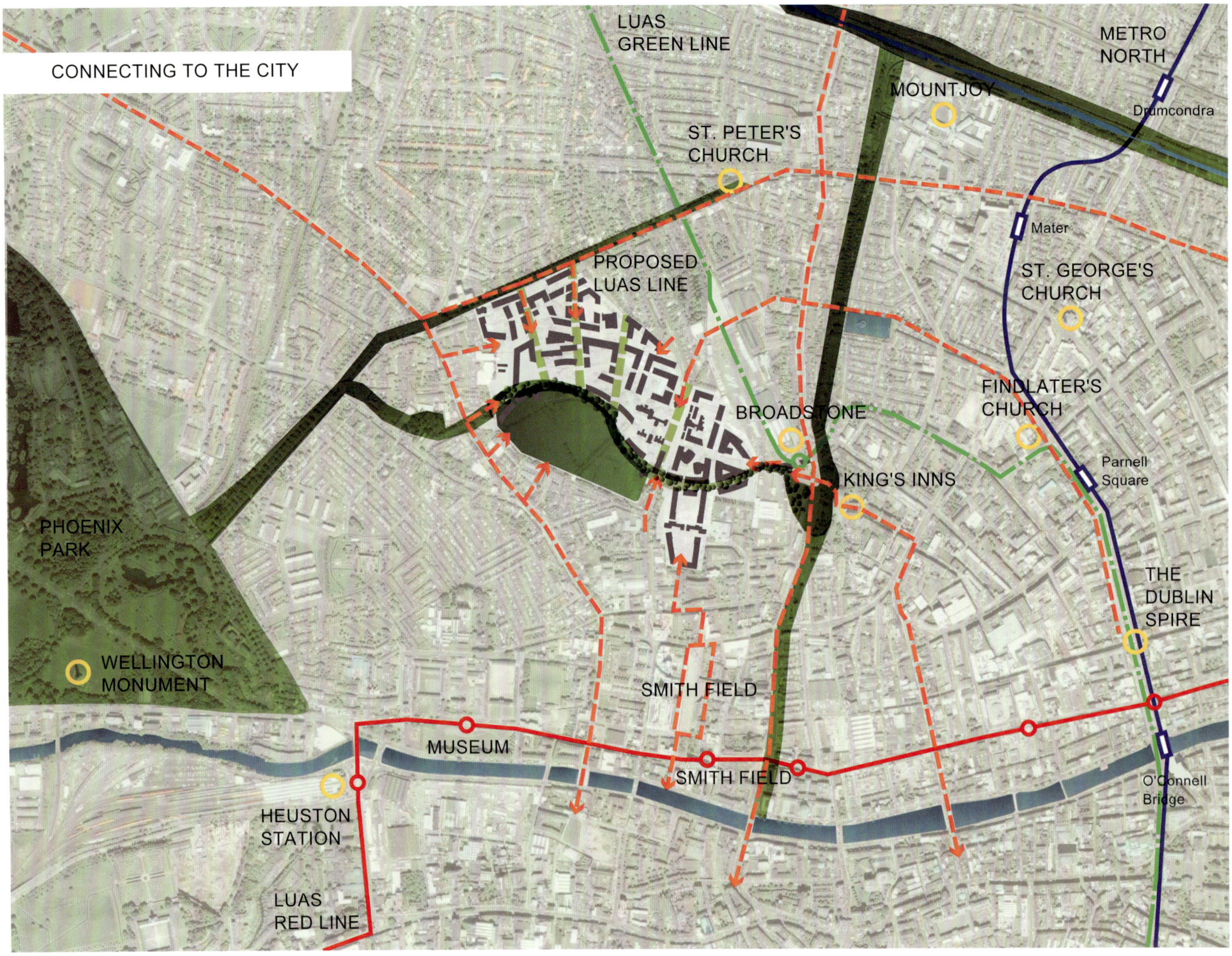

CONNECTING TO THE CITY

- LUAS GREEN LINE
- METRO NORTH
- MOUNTJOY
- ST. PETER'S CHURCH
- Drumcondra
- Mater
- PROPOSED LUAS LINE
- ST. GEORGE'S CHURCH
- BROADSTONE
- FINDLATER'S CHURCH
- KING'S INNS
- Parnell Square
- PHOENIX PARK
- THE DUBLIN SPIRE
- WELLINGTON MONUMENT
- SMITH FIELD
- MUSEUM
- SMITH FIELD
- O'Connell Bridge
- HEUSTON STATION
- LUAS RED LINE

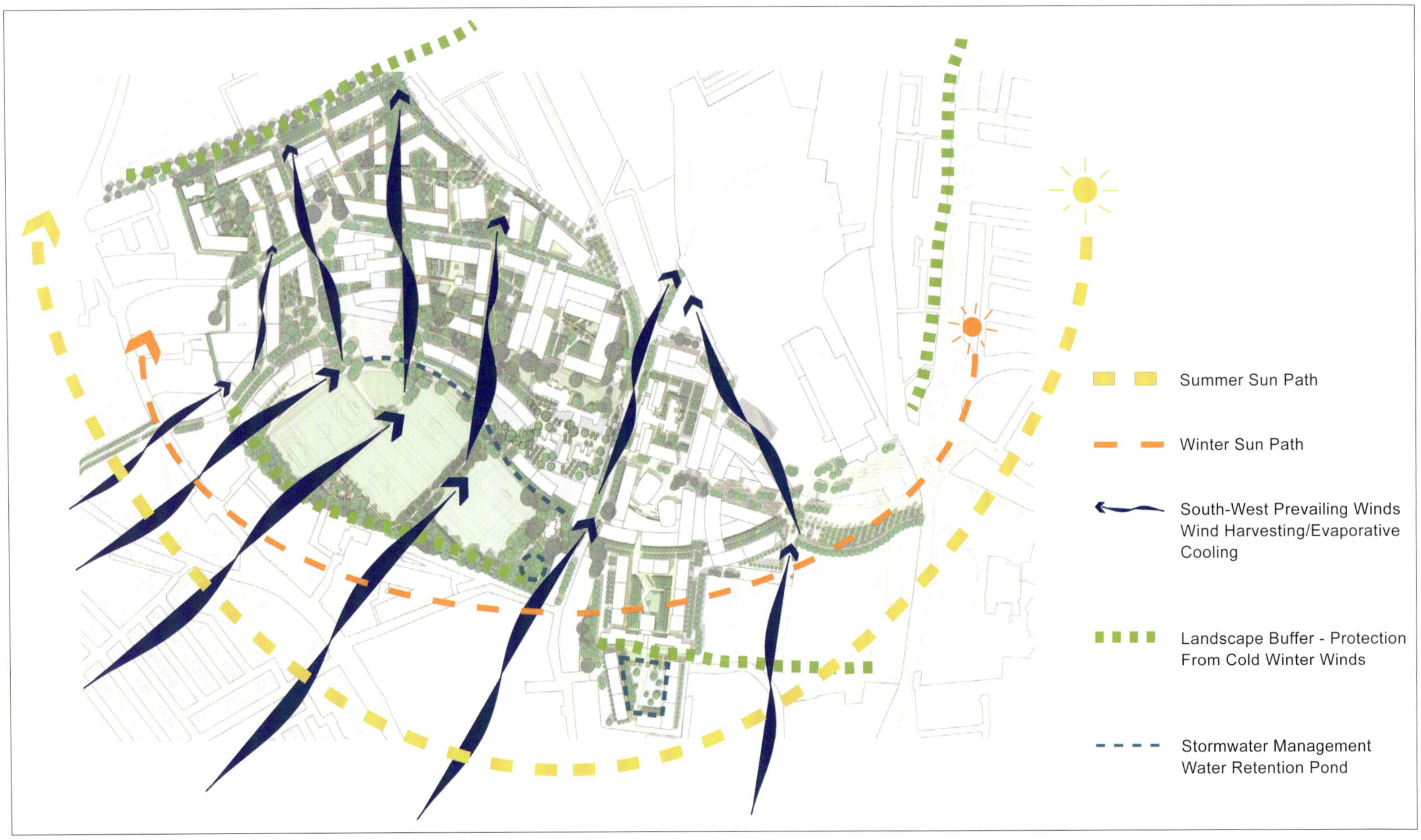

Legend:
- Summer Sun Path
- Winter Sun Path
- South-West Prevailing Winds / Wind Harvesting/Evaporative Cooling
- Landscape Buffer - Protection From Cold Winter Winds
- Stormwater Management Water Retention Pond

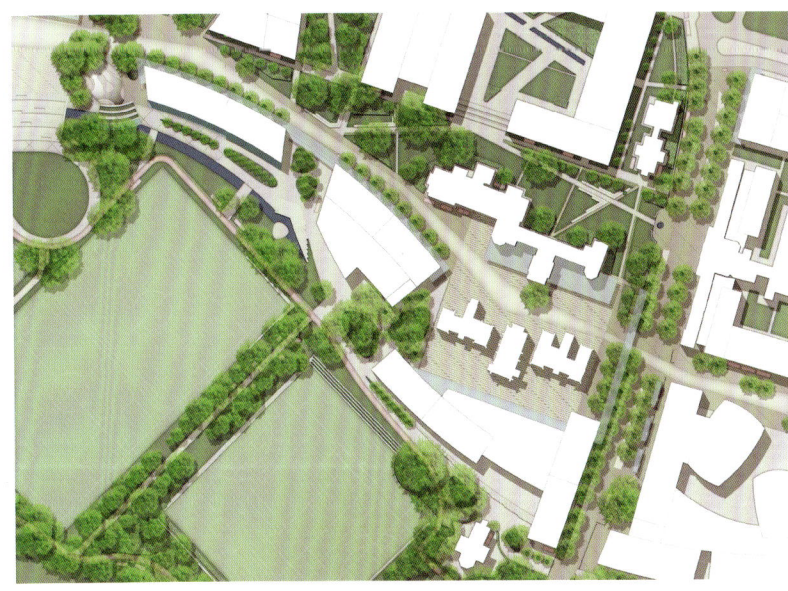

Jordan Dead Sea Development Zone Master Plan

Jury Comments:
The jury appreciated the project's emphasis on the creation of a public waterfront, unusual in this region of resorts.
The development of a planning strategy that is structured around the movement of water demonstrates an ecological sensitivity.
The master plan skillfully accommodates different populations and is incredibly comprehensive.

Notes of Interest
In order to capitalize on its cultural and political assets, the Government of Jordan has established a series of six Development Zones in which directed efforts are being made to increase foreign and domestic investment. The Dead Sea Development Zone encompasses 40 square kilometers of coastal land along the lowest body of water on earth.
The Detailed Master Plan for the Dead Sea Development Zone lays out a vision and blueprint for fostering a dynamic, robust, and sustainable tourism-based economy at the Dead Sea that will become a source of pride and revenue for the Kingdom and set the highest standard for sustainable development and innovative urban design. Critically, the plan establishes a "balanced approach" between development and conservation of this most precious resource. At the same time, it will strengthen local economies and greatly support social infrastructure for nearby existing communities.
Comprehensive design guidelines, a detailed infrastructure report, and an extensive market study enable the client to attract investment. Future development will follow a carefully choreographed phasing plan that capitalizes on existing investments, introduces infrastructure to precede development, and preserves large contiguous tracts of developable land as future land banks.
The year-long master planning process focused on critical work sessions held in Amman with local community leaders, government officials, international and local investors, and leading academics.

Collaboration: Buro Happold, Sigma Consulting, Tetra Tech
Owner: Jordan Development Zones Commission

Architect
Sasaki Associates, Inc.

Location
Amman, Jordan

Photo Credit
© Sasaki Associates, Inc.

OPEN SPACE STRATEGY

Natural assets from the framework for the Master Plan's open space strategy. Rivers, wadis, steep cliffs, and sensitive habitats are removed from the inventory of developable land.
Landmark public open spaces are planned throughout the project site, providing public access to the sea at every opportunity: a large public park, eco-tourism zones, pedestrian paths, and urban plazas.

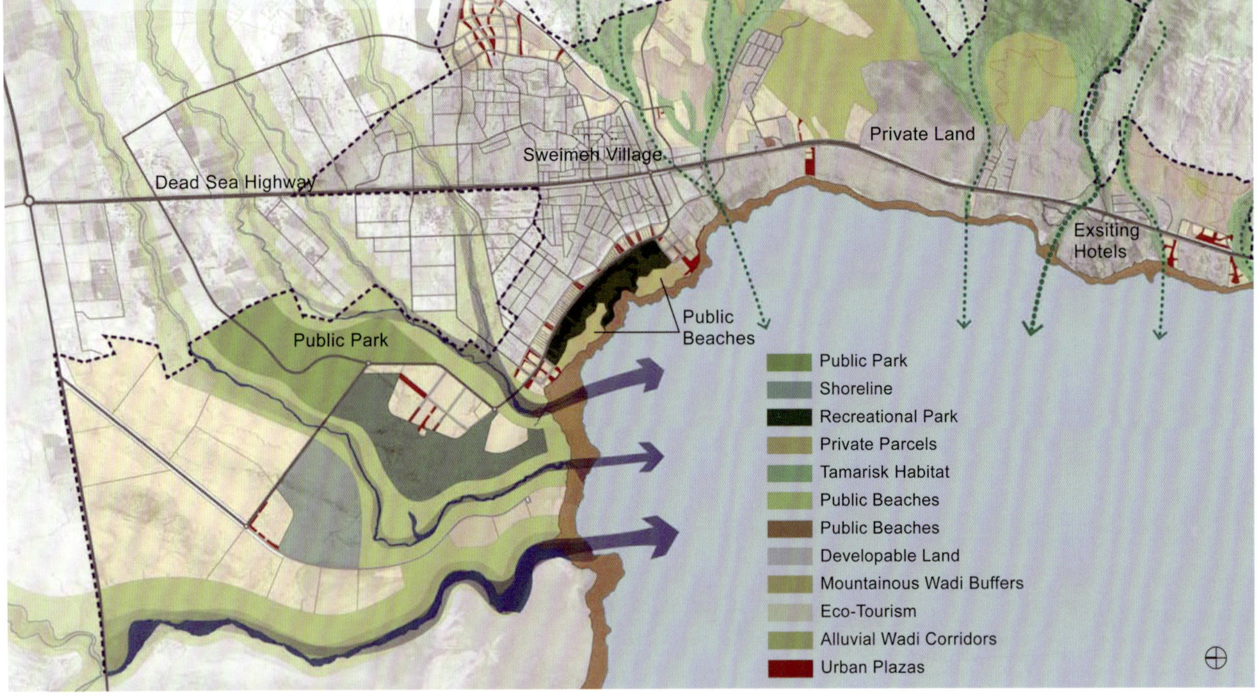

Sweimeh Village
Private Land
Dead Sea Highway
Exsiting Hotels
Public Beaches
Public Park
Public Park
Shoreline
Recreational Park
Private Parcels
Tamarisk Habitat
Public Beaches
Public Beaches
Developable Land
Mountainous Wadi Buffers
Eco-Tourism
Alluvial Wadi Corridors
Urban Plazas

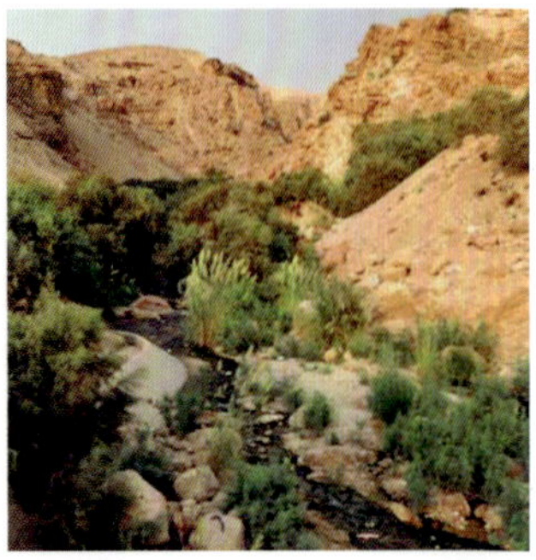

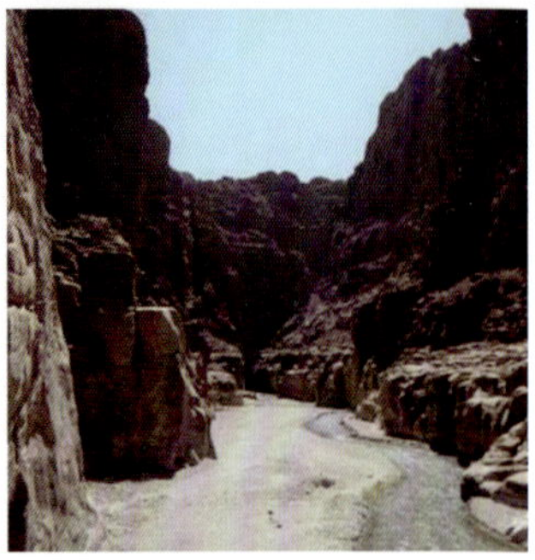

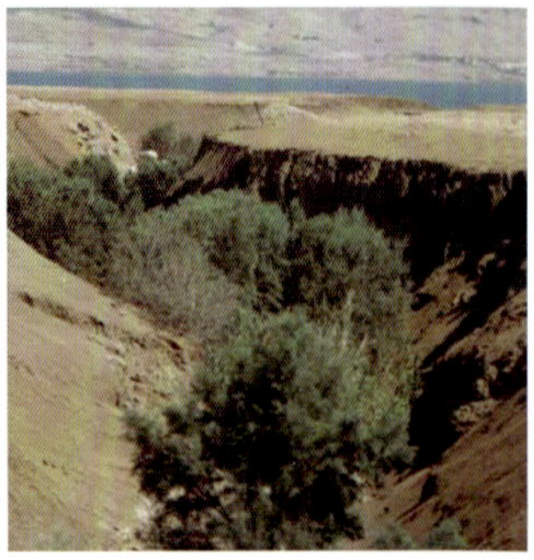

UNDERSTANDING NATURAL HYDROLOGY

The Jordan River and several smaller alluvial rivers terminate at the northern shore of the Dead Sea. Along the eastern banks of the Sea, the landscape transitions into rocky cliffs, through which mountainous wadis cut deep, dramatic incisions. It is critical to protect these complex ecological systems.

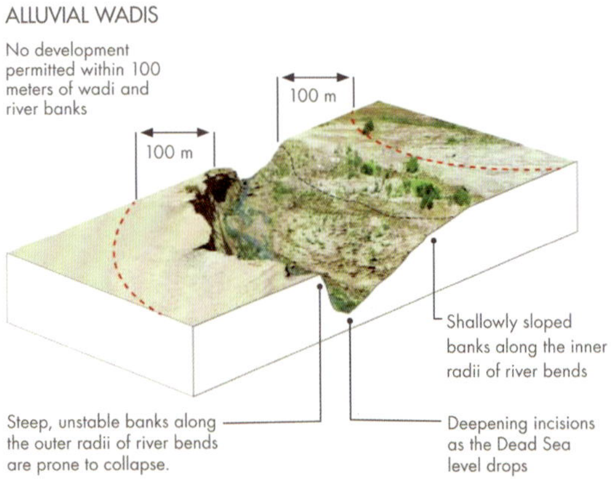

ALLUVIAL WADIS
No development permitted within 100 meters of wadi and river banks
100 m
100 m
Shallowly sloped banks along the inner radii of river bends
Steep, unstable banks along the outer radii of river bends are prone to collapse.
Deepening incisions as the Dead Sea level drops

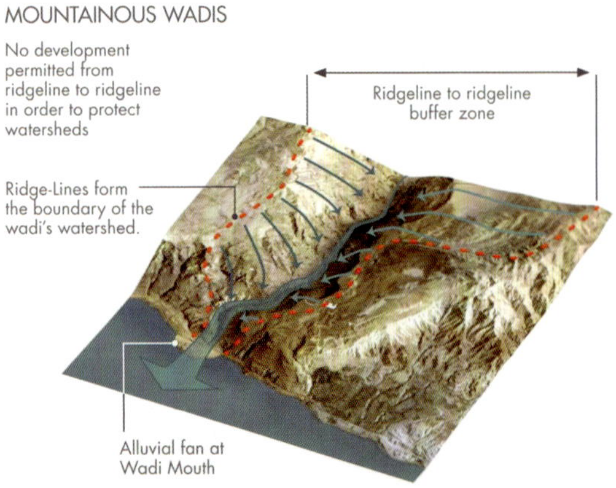

MOUNTAINOUS WADIS
No development permitted from ridgeline to ridgeline in order to protect watersheds
Ridgeline to ridgeline buffer zone
Ridge-Lines form the boundary of the wadi's watershed.
Alluvial fan at Wadi Mouth

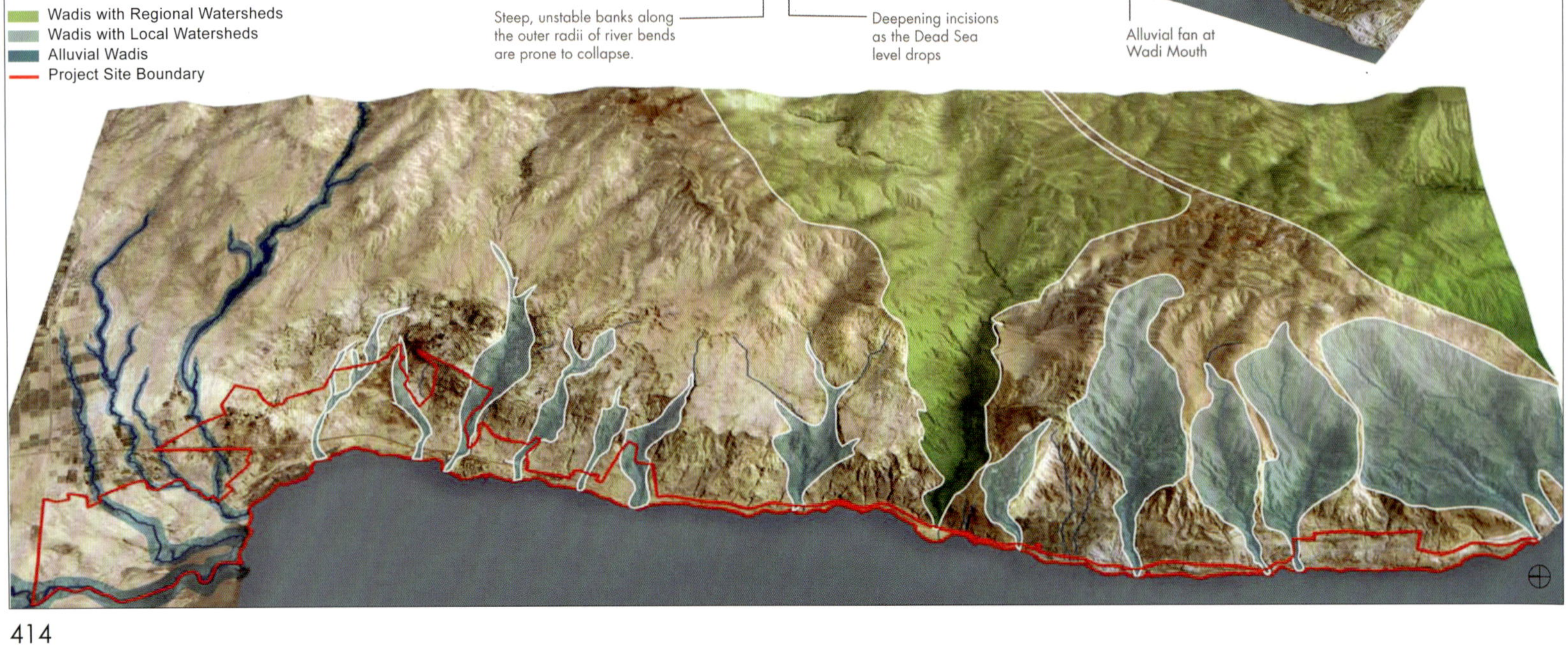

Wadis with Regional Watersheds
Wadis with Local Watersheds
Alluvial Wadis
Project Site Boundary

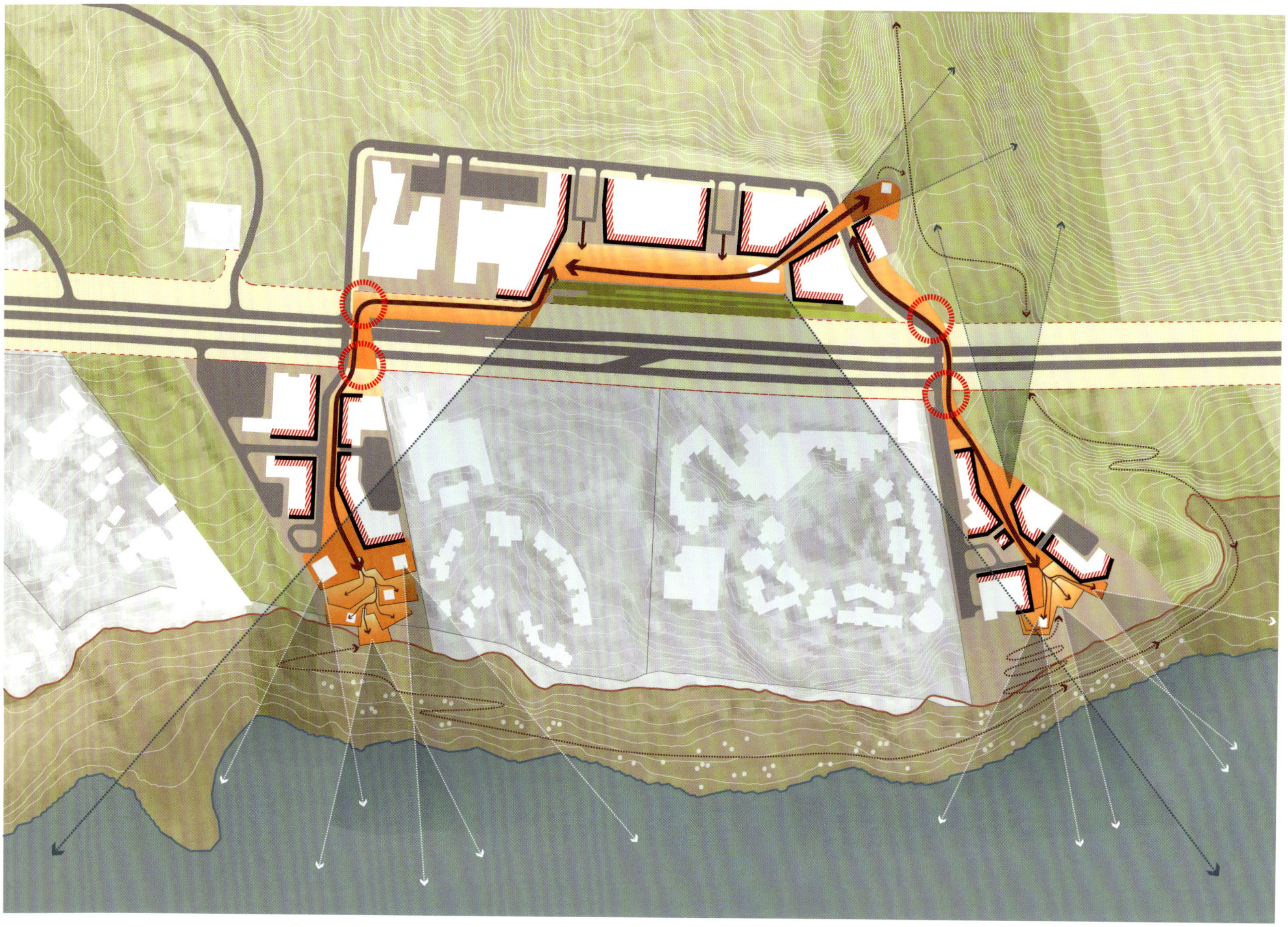

415

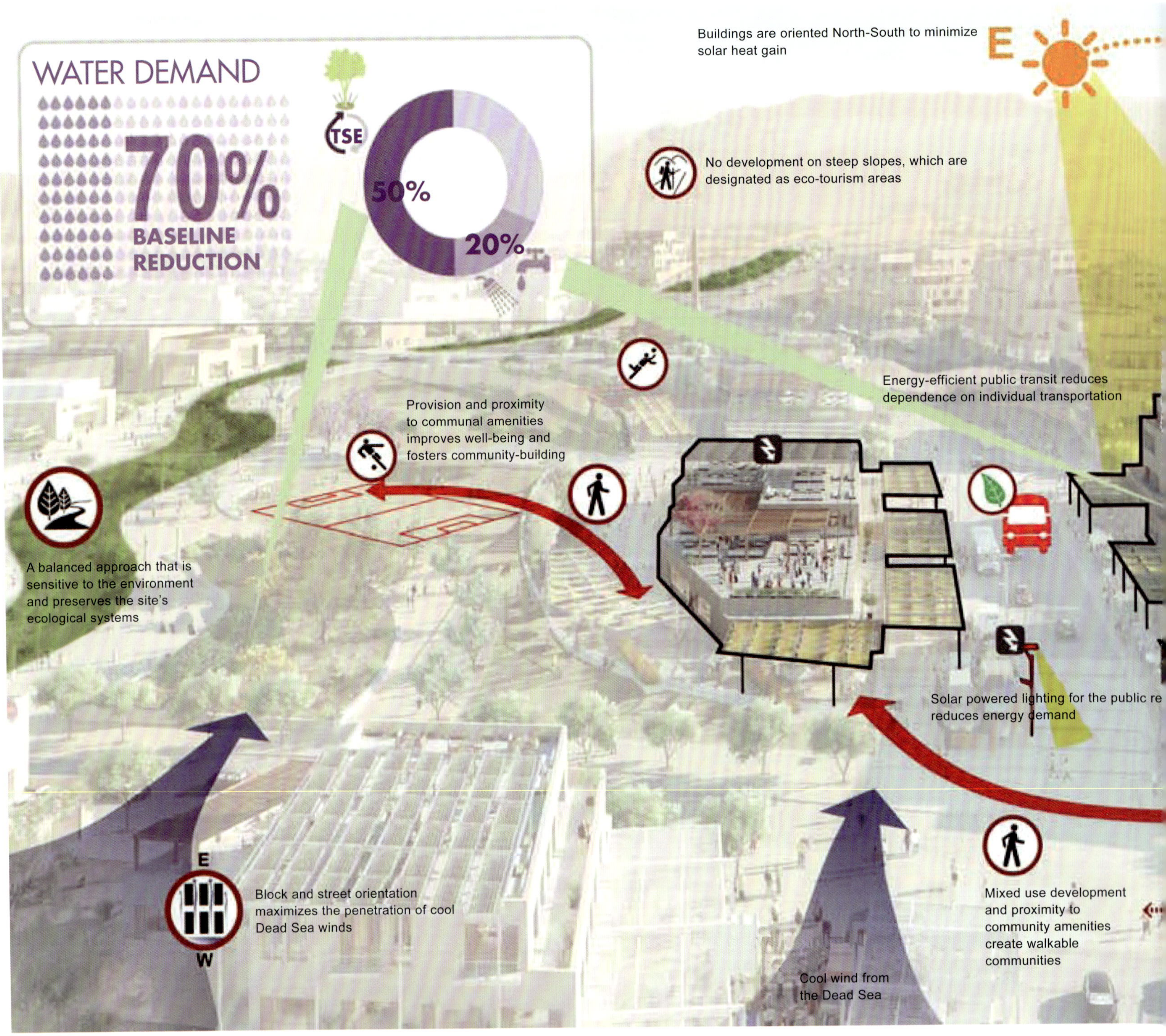

WATER DEMAND 70% BASELINE REDUCTION

50% TSE
20%

Buildings are oriented North-South to minimize solar heat gain

No development on steep slopes, which are designated as eco-tourism areas

Provision and proximity to communal amenities improves well-being and fosters community-building

Energy-efficient public transit reduces dependence on individual transportation

A balanced approach that is sensitive to the environment and preserves the site's ecological systems

Solar powered lighting for the public realm reduces energy demand

Block and street orientation maximizes the penetration of cool Dead Sea winds

Mixed use development and proximity to community amenities create walkable communities

Cool wind from the Dead Sea

EXISTING WATER CYCLE

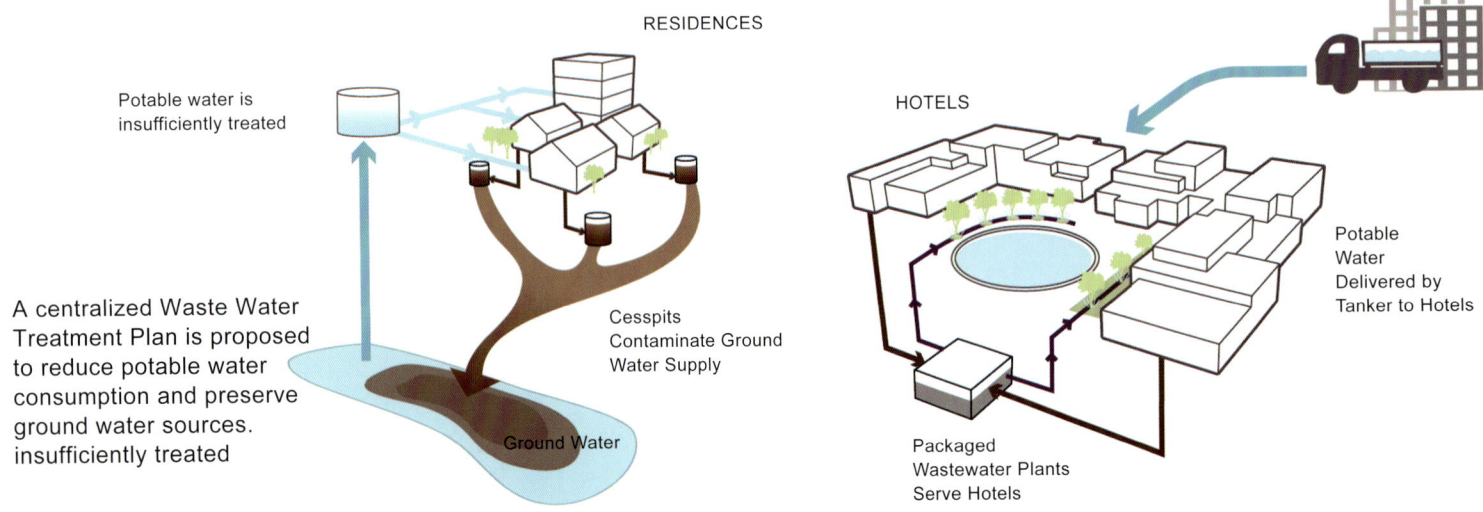

RESIDENCES

Potable water is insufficiently treated

HOTELS

Potable Water Delivered by Tanker to Hotels

A centralized Waste Water Treatment Plan is proposed to reduce potable water consumption and preserve ground water sources. insufficiently treated

Cesspits Contaminate Ground Water Supply

Ground Water

Packaged Wastewater Plants Serve Hotels

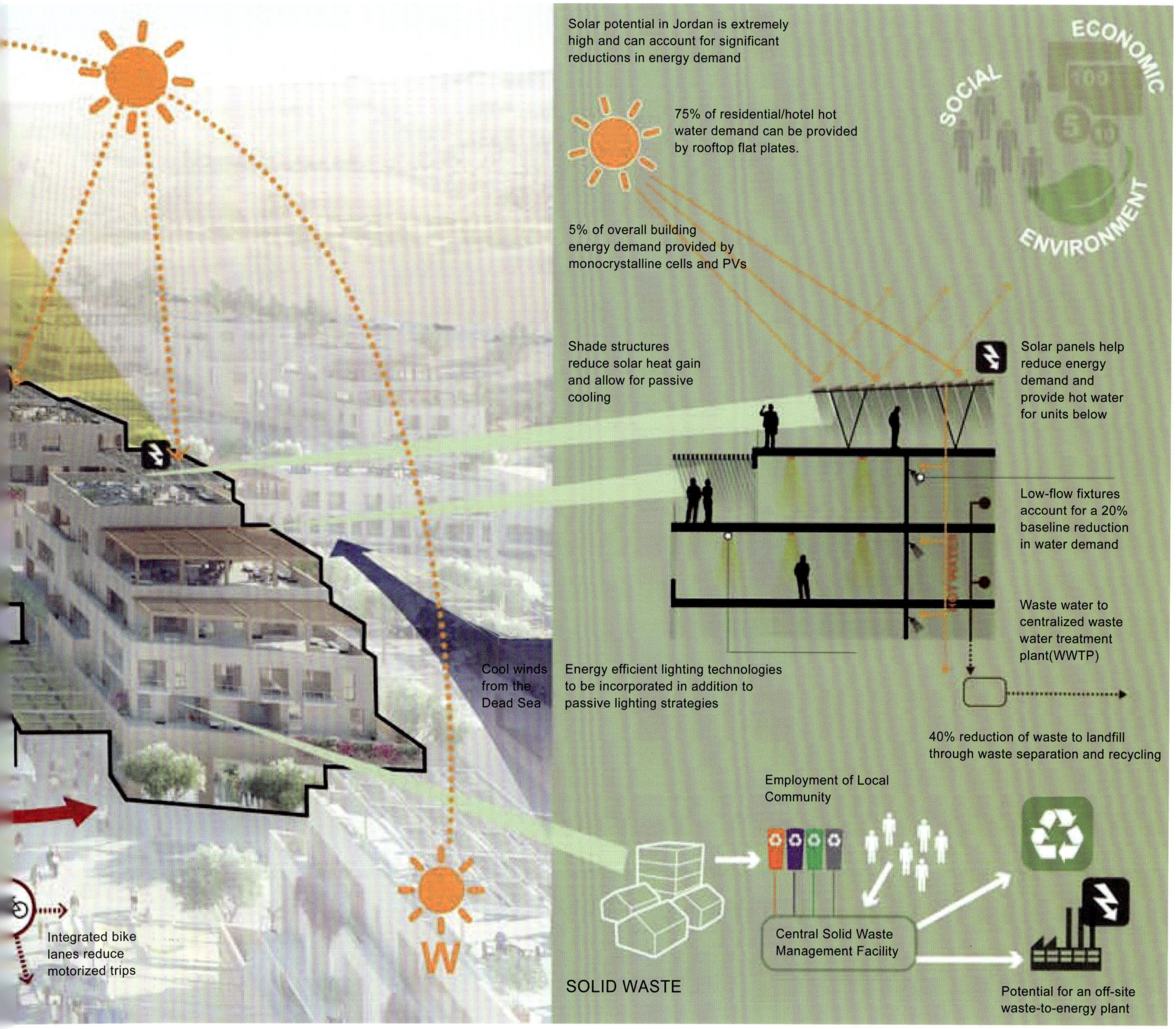

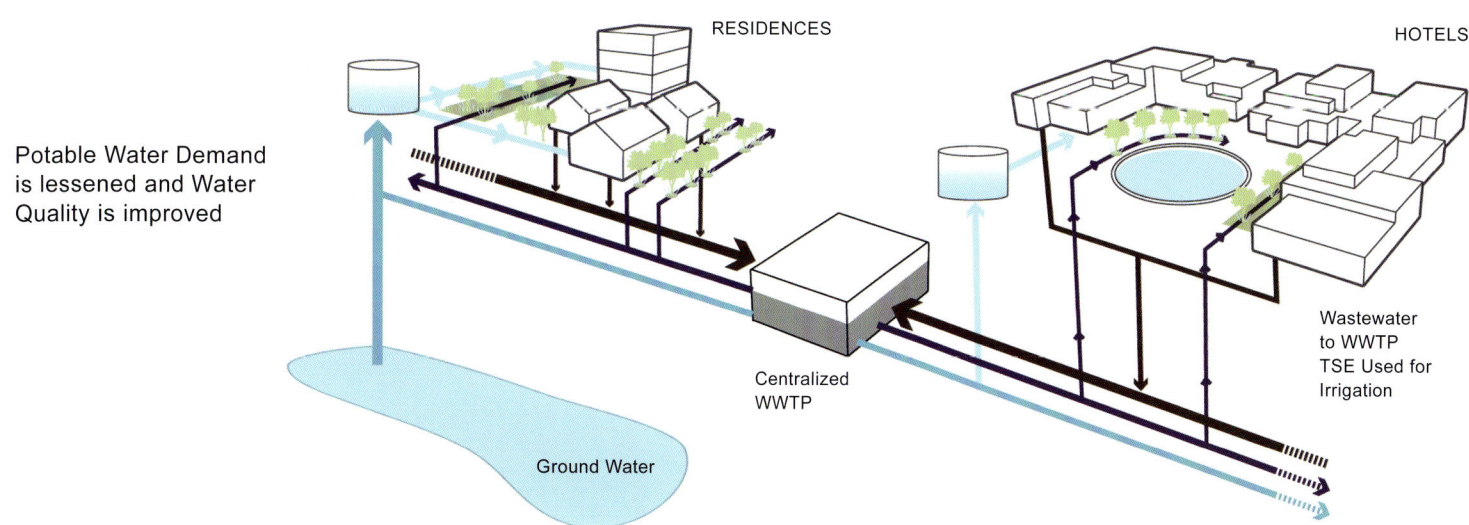

Master Plan for the Central Delaware

Jury Comments:
This is a very bold, long term vision.
The project demonstrates great connectivity back into the neighborhood fabric, integrating both existing buildings, developed open spaces, and the esplanade walk.
A good range of density has been represented, particularly along the river, and this plan has transformed the city in a substantial way.

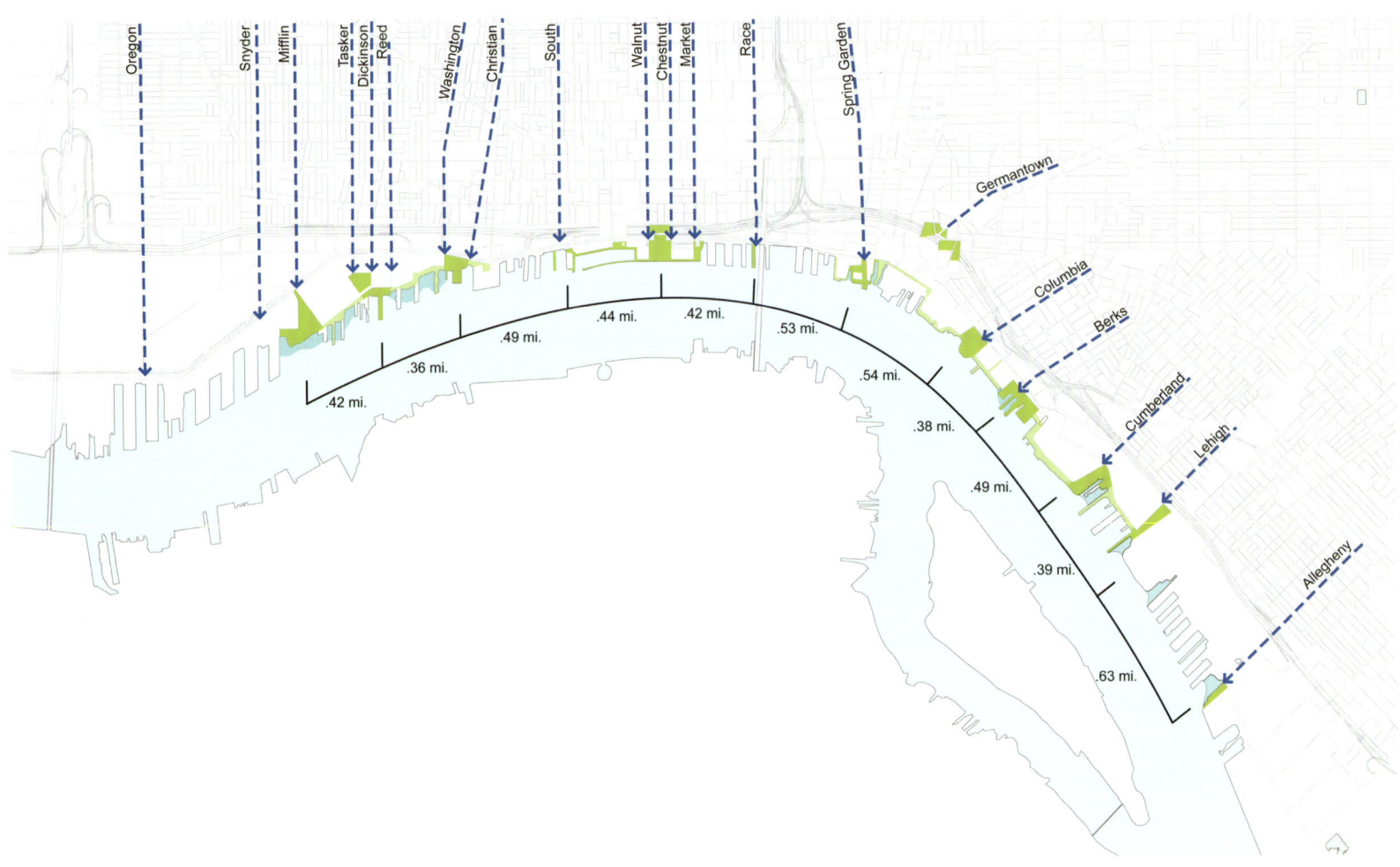

Notes of Interest
Master plan for 6 miles of the Delaware River waterfront in Center City Philadelphia, based on the Civic Vision was prepared through an extensive public engagement planning process. The goal of the plan is to provide a practical implementation strategy for the phasing and funding of public realm enhancements to the waterfront, including the locations of parks, a variety of waterfront trails, and connections to existing upland neighborhoods.
Specific zoning recommendations to shape private development as well as design guidelines for the public spaces are integral components of this project. A crucial aspect of the planning process was the creation of a dialogue with stakeholders and the incorporation of public input.
Throughout the project, the team had direct contact with neighborhood associations, elected officials, heads of major state and local agencies, as well as property owners and developers. At the end of each phase, the team conducted a public meeting to solicit feedback and engage constituents in the work's progress.

Associate Architect: Kelly/Maiello Architects & Planners
Consultant: CHPlanning, Greater Philadelphia Urban Affairs Coalition, HR&A Advisors, Hurley Franks & Associates
Cost Estimator: Davis Langdon
Engineer: KS Engineers, P.C., Parsons Brinckerhoff
Land Use Counsel: Blank Rome LLP
Programming: Karin Bacon Enterprises
Waterfront Policy Advisor: Toni L. Griffin
Owner: Delaware River Waterfront Corporation

Architect
Cooper, Robertson & Partners, KieranTimberlake, OLIN

Location
Philadelphia, Pennsylvania

Photo Credit
© Brooklyn Digital Foundry

Miami Beach City Center Redevelopment Project

Jury Comments:
Compelled with this small project with big impact, the building and its public park space has developed an extremely vital and dynamic cultural space within the city.
The inventive use of cultural programming by the symphony hall; the outdoor concert projections in the park, have made culture accessible to everyone.
The project makes good use of existing buildings and creates a strong connection back to the city, energizing and activating Miami Beach.

Notes of Interest
Opened in January 2011, the 5.86-acre Miami Beach City Center Redevelopment project consits of New World Center, an innovative facility for music education and performance with state-of-the-art technical capabilities; Miami Beach SoundScape, an adjacent 2.5-acre public park and event space; and a 556-space municipal parking structure.

The project is located on two city blocks previously used as surface parking lots. New World Center is a unique performance, education, production, and creative space with state-of-the-art capabilities, owned and operated by the New World Symphony (NWS). A global hub for creative expression and collaboration, and a laboratory for the ways music is taught, presented and experienced, the building enables NWS to continue its role as a leader in integrating technology with music education and concert presentation. It is used by NWS for educational, concert, and broadcast activities. The building features a giant, 7,000-square-foot projection wall used for outdoor presentations to audiences in the adjacent park, complemented by an immersive audio system in the outdoor viewing area.

Miami Beach SoundScape is a multi-use park that serves as an urban oasis and a gathering place for cultural and special events. It is a unified expression of passive recreation, pleasure and culture – a space that supports a multitude of day and night uses that, combined with New World Center's expansive projection wall, marries music, design, landscape and community.

Consultant: Acoustic Dimensions, Prosound and Video, Sonitus, LLC, Theatre Projects Consultants
Engineer: Coastal Systems International, Cosentini Associates, Douglas Wood Associates, Gilsanz, Murray, Steficek, LLP, Kimley Horn and Associates, Inc
General Contractor: Facchina Construction of Florida, LLC
Landscape Architect: Raymond Jungles Associates, Rosenberg Gardner Design
Lighting: LAM Partners, Inc.
Seating: Poltrona Frau
Acoustical: Nagata Acoustics America, Inc
Owner: City of Miami Beach, New World Symphony

Architect
Gehry Partners, LLP;
West 8 Urban Design and Landscape Architecture

Location
Miami Beach, Florida

Photo Credit
© Gehry Partners, LLP, © West 8 New York, © Emilio Collavino, © WorldRedEye, © Claudia Uribe, © Robin Hill, © Craig Hall

422

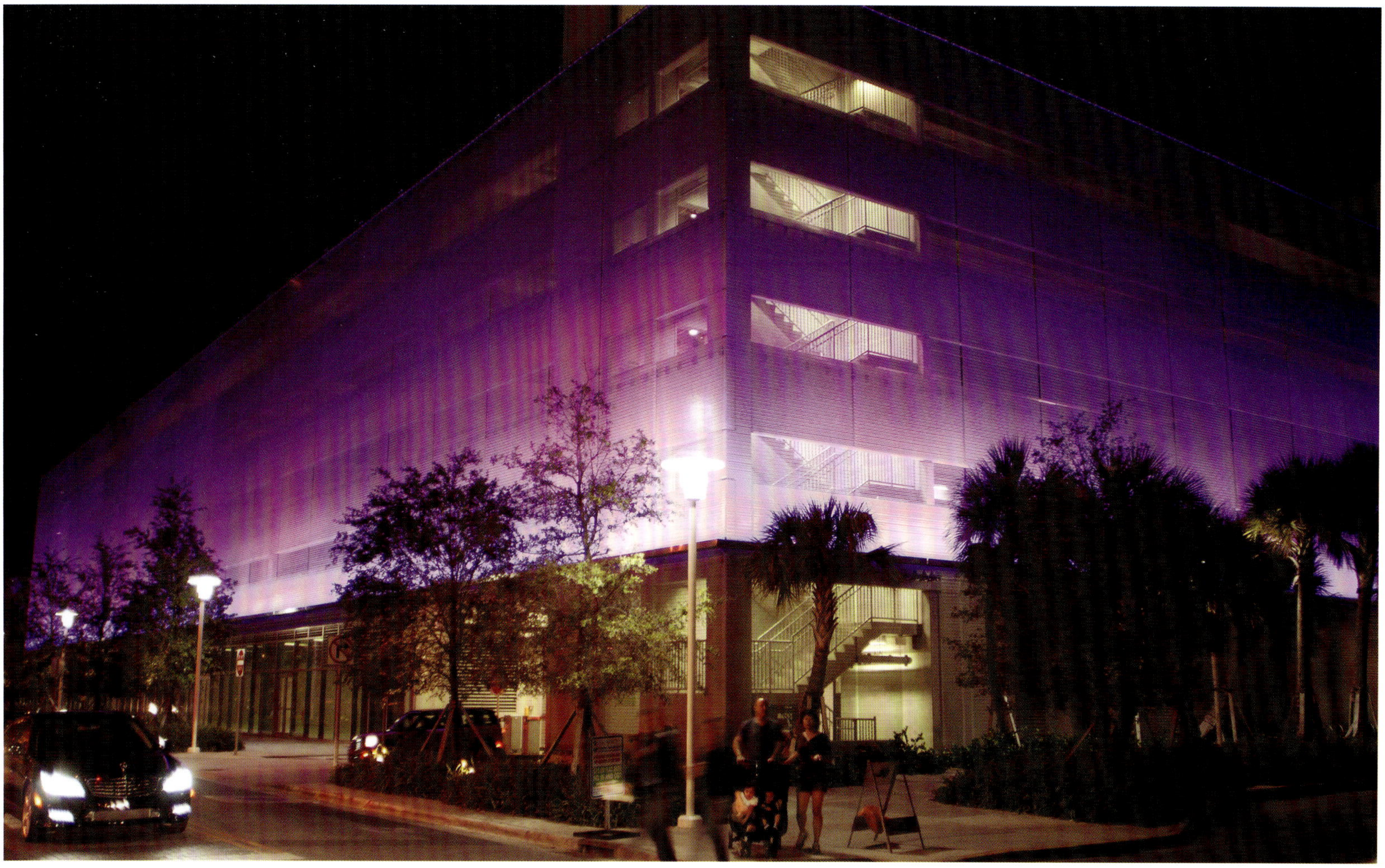

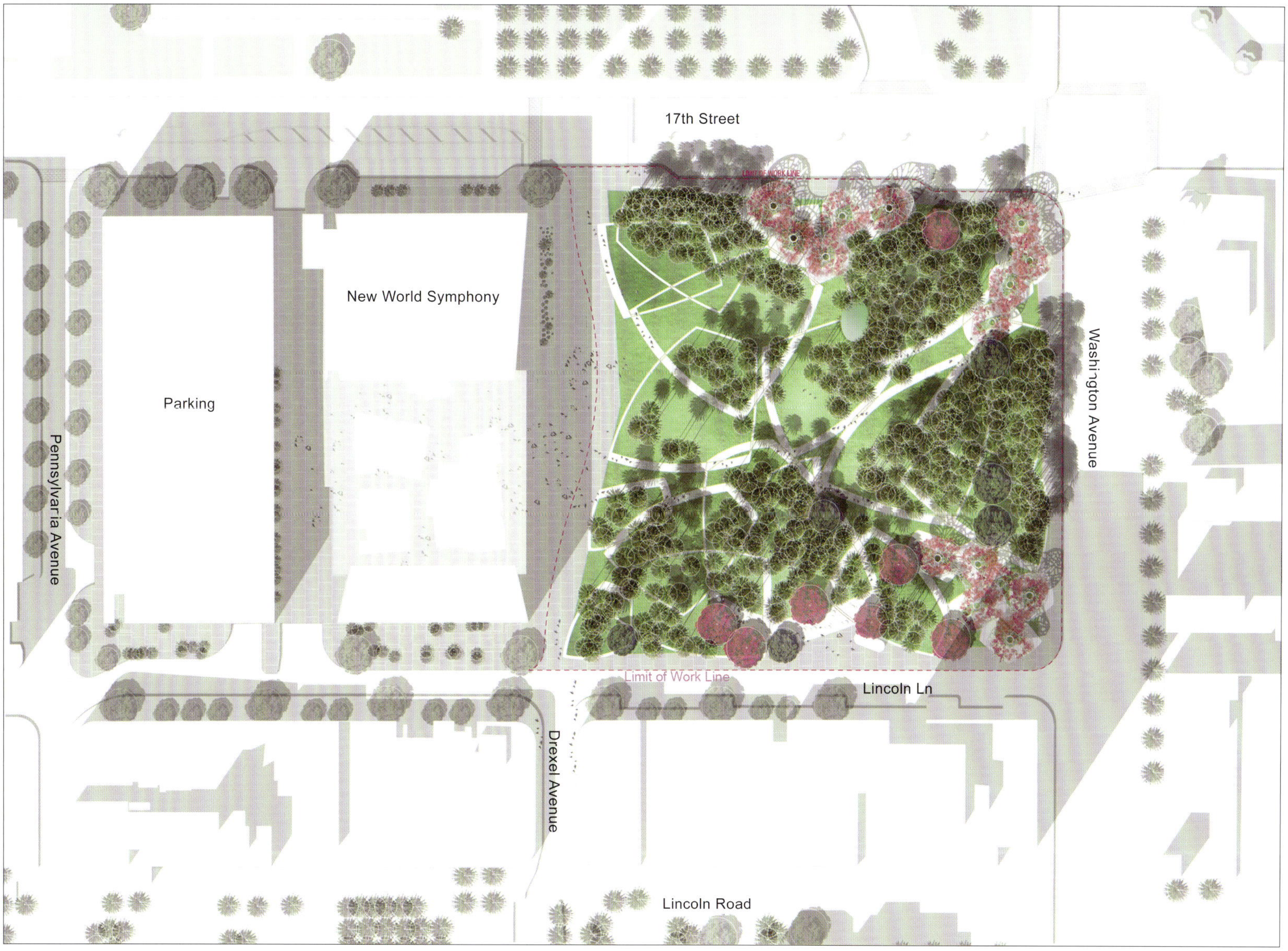

17th Street

New World Symphony

Parking

Pennsylvania Avenue

Washington Avenue

Drexel Avenue

Lincoln Ln

Lincoln Road

Limit of Work Line

Portland Mall Revitalization

Jury Comments:
Beautiful! This project asserts that urban design can really work, and exemplified this through design at both the large scale and the detail.
A strong sense of urban space has been created by the continuity of the streetscape. The environment is accessible on all levels.
It has been beautifully executed, with fine design details upgrading the good bones of the existing situation. A sense of urban play and connectivity is evident.

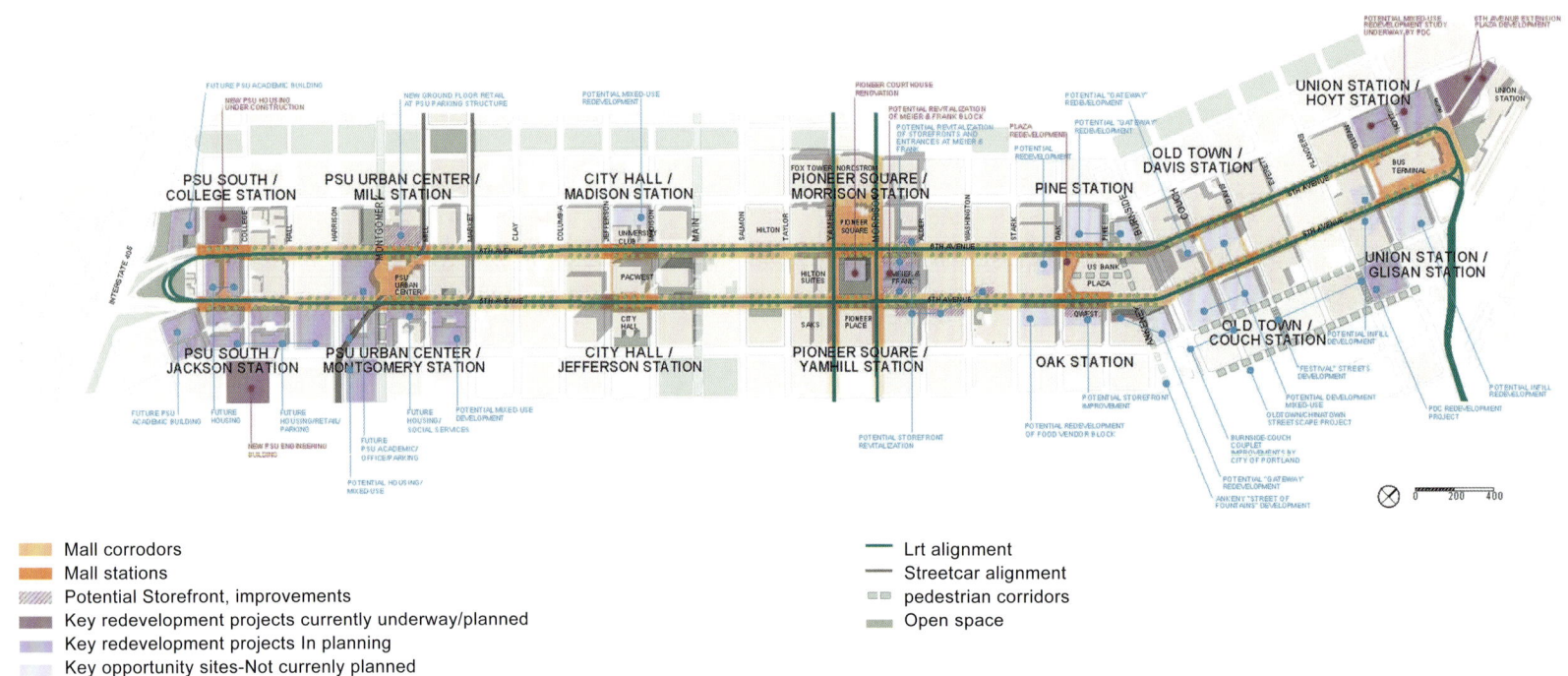

- Mall corridors
- Mall stations
- Potential Storefront, improvements
- Key redevelopment projects currently underway/planned
- Key redevelopment projects In planning
- Key opportunity sites-Not currently planned
- Lrt alignment
- Streetcar alignment
- pedestrian corridors
- Open space

Notes of Interest
Already an icon of progressive planning, the revitalized Portland Mall is significant nationally as a new benchmark in urban design, place-making and transportation infrastructure. Extending the entire length of downtown Portland, it mixes multiple modes of transportation, stimulates adjacent development and re-establishes itself as one of Portland's premier civic spaces.

The project involved renovation or rebuilding of 58 blocks and 59 intersections while providing exclusive transit lanes for bus and light rail, dedicated lanes for autos and bicycles, enhanced sidewalks for pedestrians, and parking and loading zones.

The original Mall created in 1978 was deteriorating after years of heavy use and diminishing public maintenance funding. To reverse this decline and accommodate a projected 1 million new residents by 2030, TriMet in partnership with the City of Portland, Metro, the Portland Business Alliance and the architect, teamed up to create a vision for the Mall as a Great Street.

After more than a decade of process, design and construction, the Mall's reopening was complemented by two major hotel redevelopments, national retail openings, over 40 local storefront renovations, and several institutional projects.

The revitalized Mall combines design character, aspirations, active context, operations and management of a truly great street for the 21st century.

Project Manager: Shiels, Obletz, Johnsen
Engineer: Dewhurst MacFarlane and Partners, John Knapton, KPFF Consulting Engineers, Inc., LTK Engineering Services, URS Corporation
General Contractor: Kiewit Construction Group, Inc., Stacy and Witbeck, Inc.
Landscape Architect: Mayer/Reed
Owner: Tri-County Metropolitan Transportation District of Oregon (TriMet)

Architect
ZGF Architects LLP

Location
Portland, Oregon

Photo Credit
© Bruce Forster

Reinventing the Crescent: Riverfront Development Plan

Jury Comments:
This is an innovative and radical approach to readdressing the levee on the Mississippi and reconnecting the citizens of New Orleans back to their riverfront.
The typologies that are being developed will transform the visual and physical connection of the city to the river.
The use of existing programmatic institutions and amenities to focus development along the river is particularly laudable.

1. Market Street Bridge
2. Riverpool
3. Sundeck
4. Grove
5. Movie Screen and Cinema Lawn
6. Batture
7. Playground and Snack Kiosk
8. Urban Wild
9. Perched Marsh
10. Saint Mary Street Bridge
11. Pavilion
12. Irish Channel Pier
13. Saint Andrew Street Pier
14. Wind Turbines
15. Batture
16. Observation Tower Picnic Lawn
17. Jackson Avenue Ferry Terminal

Notes of Interest
New Orleans has long been dependent on its majestic river. The banks of the Mississippi River have served many purposes throughout the city's history and are now poised to play a crucial new role. The city's economy has suffered the slow loss of maritime activity due to port consolidation and sudden, comprehensive loss of civic stability due to Hurricane Katrina in 2005.

Paradoxically, the hurricane heightened public understanding that the riverfront is in fact the "high ground" and ripe for possible redevelopment. As such, the Reinventing the Crescent Development Plan calls for the East Bank of the city's central riverfront to accommodate a continuous sequence of public open spaces, and along this sequence establish 15 special environments.

Some of these places reinforce and enhance existing public domains, such as improving the riverfront's Moonwalk and creating a better pedestrian connection between the Moonwalk and Jackson Square. Others are new urban nodes allowing the city to reconnect with the river's edge. Each of the new development nodes is strategically located to facilitate the mitigation of physical barriers that have kept citizens at an "urban arm's length" away from their river.

Associate Architects: Hargreaves Associates, Chan Krieger Scieniewicz & TEN Arquitectos
Consultant: James Richardson Economic Consulting, Julie Brown Consulting, Kulkarni Consultants, Moffatt & Nichol, Robinson et al. Public Relations, St. Martin, Brown & Associates
Owner: The New Orleans Building Corporation

Architect
Eskew+Dumez+Ripple

Location
New Orleans, Louisiana

Photo Credit
© Hargreaves Associates

POLAND FIELDS
POLAND FIELDS
BYWATER POINT
PORT OF EMBARKATION
REDEVELOPMENT

PROGRAM
Concerts & Performances
Music Festivals
Community Gardening
Running
Picnicking
Dog Walking
Parking
Street car Rides
Lawn Sports
Bike Riding

CIRCULATION
Japonica Street Bridge Overpass
St Claude Avenue Pedestrian Bridge
Streetcar Extension To Poland Av
Neighborhood Access to Poland
Fields Park
Cruise Terminal
Secure Vehicular Zone
Bywater Point Walking Trails
Levee Walk

LANDSCAPE
Shade Tree Allees
Streetcar Bosques
Parking Garden Tree Islands
Garden Tree Islands
Vegetable and Flower Gardens
Cruise Terminal Deck
Riverview Landforms
Amphitheater Lawns
Bywater Groves
Roof Garden
Existing Batture
Levee

SandRidge Energy Commons

Jury Comments:
This is a particularly refreshing project that takes on a civic role in the redevelopment of existing buildings to create a better downtown.
The reinvestment of this corporate campus project combined with preservation and strong public spaces will contribute to making Oklahoma City a better place.
The park is particularly compelling and the character of the renderings is very strong.

© Rogers Marvel Architects

Notes of Interest

SandRidge Energy, a rapidly growing natural gas and oil company, relocated from the outskirts of Oklahoma City into an abandoned area of the downtown core. The master plan for this new headquarters spans multiple buildings, and multiple city blocks, where architecture and landscape architecture weave to balance company needs and civic engagement.

The project creates a network of programs to support employees while forming a destination location within downtown. The distribution of programs serves as catalysts to encourage development of adjacent properties and integrate the company into the fabric of the city. Shared outdoor spaces enable employees, their families, and the broader community to enjoy spending time downtown.

The project is located between two major arteries – North Robinson, the city's green connector, and North Broadway, lined with commercial buildings and spaces. SandRidge Commons is an "outdoor interior" that provides a green link between these two major arteries.

This community-centered urban design project represents an approach not commonly sought; an approach that holds transferable lessons and great potential for other cities. Rather than becoming an icon and shaping only the skyline, rather than becoming a campus and shaping only an insular world, the task for SandRidge Commons was to weave program, buildings and landscapes, into the urban fabric and help improve the map of the city it calls home.

Construction Management: Lingo Construction Services
Engineer: ARUP; Frankfurt Short Bruza Associates
Landscape Architect: Hoerr Schaudt
Lighting : Microclimate and Daylighting Studies; Renfro Design Group
Owner: SandRidge Energy

Architect	Location	Photo Credit
Rogers Marvel Architects	Oklahoma City, Oklahoma	© Dbox, © Raddi Inc., © Rogers Marvel Architects

AN URBAN SHELTERBELT

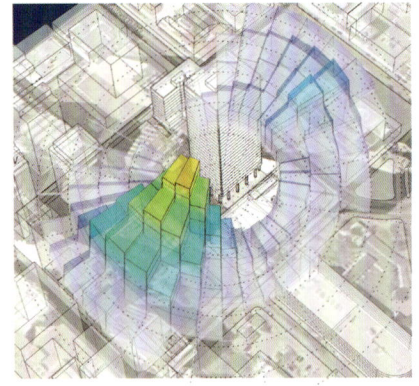
Wind patterns were analyzed to develop mitigation strategies.

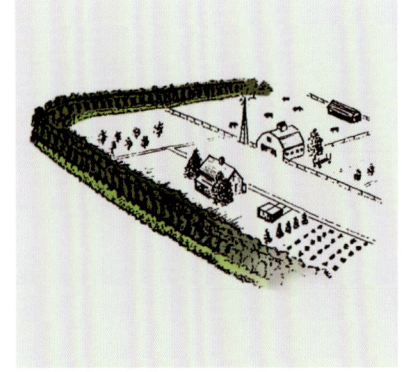
Rural windbreak strategies common to the region were studied to glean the lessons learned from decades of use in the protection of agricultural land.

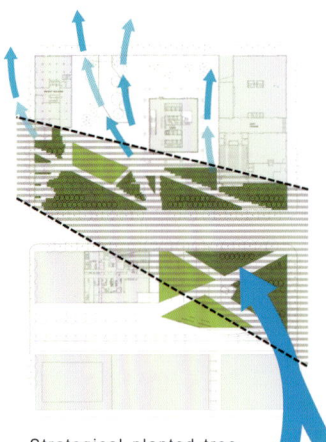
Strategical planted tree windbreaks slow down fast moving wind and shelter new public spaces.

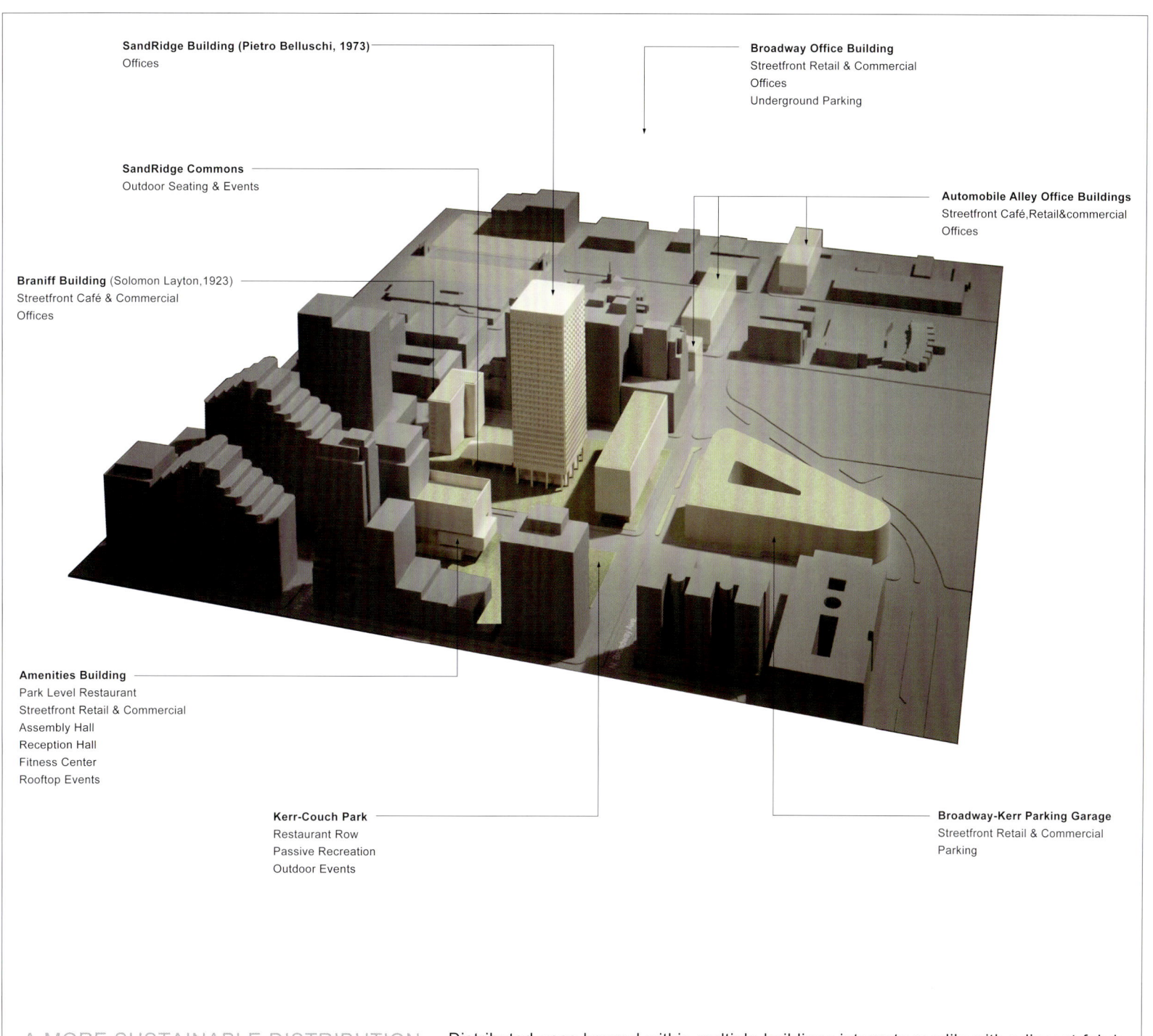

SandRidge Building (Pietro Belluschi, 1973)
Offices

SandRidge Commons
Outdoor Seating & Events

Braniff Building (Solomon Layton, 1923)
Streetfront Café & Commercial
Offices

Broadway Office Building
Streetfront Retail & Commercial
Offices
Underground Parking

Automobile Alley Office Buildings
Streetfront Café, Retail & commercial
Offices

Amenities Building
Park Level Restaurant
Streetfront Retail & Commercial
Assembly Hall
Reception Hall
Fitness Center
Rooftop Events

Kerr-Couch Park
Restaurant Row
Passive Recreation
Outdoor Events

Broadway-Kerr Parking Garage
Streetfront Retail & Commercial
Parking

A MORE SUSTAINABLE DISTRIBUTION — Distributed uses housed within multiple buildings integrate readily with adjacent fabric and offer the ability for rapid change in response to changing economic conditions.

© Raddi Inc.

Gehry Residence

Jury Comments:
Published around the world, the image of a defiantly "destroyed" California house made of unexpectedly humble materials ignited responses as far as Europe and Asia.
As often with ground-breaking efforts, the provocative house invited astonishment, admiration, and contempt. Even with a groundswell of disdain, the house eventually justified its place in architectural history by offering a strong rebuttal to the kitsch neo-historic approach of postmodernism.
It ignited a forum to consider the relationship between art and architecture, which fueled the subsequent waves of architect and artist collaborative projects in the 1980s, further expanding the role of the architect in culture.

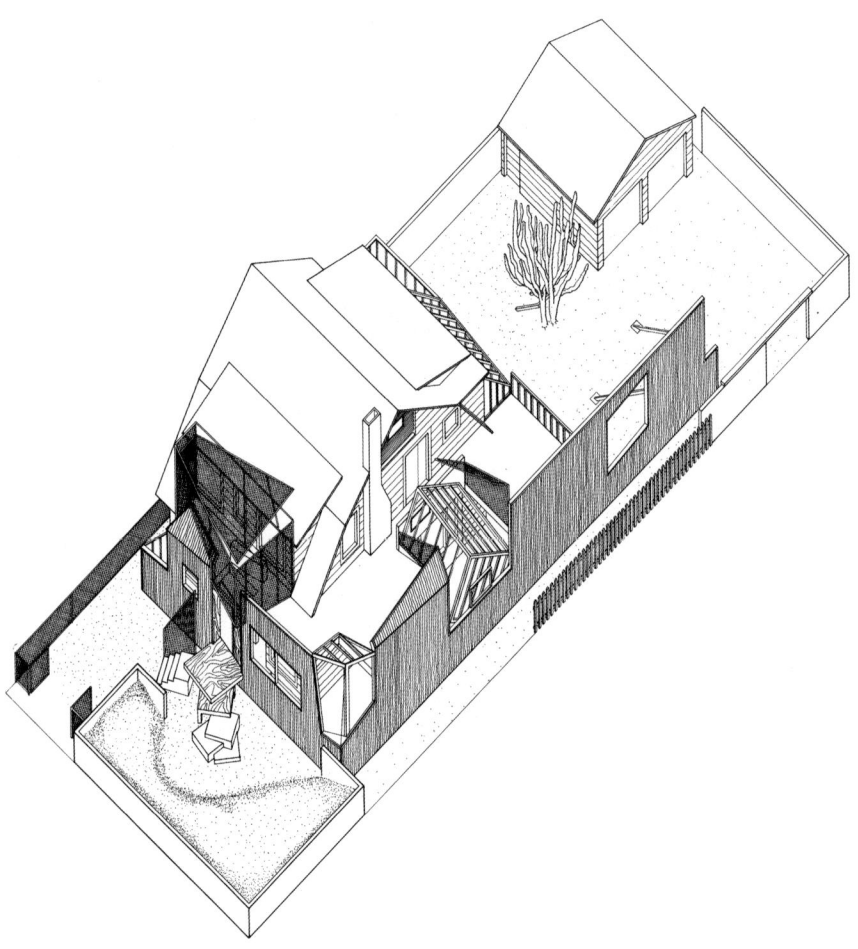

Notes of Interest
A seemingly ad hoc collection of raw, workmanlike materials wrapped around an unassuming two-story clapboard bungalow, Frank Gehry's, FAIA, home for his wife, Berta, and two sons found a literal, but unexpected, answer to the question of neighborhood context, and used it to forever re-shape the formal and material boundaries of architecture.
Enormously influential in both theory and practice, the home's fundamental material modesty and formal experimentation marks a Rubicon in the history of contemporary architecture, tearing down inherited stylistic standbys to declare a new design language for the modern suburban architectural condition. Recognizing architectural design of enduring significance, the Twenty-five Year Award is conferred on a building that has stood the test of time for 25 to 35 years as an embodiment of architectural excellence. Projects must demonstrate excellence in function, in the distinguished execution of its original program, and in the creative aspects of its statement by today's standards. The award will be presented this May at the AIA National Convention in Washington, D.C.

Architect	Location	Photo Credit
Gehry Partners LLP	Santa Monica, California	© Gehry Partners LLP

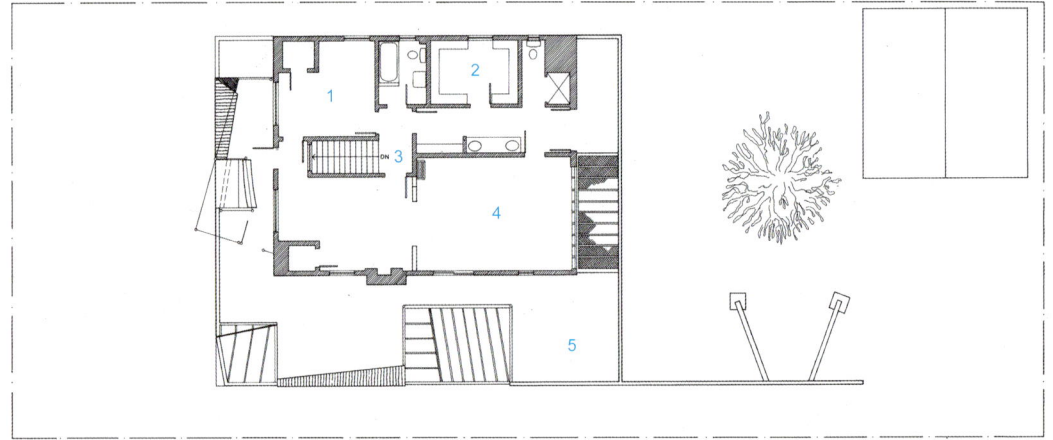

1. Bedroom
2. Closet
3. Down
4. Master Bedroom
5. Outdoor Deck

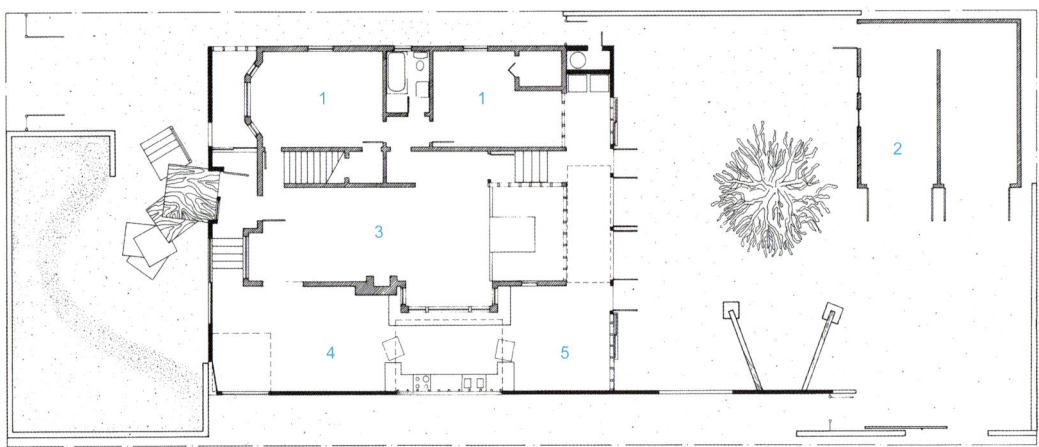

1. Bedroom
2. Garage
3. Living Area
4. Dining
5. Kitchen

INDEX

2010

Albert & Associates Architects
http://www.albertassociates.com
514 Main Atreet Hattiesburg
Mississippi 390401
Tel: 601.544.1970

Architecture Research Office
http://www.aro.net
170 Varick Street, 7th Floor New York
NY 10013
Tel: 212.675.1870

Barkow Leibinger Architects
http://www.barkowleibinger.com
SchillerstraBe94 D-10625 Berlin
Tel: 49(0)30.315712-0

Bentel & Bentel Architects
http://www.bentelandbentel.com
22 Buckram Road Locust Valley
NY 11560
Tel: 516.676.2880

Burt Hill
650 Smithfield Street
Suite 2600
Pittsburgh, PA 15222
Tel: 412.394.7000

Choi Ropiha
http://chrofi.com/
3/1 The Corso Manly NSW 2095 Australia
Enter from Whistler Street
Tel: 61.2.9977.3700

Conway+Schulte Architects
http://www.conwayandschulte.com
2300 Kennedy Street NE #240
Minneapolis, Minnesota 55413
Tel: 612.333.5867

Dake Wells Architecture
http://dake-wells.com
401 W. Walnut St.
Springfield, Missouri 65806
Tel: 417.831.9904

Daly Genik
http://www.dalygenik.com
1558 10 th St-C
Santa Monica, CA 90401
Tel: 310.656.3180

Diller Scofidio + Renfro
http://www.dsrny.com/
601 W. 26 th Street, Suite 1815
New York, NY 10001
Tel: 212.260.7971

Epstein | Metter Studios
http://www.epsteinglobal.com
600 West Fulton
Chicago, Illinois 60661-1199
Tel: 312.454.9100

FXFOWLE Architects
http://www.fxfowle.com
22 West 19th Street
New York, NY USA 10011
Tel: 212.627.1700

Gabellini Sheppard Associates
http://www.gabellinisheppard.com
665 Broadway Suite 706
New York, NY 10012
Tel: 212.388.1700

Kendall/Heaton Associates, Inc.
http://www.kendall-heaton.com

Kuwabara Payne McKenna Blumberg Architects
http://www.kpmbarchitects.com

Mack Scogin Merrill Elam Architects
http://msmearch.com
111 John Wesley Dobbs Avenue
NE Atlanta, Georgia 30303
Tel: 404.525.6869

Meyer, Scherer & Rockcastle, Ltd.
http://www.msrltd.com
710 South 2nd Street 8th Floor
Minneapolis, MN 55401
Tel: 612.375.0336

Office dA, Inc.
http://www.officeda.com

Olson Kundig Architects
http://www.olsonkundigarchitects.com
159 South Jacjson St.,Suite 600
Seattle, WA 98104,USA
Tel: 206.624.5670

Perkins Eastman
http://www.perkinseastman.com
115 Fifth Avenue
New York, NY 10003
Tel: 212.353.7200

Peter Marino Architect
http://www.petermarinoarchitect.com
150 East 58 Street
New York, NY 10022
Tel: 212.752.5444

PKSB Architects
http://www.pksb.com
330 West 42nd Street
New York, NY 10036
Tel: 212.594.2010

Polshek Partnership Architects
http://ennead.com
320 West 13 th Street
New York,New York 10014
Tel: 212.807.7171

Pugh + Scarpa
http://www.pugh-scarpa.com
4611 W. Slauson Ave.
Los Angeles, California 90043
Tel: 323.596.4700

Randy Brown Architects
http://www.randybrownarchitects.com
1925 N. 120th Street
Omaha, NE 68154
Tel: 402.551.7097

Shelton, Mindel & Associates
http://www.sheltonmindel.com
56 west 22 nd street,12 th floor
New York, NY 10010
Tel: 212.206.6406

Skidmore, Owings & Merrill LLP
http://www.som.com
224 S. Michigan Avenue Suite 1000
Chicago, IL 60604, USA
Tel: 312.554.9090

Sottile & Sottile
http://www.sottile.cc

Thomas Phifer and Partners
http://www.tphifer.com
180 Varick Street
New York, NY 10014
Tel : 212.337.0334

Tod Williams Billie Tsien Architects
http://www.twbta.com
222 Central Park South
New York, NY 10019
Tel: 212.582.2385

Wallace Roberts & Todd
http://www.wrtdesign.com

WSA Studio
http://wsastudio.com
The Jack, 982South Front Street
Columbus, Ohio 43206
Tel: 614.824.1633

_____2011
Adrian Smith + Gordon Gill Architecture
http://smithgill.com
111 West Monroe, Suite 2300
Chicago IL 60603
Tel: 312.920.1888

Allied Works Architecture
http://www.alliedworks.com
12 W 27th St, 18th Floor
New York, NY 10001
Tel: 212.431.9476

Belzberg Architects
http://www.belzbergarchitects.com
2919 1/2 Main Street
Santa Monica, CA 90405
Tel: 310.453.9611

Bernard Tschumi Architects
http://www.tschumi.com
227 West 17th Street, second floor
New York, New York 10011
Tel: 212.807.6340

Cannon Design
http://cannondesign.com
100 Cambridge Street, Suite 1400
Boston, Massachusetts 02114
Tel: 617.742.5440

Clive Wilkinson Architects
http://clivewilkinson.com
Los Angeles
144 North Robertson Boulevard
West Hollywood, CA 90048
Tel: 310.358.2200

dlandstudio llc
http://www.dlandstudio.com
137 Clinton Street
Brooklyn, NY 11201
Tel: 718.624.0244

Lehrer Architects
http://lehrerarchitects.com
2140 Hyperion Ave
Los Angeles, CA 90027-4708
Tel: 323.664.4747

Jensen Architects/Jensen & Macy Architects
http://www.jensen-architects.com
833 Market Street, 7th Floor
San Francisco, CA 94103-1827
Tel: 415.348.9650

Julie Snow Architects, Inc.
http://www.juliesnowarchitects.com
2400 Rand Tower
527 Marquette Avenue
Minneapolis, Minnesota 55402
Tel: 612.359.9430

KlingStubbins
http://www.klingstubbins.com
Washington, DC
2000 L Street, NW, Suite 215
Washington DC 20036
Tel: 202.785.5800

Kohn Pedersen Fox Associates, PC
http://www.kpf.com
11West 42nd Street
New York, NY 10036
Tel: 212.977.6500

Lake | Flato Architects
http://lakeflato.com
311 THIRD STREET
San Antonio, TX 78205
Tel: 210.227.3335

LMN + DA/MCM
http://lmnarchitects.com
801 Second Avenue, Suite 501
Seattle, Washington 98104
Tel: 206.682.3460

Marcy Wong Donn Logan Architects
http://wonglogan.com
800 Bancroft Way Suite 200
Berkeley, CA 94710
Tel: 510.843.0916

Marilys R. Nepomechie Architect
Associate Professor of Architecture at Florida International University

Marta Canaves Interior Design
7373 Sw 60th Street
Miami, FL, 33143

Montalba Architects, Inc.
http://montalbaarchitects.com
2525 Michigan Avenus, Bldg.,T4
Santa Monica, CA, 90404
Tel: 310.828.1162

Patrick Tighe Architecture
http://www.tighearchitecture.com
1632 Ocean Park Blvd
Santa Monica, CA 90405
Tel: 310.450.8823

Pei Cobb Freed & Partners Architects LLP
http://www.pcf-p.com
88 Pine Street
New York, NY 10005
Tel: 212.751.3122

Rene Gonzalez Architect
http://renegonzalezarchitect.com
670 NE 50th Terrace
Miami, FL 33137-3023
Tel: 305.762.5895

REX | OMA
http://www.rex-ny.com
20 Jay Street Suite 920
Brooklyn, NY 11201
Tel: 646.230.6557

Skidmore, Owings & Merrill LLP
http://www.som.com
224 S. Michigan Avenue, Suite 1000
Chicago, IL 60604
Tel: 312.554.9090

Steven Holl Architects
http://www.stevenholl.com
New York City
450 West 31st Street, 11th floor
New York, NY 10001
Tel: 212.629.7262

Thomas Phifer and Partners
http://www.tphifer.com
180 Varick Street
New York, NY 10014
Tel: 212.337.0334

University of Arkansas Community Design Center
http://uacdc.uark.edu
104 N. East Avenue
Fayetteville, AR 72701
Tel: 479.575.5772

Weiss/Manfredi Architecture/Landscape/Urbanism
http://www.weissmanfredi.com
200 Hudson Street 10fl
New York, NY 10013
Tel: 212.760.9002

ZGF Architects LLP
http://www.zgf.com
Portland Office
1223 SW Washington Street, Suite 200
Portland, Oregon 97205
Tel: 503.224.3860

_____2012

Andre Kikoski Architect, PLLC
http://www.akarch.com
180 Varick Street,Suite 1316
New York, NY 10014
Tel: 212.627.0240

Anmahian Winton Architects
http://aw-arch.com
650 Cambridge Street
Cambridge, MA 02141
Tel: 617.577.7400

BIG
http://www.big.dk
BIG NYC
601 West 26th Street, Suite 1255
New York, NY 10001
Tel: 347.549.4141

Center for Design Research, School of Architecture + Design, Virginia Tech
http://www.lumenhaus.com
201 Cowgill Hall
Blacksburg, VA 24060
Tel: 540.818.5012

Cooper, Robertson & Partners;
http://www.cooperrobertson.com/
311 West 43rd Street
New York, NY 10036
Tel: 212.247.1717

David Jameson Architect
http://www.davidjamesonarchitect.com
113 South Patrick Street
Alexandria, Virginia 22314
Tel: 703.739.3840

DMOD Architects
http://www.dmod.ie
Cathedral Court, New Street
Dublin 8 Ireland
Tel: 353.1.491.1700

Ennead Architects
http://ennead.com
Ennead Architects LLP
320 West 13 th Street
New York, NY 10014
Tel: 212.807.7171

Eskew+Dumez+Ripple
http://www.eskewdumezripple.com
one canal place
365 Canal Street Suite 3150
New Orleans, LA 70130
Tel: 504.561.8686

Gehry Partners LLP
http://www.foga.com
12541 Beatrice Street
Los Angeles, CA 90066
Tel: 310.482.3000

Gensler
http://www.gensler.com
Rockefeller Center
1230 Avenue of the Americas,
Suite 1500
New York, NY 10020
Tel: 212.492.1400

Goettsch Partners
http://www.gpchicago.com
224 South Michigan Avenue, Floor 17
Chicago, Illinois 60604
Tel: 312.356.0600

John Ronan Architects
http://www.jrarch.com
420 W Huron Street
Chicago, Illinois 60654
Tel: 312.951.6600

KieranTimberlake
http://kierantimberlake.com
420 North 20th Street
Philadelphia, PA 19130.3828
Tel: 215 922 6600

Koning Eizenberg Architecture
http://www.kearch.com
1454 25th Street
Santa Monica, CA 90404
Tel: 310.828.6131

Mack Scogin Merrill Elam Architects
http://msmearch.com
111 John Wesley Dobbs Avenue, NE
Atlanta, Georgia 30303
Tel: 404.525.6869

Mackay-Lyons Sweetapple Architects Limited
http://www.mlsarchitects.ca/portfolio/featuredprojects
2488 Gottingen Street
Halifax, Nova Scotia Canada B3K 3BK 3B4
Tel: 902.429.1867

Marlon Blackwell Architect
http://www.marlonblackwell.com
The Fulbright Building
217 E. Dickson St., Suite 104
Fayetteville, Arkansas 72701
Tel: 479.973.9121

Michael Maltzan Architecture, Inc.
http://www.mmaltzan.com
2801 Hyperion Avenue, Studio 107
Los Angeles, California 90027
Tel: 323.913.3098

Moore Ruble Yudell Architects & Planners;
http://www.mryarchitects.com

Morphosis Architects
http://www.morphosis.com
3440 Wesley Street
Culver City, CA 90232
Tel: 424.258.6200

OLIN
http://www.theolinstudio.com
Public Ledger Building, Suite 1123
150 South Independence Mall West,
Philadelphia, PA 19106
Tel: 215.440.0030

Patrick Tighe Architecture
http://www.tighearchitecture.com
1632 Ocean Park Blvd
Senta Monica, CA 90405
Tel : 310.450.8823

Randy Brown Architects
http://www.randybrownarchitects.com
1925 N. 120th Street
Omaha, NE 68154
Tel: 402.551.7097

Rogers Marvel Architects
http://www.rogersmarvel.com
145 Hudson Street, Third Floor
New York, NY 10013
Tel: 212.941.6718

Sasaki Associates, Inc.
http://www.sasaki.com
64 Pleasant Street
Watertown, MA 02472
Tel: 617.926.3300

Shim-Sutcliffe Architects
http://www.shim-sutcliffe.com
441 Queen Street East
Toronto, Ontario, Canada M5A 1T5
Tel: 416.368.3892

Tod Williams Billie Tsien Architects
http://www.twbta.com
222 Central Park South
New York, NY 10019
Tel: 212.582.2385

University of Arkansas Community Design Center
http://uacdc.uark.edu
104 N. East Avenue
Fayetteville, AR72701
Tel: 479.575.5772

West 8 Urban Design and Landscape Architecture
http://www.west8.nl
Schiehaven 13M, 3024 EC
Rotterdam, the Netherlands
Tel: 31(0)10.485.5801

ZGF Architects LLP
http://www.zgf.com
Portland Office
1223 SW Washington Street, Suite 200
Portland, Oregon 97205
Tel: 503.224.3860